CRIMINAL PROCEDURE

CRIMINAL PROCEDURE

J. SCOTT HARR
Normandale Community College

KÄREN M. HESS
Normandale Community College

WEST PUBLISHING COMPANY
St. Paul • New York
Los Angeles • San Francisco

Copyediting: Barbara Bergstrom
Text Design: David Farr/Imagesmythe, Inc.
Composition: Carlisle Graphics
Art: David Farr/Imagesmythe, Inc.

Photo Credits: **Cover** EKM-Nepenthe; **2** Jim Mahoney/The Image Works; **5** Ellis Herwig/ Stock, Boston; **12** Jim Mahoney/ The Image Works; **13** Cary Wolinsky/Stock, Boston; **16** Stock, Boston; **17** Scott Harr; **19** Scott Harr; **24** The Granger Collection; **28** Antman Archives/The Image Works; **31** Frederic Lewis, Inc.; **33** The Granger Collection; **34** The Granger Collection; **35** Frederic Lewis, Inc.; **46** Wide World Photos; **63** Scott Harr; **68** Alan Carey/The Image Works; **74** Jane Scherr/Jeroboam, Inc.; **83** David H. Wells/The Image Works; **86** Scott Harr; **89** EKM-Nepenthe; **102** Scott Harr; **111** Steve Malone/Jeroboam, Inc.; **122** Wide World Photos; **134** Scott Harr; **137** Scott Harr; **139** Martin E. Klimek/Jeroboam, Inc.; **148** Michael Grecco/Stock, Boston; **161** Scott Harr; **164** Scott Harr; **166** Steve Malone/Jeroboam, Inc.; **168** Peter Menzel/Stock, Boston; **178** EKM-Nepenthe; **200** Phyllis Graber Jensen/Stock, Boston; **206** Wide World Photos; **209** Jeff Albertson/Stock, Boston; **224** EKM-Nepenthe; **227** Frederic Lewis, Inc.; **232** Jim Mahoney/The Image Works; **233** P. Davidson/The Image Works; **234** Dan Chidester/The Image Works; **266** Scott Harr; **269** The Granger Collection; **274** J. Berndt/Stock, Boston; **277** Scott Harr; **282** Spencer Grant/Stock, Boston; **293** Scott Harr; **294** Scott Harr; **296** Scott Harr; **304** Scott Harr; **306** W. Marc Bernsau/The Image Works; **307** Wide World Photos; **309** Wide World Photos; **326** EKM-Nepenthe; **337** Jim Pickerell/Stock, Boston; **340** Billy E. Barnes/Stock, Boston; **341** EKM-Nepenthe; **342** Billy E. Barnes/Stock, Boston; **344** EKM-Nepenthe; **356** West Publishing Co.; **364** EKM-Nepenthe.

Library of Congress Cataloging-in- Publication Data

Harr, Scott.
   Criminal procedure / Scott Harr, Kären Hess.
      p.   cm.
   IBSN 0-314-57495-6
   1. Criminal procedure—United States. 2. Police—United States—
Handbooks, manuals, etc. I. Hess, Kären M., 1939–   . II. Title.
KF9619.8.P65H37   1990
345.73'052—dc20   89-38357
[347.30552]   CIP

Dedicated to the Profession
of Law Enforcement

It is my hope that this work will contribute something back to a profession that has given me so much. I would like to acknowledge every criminal justice professional and law enforcement student whom I have had contact with, as each of you has played an important part in the way that I view our profession.

I wish to personally acknowledge those persons who were of particular importance in the preparation of this effort: Henry Wrobleski and Karen Hess, for their continuing mentoring, faith, and encouragement; Normandale Community College staff and students; Pam Reierson, Normandale College Media Specialist, for her tireless research assistance, friendship, and commitment to the profession; Sgt. S. Schwartz for those important early lessons and direction; Capt. Ralph Schiffman for his influence; my family and friends for their patience and support; and, particularly, my dearest wife, Diane Lacy Harr, and daughter Kelsey, with whom I have always shared my dreams.

—J. Scott Harr

We both extend our deepest appreciation and heartfelt thanks to our editors at West Publishing Company, Susan Tubb and Jeff Carpenter, for their invaluable assistance and expertise in developing this book and for their friendship.

—J. Scott Harr
—Kären M. Hess

Note to Readers

Throughout this text, it is reiterated that our American law is a "living law," in fact, changing as the perceived needs of the society it serves change. As a professional in the field of criminal justice, you will be expected to know the law—even when it changes—and it will! While we have made every attempt to provide accurate, current law, the United States Supreme Court has before it at any given moment cases that could change criminal procedure overnight. This is why the text concludes with a chapter on researching the law, so you will know how to locate the law and keep current on it.

Introduction

This text is written for and dedicated specifically to the profession of law enforcement—not the public looking at the justice system from the outside; not the lawyers or legislators arguing, interpreting, or writing the law; but the cop enforcing the law.

This is not a traditional text. It is a compilation of material we feel will help law enforcement officers develop the professionalism the field now demands.

It was conceived out of the recognition that police work is not like it once was. No longer is it anything but a true profession with those choosing this noble career expected to have the same traits as such other professionals as doctors and lawyers.

We have sought to develop a text that will fill the void between complex "case law" books and basic investigation or constitutional law texts. The admittedly complex law is provided along with explanations to clarify what the law is and how it is applied in real life. Combine this with the "Do You Know" questions at the beginning of each chapter to set the stage and the discussion questions at the conclusion of each chapter, and you should leave your course with a working knowledge of this exciting area of law. The Basic Issues at the end of each chapter are included to help you look at both sides of relevant issues and to encourage you to think about our ever-changing law.

The book was not written in an ivory tower. It was written in the law enforcement community with the assistance of the profession. As a part of this system, we have attempted to provide material that police need and have continued to listen to what cops say they want to know about law and about criminal procedure.

Just as this is not a traditional text, it does not contain a traditional forward written by one individual. Because the criminal justice system in our country is an adversary system, pitting the government against the accused, it must be recognized that *both* sides play legitimate and important roles in achieving the single most important goal of the American system of law--JUSTICE.

Our two forwards represent the defense, C. Paul Jones, Minnesota Public Defender, and the prosecution, Hubert H. Humphrey, III, Attorney General of Minnesota. Each individual, in his unique perspective, represents the professionalism existing in our field. We thank them for their valuable contributions.

About the Authors

J. Scott Harr, J.D. is an author, police officer, attorney, private investigator, and member of the law enforcement department at Normandale Community College. He is also currently Assistant Public Safety Director for the City of Chanhassen.

Kären M. Hess, PhD, has written extensively in the field of law enforcement. She is a member of the English department at Normandale Community College as well as the president of the Institute for Professional Development.

Kären M. Hess and J. Scott Harr.

C. Paul Jones

Forward

More than ever before, a thorough working knowledge of the complexities of criminal procedure for those involved in the field of criminal justice is not a luxury—it is an absolute necessity. Today more quality prosecutors are available throughout the country to work with police personnel to fully develop and prepare cases and to competently present in court the results of investigations conducted by our hard-working police and laboratory technicians.

In turn, the defense bar has successfully responded to the task of providing effective, aggressive representation of those charged with crimes. In the 1960s United States Supreme Court decisions such as *Miranda* (right to remain silent), *Gideon* (right to an attorney), and *Mapp* (exclusion of evidence obtained in violation of constitutional protections) spawned and increased awareness of, and attention to, criminal JUSTICE.

This awareness and attention applied to the community in general, as well as to our judges, lawyers, legislators, and executive personnel. As a result of this attention and awareness, our police were provided with such progressive equipment as radio equipment to permit state, county, and municipal police squad car personnel to communicate with each other. They were also provided with electronic single fingerprint search equipment. Developments continue.

Not only has the sophistication level of law enforcement technology continued to evolve, but also has the sophistication level of criminals evolved. This sophistication, combined with our growing body of criminal law, results in an exceedingly complex field of criminal procedure.

The challenge is being met. Mandatory police training and licensing is becoming a reality. Annual Criminal Justice Programs such as those occurring in Minnesota have been created so that today police, prosecutors, judges and defense counsel can learn with and from each other. In essence, we all strive to achieve the same goal: JUSTICE.

Scott Harr, a police officer, attorney, and former earnest law student, has made an excellent contribution to the continuing need for improvement of all justice personnel to ensure the integrity of our delivery of criminal justice. Scott's book offers police and others a broad outlook and understanding of the entire framework of the law of which the police are an integral part. As a former state and federal prosecutor, as a current defense counsel, as a long time and current professor of law, and most importantly, simply as a member of the general public, I stand and cheer Scott for his excellent contribution.

C. Paul Jones
Minnesota State Public Defender
Professor of Criminal Law
William Mitchell College of Law

Hubert H. Humphrey, III

Forward

As Attorney General for the State of Minnesota, I have long supported the important role of good peace officer education in providing fair and effective law enforcement to our citizens. To be useful, such education must include a working knowledge of criminal and constitutional law; not just from its theoretical aspects, but from the practical viewpoint of law enforcement professionals doing their jobs every day "on the street." The desire for such knowledge is evident among peace officers I have talked to at gatherings such as Minnesota's Annual Criminal Justice Institute, and at other meetings throughout the State. This text on criminal procedure by Scott Harr and Kären Hess goes a long way toward fulfilling that need.

The authors have sought in this book to present criminal and constitutional law in a way that makes it easier to apply in the day-to-day work of law enforcement professionals. It is not only informative, but thought provoking as well. If the essence of good education is the creation of open, questioning minds that are constantly seeking better understanding, then this text will be a useful aid in that process.

Our society prides itself on being governed by principles of law rather than human whim and caprice. Among the most basic of those principles is the guarantee of rights to all citizens embodied in our Constitution. Experience has shown that there need be no conflict between protecting those rights and effective law enforcement. Indeed, time and again we have seen accurate investigations that follow the guidelines of the law bring criminals to swift justice, without any danger that the resulting convictions would later be thrown out as improperly obtained. The importance of peace officers having a good working knowledge of the law to achieve such results cannot be overemphasized.

I commend the authors for their effort at providing such knowledge. Hopefully, this text will add to the ever growing professionalism of the law enforcement community.

Hubert H. Humphrey, III
Attorney General
of the State of Minnesota

Contents in Brief

Contents

List of Figures

List of Tables

List of Cases

SECTION ONE

Protecting Your Rights

and Those of Others:

The Police Officer

and the Law

This first section provides a context from which to view how police officers are influenced by the law when dealing with criminals and criminal investigations.

The criticality of police officer safety cannot be overemphasized. Chapter 1 presents an overview of important concepts related to officer safety, concepts that should provide the underpinning for any police action, official or unofficial.

Chapter 2 presents an overview of how our laws came into being, including a brief history of the evolution of law and our legal system as well as a differentiation between criminal and civil law. Chapter 3 discusses the criminal justice system, with an emphasis on the courts and how the judicial branch of the system enforces the laws that have been enacted. The section concludes with chapter 4: a discussion of civil liability and how police officers in their official capacity may leave themselves open to being sued, and suggestions about how such lawsuits might be minimized.

Although the focus of the book is dealing with crimes and criminals, everything police officers do in this context is directly affected by the law and by the rights guaranteed to all citizens by our Constitution. Any violation of these rights can destroy a case as well as the public's faith in our profession.

CHAPTER 1

Staying Alive

"To Serve and Protect":

Officer Safety

"Your day-by-day—sometimes minute-by-minute—contact with criminals, complainants and citizens alike who are crying, cursing, bleeding, puking, yelling, spitting, biting, fighting, lying, dying, dead, drunk, doped, dirty, scared, scarred, angry, vengeful, irrational, evasive, outlandish, grieving, manipulative, taunting, demanding, defiant, cruel, neurotic, hopeless, and just plain crazy subjects your system to repeated onslaughts of disturbance. . . .

The question is—how many people could have had me today if they'd really wanted me?"—Charles Remsberg, *The Tactical Edge*

DO YOU KNOW

How many police officers have been killed in the line of duty in the last ten years? Assaulted?

What situation is most commonly associated with the killing of police officers?

What the survival triangle essential elements are?

What common responses may be made under sudden, super stress?

What the awareness spectrum is and how it relates to law enforcement?

At which level of awareness law enforcement officers should habitually operate?

What weapon is most frequently used in killing police officers?

Introduction This text seeks to teach law enforcement professionals the law of criminal procedure. Therefore, the
Chapter 1   emphasis of the chapters that follow is what the law
is and how to apply it. Without a doubt, a working
knowledge of our law is a critical requirement for being a law enforcement professional.

Never—ever—forget that the most important aspect of law enforcement is staying alive to enforce that law and to go home to your
family after doing so.

This chapter is dedicated to the basic premise that the men and
women who choose to become peace officers become heroes the day
they pin on that badge. As important as it is to learn the law, learning
to stay alive is more important. We feel a special kinship with our
readers because we have a special feeling about this profession. That is
why we have written this book. That is why we have begun this book
with a chapter on officer safety.

Just as we begin with a discussion of safety, we urge you to begin
each day with thoughts of safety. We will be urging you to stay current
with the ever-changing law of our land and to be ever aware of the
rights of its citizens. At the same time, you should stay current on
officer safety, methods, and equipment.

THE "IT CAN NEVER HAPPEN TO ME"
SYNDROME

One of the first things police officers learn while on the job is the
pervasiveness of the "it can never happen to me" syndrome. Whether
assisting victims at a serious car accident scene, investigating a
residential burglary scene, or delivering a death notification—the
police encounter a predictable victim response: "I never thought this
would happen to me!" Too many police officers go to work day after
day, year after year, with this same delusion. "I work in a small town";
or "I trust my fellow officers"; or "I'm cautious" all adds up to the same
thing—"It can never happen to me."

Combine this delusion with the fact that there is absolutely no
way to foresee when danger will arise, and the odds against officer
survival mount. Everyone's guard is up when responding to a "man
with a gun" call or to a "fight with weapons in progress." But what
about the fatally dangerous calls that do not appear dangerous?

Do you ever have any idea of just who you are stopping on even
the most routine traffic stop? Is there any way to know whether even
the most routine service call could bring you face to face with a
psychotic individual or with a person hopelessly crazy from narcotics?
While you are there "to help," you could easily be viewed as the enemy.
And when faced with a perceived threat, many people would not
hesitate to kill a cop.

Consider, for example, the man who was apprehended by the state
patrol for a variety of offenses, resulting in a very long prison term. His

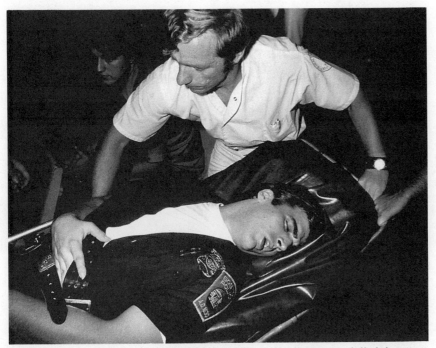

From January to June, 1989, thirty-nine law enforcement officers were killed due to criminal action. Nine were killed while investigating suspicious persons, 9 upon responding to disturbance calls, 5 during robberies, 5 while attempting arrests, 4 during drug-related situations, and 2 in ambush. Thirty-five of the thirty-nine have been cleared by law enforcement authorities. (FBI/UCR, 7-19-89)

final words during freedom were that he would kill the next trooper he could. What if you were that trooper coming into contact with him for any reason whatsoever?

I was once on a routine call. Nothing unusual had happened, and I had not expected anything to happen. My guard was down. Only later did I learn, after our detectives interrogated one of the parties present for another reason altogether, that a man had been hiding in the bathroom behind the shower curtain—armed with a machine gun. I had no way of knowing these people were heavily involved with narcotics trafficking and were ready to protect themselves, even from an officer innocently stumbling on their operation.

It is critical to face reality. Officers *DO* die, and all too frequently.

In the last ten years alone, over 1,100 law enforcement officers have been killed in the line of duty. An additional 19,000 have been injured in assaults.

According to the *Uniform Crime Reports* (1988, p. 3) the vast majority of the officers killed were white, male patrol officers with an average of nine years of service. The majority of assailants were also white males, under the age of 30, with previous arrests. At the time of the killing, approximately one-third of the assailants were on probation or parole.

Arrest situations accounted for more line-of-duty deaths than any other circumstance, followed by investigating suspicious persons, enforcing traffic laws, and responding to disturbance calls (UCR, p. 3).

THE BASICS OF SELF-PRESERVATION— STAYING ALIVE

Being shot and killed *can* happen to you as it has to so many other officers. Most officers who become victims could have either avoided the confrontation or minimized the injury and stayed alive if they had:

- Been prepared for the danger.
- Kept their guard up.
- Developed the skills needed to respond appropriately.

Complacency, together with the belief that "it can never happen to me," will result in officer injuries and deaths. So much of police work is just plain boring, and it becomes routine. The officer who drives right up to the front door of a building that has had forty false burglar alarms and starts filling out another false alarm report leaves himself wide open. What if the forty-first alarm is the real thing?

Or the chronic domestic call—you've been there so many times with nothing ensuing other than a discussion. What if this time violence erupts?

Unless you remain aware, alert, and prepared on *every* call, you are allowing yourself to fall into the same rut that many officers before you have fallen into—a rut that, without a moment's warning, can turn into a grave.

Almost everything about the job that law enforcement officers do subjects them to danger: the types of calls, the times many of these calls occur, the places they frequently occur, the visibility of the vehicle and uniform—all make police officers perfect targets.

An understanding of and appreciation for the elements of officer safety are every bit as important as understanding the elements of the laws of criminal procedure. Two excellent books on officer safety are *Street Survival: Tactics for Armed Encounters* and *The Tactical Edge: Surviving High-Risk Patrol*. Both are "must" reading for law enforce-

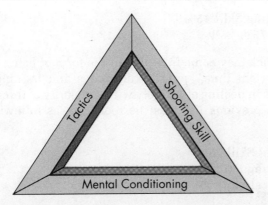

Ronald J. Adams, Thomas M. McTernan, and Charles Remsberg, *Street Survival: Tactics for Armed Encounters* (Northbrook, Ill.: Calibre Press, 1980), p. 8.

Figure 1–1   The Survival Triangle

ment officers. They go beyond the theoretical considerations summarized in this chapter to the nitty-gritty of HOW TO stay alive.

Street Survival (p. 8) depicts survival readiness as an equilateral triangle (shown above).

The survival triangle consists of mental/physical preparation, survival tactics, and shooting skill.

Each side is of equal importance, and the triangle illustrates that preparedness begins *before* the shoot-out occurs.

A few words of warning: First, effective officer survival skills involve knowledge and practice. Instincts need to be developed. As noted by Adams et al. (1980, p. 9): *"Under stress, in a crisis, you will instinctively revert to the way that you have trained."* Learn and practice.

Second, you will never be able to foresee every danger. *Expect the unexpected.* You *can* learn to minimize your risks and to train yourself to respond appropriately.

MENTAL/PHYSICAL CONDITIONING

Remsberg (1986, p. 16) suggests that "Your mind is the most dangerous weapon you carry on patrol." In *Tactical Edge*, Remsberg asserts that relative weightings "assigned to the factors that tend to determine whether UNprepared officers survive" are

- Mental Skill 5%
- Physical Skill 5%

- Shooting Skill 15%
- Luck 75%

While luck may come into play in the form of being "in the right place at the right time," proper knowledge and training will assist police officers in dealing effectively with a majority of threats. To do so, however, the previous list must be reordered as follows (Remsberg, 1986, p. 18):

- Mental Skill 75%
- Shooting Skill 15%
- Physical Skill 5%
- Luck 5%

Mind/Body Partnership

The mind can influence the body, just as the body can influence the mind. You mentally perceive fear, and your body responds accordingly. Or you feel physically apprehensive and your mind wonders why. Everyone has experienced how the mind affects the body and the body affects the mind. This relationship is critical in the law enforcement profession where crucial situations can arise abruptly.

A great deal of scientific research has been conducted on the physiological responses to psychological stimuli. Clearly, emotional stress creates physical stress. The greater the stress, the more difficulty people have controlling their responses. Most people are simply not prepared for high-stress situations.

Think of all the examples an officer sees in others. Car accident victims, even if injuries are minimal, become panic stricken. A person watching his home burn may try to run into the flames to rescue a replaceable trinket. Upon being told of the death of a loved one, many people become hysterical, physically ill, and totally out of control.

Next consider the police officer who is unexpectedly confronted with danger. Because the officer is human, the response is just like that of other victims. The less the officer is prepared, the more serious the likelihood of very serious or fatal injury. Emotions interfere with comprehension. Physical responses affect the ability to react, and suddenly their limited or artificial training plays a crucial part in the officer's survival.

Police officers may be trained in the basic skills required in the course of their job: pursuit driving, shooting, defensive tactics. But how many officers have any realistic idea of what it is like to execute these skills away from the driving course, the gun range, or the police gym? Combine extreme emotional stress with the resulting physiological responses, and the officers' response can be reduced to fatal ineffectiveness.

Remsberg (1986, p. 22) reminds us that:

Eons ago, when human biology first emerged, cavemen experienced identical psycho-physiological reactions when they confronted danger-

ous *wild animals. The arousal syndrome quickly prepared them either
to fight the threat or take flight from it. In that context, stress responses
were crucial to survival; the diversion of blood to large muscle groups,
for instance, prepared the arms for swinging and the legs for running,
both potentially life-saving movements. . . .*

*But because your response options now must usually be so different
from mere fight or flight, acute stress in your environment may
endanger—or terminate—your survival rather than help it.*

*Extra blood nourishment for your large muscles means less for your
small muscles involved in say, finger dexterity and eye-hand coordination. Thus fine motor movements that ordinarily are easy may become
impossible [firing accurately or reloading quickly]. . . . Your tightened
muscles may affect your voice, making effective verbal challenges difficult . . . or your eyes, causing excessive watering and blurring your
vision. . . .*

*The part of your brain responsible for large muscle control (essen-
tial for fighting or fleeing) gets priority at the expense of the part of
your brain responsible for abstract thought. Your ability to concentrate
is disrupted . . . your judgment suffers. . . . Your analytical thinking is
hampered.*

Remsberg (1986, pp. 21–30) goes on to note that officers who have
survived shootings experience several common phenomena resulting
from the sudden super stress.

---

*Common responses include the startle response, thought distraction,
physical distress, sensory distortion, and awareness lapse.*

The Startle Response   When you are startled it is a natural response to
jump. If you are holding a loaded gun at the time, this natural,
instinctive response can be deadly. In some instances, a shot fired by a
startled police officer sets other officers off shooting.

Another natural response is to turn toward whatever it was that
startled you. If it was someone shooting at you, this response, again,
could be deadly.

Thought Distraction   A study of survivors of shooting reports that nearly 60
percent of the officers involved had distracting thoughts at the peak of
the encounter (Remsberg, 1986, p. 24): "Can I really shoot somebody?"
"What if I only wound him and he sues me?" "Does he have kids?"

Physical Distress   Physical distress in the form of vomiting, fainting,
urinating, or defecating can occur before, during, or after acutely
stressful situations.

Sensory Distortion   According to Remsberg (1986, p. 25), "The odds are
extremely high that during your stress crisis you will perceive the

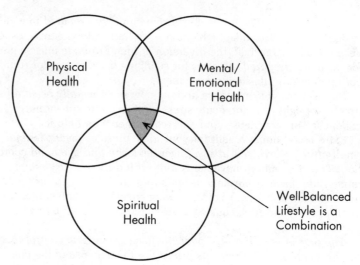

Figure 1–2   **Well-Balanced Lifestyle**

action unrealistically, in terms of what you see or hear or the amount of time the event appears to take." Size may be distorted. Visual acuity may be heightened. Sounds may be blocked out.

Awareness Lapse   It is much less common to mentally block out part or all of an extremely stressful situation.

These common reactions to stressful situations are natural, but need not be accepted. The reactions can be countered by mental conditioning, described in detail in *The Tactical Edge*.

Even the most calm and stress-free individual, does not find such a task easy. "Calm and stress-free" are terms not often associated with the law enforcement profession. Many things contribute to a potentially harmful/distracting stressful state long before the emergency situation occurs.

Nonetheless, an important part of managing your mental state is to work on creating a positive combination of mental/physical health going *into* each day's work. This might be depicted as in Figure 1–2.

Each segment contributes to the total result. You cannot discount any segment without affecting the whole. Interestingly enough, however, the law enforcement profession is such that each segment seems to be always under attack.

For example, shift work means working nights, holidays, weekends, which affects the other segments. It is not unusual for a lack of sleep to result from working swing shifts, which directly affects your physical and emotional health. Working when many others, including friends and family, are off creates additional stress—often affecting the emotional and spiritual realms. Having to play the "heavy" or "bad guy," combined with frequently seeing humanity at its worst, or having to view horrible death scenes, and the like, can affect all three areas.

Law enforcement officers have to maintain an awareness of the interaction between these areas and respond accordingly. An understanding of this "whole person" concept helps identify why the profession has such a high rate of divorce, alcoholism, and out-of-shape individuals.

This all has to be taken into consideration *before* the time when you need your physical/emotional wits about you the most.

Awareness Spectrum

Just as police officers must maintain an awareness of the interaction of their physical/mental/emotional/spiritual selves, they must also maintain an awareness of their interaction with their environment at any given time.

The awareness spectrum measures your level of alertness to your surroundings.

Remsberg (1986, pp. 47–51) uses *colors* to describe the various stages of alertness:

Condition White   a state of *environmental unawareness*. Officers in this stage are oblivious to their surroundings, daydreaming, or preoccupied with other things. The color suggests "street virginity—pure innocence and naivete. . . . Condition White may actually *encourage* attack, even on what seem to be 'safe' assignments."

Condition Yellow   a state of being *relaxed but alert*. Officers in this state are tuned into their surroundings, watchful and perceptive. They are not expecting a crisis, but they know one is always possible at any instant. They are ready for action if need be.

Condition Orange   a state of *alarm*. Officers in this state sense or know there is trouble. They are so tuned into their environment that they know all is not right. It will be impossible to take such officers by surprise.

Condition Red   "What looks wrong is wrong." Immediate action is needed. Officers coming from Condition Orange to Condition Red will act more rationally than those who were not tuned in to the potential threat. "If officers attacked in White ever realize the crisis that is upon them before they are injured or killed, they realize it too late. After eonic lag time from the startle response, they try in one giant leap to escalate from White to Red to defend themselves. But the mental and physical adjustments required are too enormous. Massive, unexpected stress is deluging their systems, and under this emergency ultra-

While every police officer will say they know that they could be involved in a shoot-out, how many really believe it could happen to THEM?

mobilization they fail to land in Red. Instead, they shoot off the color spectrum into:

Condition Black   "Panic . . . misdirected frenzy . . . paralysis. It's called Black because your mind is *blacked out* and because it symbolizes the ultimate black moment: *Lights out for you.*"

The Awareness Spectrum—Stages of Alertness *(The Tactical Edge)*

Condition White	Environmental unawareness
Condition Yellow	Relaxed but alert—ideal for patrol
Condition Orange	State of alarm
Condition Red	Something *is* wrong
Condition Black	Panic/blacked out—perhaps dead

Remsberg (1986, p. 51) stresses that "Yellow is the state of mind you should be operating in all the time you are on patrol. . . . Alertness and the tactical edge it offers actually *discourage* attack. It's ironic, but true that the officer who is habitually prepared to defend himself *rarely* has to."

Physical Fitness

Tens of thousands of articles, periodicals, books, and other resources are available on the topic of physical fitness. The fact remains, however, that the physical element of the whole person is of very great

Because so much of police work involves sitting in a car or at a desk, the importance of a regular exercise program cannot be overemphasized. Police officers have to be able to respond when the need arises.

importance—particularly to law enforcement officers. Not only will you be expected to out-perform most of the rest of the population—for example, carrying a victim away from a fire scene—but you will also be expected to do this under the worst of situations such as extreme heat or cold and under extreme stress.

There are no two ways about it. You have to be fit! Your life and the lives of those you've sworn to protect depend on it. Again, the job by its very nature detracts from this important area. You will be tired after odd work hours. You may sit for hours, days, even weeks on end in a squad car with little activity. And let's face it, cops aren't known for their good eating habits. When was the last time you took heat because the "cops are always hanging out at the vegetarian restaurant"? If the only thing open in the middle of the night is the fast food place, that's where you go.

How officers deal with stress becomes an issue itself. If it's excessive alcohol use, food, sleep, or complaining, segments of the whole person are affected, detracting from the other areas.

This text will not attempt to suggest a physical fitness regime. Rather it urges you to develop your own and stick to it. Maintain continuing involvement in an exercise program or in some active sports. Your life may depend on you being physically fit.

SURVIVAL TACTICS

In the preceding pages, you learned about being mentally and physically fit, about being at a Condition Yellow level of awareness, prepared to act at all times. The question now becomes—ACT HOW?

The purpose of this chapter is not to teach *specific* tactics, e.g., how to do a car stop or search a building. The focus is on basic survival concepts that require specific training. When considering survival tactics, every officer has to discard the stereotypes that the public and the profession itself have of police work. "Tombstone courage" is what, unfortunately, results in medals of valor or bravery. When an officer runs in without backup and accomplishes a dangerous task successfully, he or she is rewarded. But carefully scrutinized, just how far away was backup? Was immediate action required? Was the act by the lone officer brave or just stupid? What resulted in an honors ceremony could just as easily have resulted in a ceremonial funeral.

The two books recommended earlier in this chapter outline in detail specific tactics that can enhance your chances of survival. *The Tactical Edge* (p. 54) states: "Tactical Thinking that *works* involves a simple formula: you match options for defense and control to the type of threat you're facing." The book illustrates how the formula works in actual life-threatening situations.

SHOOTING SKILLS

The third leg of the triangle important to law enforcement officers is shooting skills. Americans abroad find it an unusual sight to observe police officers without guns. What could be a page 6 filler story in Detroit becomes a lead story on the international news when a "bobbie" in England uses a firearm.

Arguments about the "right to bear arms" aside, our culture permits, and perhaps encourages, the availabilty of guns and statistics show this.

According to the *Uniform Crime Reports* (1986, p. 13), of 875 law enforcement officers feloniously killed from 1977–1986, 809 were killed through the use of firearms. Table 1–1 summarizes the types of weapons used.

Table 1–1   Types of Weapons Involved in Officer Deaths (1977–1986)

Weapon	Number	Percent
Handgun	609	70%
Rifle	118	13%
Shotgun	82	9%
Knife	16	2%
Personal weapons	6	1%
Bomb	1	—
Other	43	5%

The weapon most frequently involved in the killing of a law enforcement officer is the handgun.

The most common types of handguns used were the .38 caliber and the .357 magnum. Over half of the officers killed by gunshots were within five feet of their assailants when attacked.

A friend from England was amazed to see officers equipping themselves for work here: .357 magnum revolvers, shotguns, body armor, tear gas, nightsticks, K-9s, backup guns. An expected part of the job of today's American law enforcement officer is to deal routinely with gun calls.

Unfortunately, the firearms training for police has been just that—routine. Most officers were trained, and continue to qualify, under literally ideal conditions: warm, well-lit ranges, with plenty of fire time, and under no stress.

Statistics reveal that over the last century little has changed in the ways that police tactically err in regard to armed confrontations. The fact is that the traditional patterns of instruction don't match the patterns of encounter, particularly in the area of firearms (*Street Survival*, p. 26).

It is encouraging to see more departments using creativity in conducting firearms training. Instinct shooting, dim-lights shooting, close-range shooting are all helping to address this area. Many excellent resources are available to assist in improving firearms training. What follows here is information summarized from *Street Survival*, pages 30–43, to help you understand what you will be up against.

Range Conditions vs. Typical Encounter Patterns

Distance   Most practice ranges involve targets set at 7 to 50 yards, but "spans of less than 7 yards exist between officers and suspects in almost 85 percent of actual shoot-outs."

Light   Most practice ranges are brightly lit, but more than two out of three fatal officer shootings occur during the hours of darkness or in dimly lit locations such as bars, warehouses, and basements.

Time   Most practice ranges allow ample time for positioning, aiming, and firing, but actual confrontations are "sudden affairs, over in 2 to 3 seconds."

Location   Most practice ranges have rigid safety rules, but in an actual confrontation, assailants will fire with total disregard for innocent bystanders. Police officers, in contrast, must take the safety of bystanders into consideration as they return fire.

It is important not just to practice shooting, but to shoot under as realistic conditions as possible. In a crisis situation, you will respond as you were trained and practiced. And practice makes . . . permanent!

Assailants   On the range you shoot at one target at a time. In reality, you may be confronted with two or more assailants.

Weapons   On the range no one shoots back at you. In an actual encounter "your targets not only fire back, but they generally fire first . . . and their guns may be ballistically superior. . . . Once you confront a suspect who has a gun, the odds are better than 40-60 that he will shoot at you and most probably fire the first round."

Beyond actual shooting skills, police officers must also understand basic gun safety procedures.

In addition, keeping guns at home and on your person off-duty demand special considerations.

Guns at Home

Frequently, when an officer's gun discharges "accidentally," it occurs at home. While educating your family is necessary, never forget that others will have access to your home. People are often fascinated by guns, but they are also often careless and do not know the hazard guns present. If you keep your gun at home, it is absolutely necessary that it be made inoperable, particularly if you have children in the house. It is *not* a good idea to keep your gun under your pillow or beside your bed. You can imagine the result of being startled out of sleep or after a bad dream. When you're tired, things aren't so clear.

Gun Worn Off Duty

Some departments require officers to carry weapons even when off duty. Some allow it. Some forbid it, but look the other way. Whatever your department does, carrying a weapon off duty creates some unique problems.

The obvious problem is that it is difficult to always keep it out of sight. More than once a panic-stricken shopkeeper has gotten to a phone to advise the police that "there is a man with a gun here." Common sense demands that the gun be concealed and that some identification be available. Use that common sense to react with reason should such a misunderstanding occur. Suddenly reaching for your identification or turning quickly to respond to your "fellow officers" could well result in your being shot.

Also remember a shield means nothing without the proper identification to go with it. Anyone can buy mail-order badges these days.

If you do wear a gun off duty, wear it in appropriate places, which excludes any place where drinking is part of your agenda.

Care of Your Weapon

Before leaving the topic of shooting, consider for a moment what is so routine that many officers totally forget about it—the importance of a clean, well-maintained weapon. All the preparation in the world will be of no help if your gun malfunctions because it hasn't been properly cared for, you could still end up dead.

Routine cleaning of your weapon must not be neglected! Never take for granted that your gun is in working condition. Here author Scott Harr performs routine maintenance on his duty weapon.

The fact that a gun is so seldom, if ever, used or even drawn during an officer's career, makes it easy to forget about it. Just as officers must maintain themselves emotionally and physically, they must also maintain their equipment. Not only will routine maintenance keep your weapon in operating condition, it will also keep you confidently familiar with your firearm, giving you the psychological edge that just might give you the upper hand in a crisis situation.

According to *Street Survival* (p. 370): "Your firearm is your most important piece of equipment. It can keep you alive when all else has failed. . . . When you squeeze the trigger, with perhaps only one chance to neutralize an adversary, your gun must not jam. . . misfire . . . explode or shoot crooked if it is to save you. And yet some officers who lose armed confrontations realize in their final flash of consciousness that that is exactly what has happened. Without doubt, the single greatest cause of such firearm malfunctions is poor maintenance." It is critical that you keep your gun in good condition.

LAW ENFORCEMENT EQUIPMENT

The right mental/emotional/physical training can be supplemented by the proper use of equipment. The technology relating to law enforcement equipment is changing at an incredible rate.

A decade ago few officers wore bulletproof vests; five years ago few departments even permitted the use of semi-automatic handguns. The rapid development and acceptance of such equipment, both of which are now standards in the profession in most parts of the country, illustrate the effect technology is having on the law enforcement profession.

The development of chemical agents, high-powered flashlights, newly designed nightsticks, improved handcuffs, more visible squad car lighting, stun guns, and the list goes on, reflects the necessity for the law enforcement community to keep up their awareness of such equipment.

A word of caution is in order. More technically complex equipment requires special training. Improper use of such equipment could well result in the officer and department being held liable for injuries sustained by a suspect. The topic of officer liability is discussed in depth in chapter 4.

SUMMARY

In the last ten years, over 1,100 law enforcement officers have been killed in the line of duty, and an additional 19,000 have been injured in assaults. The weapon most frequently involved in the killing of a law enforcement officer is the handgun.

The survival triangle consists of mental/physical preparation, survival tactics, and shooting skill. To be mentally and physically prepared, officers should be familiar with common responses to super-

Few areas of police work, other than the law itself, have changed as dramatically as the technology of law enforcement equipment. Emergency lighting, defensive weapons, and firearms are constantly changing in an effort by the police to keep up with the criminals.

stressful situations. These responses include the startle response, thought distraction, sensory distortion, and awareness lapse. The proper level of awareness is critical. The level of alertness to surroundings has been described as a color spectrum beginning with white—environmental unawareness; through yellow—relaxed but alert; orange—state of alarm; red—crisis situation; to black—panic, blacked out, or even dead. Condition yellow, relaxed but alert to potential threats, is the ideal state for patrol officers.

Discussion Questions

1. Why do so many officers have the "it can never happen to me" delusion?

2. Why is training so important in officer safety?
3. Why is physical fitness another critical element of officer safety?
4. Why is it important to balance the "whole person"?
5. What equipment plays a role in officer safety?
6. Do you think officers should carry guns off duty?
7. Have there been any officers killed in the line of duty in your town within the last year?

References

Adams, Ronald J., McTernan, Thomas M., and Remsberg, Charles. *Street Survival: Tactics for Armed Encounters.* Northbrook, Ill.: Calibre Press, 1980.

Remsberg, Charles. *The Tactical Edge: Surviving High-Risk Patrol.* Northbrook, Ill.: Calibre Press, 1986.

Uniform Crime Reports: Law Enforcement Officers Killed and Assaulted, 1986. Washington, DC: U.S. Government Printing Office.

B|A|S|I|C
I|S|S|U|E

WOULD GUN CONTROL REDUCE CRIME?

You have seen that handguns are the most frequently used weapon in the felonious killings of on-duty police officers. Where do you stand on the issue of gun control?

(Adapted from *Opposing Viewpoints: Would Gun Control Reduce Crime?*, St. Paul: 1984 Greenhaven Press)

Arguments FOR Gun Control

One Fewer Killing

I know that gun-control is an imperfect solution. But I know, too, that the only reason to have a gun is to kill, and if gun-control rids this world of just one gun, there might just be one fewer killing. Maybe a doctor could continue to cure, or a bartender mix drinks, or a mother see her grandchildren, or John Lennon write another song. (Richard Cohen, *Washington Post*, December 14, 1980)

Stopping the Carnage

It's time to stop the carnage. We must have federal handgun registration. This nation requires the registration of automobiles and tests the skills of drivers, but does nothing to check on who owns or uses handguns. . . . Must other children, other wives, other husbands die? Must another leader be assassinated? Surely enough have died already. Let's begin now to get rid of the weapons that make it so easy to blow our loved ones away. (John C. Quinn, *USA Today*, April 4, 1984)

A Tragic Loss of Life

The only way to prevent the tragic loss of life—the 32,000 lives a year that we're losing to handguns—is to say: "We no longer need handguns. They serve no valid purpose, except to kill people.". . . People tend not to perceive handguns to be a problem to them personally. They think that handgun deaths are something that happens to other people. It has not come home to us yet that those 32,000 people who are dying each year are our friends and our neighbors. It's much easier to take a live-and-let-live stance. (Michael Beard, *U.S. News and World Report*, December 22, 1980)

The Constitution Does Not Guarantee Personal Handguns

In 1967 the President's Commission on Law Enforcement and Administration of Justice concluded emphatically that "The U.S. Supreme Court and lower Federal courts have consistently interpreted this Amendment [the Second Amendment] only as a prohibition against Federal interference with State militia and not as a guarantee of an individual's right to keep or carry firearms." (Raymond Rogers, *Vital Speeches of the Day*, October 1, 1983)

Arguments AGAINST Gun Control

The Problem is Violence

The problem in American society is violence, not handguns. Blaming crime on handguns is like blaming wet streets for rain. To use handguns as a facile explanation for our high crime rate is to ally oneself with those who believe that our social environment is to blame for violence. For their actions, that blame lies with the environment. If we just restructure the environment, these utopians say—just remove the handguns and other unpleasant items—society will be more harmonious. Nonsense. (Mark W. Hendrickson, *New Guard*, Summer, 1982)

Armed Criminals Terrify Citizens

The net effect of New York's stiff gun-control laws has put disarmed citizens at the mercy of criminals armed with illegal, black-marketed, unregistered, untraceable guns. Or turned otherwise law-abiding citizens into lawbreakers because they now own guns illegally out of desperation for their own protection and safety from runaway crime. (Phoebe Courtney, *The American Mercury*, Winter, 1979)

The Constitution Guarantees Personal Handguns

A well-regulated militia, being necessary to the security of a free state, the right of the people to keep and bear arms, shall not be infringed. (Second Amendment to the Constitution of the United States)

And what about the Second Amendment, the one that's supposed to protect the ". . . right of the people to keep and bear arms." Legal scholars are divided over whether this is a collective or individual right, but I submit, that like the ". . . right of the people" to be free from unreasonable searches and seizures, it belongs to each of us individually. (Dan Cohen, *Minneapolis Star*, April 9, 1981)

CHAPTER 2

Crimes and How They Become So: The Origin and Evolution of Law in the United States

No man is above the law and no man is below it; nor do we ask any man's permission when we require him to obey it—Theodore Roosevelt, speech, January 1904.

DO YOU KNOW

Exactly what "law" is?

How laws serve society?

How far back the "roots" of our law extend?

Why the Code of Hammurabi, the Twelve Tables, Legis Henrici, and the Magna Carta are significant?

What common law, case law, and statutory law are?

What the Bill of Rights is and what it does?

How a statute and an ordinance differ?

What the concept of stare decisis refers to?

What three levels of jurisdiction exist in the United States?

How law can be classified?

How civil and criminal law differ?

What the difference between a crime and a tort is?

Between a felony and a misdemeanor?

What tension pervades our society?

What the difference between substantive criminal law and the law of criminal procedure is?

Introduction

Chapter 2

Most people don't run red lights, steal from their neighbors, or murder their enemies. Why? Partly because it is against the law, and if they are caught they will be punished. Since the beginning of recorded time, once people gathered, societies have set forth "rules of conduct" to maintain peace and security. According to Oran's *Dictionary of the Law*, a law is "that which must be obeyed." Or, quite simply put, law is rules that are enforced through consequences.

Dernbach and Singleton (1981, p. 2) present a more complicated definition: "Defining law is a difficult philosophical problem, but law can initially be understood as a series of rules and policies for regulating behavior in society, the creation or application of which requires the participation of the government. Rules describe what behavior is impermissible, what procedures are to be followed to accomplish certain ends, and what happens to those who do not follow them."

Ross and Ross (1981, pp. 1–2) suggest that "Law consists of the rules of community living; it is a structure of rules, regulations and accumulated decisions of the courts." It is based on the "recorded experiences of society and the community." Further, "'Laws' are rules established by a governing power to maintain peace, secure justice for its members, define the legal rights of the individual and the community, and to punish offenders for legal wrongs." They state that laws can be organized into four categories. The first is the "vast subject of contracts" relating to agreements in our business and social relations. Second are personal rights including marriage, family relations, torts, wrongful acts, and legal and civil rights. The third area is property rights including wills, estates, and real property. Finally, there is criminal law, "the principles and procedures which protect society and the community from the harmful and criminal acts of the individual. The criminal law also protects the defendant."

A law is a principle, standard, or rule made and enforced through consequences by a society.

Stuckey (1986, p. 3) contends that

A law in its simplest form is merely a guideline for human behavior. Its purpose is to encourage a person to do what is right and discourage him from doing wrong. It has been described as a social tool to mold and regulate human conduct. Legally a law is defined as an act of a legislative body written and recorded in some public repository informing people of what is right and wrong. In the case of Koenig v. Flynn, 258 NY 292 (1932) it was stated as: "that which must be

obeyed and followed by citizens, subject to sanctions or legal conse-
quences, is a law."

Laws play a necessary role in ordered civilization. People must have laws to tell them what is and what is not permissible. Laws also make it clear what the consequences will be for violating these laws. Not only does such clarification serve to protect wrongdoers from indiscriminate punishment, but it also serves to deter violating the law by setting forth prescribed punishments.

Laws serve society by educating the public regarding what the rules are, by prescribing the consequences, and thereby deterring illegal behavior.

LAWS AS A REFLECTION OF SOCIETY

Laws reflect the society that makes them whether locally or globally. Consider, for example, the laws against witchcraft during the Puritan period of our country and the extreme punishment mandated, or the laws against horse stealing in the early days of the Wild West and the automatic lynching that would follow. More recently, laws concerning such violations as drunk driving and child abuse have received increased attention. Our law has been called "living law" because it has the ability to change as our society changes.

Perhaps one of the clearest instances of our laws reflecting our social values and beliefs can be seen in *Bradwell* v. *Illinois* (1872), where the United States Supreme Court ruled that the Constitution was not violated when Illinois refused to license a qualified woman to practice law in that state: "The paramount destiny and mission of woman are to fulfill the noble and benign offices of wife and mother. This is the law of the Creator." Contrast this with a ruling a century later by Justice Brennan in *Frontiero* v. *Richardson* (1974): "There can be no doubt that our Nation has had a long and unfortunate history of sex discrimination. Traditionally, such discrimination was rationalized by an attitude of 'romantic paternalism' which, in practical effect, put women, not on a pedestal, but in a cage."

Another example of our "living law" deals with our society's acceptance of alcohol. The 18th Amendment, ratified in 1919, prohibited the manufacture, sale, or transportation of intoxicating liquors in the United States. The 21st Amendment, ratified in 1933, repealed the 18th Amendment.

The origins of our laws go much further back than the origins of our own country, however. They go very far back in the history of the world.

Laws began as soon as people congregated. Rules, even if unwritten, are a necessary part of any orderly society.

ANCIENT LAWS

Stuckey (1986, p. 4) describes the beginning of laws: "It probably did not take long for members of a primitive tribe to learn that they could not go about killing each other and have the tribe continue to exist. Therefore rules against murder were established. To satisfy man's need for food and shelter, he devised certain tools that became his property. The taking of these tools by another, depriving the owner of their use, was a serious act, so a rule against theft was enacted."

The first written laws known were set forth in the twenty-first century B.C. by the *Sumerians*. Three centuries later a Babylonian king used these laws as the basis of his historic *Code of Hammurabi*. This code, based on the premise that the strong should not harm the weak, established the principle of *lex talionis*, that is, an eye for an eye.

As time went on, people developed beliefs in gods and a whole new arena of rules sprang up. One such set of laws that has had a strong influence on our current laws is the Ten Commandments, established around 1200 B.C. These commandments prohibit such activities as lying, committing adultery, and murder. Laws related to religion are known as *ecclesiastical law* or *canon law*.

The ancient Greeks also had an important influence on our laws. They established the principle that a nation should be ruled by laws, not by men. Their numerous laws dealt with property, contracts, and business. They also established the precedent for judgment by a panel of one's peers, that is, a jury.

Following the Greeks, the Romans made even more sophisticated laws, embodied in the *Twelve Tables* in 450 B.C. Then, around A.D. 560

Emperor Justinian I collected all the preceding laws into a document, *Corpus Juris Civilis* (Body of Civil Laws), commonly called the *Justinian Code*. Another important contribution made by the Romans was the concept of *equity* ("fairness"). The Roman judges did not consider themselves to be completely bound by the law or by precedents but rather relied on fairness if they felt an existing law was inadequate. They felt that the "spirit of the law" should take precedence over the "letter of the law" if true justice was to be administered. This concept of equity is still found in our current system of laws as punishments that fit the crime are sought.

ENGLISH LAW

The most important contributor to our laws is England. Wrobleski and Hess (1986, p. 7) note that

> The early beginnings of just laws and social control were destroyed during the Dark ages as the Roman Empire disintegrated. Hordes of Germanic invaders swept into the old Roman Territory of Britain, bringing with them their own laws and customs. These German invaders intermarried with conquered English, the result being the hardy Anglo-Saxon.
>
> The Anglo-Saxons grouped their farms around small, self-governing villages that policed themselves. When criminals were caught, the punishment was often severe, as in ancient times. Sometimes, however, the tribe would let an offender prove his innocence through battle. And sometimes they allowed testimony by other tribespeople willing to swear that the accused was innocent. In addition, the practice of allowing a criminal to pay a fine for committing a crime or to work off the debt was beginning to come into vogue.

Around A.D. 600 the English were converted to Christianity. The law of the church began to be an important factor, combined with the Roman laws established during the 400 years the Romans ruled England. For several years England had a two-court system, courts of equity—free to use discretionary conscience in making judgments—and common law courts.

Dernbach and Singleton (1981, pp. 46–47) state that "The common law is the body of rules and principles found exclusively in judicial decisions. It is not created by legislatures, and it is not found in constitutions; the common law is judge-made law." Common law remains an important part of the modern American legal system, as case law decisions form and shape legal interpretations.

Common law is judge-made case law that originated in England and reflects custom and tradition. It may or may not have been written at that time.

After the last successful Norman invasion of England in 1066, England began developing its own legal system. Parliament began passing laws related to specific crimes and their penalties. Consequently, English common law became a mixture of custom and tradition and acts of Parliament, along with decisions by judges. This distinction between acts of Parliament and decisions by judges results in two different kinds of laws: statutory law and case law. Like common law, statutory and case law remain important parts of our modern legal system.

Statutory law is based on legislation passed by governments. Case law is based on decisions reached by courts in similar situations.

The decisions contained in case law are often referred to as *precedents* and serve to influence future cases.

King Henry I, who ruled England from 1100 to 1135, made important statutory laws. He became known as Henry the Lawgiver after he issued the *Leges Henrici*. This royal decree established that a criminal should be punished by the state rather than by his victim, thus making the enforcement of the law a public matter.

Another English king made a significant contribution to our system of laws, although not by his own choice. King John abused his power by selling royal positions, increasing taxes without the consent of the barons, and deciding court cases according to his whims rather than by law. To increase his revenues King John frequently made certain acts into crimes to confiscate the property of the landowner. This greedy, tyrannical leader was referred to as "the cruel leader."

In 1215 a group of barons and church leaders raised an army and forced King John to sign a document guaranteeing that no free man would be imprisoned except by judgment of his peers or by the law of the land. This document, the Magna Carta, assured the people that indiscriminate governmental power would not be exercised against them and that a predictable legal process would be used, assuring "due process."

The Magna Carta gave the English due process of law.

"Due process" is the foundation on which our legal system is built. It has been purposely left undefined in the great historical documents of the Magna Carta and the United States Constitution so

The right of due process of law was established in England and embodied in the Magna Carta. The principles contained in this historic document still influence the very essence of American law.

that the working definition could be continuously developing. While so important, with an understanding of the law, Ballentine's *Law Dictionary* states . . .

> One of the most famous and perhaps most often quoted definition of "due process of law" came from Daniel Webster in his argument in the Dartmouth College case (1819), wherein he declared that by due process of law is meant "The law which hears before it condemns, which proceeds upon inquiry, and renders judgment only after trial" (Black's Law Dictionary). A simple concept of due process is "the right to hear and the right to be heard."

The Magna Carta (also spelled Charta) included the right of habeas corpus, promising not to confine a person for a long time without a hearing. Although it is often stated that the document also provided for the right to a jury trial, what it actually did was provide that anyone accused of a crime had the right to have the charge reviewed by a council of peers, usually sixteen to twenty-four people. This council was known as a grand jury, and this group decided if the accused should stand trial. The trial itself, however, was whatever was customary, for example, trial by ordeal or by battle. The Magna Carta was used as a model for our Bill of Rights and provides a firm base upon which our law is built.

During this time in England the king's law (secular law) existed side-by-side with ecclesiastical law (religious law). All Englishmen were subject to both secular and ecclesiastical laws. Frequently rivalries arose concerning who had jurisdiction over a case. The final appeal in secular courts was to the king; in ecclesiastical court, to the Pope in Rome. As Stuckey (1986, p. 21) notes: "The inevitable result of this final appeal to the Pope was to give recognition to the fact that the canon law was a world-wide system and was not limited to any national boundary. The kings were jealous of the Pope's outside influence, over which the kings had little control, so they often tried to restrict this outside influence." The frequent controversies between the church and the king is one of the primary reasons for our strict separation of church and state.

THE EVOLUTION OF LAW IN THE UNITED STATES

During the colonial period in the United States, each colony had a legislature with limited power and a British governor who was under the authority of the English king or queen. Each colony was unique and, importantly, had a distinct political organization. They did not embrace English law entirely, notes Farnsworth (1983, p. 6), because of three impediments. First was a dissatisfaction with some aspects of English justice. Many had, in fact, immigrated to the New World to escape religious, political, or economic oppression. The second impediment was a lack of trained lawyers. The third was the primitive living conditions in the colonies.

In addition, England had given the colonies the power to pass their own legislation. Therefore, during the seventeenth century each colony developed its own system of laws, usually based on a "general sense of right as derived from the Bible and the law of nature" (Farnsworth, 1983, p. 7). In the mid–eighteenth century, the colonists came to view England as increasingly oppressive, imposing high taxes, enforcing unwanted commercial regulations, and trying to control new territories frequently through military rule. English soldiers were sent to the colonies to enforce the laws and to collect taxes. Anyone who objected to the excessive taxation was taken to England for trial. As noted by Stuckey (1986, p. 30), "Suspected objectors were frequently

Modern American law has its roots in English common law, that is, judge-made case law. In many respects, the primary difference between a modern American courtroom and its colonial counterpart is as simple as the clothing and hair styles worn.

subjected to searches and seizures without cause and imprisoned without justification."

Feeling that their freedom was no longer secure, fifty-four colonists came together in 1774 in Philadelphia in the First Continental Congress. According to Farnsworth (1983, p. 2):

> The colonists were anxious to assure their enjoyment of rights that the English had under case law and under the English Bill of Rights of 1689. . . .
>
> By 1775, when the Second Continental Congress convened, fighting between the colonists and the British had already begun. Despite its dubious status, this body assumed authority over the colonies as a whole and instigated preparations for war. In spite of the hostilities, there was reluctance to break with England and only after long delay were all of the colonies brought into line and independence declared in July, 1776. The Declaration of Independence detailed the colonists' grievances and epitomized much of the revolutionary theory.

When the colonists rebelled in 1776 and broke away from England, they had to form their own system of government and laws. The revolution did not unite the colonies; it simply cut them free from England. Each state proceeded to make its own constitution and jealously guarded its autonomy. It was not until ten years later in 1787 that the Constitution of the United States was written.

The United States Constitution

The Preamble to the Constitution sets forth the reasons for the independent colonies joining into a union:

The Boston Tea Party reflects the willingness of Americans to stand up for their convictions to establish a system of justice that ensures the freedom that is the essence of the United States.

We the People of the United States, in Order to form a more perfect Union, establish Justice, insure domestic Tranquility, provide for the common defence [sic], promote the general Welfare, and secure the Blessings of Liberty to ourselves and our posterity, do ordain and establish this Constitution for the United States of America.

The Constitution, in effect, merged the individual colonies into a single nation. Farnsworth (1983) suggests that the most crucial decision of the Constitutional Convention was "To have a central government with widened powers designed to operate on individuals rather than states." In other words, the federal system of government existed side-by-side with the state governments and was given limited powers. In fact, the limitation of federal government powers was of primary importance.

The articles of the Constitution did not guarantee any basic human rights, but basically set forth procedure. Because the colonists were still very mindful of how they had been treated under English rule, they quickly added ten amendments to the Constitution. These ten amendments are known as the Bill of Rights and are a critical part of the United States system of justice, providing the guarantees that Americans cherish.

The Bill of Rights, the first ten amendments to the Constitution, guarantee United States citizens certain rights by limiting the power of the government.

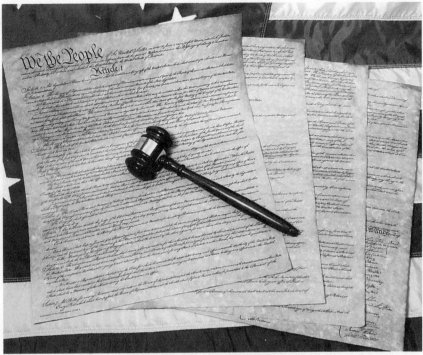

Isn't it incredible that a document written over two hundred years ago continues to affect and direct the profession of law enforcement daily.

The following amendments are most applicable to the study of criminal procedure:

- *The First Amendment* guarantees freedom of speech, of the press, and of assembly.
- *The Fourth Amendment* prohibits unreasonable searches and seizures and requires establishing probable cause.
- *The Fifth Amendment* prohibits double jeopardy and being compelled to testify against oneself and guarantees due process.
- *The Sixth Amendment* guarantees rights during a criminal trial, including the rights to a speedy, public trial by an impartial jury; to know the charges; to be confronted with witnesses against oneself; and to have a defense attorney.
- *The Seventh Amendment* guarantees the right to trial.

Although the Bill of Rights originally applied to only the federal government, the Fourteenth Amendment made some provisions of the first ten amendments applicable at the state level. You'll look at these amendments as they apply to specific criminal procedures later in the book.

The Three Branches of Government

The Constitution structured the federal government into three branches: executive, legislative, and judicial.

The *executive branch* is responsible for the efficient running of the country. At the federal level the head is the president of the United States. At the state level it is the governor, and at the local level it is often a position such as the mayor. The chief executive is elected and holds office for a pre-determined number of years.

The *legislative branch* is responsible for passing laws to ensure the safety and prosperity of the country, state, or locality. At the federal level this is the Congress of the United States, which has two divisions, the Senate and the House of Representatives. At the state level it is the legislature, also frequently having the same two divisions as at the federal level. Laws passed by the Congress of the United States or by state legislatures are called statutes. At the local level, the legislative branch is frequently embodied in a county board or a city council. Laws passed by these local legislatures are called *ordinances*. Legislation has become increasingly important in American law because of the benefits that codified laws (codes) provide, for example, ease of research, clarity of definition, and ability to alter.

Laws passed by state and federal governments are called statutes; laws passed by local governments are called ordinances.

The *judicial branch* is entrusted with interpreting the laws, determining when they have been broken, and, if so, setting forth penalties. In a common law system such as that of the United States, a judicial decision has two functions (Farnsworth, 1983, pp. 44–45):

> *The first, which is not, to be sure, peculiar to the common law, is to define and to dispose of the controversy before the court, . . . the second function of a judicial decision, and one that is characteristic of the common law, is that it establishes a precedent so that a like case arising in the future will probably be decided in the same way.*

Relying on previous cases should help assure that everyone is treated equally under the law. It should also help to predict the outcome of a given case; and it should be more efficient, saving time and energy. Finally, it shows respect for the decisions of past judges, acknowledging that society frequently looks back to predict the future.

The concept of present cases relying on past cases is that of *stare decisis*, which literally means, "the decision stands."

Stare decisis means that present cases rely on decisions made in past cases (that is, on precedents).

Dernbach and Singleton (1981, p. 21–22) tell us that

> stare decisis *requires that a court follow its own decisions and the decisions of higher courts within the same jurisdiction. This assures that the law is known, with results being predictable.*

A state trial court, for example, must follow its own decisions and the decisions of the appellate courts in that state.

> *Precedent, then can be of two types—binding or persuasive. Where the doctrine of* stare decisis *applies, precedent is binding and a court's options are limited. . . . Where the doctrine of* stare decisis *is not applicable, as with decisions from other jurisdictions or lower courts in the same jurisdiction, courts are free to follow previous decisions or ignore them. Although courts are not bound by such decisions, they remain persuasive because their reasoning can illuminate possible solutions to a problem (Dernbach and Singleton, p. 22).*

The Three Areas of Jurisdiction

In addition to establishing three branches of government, our legal system has established three areas of jurisdiction: federal, state, and local. "Jurisdiction," say Ross and Ross (1981, p. 6), "is the legal authority of a public body to act."

The three jurisdictions in the United States are the federal, state, and local governments.

The United States Constitution provides the basic framework upon which *all* law is constructed. At the federal level, laws are passed (promulgated) by Congress, codified as the United States code. At the state level are the individual state constitutions, with laws passed by their legislatures being set forth in state statutes.

Each state is autonomous as long as it does not violate federal law. The trend has been toward greater uniformity of laws among the states by the passage of "Uniform" or "Model" laws, such as the Model Arson Act, Uniform Building Code, and the Model Penal Code.

Finally, at the local level, each community, be it a village, town, or city, passes ordinances to govern the conduct of citizens of that community. They have the power to control building construction, including electricity and plumbing, as well as local zoning and traffic.

Whether federal, state, or local, laws reflect the perceived needs of the people they serve.

Specific courts have also been established to parallel each of these three levels of jurisdiction, as will be discussed in chapter 3.

Within the three jurisdictions, a hierarchy of legislation has been established as follows (Farnsworth, 1983, pp. 55–57):

- The Constitution of the United States
- Treaties made by the United States
- Federal statutes
- Federal executive orders
- State constitutions
- State statutes
- State administrative rules and regulations
- Municipal charters, ordinances, rules, and regulations

"A court may," suggests Farnsworth (p. 55), "refuse to apply a legislative enactment to a case on the ground that the enactment is invalid because it conflicts with some more authoritative legislative source. For this reason it is important to have an understanding of the hierarchy of these sources."

The United States Constitution remains the supreme law of the land, with federal treaties and statutes having to comply with United States constitutional law. In turn, all other laws must comply with the United States Constitution and generally with federal treaties and statutes.

Obviously such a hierarchy is necessary so the broad framework of the United States Constitution will govern all laws, and that other federal laws will affect the entire country. Individual states, as well as municipalities, are then permitted to regulate their own jurisdictions when local issues, rather than nationwide issues, are being dealt with.

CLASSIFICATIONS OF LAW

Laws can be classified in the following ways:

- by type: written and common law
- by source: constitutional, statutory, and case law; ecclesiastical or cannon law
- by the parties involved: public and private law
- by substance: civil and criminal law

Law may be classified by type (written/common), by source (constitutional/statutory/case), by the parties involved (public/private), and by substance (civil/criminal).

Written law is law made by legislative bodies and embodied in constitutions, by-laws, treaties, statutes, and ordinances. It is synonymous with statutory law. It does not involve specific cases. Common law is law made by courts, with earliest case law not even being recorded. It is synonymous with case law and does involve specific court decisions.

The public/private classification is based on the scope of the law. "Statutes may be called public because the rights conferred are of general application, while laws known as private affect few or selected individuals or localities" (*Garner v. Teamsters, Chauffeurs and Helpers Local Union No. 776* [1953]). *Private laws* include such areas as contracts, negligence, wills, and sometimes divorce. *Public laws*, on the other hand, involve the relations of individuals among themselves and with the government.

The civil/criminal classification is the one of most interest in this text. You will be learning to deal with criminal matters legally, and legally usually involves the suspect's civil rights. If you do not deal legally with criminal matters, you may find yourself the target of a civil lawsuit. The two are integrally related.

Black's *Law Dictionary* defines civil law as "laws concerned with civil or private rights and remedies, as contrasted with criminal laws." In civil lawsuits, one individual or group has a complaint against another individual or group. A civil wrong is called a *tort*. It is a personal matter, and the wronged party seeks restitution or compensation, usually in the form of money. A tort is a wrong against an individual.

A crime, in contrast, is a wrong against society. It is an act or omission defined and made punishable by law. According to Black's *Law Dictionary*, criminal law is "that law which for the purpose of preventing harm to society, (a) declares what conduct is criminal, and (b) prescribes the punishment to be imposed for such conduct." Criminal laws are often referred to as the *penal code,* or criminal statutes. When a criminal law is broken, the complex procedural machinery for the administration of justice is set in motion.

A crime is a wrong against society. A tort is a wrong against an individual. An act may be both a crime and a tort.

People who commit crimes and are found guilty by the court are punished by the government in the form of a fine, imprisonment, or both. People who commit torts and are found liable by the court are made to make restitution to the victim. They may also be the subject of other sanctions. A single act may be both a crime and a tort. For example, if someone were to hit you, that person could be charged with the crime of assault and, if found guilty, be made to pay a fine and/or be imprisoned. This is a crime because it is considered a wrong against society as a whole. In addition, you could sue the person for committing the tort of battery, seeking damages (money) and, if found liable, the person would have to make financial compensation to you in the amount decreed by the court.

CLASSIFICATIONS OF CRIME

"Criminality is a universal phenomenon, as the Bible, Homer, the Icelandic saga, Chinese history, American Indian legends, and other oral and written traditions attest" *(Two Hundred Years of American Criminal Justice).*

Crimes are often divided into three categories: felonies, misdemeanors, and lesser infractions or petty misdemeanors.

A felony is the most serious crime and carries the most serious penalties of death or imprisonment, generally for no less than one year in a state or federal prison. Felonies include arson, serious assault, burglary, murder, rape, robbery, and theft (above a certain value). Felonies are often further classified as simple or aggravated based on the degree of danger or harm involved.

Misdemeanors are less serious crimes and carry a sentence of less than a year in a jail. Misdemeanors are often classified as gross or petty based on the monetary value involved. Petty misdemeanors are sometimes called infractions, the least serious crimes, usually carrying a fine and/or probation but no imprisonment.

The importance of differentiating between such classifications of criminal acts is not only in the severity of the sentences imposed, but in the criminal procedures that apply. For instance a felony level crime is sometimes handled differently than is a misdemeanor level crime. More on this will be discussed later. Exact definitions of such crime classifications are found within statutory criminal codes.

A *felony* is a more serious crime, generally punishable by a prison sentence of more than one year. A *misdemeanor* is a lesser crime, generally punishable by a fine or a jail sentence not to exceed one year.

CRIME IN THE UNITED STATES

The United States has been called the most crime-ridden country in the world. Stuckey (1986, p. 7) suggests three reasons this impression exists: "Freedom of the press, which devotes much space and time to coverage of criminal activities; maintaining outstanding records and statistics on crime; and efficient law enforcement agencies, making many arrests which, in turn, are recorded in files and publicized in the news media." After presenting these reasons, he expands on why we have so much crime in the United States:

One reason for the United States' high crime rate is that our society contains mixed emotions concerning law and order. Perhaps there is no place on earth where people wish to live more comfortably and peacefully with others than in the United States, yet no group of people resent more than we do being told what we can and cannot do. We want to be protected by the authority vested in our government, particularly in law enforcement, and at the same time we do not hold authority in particularly high esteem. Too many of our citizens want their families to be safe from the hoodlum but do not want their favorite bookie arrested. They want their streams stocked with fish at all times, but they like to brag about "bagging" more than the limit. Americans want Junior to grow up as a wholesome law abiding citizen, but while on the Sunday drive they station him in the back seat to be the lookout for "cops" while Dad speeds. Too many want the law to control the "other guy" but want complete freedom of movement for themselves. These same people expect to be aided in an emergency but do not want to become involved in others' problems. In summary, as a nation our people love freedom and individuality—without restraint.

A tension between individual and societal rights pervades our country.

It is one challenge of law enforcement to balance these rights.

SUBSTANTIVE CRIMINAL LAW VS. THE LAW OF CRIMINAL PROCEDURE

One other important distinction must be made before moving on to look at the third branch of government, the judicial system, charged with carrying out the laws made by the legislative branch. That is the distinction between substantive criminal law and the law of criminal procedure.

Substantive criminal law serves to define specific crimes and their penalties. The law of criminal procedure deals with the process of enforcing substantive criminal law.

Substantive Criminal Law

For a law to be enforced it is absolutely essential that the elements that make up a particular offense be clearly and specifically defined. A law that is too vague or overbroad will be found to be unconstitutional. Similarly, the applicable law is required to specify the punishment that could result from violating the law.

Substantive criminal law benefits society by defining what acts are against the law. It sets forth the specific elements of such offenses as the serious felonies: aggravated assault, arson, auto theft, burglary, murder, forcible rape, larceny-theft, and robbery.

It also deals with such important matters as accomplice liability, the necessity of intent, and the possible defenses of intoxication and mental illness.

The Laws of Criminal Procedure

This text focuses on the laws of criminal procedure, that is, the process of enforcing substantive criminal law. Criminal procedure begins with the earliest investigation of a crime and terminates with the final disposition of an offender.

While *defining* criminal offenses is of great importance, the procedural system by which an individual is determined to be guilty of the offense or not, is equally important. Our law has always been greatly concerned with making as certain as possible that only the guilty are convicted. For this reason the government, as the prosecuting authority, must adequately bear the heavy burden of proving its case "beyond a reasonable doubt." This is by no means an easy, nor always an attainable, burden for the state to bear.

At times the guilty go free. It is the sincere hope of our system, however, that even fewer innocent people are convicted. It is, indeed, a system that is admittedly flawed; it does not always produce the results that everyone wants to see. In an adversary system such as we have elected to live under, there will always be a winner . . . and always a loser. But, as has been said often, while our system may not be perfect, it is the best that exists.

SUMMARY

A law is a principle, standard, or rule made and enforced by a society. Laws serve society by educating the public about what the rules are, by prescribing the consequences of violating the rules, and thereby deterring illegal behavior.

Common law is judge-made case law that originated in England and reflects custom and tradition. It may or may not have been written at that time. Statutory law is based on legislation passed by governments. Case law is based on decisions reached by courts in similar situations.

The Magna Carta gave Englishmen due process of law. It served as a model for our Constitution and Bill of Rights, the first ten constitutional amendments that give United States citizens certain rights.

The three jurisdictions in the United States are the federal, state, and local governments. Laws passed by the federal government and by state governments are called statutes; laws passed by local governments are called ordinances. The concept of *stare decisis* means that present cases rely on decisions made in past cases, that is, on precedents.

Laws may be classified by type (written/common), by source (constitutional/statutory/case), by the parties involved (public/private), and by substance (civil/criminal). A crime is a wrong against society. A tort is a wrong against an individual. An act could be both a crime and a tort. Crimes may be classified as felonies or misdemeanors. A felony is a more serious crime, generally punishable by a prison sentence of more than one year. A misdemeanor is a lesser crime, generally punishable by a fine or a jail sentence not to exceed one year.

One other important distinction is that between substantive criminal law and the law of criminal procedure. Substantive criminal law serves to define specific crimes and their penalties. The law of criminal procedure deals with the *process* of enforcing substantive criminal law.

Discussion Questions

1. Why is law needed?
2. What is meant by our "living law"?
3. What differences exist between common law and codified law?
4. What differences exist between civil law and criminal law?
5. What does "due process of law" mean?
6. What are the various law enforcement jurisdictions and how do they interact?

References

Dernbach, John C., and Singleton, Richard V., II. *A Practical Guide to Legal Writing and Legal Method.* Littleton, Colo.: Fred B. Rothman & Co., 1981.

Farnsworth, E. Allan. *An Introduction to the Legal System of the United States.* New York: Oceana Publications, Inc., 1983.

Oran, Daniel. *Oran's Dictionary of the Law.* St. Paul, Minn.: West Publishing Company, 1983.

Ross, J. Martin, and Ross, Jeffrey S. *Handbook of Everyday Law.* New York: Harper & Row Publishers, 1981.

Stuckey, Gilbert B. *Procedures in the Justice System.* 3d ed. Columbus, Ohio: Charles E. Merrill Publishing Company, 1986.

Wrobleski, Henry M., and Hess, Kären M. *Introduction to Law Enforcement and Criminal Justice.* 2d ed. St. Paul, Minn.: West Publishing Company, 1986.

You and the Law. 3d ed. Pleasantville, N.Y.: The Reader's Digest Association, Inc., 1984

DOES THE CRIMINAL JUSTICE SYSTEM WORK FOR OR AGAINST OFFENDERS?

On one hand are those who say the criminal justice system "coddles" criminals; that their rights interfere with justice being done. On the other hand are those who say the criminal justice system *must* protect the rights of persons accused of crimes.

(Adapted from Opposing Viewpoints—Is the Criminal Justice System Fair?)

Arguments that the System Favors Offenders

Charles Gould states: "I am unalterably opposed to legal loopholes which permit hardened, vicious criminals with long records of serious infractions to escape just and proper punishment."
   Gould also states:

> The warped logic of the men and women who are more concerned with bleeding hearts than with bleeding bodies goes something like this: "It is the system that is to blame. It is the ghetto. It is the lack of education. It is prejudice and poverty that forces young people to break the law."
>   In effect, they argue that you and I are guilty! It is easy to see how this faulty reasoning permits vicious criminals to rationalize and justify their violent acts. With this topsy-turvy kind of thinking, robbery, rape and murder become "moral acts against an immoral society."
>   Well, count me out! As I accept no credit for the great and good things done by tens of millions of men and women, neither do I accept blame for the actions of the evil persons with twisted minds who brutalize our streets.

Collapsing System

> In 1981, there were 13 million serious crimes and only 2 million arrests (17 percent). But only about 160,000 felons actually went to jail—1 percent of serious crimes.
>   This means, 99 percent of all serious crimes were committed with impunity—a "success rate" that could never be matched by honest, diligent citizens engaged in any activity in the private sector.
>   Anyone who doesn't understand that felons know this is fatu-

ously naive. The roving bands of young thugs are a testament to a massive breakdown in the criminal justice system. (Warren T. Brookes, Reprinted with permission of Heritage Features Syndicate, May 1985)

Arguments that the System Must Protect Offenders

It is a well-known, basic proposition that in our criminal justice system every person is presumed innocent until proven guilty. Bertram Harnett says:

> Shortcuts across constitutional rights are dangerous ground, since the freedom of all of us is linked together. Those who would trade liberty for security must know that all the cliches about vigilance being the price of liberty are true, for what the government can do to one it can do to another. People become lulled where violent crimes are involved; after all, how many such criminally accused does the average person really know? It is only when civil rights deprivations strike home that most people become alert to their personal significance. Just as the national will to continue the Vietnam War crumbled as the military draft began to cut heavily into the middle classes, the criminal involvement of "nice" youngsters with drugs and "nice" adults with white-collar crimes has driven to unlikely homes the reminders of freedom's necessities. . . .
>
> Trial judges often take the blame for sloppy police work or poor preparation by the prosecution. If an acquittal results from a failure of evidence, the judge is likely to find himself blamed, particularly if provocative journalism has formed public opinion in the belief of guilt. The basic point, often overlooked, is that the accused person may simply not have been proven to be guilty. (*Law, Lawyers, and Laymen.* 1984, Harcourt, Brace Jovanovich, Inc.)

Protecting the Accused Offsets Government's Power—

> Government's power to investigate, arrest, charge, try and punish its citizens is awesome. Power so overwhelming is subject to abuse. And abuse, whether deliberate or inadvertent, can deny justice to an individual accused of crime. That is why this country has attempted to build "massive safeguards" of defendants' rights into its criminal justice system. Those safeguards, too, are subject to abuse, but the balance of power remains with the government. (*Minneapolis Tribune*, February 10, 1981)

CHAPTER 3

Dealing with Those

Who Break the Law:

Our Courts and the

Criminal Justice System

It is better that ten guilty persons escape than that one innocent suffer.—Blackstone, *Commentaries*

DO YOU KNOW

What an inferior court is?

What the two main functions of courts are?

What the difference between original and appellate jurisdiction is?

What the term *venue* means?

How many levels our court structure has and what they are?

What the hierarchy is within and among the levels?

Who the officers of the court are?

What the three parts of the criminal justice system are?

Who usually begins the criminal justice process?

How important police discretion is in the criminal justice process?

Who controls the pretrial progress of most adult cases?

What the major purpose and task of corrections are?

Introduction

Chapter 3

The United States Constitution (Art. III, Sec. 1) created our federal judicial system: "The judicial Power of the United States shall be vested in one supreme Court, and in such inferior Courts as the Congress may from time to time ordain and establish." Likewise, the constitutions of the individual states created state supreme courts and inferior courts, often very similar to those at the federal level.

The term inferior court refers to courts beneath the supreme courts.

When someone is arrested for a crime and charged, unless the case is plea bargained, the case will end up in a court. Just what court that is will depend not only on the charge but also on the applicable federal or state jurisdiction. Although these court structures vary from state to state, they are more alike than different. Most of the differences are in what things are called rather than in how they work. Basically, all courts serve two main functions.

The two main functions of courts are settling controversies between parties and deciding the rules of law that apply in a specific case. (The parties may be individuals and/or governments.)

As noted by Dernbach and Singleton (1981, p. 6): "Courts in our society decide what the law means and how it should be applied to specific situations. Sometimes courts interpret rules that are codified in statutes, regulations, or constitutions. At other times they make their own rules as they decide cases, forming a body of judge-made law."

JURISDICTION

What kind of cases a court can hear depends on its jurisdiction, a concept introduced in the last chapter. Recall that the Constitution established three areas of jurisdiction: federal, state, and local. Jurisdiction is more than that. "Jurisdiction," says Rolando V. del Carmen (1987, p. 10), "refers to the power of a court to try a case. A court's jurisdiction is defined by the totality of the law that creates the court and limits its powers." Jurisdiction, in addition to being federal, state, or local, may also be original or appellate.

Original jurisdiction *means the court has the authority to hear cases first, try them, and render decisions.* Appellate jurisdiction *means the court has the authority to review and affirm or reverse the actions of a lower court.*

As noted by Jacobstein and Mersky (1981, p. 14):

> In general there are trial courts and appellate courts. The former are the courts where the trial is first held. . . . It is here the parties appear, witnesses testify, and the evidence is presented. The trial court usually determines any questions of fact that may be in dispute and then applies the applicable rules of law.
>
> Once the trial court reaches its decision, the losing party has a right of appeal to an appellate court. Generally, the appellate court can only decide questions of law and its decision in each case is based on the record made below. Appellate courts do not receive new testimony or decide questions of fact, and in most jurisdictions only the appellate courts issue written opinions.

Other divisions of jurisdiction also exist. Courts may have general or limited jurisdiction. As the names imply, courts with *general jurisdiction* may hear a broad range of cases; those with *limited jurisdiction* may hear a much narrower range of cases. Courts may also have exclusive or concurrent jurisdiction. *Exclusive jurisdiction* means that only that specific court can hear a specific case. *Concurrent jurisdiction* means that two separate courts have jurisdiction.

Both the federal and state courts have levels, with the supreme courts being at the top. The supreme courts are generally appellate courts but in some cases may have original jurisdiction. Below the supreme courts are courts of general jurisdiction. These courts have original jurisdiction over areas specified in the constitution or statutes and are called trial courts. These courts have jurisdiction over serious criminal cases, i.e., those involving felonies. Courts of general jurisdiction also have appellate jurisdiction over the courts below them, called the inferior courts. Because of increasing cases being litigated, there are often intermediate appellate courts on the state and federal level.

Inferior courts have limited jurisdiction over specific areas, and their decisions are subject to review by the higher courts. They may be called district courts, county courts, municipal courts, justice courts, juvenile courts, or probate courts. They may also have jurisdiction over minor criminal cases such as misdemeanors.

Beneath the state courts are local courts, also having limited jurisdiction. These may include traffic courts, magistrate's courts, police courts, small claim courts, justice courts, justice of the peace courts, city courts, or municipal courts.

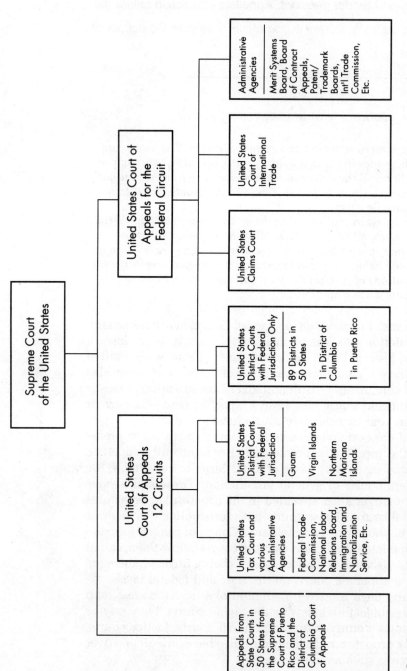

From *Criminal Procedure for Law Enforcement Personnel,* by Rolando V. del Carmen. Copyright © 1987 by Wadsworth, Inc. Reprinted by permission of Brooks/Cole Publishing Company, Pacific Grove, CA 93950.

Figure 3–1   The United States Court System

The term jurisdiction may also refer to a geographical area. Stuckey (1986, p. 37–38) suggests that: "This dual use of the term 'jurisdiction' stems from the fact that it is an all-encompassing word, embracing every kind of judicial action."

VENUE

A more precise term to describe the geographical area in which a case may be heard is venue.

Venue refers to the place a case comes to trial and the area from which the jury is selected.

Usually the venue is within the county in which a crime was committed. Sometimes it is difficult to tell exactly where this was, so states have established guidelines to solve this problem. For example, if a crime is committed in two counties or on the border between two counties, the trial can be held in either one.

Sometimes a defendant will ask for a change of venue, that is, to have the trial outside the geographical area where the crime was committed. This happens most frequently in highly sensationalized crimes with much pretrial publicity where it is feared that the jurors will be biased.

Having looked at venue, the geographical area in which a case may be heard, and jurisdiction, the inherent power of a court to try a case, turn your attention now to our court system, starting at the lowest level and working up to the top—the United States Supreme Court.

LOCAL COURTS

Local courts include municipal courts, inferior courts of limited jurisdiction, and county courts.

Municipal Courts   These courts hear ordinance violations, minor criminal cases, traffic cases, and sometimes more major cases. Their authority is usually limited to the city or county where the court is located.

Inferior Courts of Limited Jurisdiction   These courts include probate courts, family courts, police courts, justice of the peace courts, and traffic courts. A few states still have police courts, courts that try misdemeanor offenses and conduct preliminary examinations to decide if there is sufficient evidence to bring the case to trial in a higher level court. Some states have established these inferior courts of limited jurisdiction to eliminate the expense and inconvenience of having to travel to a county or district court.

County Courts   County courts often have exclusive jurisdiction over misdemeanor cases and civil cases involving a limited amount of money. In some states county courts also are probate courts and juvenile courts. Some states have combined various courts under the umbrella of the county courts.

THE STATE COURT SYSTEM

Farnsworth (1983, p. 33) notes that "The great bulk of all litigation comes before the state courts." At the state level are general jurisdiction trial courts, intermediate appellate courts, and supreme courts.

General Jurisdiction Trial Courts   These courts are called superior, circuit, or district courts, or courts of common pleas. They have jurisdiction over almost all cases, civil and criminal, that are not under the jurisdiction of a special court. In many states, especially those lacking local courts, this is the court to which serious criminal cases would first be assigned.

Intermediate Appellate Courts   These courts were created to reduce the case loads of the state supreme courts. Cases that are appealed generally go to the intermediate appellate court first.

State Supreme Courts   State supreme courts are the highest court in a state and are generally called supreme courts, although some states call them courts of appeals. These courts are given their power by the individual state constitutions. They generally oversee the intermediate appellate courts and have very few areas of original jurisdiction. If someone petitions the supreme court to review the decision of an appeals court, this is called a *petition for certiorari*. The supreme courts are not obligated to hear all such cases and, in fact, review only a small percentage of petitions for certiorari.

THE FEDERAL COURT SYSTEM

The federal court system consists of a number of specialized courts, a number of district courts with general jurisdiction, twelve circuit courts of appeals, and the United States Supreme Court.

Special United States Courts   Congress has created several specialized courts that you will probably never have any dealings with. They include the Court of Military Appeals, the Court of Claims, the Court of Customs and Patent Appeals, the Customs Court, and the Tax Court.

United States District Courts   The district courts are trial courts with general, original, federal jurisdiction. They try both civil and criminal cases. In civil cases, however, the plaintiff and defendant must be from different

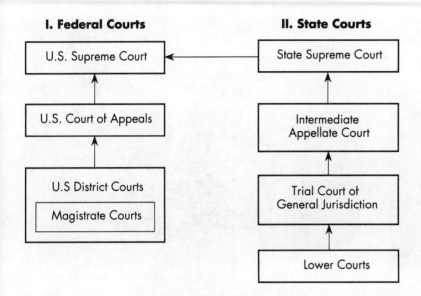

I. Federal Courts

U.S. Supreme Court	

U.S. Court of Appeals

U.S District Courts

Magistrate Courts

II. State Courts

State Supreme Court

Intermediate
Appellate Court

Trial Court of
General Jurisdiction

Lower Courts

From *You and the Law*, Copyright © 1984 The Reader's Digest Association, Inc. Reprinted by permission.

Figure 3–2   The Dual Court System: A Simplified Flow Chart

states and the amount of the lawsuit must be over $10,000. The federal district courts try a very limited number of criminal cases. The *Guide to the Federal Courts* (1984, p. 9) states that only about 6 percent of criminal activity is covered by federal statutes.

Each state has at least one district court. Some large states have four. The total number of district courts is ninety-one—eighty-nine in the states, one in the District of Columbia, and one in Puerto Rico.

United States Courts of Appeals   Like the intermediate appellate courts at the state level, the United States District Courts were created to ease the caseload of the Supreme Court. Each state is assigned to one of eleven districts or *circuits*. The District of Columbia has its own circuit and court. These courts have jurisdiction over final decisions of federal district courts. They are the court of last resort for most federal cases.

The United States Supreme Court   The Supreme Court has eight associate justices and a chief justice. The justices are appointed for life terms by the president, with the approval of Congress. The Court begins hearing cases in October of each year and stays in session until it has heard all the cases, usually by midsummer.

Its chief function is as an appellate court. It receives between two thousand and four thousand cases a year but usually accepts only 10 percent for review. Over a third of the cases received are from state supreme courts. The Supreme Court is restricted by act of Congress to hear only certain types of appeals from federal appeals courts and state supreme courts. Basically, the cases must involve a federal or state statute alleged to be unconstitutional. There is no right to have a case

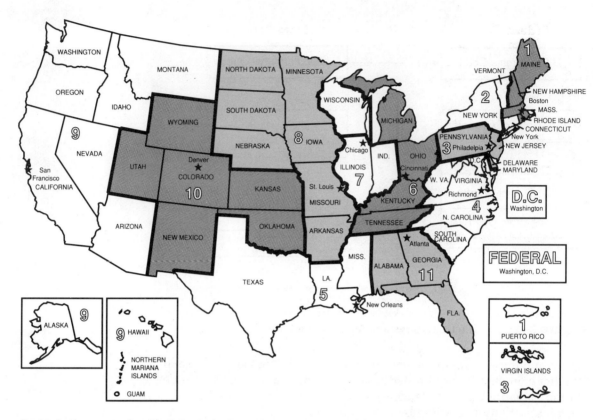

Reprinted with permission from West's Law Finder, Copyright © 1980 by West Publishing Company.

Figure 3–3 Federal Judicial Circuits

heard by the Supreme Court. It hears only cases of extreme national importance in order to set important policy.

The Supreme Court has dealt with such controversial issues as abortion, busing, and school prayer. Bills have been introduced in Congress to prevent the Supreme Court from ruling on such "moral" issues, leaving it up to the individual states.

The Supreme Court is the only court empowered to handle lawsuits between two states.

Level of Authority	Between Systems	Within Systems
Highest	Federal	Supreme Court
		Appellate
Middle	State	General
Lowest	Local	Inferior

The structure of the judicial system from federal to state is illustrated in figures 3–4 and 3–5.

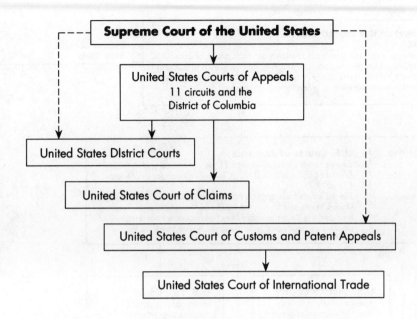

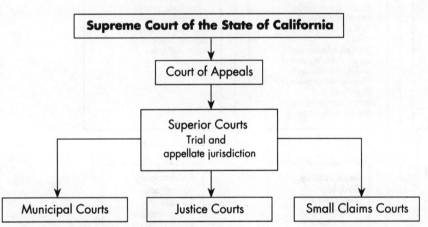

J. Myron Jacobstein and Roy M. Mersky. *Legal Research Illustrated*. Foundation Press, 2nd ed. 1981, p. 21. Reprinted with permission.

Figure 3—4   Court Organization Chart

OFFICERS OF THE COURT

Our judicial system does not consist simply of buildings. Within the courthouses are individuals charged with carrying out the administration of justice.

The officers of the court are judges, lawyers, clerks of court, sheriffs, marshals, and bailiffs.

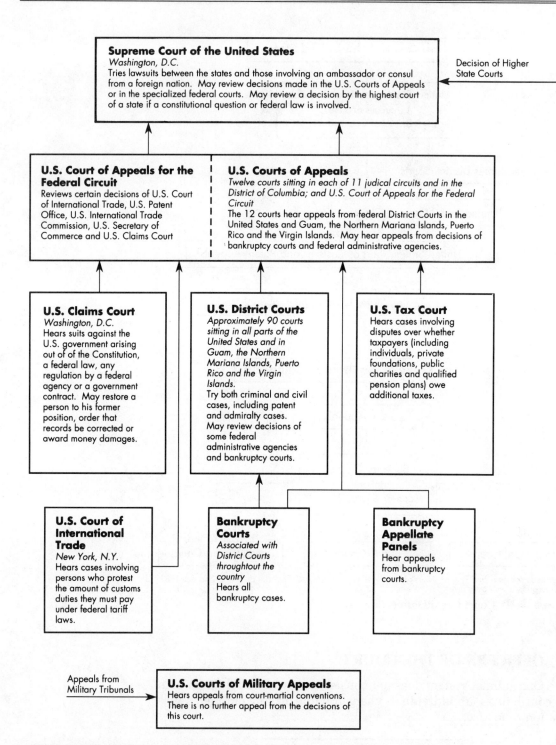

Supreme Court of the United States
Washington, D.C.
Tries lawsuits between the states and those involving an ambassador or consul from a foreign nation. May review decisions made in the U.S. Courts of Appeals or in the specialized federal courts. May review a decision by the highest court of a state if a constitutional question or federal law is involved.

Decision of Higher State Courts

U.S. Court of Appeals for the Federal Circuit
Reviews certain decisions of U.S. Court of International Trade, U.S. Patent Office, U.S. International Trade Commission, U.S. Secretary of Commerce and U.S. Claims Court

U.S. Courts of Appeals
Twelve courts sitting in each of 11 judical circuits and in the District of Columbia; and U.S. Court of Appeals for the Federal Circuit
The 12 courts hear appeals from federal District Courts in the United States and Guam, the Northern Mariana Islands, Puerto Rico and the Virgin Islands. May hear appeals from decisions of bankruptcy courts and federal administrative agencies.

U.S. Claims Court
Washington, D.C.
Hears suits against the U.S. government arising out of of the Constitution, a federal law, any regulation by a federal agency or a government contract. May restore a person to his former position, order that records be corrected or award money damages.

U.S. District Courts
Approximately 90 courts sitting in all parts of the United States and in Guam, the Northern Mariana Islands, Puerto Rico and the Virgin Islands.
Try both criminal and civil cases, including patent and admiralty cases. May review decisions of some federal administrative agencies and bankruptcy courts.

U.S. Tax Court
Hears cases involving disputes over whether taxpayers (including individuals, private foundations, public charities and qualified pension plans) owe additional taxes.

U.S. Court of International Trade
New York, N.Y.
Hears cases involving persons who protest the amount of customs duties they must pay under federal tariff laws.

Bankruptcy Courts
Associated with District Courts throughtout the country
Hears all bankruptcy cases.

Bankruptcy Appellate Panels
Hear appeals from bankruptcy courts.

Appeals from Military Tribunals

U.S. Courts of Military Appeals
Hears appeals from court-martial conventions. There is no further appeal from the decisions of this court.

From *YOU AND THE LAW,* Copyright © 1984 The Reader's Digest Association, Inc. Reprinted by permission.

Figure 3–5   The Federal and State Court Systems

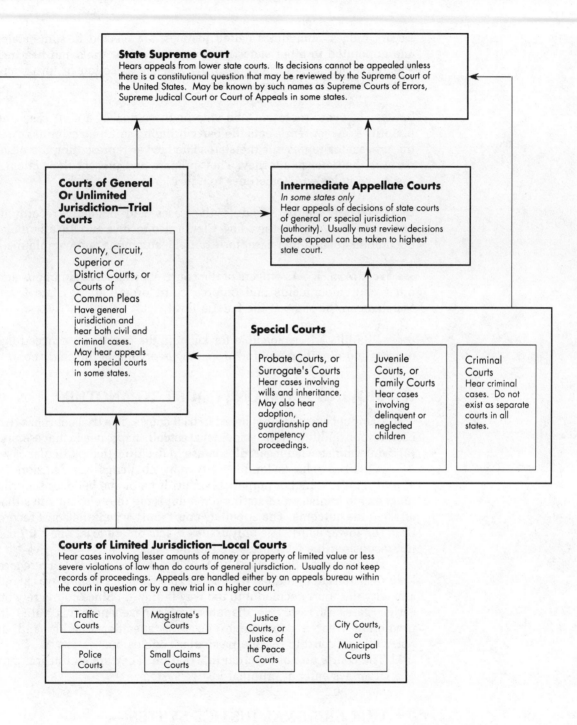

State Supreme Court
Hears appeals from lower state courts. Its decisions cannot be appealed unless there is a constitutional question that may be reviewed by the Supreme Court of the United States. May be known by such names as Supreme Courts of Errors, Supreme Judical Court or Court of Appeals in some states.

Courts of General Or Unlimited Jurisdiction—Trial Courts

County, Circuit, Superior or District Courts, or Courts of Common Pleas Have general jurisdiction and hear both civil and criminal cases. May hear appeals from special courts in some states.

Intermediate Appellate Courts
In some states only
Hear appeals of decisions of state courts of general or special jurisdiction (authority). Usually must review decisions befoe appeal can be taken to highest state court.

Special Courts

Probate Courts, or Surrogate's Courts Hear cases involving wills and inheritance. May also hear adoption, guardianship and competency proceedings.

Juvenile Courts, or Family Courts Hear cases involving delinquent or neglected children

Criminal Courts Hear criminal cases. Do not exist as separate courts in all states.

Courts of Limited Jurisdiction—Local Courts
Hear cases involving lesser amounts of money or property of limited value or less severe violations of law than do courts of general jursdiction. Usually do not keep records of proceedings. Appeals are handled either by an appeals bureau within the court in question or by a new trial in a higher court.

Traffic Courts

Magistrate's Courts

Justice Courts, or Justice of the Peace Courts

City Courts, or Municipal Courts

Police Courts

Small Claims Courts

Judges   Judges, sometimes called justices, are elected in some states and appointed in other states. Judges preside over trials and hearings and render decisions. They also oversee the selection of juries and instruct them during jury cases.

Lawyers   Lawyers represent one side or the other. In a civil case, the plaintiff's lawyer represents the party bringing suit. In a criminal case, the prosecutor represents the state. The lawyer representing the other party is the defense attorney. They prepare and present their clients' cases to a judge and sometimes to a jury.

Clerks of Court   Clerks schedule the cases and officially record all business conducted by the court. Clerks also receive and file all official documents related to a case, for example, summons and complaints.

Sheriffs and Marshals   As officers of the court, sheriffs serve summons and other court documents and enforce court orders at the state level. Marshals do the same at the federal level.

Bailiffs   Bailiffs are responsible for keeping the courtroom proceedings orderly and dignified and for protecting everyone in the courtroom.

MOVING FROM ONE COURT TO ANOTHER

Criminal cases are first heard in trial courts. The trial court has two basic responsibilities: (1) it decides what actually happened in the case, and (2) it determines what legal rules to use in deciding that particular case.

A person who is found guilty may challenge the decision by appealing it to a higher (appellate) court if he or she believes the trial judge made a mistake in stating or in applying the relevant rules that affected the outcome. The appellate court must accept the court record from the lower court. The only issues it acts on are legal ones. It does not reconsider the facts presented in the case.

Dernbach and Singleton (1981, p. 7) point out that "Courts record their decisions in opinions, which describe what the dispute was about and why the court decided it in the way it did. . . . Since courts rely on earlier cases in resolving disputes, cases have enormous value in predicting what a court might do in a specific situation and in persuading a court to reach a particular conclusion."

The courts do not function in isolation. They are an integral part of a larger system, our criminal justice system.

OUR CRIMINAL JUSTICE SYSTEM— AN OVERVIEW

Adapted from the President's Commission on Law Enforcement and Administration of Justice, *The Challenge of Crime in a Free Society* 7, 10-12 (1967).

The criminal justice system America uses to deal with crimes it cannot prevent and criminals it cannot deter was not designed or built one piece at a time. Its philosophic core is that the government may punish a person only if it has proved by an impartial, deliberate process that that person has violated a specific law.

Many layers of institutions and procedures have grown up around that core. Some are carefully constructed; others are makeshift. Some were inspired by principle; some simply served a useful purpose. Parts of the system—magistrates' courts, trial by jury, bail—are very old. Other parts—juvenile courts, probation and parole, professional police officers—are relatively new. The entire system is an adaptation of English common law to America's peculiar structure of government allowing each community to construct institutions to meet their own special needs. Every village, town, county, city, and state has its own criminal justice system. There is also a federal system. All operate somewhat alike, but none operate exactly alike.

Society uses its criminal justice system to enforce the standards of conduct needed to protect individuals and the community. The system operates by apprehending, prosecuting, convicting, and sentencing community members who break the law. The action taken against lawbreakers serves three purposes in addition to punishment. (1) It removes dangerous people from the community. (2) It deters others from criminal behavior. And (3), it gives society a chance to try to rehabilitate lawbreakers.

The greatest difference among different countries' criminal justice systems is the kind and amount of protection offered to individuals during the process of determining guilt and imposing punishment. The American system stresses preserving local autonomy and protecting individuals accused of breaking the law. It often does so at the expense of efficiency and effectiveness. For example, it has been relatively unsuccessful in preventing organized crime figures or international terrorists from preying on society.

The criminal justice system has three separately organized parts—the police, courts, and corrections—each with distinct tasks.

These three parts are NOT independent of each other. What each does and how directly affect the work of the others. The courts can deal only with those whom the police arrest. Corrections can deal only with those delivered to it by the courts. How well our correctional system reforms convicts determines if they will again commit crimes and become police business. Police activities are closely watched by the courts. Reforming or reorganizing any part or procedure of the system changes other parts and procedures. Furthermore, the criminal process is an orderly progression of events. Some, like arrest and trial, are very visible. Some, though very important, occur out of public view.

Figure 3–6 illustrates in simplified form the criminal justice process and the many decision points along the way. Because felonies, misdemeanors, petty offenses, and juvenile cases generally follow quite different paths, they are shown separately.

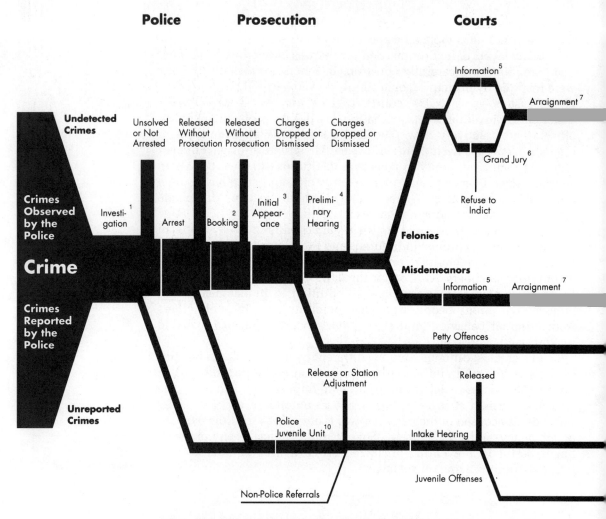

Report by the President's Commission on Law Enforcement and Administration of Justice: The Challenge of Crime in a Free Society 8, 9 (1967).

Figure 3–6   The Criminal Justice Process

Corrections

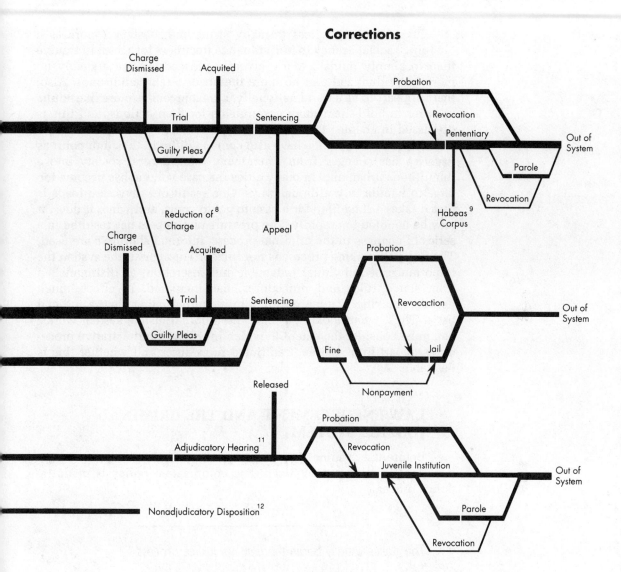

Juvenile court is less formally structured, designed more as a "helping" social agency to individualize treatment for youth in trouble than to simply punish. Many juvenile proceedings are arguably no more individualized and no more therapeutic than adult ones. Also, there appears to be a trend nationally to treat juveniles more like adults in order to hold them more accountable for their actions, and this is discussed in chapter 11.

Theory and practice have also come to differ in the adult court as America has changed from a relatively relaxed rural society into a tumultuous urban one. In many cities the case volume has become too large to handle in traditional ways. One result of heavy case loads is that it takes a long time for a case to get to court, and when it does, it may be handled too rapidly. The pressure of numbers has resulted in a series of changes in the criminal process. Informal shortcuts are used. The decision-making process is routinized. Throughout the system the importance of individual judgment and discretion, as distinguished from stated rules and procedures, has increased. In effect, much decision making is done on an administrative rather than a judicial basis. Thus, when looking at how the criminal justice system works, you must consider the extent to which invisible, administrative procedures depart from visible, traditional procedures and whether this is desirable.

LAW ENFORCEMENT AND THE CRIMINAL JUSTICE SYSTEM

Before the criminal justice process even begins, something happens that is seldom recognized: law enforcement policy is made by police officers.

The police usually begin the criminal justice process.

Police officers do not—in fact, cannot—arrest every offender they encounter. It is doubtful that they arrest most. A criminal code, in practice, is not a set of specific instructions, but a rough map of the territory in which police officers work. How police officers move around that territory depends largely on their personal discretion.

Police officers' duties compel them to exercise personal discretion many times daily. Crime does not look the same on the street as it does in a legislative chamber. How much noise or profanity makes conduct "disorderly"? When must a quarrel be treated as a criminal assault: at the first threat, the first shove, the first blow, after blood is drawn, or when a serious injury is inflicted? How suspicious must conduct be before there is "probable cause"?

Minnesota State Trooper making an arrest, thus initiating the suspect into the criminal justice system and its complexities.

All police officers are interpreters of the law. Police discretion plays a critical part in the justice process.

All police officers are also arbiters of social values. They meet situation after situation in which arresting someone is questionable. Obviously a boy throwing rocks at a school's windows is committing vandalism. But it is often not at all obvious whether a police officer will better serve the interests of the community and of the boy by taking him home to his parents or by arresting him. Who are the boy's parents? Can they control him? Is he a frequent offender who has responded badly to leniency? Is vandalism so epidemic in the neighborhood that he should be made an example? With juveniles especially, the police exercise great discretion.

Finally, how police officers work is influenced by practical matters:

- the legal strength of the available evidence,
- the willingness of victims or witnesses to be involved,
- the willingness of witnesses to testify,
- the temper of the community,
- the time and information at the police officer's disposal.

Much is at stake in how police officers exercise this discretion. If they decide conduct is not suspicious enough to justify intervention, the chance to prevent a robbery, rape, or murder may be lost. If they overestimate the seriousness of a situation or they act out of panic or prejudice, their actions may touch off a riot. They may even hurt or kill someone unnecessarily.

THE COURTS AND THE CRIMINAL JUSTICE SYSTEM

If police officers arrest someone, whether that person progresses further in the criminal justice system is usually up to the courts. The decision is made by a magistrate and/or a prosecutor.

The Magistrate

In direct contrast to police officers, the magistrate before whom a suspect is first brought usually exercises less discretion than the law allows. Magistrates are entitled to inquire into the facts of the case, but they seldom do or can. Many magistrates, especially in big cities, have such full calendars they can look carefully at only extraordinary cases.

In practice the most important things magistrates do are to set the amount of a defendant's bail and in some jurisdictions to appoint counsel. Often neither action gets the careful attention it deserves. In many cases the magistrate accepts a waiver of counsel without insuring that the suspect knows the significance of legal representation.

Bail is supposed to free an untried defendant and yet make sure he appears for trial. The Eighth Amendment to the Constitution declares that bail must not be "excessive." Appellate courts have declared that not just the seriousness of the charge, but the suspect's personal, family, and employment situation be considered when setting bail. Yet most magistrates set it according to standard rates. In fact, most misdemeanor bonds are "scheduled" or set in advance and bear no relation to the individual defendant.

The Prosecutor

The key administrative officer in processing cases is the prosecutor. The prosecutor represents the state, (i.e., the government) in the case against the defendant. The prosecutor is an officer of the court and may be an actual government employee or work for a private firm contracting with the jurisdiction to represent the people. The prosecutor monitors the progress of the case based on the available facts, determining how far justice will demand that the case be pursued throughout the system.

Prosecutors control the pretrial progress of most adult cases. They decide whether to drop a case or press charges—and what charges to press.

When the charge is reduced, as it is in two-thirds of all cases in some cities, it is usually the prosecutor who reduces it. Often this reduction is the result of plea bargaining.

Plea Bargaining

In plea bargaining, prosecutors reduce the original charge or recommend a more lenient sentence in return for a plea of guilty. One reason plea bargaining exists is that there are ten times more cases than there are prosecutors, judges, or courtrooms to handle them. Plea bargaining can be anything from a series of careful conferences to a hurried consultation in a courthouse corridor. Whether plea bargaining is a fair, effective way to dispose of criminal cases depends heavily on whether defendants are provided early with competent, conscientious counsel.

If the case goes to trial and the defendant is found guilty, a critical phase of the criminal justice process is the sentencing.

Sentencing

An enormously consequential decision is the *sentencing* decision of a judge. Most states have some sort of mandatory sentencing provisions, as summarized in table 3–1.

However, the law also recognizes the importance of fitting sentences to individual defendants by giving judges, in some cases, considerable latitude. Unfortunately, judges often lack time and sufficient information about defendants. Perhaps the greatest lack of all, however, is lack of correctional alternatives. Some lower courts have no probation officers. Those that do have such heavy case loads that a sentence of probation means, in fact, releasing an offender into the community with almost no supervision. Few states have a sufficient variety of correctional institutions or treatment programs to inspire judges with the confidence that sentences will lead to rehabilitation.

CORRECTIONS

The correctional apparatus for guilty defendants is the most isolated part of the criminal justice system. Much of it is physically isolated. Its institutions usually have thick walls and locked doors. They are often in rural areas, remote from the court and community. They are

Table 3—1   **Most States Have Some Mandatory Sentencing Provisions**

	Type of sentencing	Mandatory sentencing	Mandatory offenses
Alabama	Determinate	Yes	Repeat felony
Alaska	Determinate, presumptive	Yes	Murder, kidnaping, firearms, repeat felony
Arizona	Determinate, presumptive	Yes	Firarms, prior felony convictions
Arkansas	Determinate	Yes	Robbery, deadly weapons
California	Determinate, presumptive	No	
Colorado	Determinate, presumptive	No	
Connecticut	Determinate	Yes	Sex assault with firearm, burglary, repeat felony, assault on elderly
Delaware	Determinate	Yes	Murder, kidnapping, prison assault, robbery, narcotics, deadly weapon, habitual criminal, obscenity, others
Florida	Indeterminate	Yes	Drug
Georgia	Determinate	Yes	Armed robbery, burglary, drugs
Hawaii	Indeterminate	No	
Idaho	Determinate	Yes	Firearm, repeat extortion, kidnap or rape with bodily injury
Illinois	Determinate	Yes	Major offenses, specified felonies and offenses, repeaters, weapons
Indiana	Determinate, presumptive	Yes	Repeat felony, violent crime, deadly weapons
Iowa	Indeterminate	Yes	Forcible felonies, firearms, habitual offenders, drugs
Kansas	Indeterminate	Yes	Sex offense, firearms
Kentucky	Indeterminate	No	
Louisiana	Indeterminate	Yes	Drugs, violent crime
Maine	Determinate	No	
Maryland	Determinate, guidelines	Yes	Repeat violent offenders, handgun
Massachusetts	Indeterminate	Yes	Firearm, auto theft, drug trafficking
Michigan	Indeterminate	Yes	Murder, armed robbery, treason, firearms
Minnesota	Guidelines	No	
Mississippi	Determinate	Yes	Armed robbery, repeat felony
Missouri	Determinate	Yes	Dangerous weapon, repeat felony
Montana	Indeterminate	Yes	Firearms
Nebraska	Indeterminate	No	
Nevada	Determiante	Yes	2nd degree murder, 1st degree kidnaping, sexual assault, firearm, repeat felony
New Hampshire	Indeterminate	Yes	Firearms
New Jersey	Determinate, presumptive	Yes	Sexual assault, firearms
New Mexico	Determinate, presumptive	Yes	Firearms
New York	Indeterminate	Yes	Specified violent and nonviolent felonies
North Carolina	Determinate, presumptive	Yes	Armed robbery, 1st degree burglary, repeat felony with firearm
North Dakota	Determinate	Yes	Firearm
Ohio	Indeterminate	Yes	Rape, drug trafficking
Oklahoma	Determinate	Yes	Repeat felony
Oregon	Guidelines, Indeterminate	Yes	Drugs
Pennsylvania*	Guidelines, indeterminate	Yes	Selected felonies with firearms, within 7 years of prior convictions, in or near public transportation
Rhode Island	Indeterminate	No	
South Carolina	Determinate	Yes	Armed robbery, drugs, bomb threat
South Dakota	Indeterminate	No	
Tennessee	Determinate, indeterminate	Yes	Specified felonies, firearms, repeat felony
Texas	Determinate	Yes	Repeat felony, violent offenses
Utah	Indeterminate	No	
Vermont	Indeterminate	Yes	Drugs, violent crime
Virginia	Indeterminate	No	

	Type of sentencing	Mandatory sentencing	Mandatory offenses
Washington	Indeterminate	Yes	Firearms, rape, repeat felony
West Virgina	Indeterminate	Yes	Firearms in felony
Wisconsin	Indeterminate	No	
Wyoming	Indeterminate	No	

*Pennsylvania updated as of December 1982.

Sources: *A survey of mandatory sentencing in the U.S.,* Richard S. Morelli, Craig Edelman, Roy Willoughby, Pennsylvania Commission on Crime and Delinquency. *September 1981. Judical and executive discretion in the sentencing process: Analysis of felony State code provisions.* Criminal Courts Technical Assistance Project (Washington: American University, January (1982). *A national survey of parole-related legislation.* Michael Kanvensohn, (San Francisco: Uniform Parole Reports, December 1979).

States primarily use three strategies for sentencing

*Indeterminate sentences usually *provide a minimum and a maximum* term, either of which *may be reduced* by "good time" (time credits gained by inmates for good conduct or special achievement) or by a decision of the parolling authorities. The maximum sentence may be set as a range (for example, 5 to 10 years) rather than a specific number of years.

*Determinate sentences usually provide a *fixed term* that may *be reduced* by good time or parole. Judicial discretion may be available to grant probation or suspend the sentence. Sentencing laws generally provide a maximum (or a range) for sentence duration. Determinate systems are usually based on a definite length for a sentence that can be increased or decreased for aggravating or mitigating factors or on guidelines that define sentence lengths, deviations from which must be justified by sentencing judges.

*Mandatory prison sentences are defined by law and must be given upon conviction; the *judge is not permitted to grant probation or to suspend the sentence.*

Most States apply a combination of sentencing strategies

Many States may have a predominant orientation toward one strategy (for example, indeterminate) and require another strategy (for example, mandatory sentences) for specific offenses. The strategies utilized by States are constantly evolving, thus complicating overall classification. As of September 1981, for example, some States that required mandatory prison sentences for certain offenses used a predominantly indeterminate strategy while others used a determinate strategy.

also isolated in that their officials have no everyday working relationships with officials from the system's other branches, like those commonly existing between police and prosecutors, or prosecutors and judges.

Corrections is further isolated in that what it does with, to, or for those under its supervision is governed by very broadly written statutes and is seldom scrutinized by appellate courts. Finally, it is isolated from the public partly by its invisibility and physical remoteness; partly by the lack of drama in most of its activities; but perhaps most importantly by the fact that the correctional apparatus is often used—or misused—by both the criminal justice system and the public as a rug under which disturbing problems and people can be swept.

Although rehabilitating criminals is presumably the major purpose of corrections, the custody of criminals is actually its major task.

On any given day well over a million people are being "corrected" in America, two-thirds on probation or parole and one-third in prisons or jails. However the majority of correctional money is spent and the vast majority of correctional personnel work in prisons and jails. Further, the vast majority of correctional personnel work at administrative or custodial jobs, and many jails have only custodial and administrative personnel.

This emphasis on custody means that the enormous potential of the correctional apparatus for making creative decisions about its

Jail. The ultimate means of losing one's valued rights of freedom. It is amazing that the concept of recidivism exists given the stark reality of jails.

treatment of convicts is largely unfulfilled. This is true of offenders in custody as well as those on probation and parole. In the juvenile correctional system the situation is somewhat better. Juvenile institutions have a higher proportion of treatment personnel, and juvenile probation and parole officers generally have lighter case loads than those who deal with adult offenders.

Except for sentencing, no decision in the criminal process has more impact on convicted offenders than the *parole* decision. This determines how much of the maximum sentence a prisoner serves. This is another invisible administrative decision seldom open to attack or subject to review. Parole decisions are made by parole board members who are often politically appointed. Although many are skilled and conscientious, they generally can spend no more than a few moments on a case. Since there is virtually no appeal from their decisions, they may be arbitrary or discriminatory. Just as carefully formulated and clearly stated law enforcement policies would help police officers, charge policies would help prosecutors, and sentencing policies would help judges, so parole policies would help parole boards perform their important duties.

THE STATUS OF OUR CRIMINAL JUSTICE SYSTEM

America's system of criminal justice is overcrowded and overworked, undermanned, underfinanced, and very often misunderstood. It needs more information, more knowledge, and more technical resources. It needs greater coordination among its many parts. It needs more public support, including the help of community programs and institutions in dealing with offenders and potential offenders. The system needs, above all, the willingness to reexamine old ways of doing things, to reform itself, to experiment, to run risks, to dare. It needs vision. It needs to be as viable as the "living law" it serves.

Police officers are a critical part of this system. Understanding the total context in which police officers function should help assure that they fulfill their role professionally.

SUMMARY

An inferior court is a lower court. The two main functions of courts, regardless of level, are settling controversies between parties and deciding the rules of law that apply in a specific case. (The parties may be individuals and/or governments.) Original jurisdiction means the court has the authority to hear cases first, try them, and render decisions. Appellate jurisdiction means the court has the authority to review and affirm or reverse the actions of a lower court.

Venue refers to the place in which a case comes to trial and the area from which the jury is selected. (The term *jurisdiction* is sometimes also used in this context.)

Our court system consists of three levels—local, state, and federal. State courts can overrule local courts, and federal courts can overrule state courts. Local, state, and federal court systems also have levels, with the lowest levels being the inferior courts, progressing in authority to courts of general jurisdiction, appellate courts, and, finally, to the highest authority, supreme courts.

Officers of the court, at various levels, are judges, lawyers, clerks of court, sheriffs, marshals, and bailiffs. The court is part of a larger system, our criminal justice system.

The criminal justice system has three separately organized parts—the police, courts, and corrections—each with distinct tasks. The police usually begin the criminal justice process. All police officers are interpreters of the law. Police discretion plays a critical role in the justice process. Prosecutors control the pretrial progress of most adult cases, deciding whether to drop a case or press charges and, if so, what charges.

The third segment of the criminal justice system is corrections. Although rehabilitating criminals is presumably the major purpose of corrections, the custody of criminals is actually its major task.

Discussion Questions

1. What are the main purposes of the courts?
2. What is the importance of "jurisdiction"?
3. Why is it necessary to have so many people involved in our judicial system?
4. What aspects of the American criminal justice system make it unique?

5. What is "discretionary law enforcement"?
6. In an era of strict law enforcement, why does "plea bargaining" remain?
7. What area within the criminal justice system needs the most reform?
8. Do you agree with the quotation at the beginning of this chapter?

References

del Carmen, Rolando V. *Criminal Procedure for Law Enforcement Personnel.* Monterey, Calif: Brooks/Cole Publishing Company, 1987.

Dernbach, John C., and Singleton, Richard V., II. *A Practical Guide to Legal Writing and Legal Method.* Littleton, Colo.: Fred B. Rothman & Co., 1981.

Farnsworth, E. Allan. *An Introduction to the Legal System of the United States.* New York: Oceana Publications, Inc., 1983.

Guide to the Federal Courts. Washington, D.C.: WANT Publishing Company, 1984.

Jacobstein, J. Myron and Mersky, Roy M. *Legal Research Illustrated.* 2nd ed. Westbury, New York: Foundation Press, 1981.

President's Commission on Law Enforcement and Administration of Justice, *The Challenge of Crime in a Free Society.* Washington, DC: U.S. Government Printing Office, February 1967.

Stuckey, Gilbert B. *Procedures in the Justice System.* 3d ed. Columbus, Ohio: Charles E. Merrill Publishing Company, 1986.

You and the Law. 3d ed. Pleasantville, New York: The Reader's Digest Association, Inc., 1984.

THE ROLE OF CORRECTIONS—PUNISH OR REHABILITATE?

Another controversial area is whether our criminal justice system should seek to punish or to rehabilitate offenders. Or does the system's treatment depend on the offender?

(Adapted from Opposing Viewpoints—What is the Purpose of Prisons?)

Arguments for Punishment

Prisons Should Punish

The most desirable penal policy is that of just punishment, the swift punishing of blameworthy behavior. (Francis T. Murphy, *New York State Bar Journal,* 1984)

Punishment Advances Human Dignity

But why punish [criminals]? . . . The answer, I think, is clear: We want to punish them in order to *pay them back.* We think they must be made to pay for their crimes with their lives, and we think that we, the survivors of the world they violated, may legitimately exact that payment because we, too, are their victims. By punishing them, we demonstrate that there are laws that bind men across generations as well as across (and within) nations, that we are not simply isolated individuals, each pursuing his selfish interests and connected with others by a mere contract to live and let live. (Walter Berns, *For Capital Punishment,* 1979)

Punishing the Criminal

We should do better to look at the [prison] problem from a just deserts point of view and ask ourselves, do not these criminals who have long records and have committed unspeakable crimes, deserve to be punished more severely, and in a way that is appropriate to their crimes? We do not seek to "cure" the criminal, but rather for him to atone for his crime. The term of imprisonment must be one that keeps up front, very clearly in view, that the criminal is there to *be punished.* (Graeme R. Newman, *Just and Painful,* 1983)

Arguments for Rehabilitation

Prisons Should Rehabilitate

When society places a person behind walls and bars it has an obligation . . . to change that person before he or she goes back into the stream of society. (Warren E. Burger, remarks at Pace University, June 11, 1983)

Society Needs More Than Warehouses

We're deluding ourselves if we continue to lock people up at great cost, let them sit idle and hope that crime will just disappear. It won't. When an ex-convict returns to society unskilled, unmotivated and unaccustomed to earning a living; it's a safe bet that he will commit more crimes. New outlets for prison labor must be explored and expanded. (Gordon Mehler, *New York Times*, July 17, 1984)

Costs of Confinement

Today the confinement of the 400,000 inmates of American prisons costs the taxpayers of this country, including the innocent victims of crimes, who help pay for it, more than twelve million dollars a day! . . . We do not need the help of behavioral scientists to understand that human beings who are taught to produce useful goods for the market place, and to be productive are more likely to develop the self-esteem essential to a normal, integrated personality. This kind of program could provide training in skills and work habits, and replace the sense of hopelessness that is the common lot of prison inmates. . . . Life is filled with rewards for cooperation and penalties for noncooperation. Prison sentences are shortened and privileges are given to prisoners who cooperate. What I urge are programs in which the inmate can earn and learn his way to freedom and the opportunity for a new life. (Warren E. Burger, remarks at the commencement exercises at Pace University, June 11, 1983)

CHAPTER 4

The Officer's Badge:

A Shield or a Target?

Police Liability

As a Law Enforcement Officer, my fundamental duty is to serve mankind; to safeguard lives and property; to protect the innocent against deception, the weak against oppression or intimidation, and the peaceful against violence or disorder; and to respect the Constitutional rights of all men to liberty, equality, and justice.

—International Association of Chiefs of Police Law Enforcement Code of Ethics

DO YOU KNOW

What Section 1983 is and how it relates to liability?

Who has immunity from civil lawsuits?

Who can be sued?

What a "collective deep pocket" is?

What the three categories of tort law are?

With which intentional torts law enforcement officers are most frequently involved (and their elements)?

What the difference between libel and slander is?

What the simple definition of negligence is?

What activities may lead to negligence lawsuits?

Whether deadly force can be used to stop a "fleeing felon" and the precedent case?

What common defenses are used in police civil liability cases? Can the police sue back?

How to minimize legal liabilities?

Introduction

Chapter 4

- A routine traffic stop erupts, without warning, into a high-speed chase. The result: a bystander is hit and killed.
- After dozens, maybe hundreds, of unfounded residential alarms, an open door leads to an unexpected confrontation within this darkened house and shots are fired. The result: a homeowner is hit and killed.

These scenarios have gone through the minds of every law enforcement officer. Perhaps no other profession routinely encounters so many opportunities for problems to occur. The type of calls responded to, the areas in which they occur, and the variety of equipment used create volatile situations that may result in injury or death. When the undeniable possibility becomes a reality, who will be blamed?

- The officer?
- The chief?
- The city?
- A bystander?
- The supervisor?
- The department?
- The suspect?

Only naive or deluded police officers believe they would never be sued. The past two decades have produced an unprecedented increase in suits brought against the police. It is presently estimated that over 30,000 lawsuits are initiated against law enforcement annually (Silver, 1986, p. xi). A decrease in this figure is unlikely.

One important statute on which lawsuits are often based is known as Section 1983, the Civil Rights Act.

SECTION 1983—THE CIVIL RIGHTS ACT

Statute 42 of the United States Code, Section 1983, passed after the Civil War in 1871, states:

> *Every person who, under color of any statute, ordinance, regulation, custom, or usage, of any State or Territory, subjects, or causes to be subjected any citizen of the United States or other person within the jurisdiction thereof to the deprivation of any rights, privileges, or immunities secured by the Constitution and laws, shall be liable to the party injured in an action at law, suit in equity, or other proper proceeding for redress.*

In plain English, any person acting under the authority of law who violates another person's constitutional rights can be sued.

Blackmun (1986) notes the historical and present importance of this act:

> Then [in 1871] § 1983 was part and parcel of the Radical Republican assault on the ashes of the Old South. Today, § 1983 properly stands for something different—for the commitment of our society to be governed by law and to protect the rights of those without power against oppression at the hands of the powerful. . . . What a vibrant and exciting old statute it is. As Edmond Cahn so aptly observed, "Freedom is not free." Whatever is the fate of § 1983 in the future, I do hope that it survives both as a symbol and as a working mechanism for all of us to protect the constitutional liberties we treasure.

The two basic requirements for a § 1983 action are (1) the plaintiff must be deprived of a constitutional right, and (2) the defendant must deprive the plaintiff of this right while acting under the "color of the law" (Adickes v. Kress and Co.[1970]).

The question then arises, must the defendant be an individual, or can it be a city?

WHO IS LIABLE?

In 1961, in *Monroe* v. *Pape*, the Supreme Court ruled that municipalities could not be sued. They had absolute immunity from civil rights actions under Section 1983. The doctrine of "sovereign immunity" (literally "the king can do no wrong") has protected governmental bodies from being sued. This position was reversed in 1978.

In 1978, in Monell v. New York City Department of Social Services, the Court said that local municipalities were liable under Section 1983.

According to *Monell*, cities, counties, and other local governmental bodies could be sued for damages under the authority of Section 1983. Schnapper (1986, p. 28) describes the background of this case.

In Monell itself, the plaintiffs complained that the New York City De-
partment of Social Services had as a matter of official policy required
pregnant employees to take unpaid leaves of absence before such
leaves were medically necessary. The practice at issue had been origi-
nated by an unnamed lower-level personnel official, but had been ad-
hered to throughout the agency. The Court held, in a refrain repeated
in slightly different ways throughout its opinion, that the language of
section 1983—"plainly imposes liability on a government that under
color of some official policy, 'causes' an employee to violate another's
constitutional rights."

Seng (1984, p. 37) describes how the *Monell* ruling affects law
enforcement officers' actions and liability as well as that of their
department and their city. In his example, a Jehovah's Witness was
arrested by a police officer for violating a city ordinance banning the
distribution of leaflets on public streets. The defendant could not post
bond and was jailed until he went before the local magistrate. He was
found guilty and fined fifty dollars. On appeal, however, his conviction
was reversed. Until this time, he was a classic example of an innocent
victim with no remedy for damages. He could not sue the city council
members who passed the ordinance, the prosecutor who charged him,
or the judge who found him guilty.

Legislators, prosecutors, and judges have absolute immunity from
suit.

Similarly, the arresting officer's convincing defense was that he
was enforcing an official city policy in good faith. *Monell* and *Owen,*
however, provided the Jehovah's Witness a remedy against the city,
regardless of whether its officials knew or even should have known that
the ordinance was unconstitutional (*Owen* v. *City of Independence*
[1980]).

Such challenges are becoming more and more frequent. Consequently, law enforcement officers, their departments, and their municipalities need to be sure that local ordinances do *not* violate citizens'
constitutional rights if they wish to avoid the risk of being sued.
Sovereign immunity is clearly being eroded at a swift pace.

Police officers, police departments, and the city can be sued.

The concept of *risk management* is not new to private industry.
The need to identify risks and limit losses is a necessary part of doing

business. Only recently, however, has law enforcement realistically responded to the very real possibility of being the target of extremely expensive legal actions. The mere fact that police agencies and their employing body of government are well insured makes them very obvious targets.

Statistics clearly indicate that the possibility of being sued is increasing at an alarming rate. Not only may individual officers be named in the action, but also their supervisors, the chief of police, the police department, the municipality, and anyone else involved may be named.

Suing every possible party creates a "collective deep pocket" from which astronomical judgments can be collected.

The city is not always liable for the actions of its police officers, however, as decided in *City of Oklahoma City v. Tuttle* (1985). In fact, the governmental body must have a causal part of the injury. In this case an Oklahoma City police officer shot an unarmed civilian who the city admitted had not committed a crime. The widow sued the police officer and the city, claiming that the shooting resulted from poor training and supervision of rookie officers. The court ruled that a single act could not, by itself, establish an inadequate training policy.

CIVIL LAW: A CLOSER LOOK

While police officers could be and have been charged with committing a crime while on duty, the vast majority of suits brought against the profession are civil.

Most civil (tort) law in the United States developed through common law and is often supported or clarified through interpretation by statutory law. Recall that statutory law is developed by legislatures and appears in the form of statutes. Common law is judge-made law, developed case by case over many centuries.

The American colonists brought with them the common law of England, which remains the basis of our law. It is entirely possible that a lawsuit today involving space-age cars on the most modern freeways could find the pivotal legal issue of the case being determined by a 200-year-old case involving horses and buggies.

In most civil cases, the law developed in past cases, not statutes, determines what the present law is. And that is one reason civil law can be so complex and difficult to understand: there are few statutes to rely on.

In addition, the burden of proof differs in civil and criminal court. The "beyond a reasonable doubt" standard in criminal law is higher than the common civil standard of "by a preponderance of the evidence." It is possible that an assailant could be found liable in civil court and acquitted in criminal court. The plaintiff may be able to prove the lesser standard, but not the higher standard. In other words, it is easier to sue someone civilly than to prosecute someone criminally.

Addicks (1981, p. 180) says two distinctions are important in determining the personal liability of city officers and employees for acts committed while on duty: (1) the distinction between discretionary and ministerial acts, and (2) the distinction between "nonfeasance" and "misfeasance" or "malfeasance."

It is well established that if a police officer is carrying out a duty that calls for using judgment or discretion in regard to how the duty is to be performed, the officer is not liable for damages to an individual unless guilty of willful wrong or gross negligence.

There is liability, however, when the duty is ministerial; that is, the way the duty is to be performed is prescribed. If an officer fails to follow the prescribed procedure and an injury results, the officer is liable. For example, if a department has a policy that an officer is not to fire a gun from within a moving patrol car, and the officer does shoot from his moving patrol car, that officer is liable if the action results in damage or injury to innocent bystanders. The employer could also be named in the suit.

Addicks (1981, p. 181) explains further that misfeasance is an act of misconduct; whereas nonfeasance is a failure to take action. For example, using excessive force in making an arrest would constitute misfeasance. A partner simply standing by and doing nothing to stop the excessive force constitutes nonfeasance.

Civil law has three categories: strict liability, intentional wrongs, and negligence.

Strict liability refers to instances in which a wrongdoer (called a tortfeasor) is held liable to the injured party, whether or not the wrongdoer actually did anything wrong. Strict liability, also called liability without fault, most often involves ultrahazardous activities such as using explosives or keeping wild animals. The idea behind strict liability is that if people want to engage in such inherently dangerous activities, they should bear the responsibility for any damage that results. This area has yet to be a major problem for police officers. However, with the increasing use of high-tech law enforcement equipment, it is conceivable that such strict liability would become a more popular course of action for injured plaintiffs. Law enforcement is most frequently involved in the categories of intentional wrongs and negligence.

INTENTIONAL WRONGS

Intentional means, quite simply, "on purpose" or "done by design," and *wrong* in this case means "against the law." Technically, an act is considered to be an intentional wrong if someone sets out to bring about a result that will invade the interests of another in a way that the law will not allow (Prosser, 1971, p. x). The act need not cause a serious injury, and hostile intent is not required. Any purposeful invasion of a protected interest is sufficient to bring about a lawsuit. According to Silver (1986, SS 1.07): "Perhaps more than any other occupation, police work is highly intrusive into human activity. It is not surprising, therefore, that there is a continuous stream of intentional tort litigation against the police."

Keep in mind that the same wrongful act could constitute both a crime (wrong against society) and a tort (wrong against the individual). To repeat, an officer *could* conceivably be charged with a crime, but is much more likely, for a number of reasons, to be sued civilly. Therefore, this text concentrates on the civil suits in this chapter.

Intentional civil wrongs (torts) affecting law enforcement include assault, battery, false imprisonment, false arrest, malicious prosecution, intentional infliction of emotional distress, trespass, illegal electronic surveillance, invasion of privacy, and defamation.

In each of these intentional torts, specific elements must be present. And in each, a specific interest is being protected.

Assault

Because law enforcement often involves use of force in apprehending suspects, police officers may leave themselves open to charges of assault. The elements of civil assault are different than criminal assault, as force is not an aspect of it.

The elements of ASSAULT are

1. An action creating reasonable apprehension of immediate harmful or offensive contact to another

2. Intent to cause such apprehension

For example, the menacing shaking of a fist at someone can be assault. No striking or attempted striking is required. The question is simply, "Was the victim reasonably apprehensive of intended present harmful or offensive conduct?" A ninety-pound weakling most definitely can assault a large, muscular lifeguard by acting so that the lifeguard was reasonably apprehensive of having sand kicked in his face.

For an assault to occur, some action must be present. Words alone, no matter how violent, are not an assault. In fact, words may serve to negate an assault by making the apprehension unreasonable. For example, our ninety-pound weakling, while moving his tiny foot about in the sand, tells the lifeguard, "If I weren't such a nice guy, I'd kick sand in your face."

The apprehension must also be immediate. Either future threats or long-distance threats, such as those made over the telephone or by letter, are not usually an assault. (They may, however, constitute "intimidation or harassment by phone.")

Battery

Closely related to assault is the tort of battery. In fact, they are often used in conjunction: assault and battery.

The elements of BATTERY are

1. *An action creating unpermitted harmful or offensive contact to another*

2. *Intent to cause such contact*

An example of battery is striking someone who has not consented to be hit. People are entitled to have others keep their hands off them. While a certain amount of unauthorized pushing and shoving is an inevitable part of moving about in our crowded society, the law prohibits intentional harmful or offensive contact.

Simply tapping someone on the back to get his or her attention is not a battery. But jumping out of the bushes along a deserted road in the dark of night to tap a passerby on the back could be a battery. The contact need not cause actual harm such as a bloody nose. Battery includes any contact the plaintiff finds offensive or insulting, such as being spit on, having one's hat or other article of clothing forcibly removed, being forced to sit down, or even being tripped in jest.

The contact is not unpermitted if the person has agreed to it, for example, in a professional boxing match or a football game.

Assault and battery are two separate intentional torts that may result from one continuing act. For instance, a person who starts to swing at another with a fist so the victim sees it has committed assault. Battery occurs on contact. If the victim's back is turned as the blow is

What is "unreasonable" or "excessive" force? Different people in different positions view it differently. Police officers must carefully weigh the factors present, recognizing that their actions will be carefully scrutinized by others.

delivered and the person is unaware of it until the contact, no assault takes place, only battery. Thus, civil and criminal law terminology are not always interchangeable.

Assault, Battery, and the Law Enforcement Officer's Liability

Hagglund (1984, pp. 14–16) states that

The intentional torts of assault and battery most often arise in the situations of pursuit and arrest. . . . A police officer who intentionally contacts a suspect in a manner which is either excessive or unpermitted or unjustified under the circumstances, may have committed the torts of assault and/or battery. . . .

He goes on to note that police officers are

privileged to use reasonable force in effecting arrests.
To satisfy the burden of showing the existence of the privilege, the officer must show that he was acting in the course of his duty in attempting to effect a lawful arrest and that he made a reasonable effort to identify himself if his capacity was not readily apparent. Until that identity is revealed, an individual has a right to look upon the policeman as any other citizen and use reasonable force in defending himself. In Celmer v. Quarberg [1973], the plaintiff was on a deserted farm and was confronted by a plainclothes police officer wielding two pistols. He concluded that the officer was a "crazed farmer." The officer did not

sufficiently identify himself as a police official when he approached the plaintiff, and the plaintiff attempted to flee and suffered serious injuries. The Wisconsin court affirmed a jury verdict in favor of the plaintiff, noting that the right and privileges granted to police officers in the pursuit of their duty have legitimate effect only in those instances in which the officer, accompanied by his identity as a police officer, approaches the private citizen. . . .

The issue of whether or not the force used was reasonable is a jury question. . . . In Agee v. Hickman [1974] the court aptly noted: " . . . when a man under arrest doubles his 'fist and squares away,' there is no legal or practical reason that the officer has to give him the first 'lick' before using reasonable force to overcome the show of force."

False Imprisonment

Because police officers may have to detain people against their wishes, they may be sued for false imprisonment.

The elements of FALSE IMPRISONMENT are

1. *An action confining or restraining someone to a bounded area*

2. *Intent to do so*

For example, someone, without authority, prevents someone else from leaving a particular area.

Confinement or restraint may occur by using physical barriers or force or threats of force against a person, his or her property, or his or her family. Being restricted to a "bounded area" means there is no known way for the person to escape. For instance, attempting to lock a person in a room that has an unlocked, unguarded rear door is not imprisonment.

In addition, plaintiffs must know at the time that they are being restrained. The threatened use of force may also be indirect, such as words or acts that would reasonably cause the person to believe he or she was not free to go. For example, the lifeguard who has had enough and demands that the weakling stay put "or else," or moves about him in a way so he cannot escape to the showers, could be liable for false imprisonment.

False Arrest

False arrest is similar to false imprisonment. The very nature of an arrest constitutes confinement. The difference between false arrest and false imprisonment is that in false arrest, the legal authority does not exist for the detention. It is entirely possible that police could legally arrest an individual based on probable cause for an offense such as public intoxication. However, on learning or failing to learn that in fact the person is a diabetic, continued detention could constitute false imprisonment (Tufte v. City of Tacoma, 1967). Legal authority is required to defeat charges of both false arrest and false imprisonment, an obvious law always ignored by the police on television when the captain orders the patrol officers to "bring the suspect in for questioning"—before any arrest warrant or other legal authority exists for such action.

Officers in such a situation could find themselves being sued for a myriad of civil wrongs, including assault and battery, trespass, false imprisonment, and intentional infliction of emotional distress.

False Imprisonment, False Arrest, and Police Officer Liability

Hagglund (1984, p. 16) notes that "The greatest number of tort actions against police officers and their employers are for false arrest and false imprisonment." These cases usually arise when the arrest is made without an arrest warrant. An arrest without a warrant is presumed to be invalid, with the burden to prove otherwise on the defendant (Silver). Showing probable cause justifies a warrantless arrest in certain circumstances, but a presumably or apparently valid warrant or other legal authority will preclude a false arrest claim (Silver). Lawful arrests are discussed in detail in chapter 6.

Malicious Prosecution

The elements of malicious prosecution are similar to those for false arrest. The difference is in the interests protected by each. A leading case decided in the New York Court of Appeals stated that false arrest/imprisonment protects one's interest in being able to move freely about, while malicious prosecution protects one from unjustifiable litigation (*Broughton v. State*).

According to Hagglund (1984, p. 22):

In order to maintain a successful action against a police officer for malicious prosecution, the plaintiff must show:

1. *A criminal proceeding instituted by the defendant against the plaintiff.*
2. *Termination of proceedings in favor of the plaintiff.*
3. *Absence of probable cause for the bringing of the proceeding.*
4. *"Malice" or a primary purpose other than bringing an offender to justice.*

Intentional Infliction of Emotional Distress

This area of civil law is developing slowly, with some courts as yet reluctant to recognize it.

Neither the police nor the private citizen may arbitrarily enter the property of another. The exceptions must be known to law enforcement officers to avoid both civil liability and the consequences of the exclusionary rule.

The elements of INTENTIONAL INFLICTION OF EMOTIONAL DISTRESS are

1. *An action that is extreme and outrageous conduct*

2. *Intent to cause severe emotional distress*

The act must involve conduct that is so outrageous that it "transcends all bounds of decency." Many cases result from extreme business conduct (as used by collection agencies, for example), or from the misuse of authority (Conviser, Levine, and Chess). While physical injuries are not required, severe emotional distress must be proven, and this is difficult.

Trespass

Official police business may require officers to enter private property, sometimes leaving themselves open to charges of trespass.

The elements of TRESPASS ARE

1. *An action resulting in the physical invasion of land of another*

2. *Intent to do so*

The defendant need not actually step on the land. Throwing objects onto the property can constitute this tort.

In addition, "land" includes a reasonable space above and below the surface. Therefore, trespass could include stringing wires over someone's land, shooting a bullet over the top of such land, or tunnelling under the surface of someone else's property. Trespass does not require injury to the property as the intrusion itself is the actual wrong.

Illegal Electronic Surveillance

Wiretapping and electronic "bugging" may result in charges of trespass or of invasion of privacy. In *Katz* v. *United States* (1967), the court ruled that an electronic "bug" placed outside a public telephone booth violated the defendant's Fourth Amendment right to a reasonable expectation of privacy. Not all electronic surveillance is illegal, however. In 1968 Congress passed Title III of the Safe Streets Act permitting controlled use of electronic surveillance devices. Usually such electronic surveillance requires a warrant based on probable cause to believe that a criminal conversation will take place. Electronic surveillance is discussed in chapter 12.

Defamation

Law enforcement officers must be careful of statements they make about people's character, or they may find themselves sued for defamation.

The elements of DEFAMATION are

1. *Defamatory language by the defendant about the plaintiff*

2. *Published (or communicated) to others*

3. *Damaging the reputation of the plaintiff*

Defamatory language is language that adversely affects another's reputation. The assertion must be about the plaintiff and must be communicated (published) to a third person who understands it. Merely saying "I know someone who . . . " is not sufficient. Nor is uttering a grossly defamatory statement to someone in Chinese if they do not understand Chinese. Anyone who repeats the defamatory statement can become liable as well.

Defamation can be either libel or slander.

Libel *is written defamation.* Slander *is oral defamation.*

If the defamation is written (libel), the law views it as very serious because written material is more permanent. Therefore, a plaintiff need not prove specific damages. General damages are presumed simply because the statement was made.

Spoken defamation (slander), in contrast, must generally result in actual damages that can be proven to have financially affected the plaintiff. In other words, special damages must be proved.

A difference is that courts do not want to infringe on spoken words to the same degree as written words. In several distinct categories of spoken defamation, however, damages *are* presumed without further proof:

1. A statement directly relating to the plaintiff's business or profession. Example: Butcher Bill sells diseased meat. Doctor Danielson is an inept surgeon. Officer Jim is on the take.
2. A statement that the plaintiff has a "loathsome disease" such as a venereal disease, leprosy, or perhaps AIDS.
3. A statement that the plaintiff was/is guilty of a crime involving moral turpitude, that is, immoral, depraved, vile. For example, prostitution or child abuse.
4. A statement that a woman is unchaste.

The preceding categories of slander are considered "slander per se," and require no finding of specific damages. It is considered to be damaging enough that the words were spoken, so general damages are presumed.

Silver (1986, p. 1–22) notes that "If a report is made in the course of routine or traditional police activities, the reporting officer will be liable for any defamatory falsehood only if he has acted maliciously. Thus, any misstatement of fact which is known to be untrue when made, or which is made in reckless disregard of the truth, will be actionable." Factual assertions are much safer to state than are assumptions or conclusions.

Private vs. Public Persons

It has been held that private individuals deserve more protection from defamation than *public figures*. For a public official or public figure to recover in an action for defamation, they must prove the defendant made the statement with malice. *Malice* is defined as knowing the statement was false or issuing the statement with a reckless disregard for its truth or falsity. The requirement to prove malice is not imposed on private persons. Public figures are presumed to know that they may be the topic of discussion, as well as having a more available forum from which to respond.

The rule of thumb regarding defamation in today's litigious society is to be very cautious when stating anything that could be considered to harm the reputation of someone else. An increasing number of law enforcement agencies are incorporating the position of a

The law of negligence applies to the public and the police. Accidents are carefully reviewed to determine cause. Accidents involving police emergency responses are a frequent source of law suits.

specially trained "public information officer" to disseminate information to the press.

NEGLIGENCE

The other general category of civil charges frequently involving law enforcement officers is that of negligence.

The elements of NEGLIGENCE are

1. The existence of a duty to use due care

2. A breach of that duty

3. The breach of duty must be both the actual and proximate cause of injury

4. Damages must result to the plaintiff

Attorneys continually argue about what is and is not negligent behavior. Silver (1986, p. 1–35) asserts: "Negligence may attend all police functions, especially those related to highway control and accident scenes."

Simply stated, negligence is the failure to use due care to prevent foreseeable injury that results in injury.

According to Conviser, Levine, and Chess, p. 30, "Torts":

Every one of us has a presumed legal duty to avoid acting in a way that could result in injuring another. The legal duty that case law has developed is "due care to avoid foreseeable risk." The plaintiff must successfully argue that the defendant had reason to believe his or her conduct would create a foreseeable risk of harm. There is generally no duty if the risk is not foreseeable.

The Reasonable Person

Civil law is based on a standard of behavior called "reasonable." The courts have created a fictional person by which to compare all human behavior. Although nonexistent, this individual is universally known as the "reasonable person of ordinary prudence" (Prosser). This creature has been described as a reasonable man, a prudent man, or a man of ordinary sense using ordinary care and skill (Prosser). Whatever phase is selected, we are all required to do what such a person would do—behave reasonably to prevent foreseeable risk of injury to others.

Herbert (1930, pp. 12–16) describes the reasonable person this way:

This excellent but odious character stands like a monument in our courts of justice, vainly appealing to his fellow-citizens to order their lives after his own example. . . . He is an ideal, a standard, the embodiment of all those qualities which we demand of the good citizen. . . . He is one who invariably looks where he is going, and is careful to examine the immediate foreground before he executes a leap or a bound; who neither star-gazes nor is lost in meditation when approaching trapdoors or the margin of a dock; . . . who never mounts a moving omnibus and does not alight from any car while the train is in motion . . . and will inform himself of the history and habits of a dog before administering a caress . . . who never drives his ball until those in front of him have definitely vacated the putting-green which is his own objective; who never from one year's end to another makes an excessive demand upon his wife, his neighbors, his servants, his ox, or his ass; . . . who never swears, gambles or loses his temper; who uses (or does?) nothing except in moderation, and even while he flogs his child is meditating only on the golden mean.

In short, we all must, day in and day out, in all our business and personal activities, behave as would a reasonable person! Professionals, including doctors, lawyers, and police officers, are often held to even higher standards than our "ordinary person." They are expected to act as other members of that profession would behave in the same or similar locality.

The routine police duties that most frequently lead to negligence lawsuits are care of incapacitated persons, duty to render emergency aid, caring for arrestees, aiding private citizens, investigating unusual circumstances, and operating emergency vehicles.

Negligence during Police Emergencies

The primary source of lawsuits in this area is in the operation of emergency vehicles. If police are responding to an emergency, they have the authority to ignore certain traffic rules such as posted speed limits, stop signs and signals, and lane restrictions. Usually they are required to use an audible and visual signal when ignoring these traffic rules. As noted by Silver (1986, pp. 3–9): "Statutes require that emergency operations be undertaken with 'due regard' for others' safety. Increasingly, police are being held liable for negligent chases." The safe ("not negligent") officer remembers that red lights and siren only *request* the right of way. They do not guarantee it.

Negligence and the Use of Deadly Force

Territo (1984, p. 111) says: "No aspect of policing elicits more passionate concern or more divided opinions than the use of deadly force. Many community groups and minority organizations believe police killings of civilians are excessive and often unjustifiable; many police agencies are apprehensive and angry about unprovoked fatal assaults on patrol officers." Few other aspects of the profession elicit such public scrutiny.

Farber and Manak (1986, p. 151) note that

> In March, 1985, the United States Supreme Court initiated what must be viewed as a new era in the law of deadly force in the United States. In Tennessee v. Garner, . . . the Court ruled a state statute embodying the common law "fleeing felon" rule was unconstitutional as applied to the shooting of an unarmed fifteen-year-old running from the scene of a burglary. Deadly force utilized to prevent the escape of suspected felons, the Court concluded, "may not be used unless it is necessary to prevent the escape and the officer has probable cause to believe that the suspect poses a significant threat of death or serious physical injury to the officer or others."

In this case, two police officers responded to a call regarding a prowler. When they arrived the caller said she had heard someone trying to break into a neighboring house. One officer went to the back of the house and saw the suspect run across the yard and stop below a high fence. Using his flashlight, the officer could see the suspect's face and hands and believed him to be an unarmed seventeen- or eighteen-year-old boy. The officer identified himself as police and ordered the boy to halt. When the boy began climbing the fence, the officer shot, striking him in the back of the head and killing him. The boy was a 100 lb., 5'4" fifteen-year-old. He had taken ten dollars and a purse from the house, but he was unarmed. The boy's father filed a federal civil rights lawsuit against the officer, the Memphis police department, the director of the department, and the mayor. He won.

As noted by Farber and Manak:

> The Court stated that the officer "could not reasonably have believed" that the suspect—"young, slight, and unarmed—posed any threat" either to the officer or to others. . . .
>
> As a result, the Court felt that the earlier concept—"that use of deadly force against a fleeing felon is merely a speedier execution of someone who has already forfeited his life"—had been so undermined as to no longer be supportable.
>
> "A police officer may not seize an unarmed, nondangerous suspect by shooting him dead," the Court stated. "The Tennessee statute is unconstitutional insofar as it authorizes the use of deadly force against such fleeing suspects."

The "fleeing felon" rule, authorizing police to shoot at a felon who is attempting to escape, was ruled unconstitutional in Tennessee v. Garner because the suspect was not armed and not dangerous.

According to Farber and Manak (p. 153), the Court's opinion noted that "as many as twenty-three states, at the time, had statutes or court decisions which would allow officers to use deadly force to prevent the escape of a fleeing felon—regardless of whether or not the suspect was armed or the crime committed involved violence."

They go on to warn: "A department which does not immediately review—and, if necessary, rewrite—its policy on the use of deadly force to conform with *Garner* is potentially playing with a firestorm of civil liability."

COMMON DEFENSES IN CIVIL LAW SUITS

According to del Carmen (1987, pp. 411–14), three defenses are commonly available in state tort and Section 1983 cases.

*Common defenses in civil law suits are (1) probable cause, (2)
official immunity, and (3) good faith.*

The *probable cause defense* applies only to illegal search and
seizure, false arrest, and false imprisonment. As noted, if police are
acting with a warrant they are usually not liable. Legal searches,
seizures, and arrests are the subject of chapters 5, 6, and 7.

Official immunity, as already noted, is available only to legislators, prosecutors, and judges, not police officers.

The *good faith* defense is the most common defense in Section
1983, but cannot be used in state tort lawsuits. As the name implies, good
faith means the officer acted with honest intentions, meaning no harm.

COUNTERSUITS BY POLICE OFFICERS

A headline in the February 20, 1985, *New York Times* reads: "New
York Now Suing Some Who Bring Brutality Cases." The article states:

> *New York City, in a policy change, has begun to countersue some peo-
> ple who have brought civil suits in which they accuse police officers of
> brutality. . . . In the countersuits, the city has contended that it was
> the officers, not the civilian complainants, who were attacked. . . .*
>
> *The right to countersue for officers has been challenged as a
> conflict-of-interest violation. . . . "It will frighten average people from
> seeking redress from a wrong done to them by a cop," said Mr. Meyer-
> son, a former staff lawyer for the National Association for the Ad-
> vancement of Colored People. . . .*
>
> *The senior assistant corporation counsel in charge of litigation, . . .
> in an affidavit defending the change, said, "Violent individuals who
> assault officers will not be permitted the unearned security of being
> effectively immune from liability."*

The police can countersue.

There are, however, disadvantages in filing lawsuits against arrestees or suspects, including the fact that officers have to hire their own lawyers and the fact that people who are in trouble with the law may be poor.

MINIMIZING LEGAL LIABILITIES

Specific ways police officers can minimize lawsuits are listed by
del Carmen (1987, pp. 420–21):

1. *Know and follow your department's manual or guidelines. If you do, you will have a strong claim to a "good faith" defense.*
2. *Act within the scope of your duties.*
3. *Act in a professional and responsible manner at all times. When faced with a difficult situation, use reason instead of emotion.*
4. *Know the constitutional rights of your constituents and respect them.*
5. *Consult your legal counsel or supervisor if you have doubts about what you are doing. Be able to document the advice given.*
6. *In sensitive cases, document your activities. Keep good written records.*
7. *Establish and maintain good relations with your community.*
8. *Keep yourself well informed on current issues and trends in civil and criminal liability cases.*

To minimize lawsuits: (1) know and follow your department's guidelines; (2) stay in the scope of your duties; (3) always act professionally; (4) know and respect your constituents' rights; (5) if in doubt, seek advice; (6) keep good records of your activities; (7) maintain good community relations; and (8) keep up to date on civil and criminal liability cases.

THE LIVING LAW

Before leaving the topic of civil liability, it is important to remember that the common law that is the basis for civil law is what allows it to be termed "living law." Unlike statutes that remain the same until changed by the legislature, the common law is allowed—in fact encouraged—to change as society's needs change. While such law will continue to have its roots in ancient English common law, the differences in each case, no matter how slight, permit the court hearing it to consider present needs of society in deciding how to rule on that case.

While the standard of care for the operation of a motor vehicle may require the same duty to keep a safe lookout for pedestrians as would that for the driver of a team of horses in the 1800s, current law has to consider the obvious differences such as the speed of cars versus horses, the weight of the metal cars, the injury that a car would cause hitting a pedestrian, and the like. It is through this ability of the law to consider each case on its own, while requiring that it be compared to every case that has gone before it, that the standards of society are reinforced or changed as seen fit by the legal process. This changeability also makes del Carmen's eighth suggestion so important. Do keep informed on current issues and trends in civil and criminal liability cases.

SUMMARY

Section 1983 of the U.S. Code is the Civil Rights Act. The two basic requirements for a § 1983 action are (1) that the plaintiff be deprived of a constitutional right, and (2) that the defendant deprived the plaintiff of this right while acting under the "color of the law." *Monell* v. *New York City Department of Social Services* (1978) established that local municipalities were liable under Section 1983. When a plaintiff sues every possible person remotely connected to the case, this creates a "collective deep pocket" from which astronomical judgments can be collected.

Civil (tort) law has three categories: strict liability, intentional wrongs, and negligence. It is the latter two that most affect police officers. Intentional wrongs (torts) affecting law enforcement include assault, battery, false imprisonment, false arrest, malicious prosecution, intentional infliction of emotional distress, trespass, illegal electronic surveillance, invasion of privacy, and defamation. Defamation can be either libel (written) or slander (oral).

Negligence has four elements: (1) the existence of a duty to use due care, (2) a breach of that duty, (3) the breach of duty must be both the actual and proximate cause of the injury, and (4) damages to the plaintiff must result. Simply stated, negligence is the failure to use due care to prevent foreseeable injury that results in injury.

The routine police duties that most frequently lead to negligence lawsuits are care of incapacitated persons, duty to render emergency aid, caring for arrestees, aiding private citizens, investigating unusual circumstances, and operating emergency vehicles.

The "fleeing felon" rule, authorizing police to shoot at a felon who is attempting to escape, was ruled unconstitutional in *Tennessee* v. *Garner* because the suspect was not armed and not dangerous.

Common defenses in civil law suits are (1) probable cause, (2) official immunity, and (3) good faith. The police can countersue.

To minimize lawsuits: (1) know and follow your department's guidelines; (2) stay in the scope of your duties; (3) always act professionally; (4) know and respect your constituents' rights; (5) if in doubt, seek advice; (6) keep good records of your activities; (7) maintain good community relations; and (8) keep up to date on civil and criminal liability cases.

Discussion Questions

1. Why is a "1983 action" an important concept for police officers to understand?
2. Acknowledging the complexities of civil law, what applicability does the law of negligence have to the law enforcement officer?
3. How could a person be both civilly and criminally liable?
4. In using the "reasonable person" standard to determine if someone would be liable for specific actions, how is "unreasonableness" determined?

5. Should our criminal justice system include such "safeguards" as the "1983 action"?
6. Have any lawsuits been brought against your police department in the past year?
7. Have you ever personally been sued? Sued anyone?

References

Addicks, Mentor C., Jr. *Handbook for Minnesota Cities.* 4th ed. St. Paul: League of Minnesota Cities, 1981.

Ballentine, James A. *Ballentine's Law Dictionary.* 3d ed. Edited by William S. Anderson. Rochester, N.Y.: The Lawyers Co-Operative Publishing Company, 1969.

Blackmun, Harry A. "Section 1983 and Federal Protection of Individual Rights—Will the Statute Remain Alive or Fade Away?" Speech delivered in 1984 and reprinted in Lobel's *Civil Rights Litigation and Attorney Fees Annual Handbook.* Vol. 2. New York: Clark Boardman Company, Ltd., 1986.

Conviser, Richard J.; Levine, Steven H.; and Chess, Stanley D. "Torts." *BAR/BRI Bar Review.* Harcourt Brace Jovanovich, 1986.

Carpenter, *International Invasion of Interest of Personality,* 1934, 13, Or. L. Rev. 227, 237, Restatement of Torts, ss24, Comment C.

del Carmen, Rolando V. *Criminal Procedure for Law Enforcement Personnel.* Monterey, Calif.: Brooks/Cole Publishing Co., 1987.

Farber, Bernard J., and Manak, James P. "Police Liability for Use of Deadly Force in the Wake of *Tennessee v. Garner.*" In Lobel's *Civil Rights Litigation and Attorney Fees Annual Handbook.* Vol. 2. New York: Clark Boardman Company, LTD, 1986.

Fyfe, James J. "Police Use of Deadly Force." In Territo's *Police Civil Liability,* 111–17. Hanrow Press, 1984.

Hagglund, Clarance E. "Liability of Police Officers and their Employers." In Territo's *Police Civil Liability,* 12–33. Hanrow Press, 1984.

Herbert, A. P. *Misleading Cases in the Common Law,* 12–16. 1930.

Lobel, Jules, ed. *Civil Rights Litigation and Attorney Fees Annual Handbook.* Vol. 2. New York: Clark Boardman Company, Ltd., 1986.

"Police Misconduct: Municipal Liability Under Section 1983." *Kentucky Law Journal,* 74 (1985-86): 651–66.

Prosser, William L. *Handbook of the Law of Torts.* 4th ed., St. Paul, Minn.: West Publishing Company, 1971.

Prosser, William L., and Keeton. *On Torts.* 5th ed. St. Paul, Minn.: West Publishing Company, 1984.

Schnapper, Eric. "Municipal Liability: From *Monell* to *Tuttle* and *Pembaur.*" In Lobel's *Civil Rights Litigation and Attorney Fees Annual Handbook.* Vol. 2. New York: Clark Boardman Company, Ltd., 1986.

Seng, Michael P. "Municipal Liability for Police Misconduct." In Territo's *Police Civil Liability,* 34–54. Columbia, MD: Hanrow Press, 1984.

Silver, Isidore. *Police Civil Liability.* New York: Matthew Bender, 1986.

Territo, Leonard, ed. *Police Civil Liability.* Hanrow Press, 1984.

HOW MUCH SUING GOES ON AND IS IT USUALLY JUSTIFIED?

Is the United States lawsuit crazy, or are there simply more people and more circumstances requiring lawsuits?

(Adapted from Opposing Viewpoints, Is the Litigation Crisis Destroying the Legal System?)

America Is a Litigious Society and Most Lawsuits Are Not Justified

The fact that Americans are extremely litigious cannot be disputed. In the last ten years we have heard constant complaints about crowded court calendars and burgeoning dockets. On the federal level there have even been proposals to create an intermediate appellate court between the Court of Appeals and the Supreme Court.

Impossible to Right All Wrongs   So what are we trying to accomplish with our legal system? Like no other society, we have attempted to use it to right all the wrongs and to remedy all the injustices of our society. And we use it not only more frequently but also for a greater variety of issues. We use law to eradicate inequality, and we use law to regulate a host of social, economic, and even medical problems that are customarily resolved in non-legal ways in other countries.

Excerpted from Charles Whitebread and John Heilman, "Why Are We So Litigious?" *Los Angeles Times,* Dec. 21, 1983

As Tort Law Operates Now, It Is More Like a Lottery Than a Rational System of Justice People with identical grievance can collect radically different amounts. What you collect depends on such factors as where you live, the assets of the defendant, what judge you get and the amount of your lost earnings. . . . And much of the income redistribution caused by tort cases is from everyone else to the lawyers—if you include what the defendants' lawyers get paid. For instance, according to a Rand Corporation study, in all the current litigation over asbestos, the average cost to the defendant has been $101,000. Of that, $37,000 has gone to the defendant's lawyers, $25,000 to the plaintiff's lawyers, and $39,000 is left for the plaintiff.

Worst of all, the tort system teaches a cramped lesson about justice and injustice. Most of the suffering in our society is part of everyday life. Relief from suffering needn't depend on finding someone to blame. The instinct that says it's wrong for people to suffer unnecessarily should be directed into politics, not into lawsuits.

Excerpted from Michael Kinsey, "Craziness in the Courtroom," *The New Republic*, November 18, 1985

An Oregon jury ordered Ford to pay $1.5 million to the estate of a woman who was killed when a runaway horse she hit crashed through the roof of her Ford Pinto. Although Ford argued that the case was "one in a million" and no car could withstand such an impact, the jury found the auto maker liable.

Excerpted from *Reader's Digest*, May 1986

America Is Not Overly Litigious and Most Lawsuits Are Justified

The myth is that America is experiencing a "litigation explosion" in its trial courts that forecasts certain doom of its legal systems. This explosion theme was introduced in the early 1970s, but it is based on speculation and unsupported pronouncement. . . . Litigation actually occurs in a very tiny percentage of all disputes.

Over the centuries many things have been said about lawyers, and few have been flattering. . . . Jeremy Bentham, an eminent 19th-century British political scientist, said that "lawyers are the only persons in whom ignorance of the law is not punished." . . . One myth about lawyers, however, must be dislodged. That myth is that "all lawyers are contentious, litigious, and therefore are not amenable to alternatives to litigation." The truth is that most lawyers are in favor of negotiated settlements for disputes, with or without intervention of third parties.

Excerpted from John W. Cooley, "Puncturing Three Myths About Litigation," *ABA Journal*, December 1984

Americans are portrayed as being excessively, almost pathologically litigious, willing to "sue the bastards" with the slightest provocation and over the most trivial matters. There is, however, a growing skepticism about the alleged explosion and the attendant crisis. In fact, a number of researchers and commentators are even questioning the very idea of a litigation explosion.

Excerpted from Stephen Daniels, *The Judges' Journal*, Spring 1985

Litigation and Corporate Conscience   Civil litigation has . . . been instrumental in improving the environment, promoting safety, and protecting consumers from a wide variety of daily hazards. It was a lawsuit that compelled the Reserve Mining Company to stop dumping asbestos waste into Lake Superior and to pay for filtering the water used by the residents of Duluth, Minnesota. . . . Litigation or the fear of litigation has compelled auto manufacturers to recall thousands of defective machines that could have caused injury or death to the drivers and passengers, other motorists, and pedestrians. . . . Litigation is the spur to an enlightened corporate conscience.

Excerpted from Lois G. Forer, *Money and Justice*, 1984

Tort Law Is Not Like a Lottery   It turns out that jurors weren't quite so silly as the anecdotes make them sound. It turns out that if you had been on the jury you might have voted for the plaintiff. . . . There's the one about the horse hitting the Pinto. That's *Green vs. Ford Motor Co.* . . .

The story of the Green family is a sad one. Mr. Green was driving his wife home from the hospital where she had just been delivered of a baby. She was struck on the temple when the roof collapsed under the weight of the horse and was killed. Mr. Green proved in court that the Pinto's roof could not withstand the 5,000 pounds of pressure specified by the National Transportation Safety Board and that the company's records of vehicles which failed this test had been destroyed.

Excerpted from Tom Braden, "Insurance Horror Stories," *The Washington Times,* April 4, 1986

SECTION TWO

Operating within the Law

during Criminal

Investigations

Section One described the total context within which law enforcement officers must function as they perform their duties. Keep in mind that officer safety should always be an overriding consideration.

Section Two discusses the various aspects of criminal investigation law enforcement officers engage in and how the law affects their work. The first three chapters focus on basic search and seizure issues and the provisions of the Fourth Amendment prohibiting unreasonable search and seizure. Chapter 5 introduces stop and frisk, the gray area preceding many arrest situations, as well as the Fourth Amendment, which governs searches and seizures and the exclusionary rule by which the courts enforce the Fourth Amendment. Chapter 6 focuses on lawful arrests with an emphasis on probable cause and the critical role it plays. In Chapter 7 legal searches are the central theme, with a return to the Fourth Amendment and the exclusionary rule as they relate to searches.

The next three chapters deal with the investigative process and the laws governing investigative procedures. Chapter 8 discusses confessions and the well-known *Miranda* decision as well as the Fifth Amendment rights that are important to investigations. Chapter 9 deals with the identification process and laws related to it, including issues related to eyewitness identification, lineups, and self-incrimination in identification. Chapter 10 presents the law of evidence and returns to an in-depth look at the exclusionary rule.

The remaining chapters in this section focus on specialized topics. Chapter 11 looks at our juvenile justice system, a separate entity within our criminal justice system, having some important differences and some controversial approaches. The section concludes with a discussion in Chapter 12 of special problems encountered in criminal investigations, including electronic surveillance, the use of informants, and entrapment.

CHAPTER 5

Stop and Frisk and

the Fourth Amendment

It is simply fantastic to urge that such a procedure [stop and frisk], performed in public by a police officer, while the citizen stands helpless, perhaps facing a wall with his hands raised, is a "petty indignity."—United States Supreme Court *(Terry)*

DO YOU KNOW

What time frame the law of stop and frisk applies to?

What landmark case established stop and frisk?

What basic principles were established by the Terry decision?

What limitations are imposed on stop and frisk?

What the parameters of a stop are?

If the Miranda warning must be given during a stop?

What the parameters of a frisk are?

When vehicles can be stopped?

What rights are protected by the Fourth Amendment?

How to define reasonable?

What the exclusionary rule is and how it affects law enforcement officers?

Introduction

Chapter 5

Even the newest rookie cop knows that an ideal arrest scenario seldom presents itself. It is, in fact, so infrequent that an officer happens upon a crime in progress that such occasions become noteworthy in that officer's career.

The fact is that most arrests are the result of good hard police work—the kind that, in spite of technological advances, has remained virtually unchanged for centuries. It is by working an area in a way so as to observe suspicious activity and responding accordingly that crimes are discovered and cases solved.

The next chapter (6) deals specifically with the law of arrest—the body of law that applies when there is sufficient probable cause to take a suspect into custody. But what about that gray area prior to establishing probable cause? That gray area is the focus of this chapter.

Officers talk about developing a "sixth sense"—an ability to *know* that something is not right. What they are really talking about are observational skills officers develop. Sergeant Sylvester (Chip) Schwartz, Edina Police Department, Edina, Minnesota, discusses the need for an officer to develop "soft vision"—surveying all that is present while on patrol, while paying specific attention to those events that the officer is trained to make note of. Tire tracks in fresh snow; furtive conduct by a pedestrian; a discarded parcel; a door ajar: to the average citizen such observations mean nothing. To the trained eye of the law enforcement professional, however, they mean an opportunity to delve further into what just may be criminal activity.

The law of stop and frisk deals with that time frame during which officers follow up on their suspicions, but before the time that the requisite probable cause is established to justify an arrest.

The law of stop and frisk permits officers to act on their suspicions rather than to turn away, awaiting that infrequent, obvious crime to be committed before their very eyes.

The landmark case of *Terry* v. *Ohio* (1968) provides both a classic example of how a stop-and-frisk situation may arise and how the law deals with it.

THE PRECEDENT CASE: TERRY VS. OHIO

One afternoon in 1963 Detective Martin McFadden, Cleveland Police Department, saw two men standing outside a jewelry store, talking. To the casual observer, the men were simply talking to each other. But to Detective McFadden, a thirty-nine-year veteran on the police force, with thirty years as a detective, the men looked suspicious. He watched as one man walked to the window, looked in for a while, then went up to the corner, back to the store, and then back to the other man. He repeated this routine several times as Detective McFadden continued to watch. At one point a third man joined them briefly then left, and the two men began repeating their routine. McFadden was suspicious that they were casing the store for a robbery and was about to investigate when the two men began walking toward the store where the third man was waiting.

McFadden approached the three men, identified himself as a police officer, asked their names, and then grabbed one of the men, placing the man between himself and the other two. He did a quick pat-down of the man—later identified as John Terry—and felt what could be a gun in Terry's pocket, but he couldn't remove it. He ordered the three into the store at gunpoint, removed Terry's coat, and took a .38-caliber revolver from its pocket. When he patted down the other men, he found a revolver in the coat of one of them, identified as Chilton. Both were formally charged with carrying concealed weapons.

Their lawyers argued that the guns had been illegally seized and that, therefore, they could not be used as evidence. Without that evidence, there would be no case. The Ohio trial judge, however, found both guilty as charged. Chilton and Terry appealed their conviction to the United States Supreme Court, but before the case was heard, Chilton died, so the decision referred only to Terry.

When the case reached the United States Supreme Court, the legal issue was simply phrased "whether it is always unreasonable for a policeman to seize a person and subject him to a limited search for weapons unless there is probable cause for an arrest."

The United States Supreme Court upheld the Ohio verdict. The Court said McFadden had "acted reasonably" because based on his experience and training the men's actions supported McFadden's suspicion that they were planning a robbery, the robbery would probably involve weapons, and nothing happened to make him think differently. He had to act quickly when he saw the three men gather at the store. The Court noted:

> *Each case of this sort will, of course, have to be decided on its own facts. We merely hold today that where a police officer observes unusual conduct which leads him reasonably to conclude in light of his experience that criminal activity may be afoot and that the persons with whom he is dealing may be armed and presently dangerous, where in the course of investigating this behavior he identifies himself as a policeman and makes reasonable inquiries, and where nothing in the initial stages of the encounter serves to dispel his reasonable fear for his own or other's safety, he is entitled for the protection of himself and others in the area to conduct a carefully limited search of the outer clothing of such persons in an attempt to discover weapons which might be used to assault him.*
>
> *Such a search is a reasonable search under the Fourth Amendment, and any weapons seized may properly be introduced in evidence against the person from whom they were taken.*

The Terry decision established that police officers who have reasonable suspicion that someone is about to commit a crime may stop the person and possibly "frisk" them for weapons.

GUIDELINES ESTABLISHED BY THE TERRY DECISION

Guidelines established by *Terry v. Ohio* that determine if a stop and frisk is valid have been outlined by del Carmen (1987, pp. 119–120):

1. *Circumstances. The police officer must observe unusual conduct that leads him or her reasonably to conclude, in the light of his or her experience, that: (a) criminal activity may be afoot, and (b) the person with whom he or she is dealing may be armed and presently dangerous.*
2. What police officer must initially do. *In the course of investigating such behavior, the officer must: (a) identify himself or herself as a police officer, and (b) make reasonable inquiries.*
3. Extent of what an officer can do. *If these first two requirements are satisfied, the officer, for the protection of himself or herself and others in the area, may conduct a carefully limited search of the outer clothing of the person in an attempt to discover weapons that might be used to assault him or her.*

He goes on to note that no "fishing expeditions" are allowed: "The frisk cannot be used to see if some type of evidence can be found on the suspect. Its only purpose is to protect the police officer and others in the area from possible harm. A frisk for any other reason is illegal and leads to the exclusion of any evidence obtained, regardless of how incriminating the evidence may be."

Ferdico (1985, p. 291–92) suggests a partial list of factors that might favor the decision to frisk a person:

1. *The suspected crime involves the use of weapons [as in Terry].*
2. *The suspect is nervous or "rattled" over being stopped.*
3. *There is a bulge in the suspect's clothing.*
4. *The suspect's hand is concealed in a pocket.*
5. *The suspect does not present satisfactory identification or an adequate explanation for suspicious behavior.*
6. *The area the officer is operating in is known to contain armed persons.*

Ferdico cautions that (p. 292) "Any one of these things taken alone may not give sufficient grounds to frisk a suspect, but a combination of some of these elements or others, evaluated in light of the officer's knowledge and experience, might provide a justification to frisk."

THE STOP

The purpose of a stop is to prevent crime. As stated in the *Terry* decision,

> In justifying the particular intrusion [the stop] the police officer must be able to point to specific and articulable facts which, taken together with rational inferences from all those facts, reasonably warrant that intrusion.

The *Terry* court based such a determination on a "reasonable person" standard, stating, "Would the facts available to the officer at the moment of the seizure or the search, warrant a man of reasonable caution in the belief that the action taken was appropriate?"

In other words, an officer may not stop someone just for the sake of stopping them, or because the person is a white person in a black neighborhood, or because the officer does not like the looks of the individual. On the other hand, factors such as unusual, suspicious activity; looks similar to a "wanted poster," a known felony record, and the like, many add up to provide the necessary "articulable reasonable suspicion" necessary for a stop.

A stop is a brief detention of a person based on "specific and articulable facts" for the purpose of investigating suspicious activity.

The question then becomes, how long may the person be detained? The answer: however long it takes—within reason. It must be no longer than necessary for the officers to obtain the needed information. In *Florida* v. *Royer* (1983) the court said: "[A]n investigative detention must be temporary and last no longer than is necessary to effectuate the purpose of the stop. Similarly, the investigative methods employed should be the least intrusive means reasonably available to verify or dispel the officer's suspicion in a short period of time."

Although in *Terry*, the stop was made for the purpose of preventing a crime, a stop may also be made for the purpose of crime detection. LaFave and Israel (1985, p. 176) say, "When immediately after the perpetration of a crime the police may have no more than a vague description of the possible perpetrator, it seems irrational to deprive the officer of the opportunity to 'freeze' the situation for a short time, so that he may make inquiry and arrive at a considered judgment about further action to be taken."

They go on to note:

> Another issue is whether an interaction would remain a "Terry Stop" if force or threat of force is used by the police. Regardless of whether

the action is actually called a "stop" or an "arrest" by the police, the real question is what was done by the police. If the stop is briefly made for investigative purposes, it would remain a "stop," even if a suspect is surrounded, officers have weapons drawn, and certain force is used. The courts consider the display of weapons by police officers case by case.

As noted by Frase et al. (1986, pp. 257–58): "Terry did not address the question of what happens if the police make a valid investigative stop but the suspect refuses to answer questions or tries to leave. Justice White was of the opinion that 'the person stopped is not obliged to answer, answers may not be compelled, and refusal to answer furnishes no basis for an arrest, although it may alert the officers to the need for further observation.'"

Another question that arises is whether the Miranda warning needs to be given to individuals who are temporarily detained by the police. Ferdico (1985, p. 301) describes a case where this question arose:

Police officers had been alerted via radio to be on the lookout for a white Mustang with California license plates believed to be driven by a person involved in a robbery in a nearby town. When the officers spotted a car fitting that description, they stopped the defendant, asked him for identification, and asked if he had been in the town where the robbery occurred. Defendant replied that he had. No Miranda warnings had been given prior to the questions. Defendant was convicted of robbery and appealed.

The court found nothing in the questioning that amounted to an in-custody interrogation calling for Miranda warnings:

"Miranda does not bar all inquiry by authorities without previous warnings. . . . In our opinion Miranda was not intended to prohibit police officers from asking suspicious persons such things as their names and recent whereabouts without fully informing them of their constitutional rights" (Utsler v. State—South Dakota—1969).

The Miranda warning need not be given during a stop.

The Supreme Court of Washington agreed in State v. Lane (1970) when it stated, "We hold that it is not a violation of either the letter or spirit of Miranda for police to ask questions which are strictly limited to protecting the immediate physical safety of the police themselves and which could not reasonably be delayed until after warnings are given." A routine traffic stop does not require Miranda because it is not considered to be a custodial situation, per Berkemer v. McCarty (1984).

THE FRISK

The purpose of a frisk is protection. It does not automatically occur with every stop. Officers should frisk an individual ONLY if nothing in the initial stages of the stop reduces his reasonable suspicion that the person is about to commit a crime *and the officer suspects the person may be armed and dangerous*. For example, if an officer stopped a person who was running down an alley in the middle of the night carrying a paper bag and the person gave vague answers, was extremely nervous, and reaching for his pocket, the officer might well conduct a frisk. If, on the other hand, the person gave straight answers—he was late to work and his lunch was in the paper bag—a frisk would NOT be reasonable and should not be performed.

A frisk is a reasonable search for weapons for the protection of the police officers and others.

As noted by the Court in the *Terry* decision, "[I]t would appear to be clearly unreasonable to deny the officer the power to take necessary measures to determine whether the person is in fact carrying a weapon and to neutralize the threat of physical harm."

According to LaFave and Israel (1985, p. 182),

> In determining the lawfulness of a frisk, two matters are to be considered: (1) whether the officer was rightfully in the presence of the party frisked so as to be endangered if that person was armed; and (2) whether the officer had a sufficient degree of suspicion that the party frisked was armed and dangerous.

So, in order for an officer to be able to frisk someone, that person must have first been legally stopped by the officer. The mere fact that an officer sees a bulge under a pedestrian's coat will not justify a frisk. However, once a person is legally stopped by an officer, all that is required to justify a frisk is that the officer's observations lead him to "reasonably conclude" that the person with whom he is dealing *may* be armed and presently dangerous (*Terry*). This will always depend on the specific situation but could include such circumstances as a suspicious bulge in the suspect's clothes, the nature of the crime being investigated, suspicious activity such as reaching for a pocket, or knowledge that the suspect had been armed in the past. The officer need not be in actual "fear"—he or she need only to be able to reasonably conclude that the suspect *may* be armed and dangerous.

As Ferdico (1985, p. 291) cautions, "The most important thing for law enforcement officers to remember is that their authority to frisk is a limited and narrowly drawn authority."

Frisking Someone of the Opposite Sex

Frisking someone of the opposite sex is a difficult situation. Such frisking may bring about a charge of sexual harassment or indecent handling. Some options are obvious. If the individual is wearing a coat or jacket, you can ask him or her to remove it and then pat it down. Pat down the clothing of a person of the opposite sex only with a very strong suspicion that the person is armed and dangerous.

Purses and handbags should be squeezed to see if a weapon is concealed within. If a hard object is felt, the purse or handbag may be opened and searched.

STOP AND FRISK AND VEHICLE DRIVERS

Delaware v. *Prouse* (1979) established that

> . . . *except in those situations in which there is at least clear articulable, reasonable suspicion that a motorist is unlicensed or that an automobile is not registered, or that either the vehicle or an occupant is otherwise subject to seizure for violation of law, stopping an automobile and detaining the driver in order to check his driver's license and the registration of the automobile are unreasonable under the Fourth Amendment.*

Instances in which motorists may be stopped are summarized by Frase et al. (1986, p. 262): "Courts have approved stopping a car because it had expired license plates, because it had defective turnlights, because the license was tied on with baling twine, because there was a beer can on its roof, and because of erratic driving. A car may also be stopped if it matches the description of a car seen at a crime or if it is coming from the direction of a place where a crime has just been committed."

Police may legally stop motorists they see violating traffic laws or who they suspect are driving under the influence of alcohol. They may also stop a motorist they reasonably suspect does not have a license. And they may stop a motorist they believe may be driving an unregistered car. Unless the preceding exist, they may NOT stop a driver simply to check his driver's license and registration.

Officers may stop motorists who violate traffic laws, who appear to be driving under the influence of alcohol, or who they suspect do not have a driver's license or a valid registration for the car.

Officers who stop motorists for traffic violations CAN, for safety, order drivers out of their vehicles. In *Pennsylvania* v. *Mimms* (1977), the Pennsylvania court held that without any showing that a particular

Traffic stops, particularly those that escalate to a more serious level, present procedural problems and constitute a direct threat to officers' safety.

suspect may be armed, an officer may require a person lawfully stopped to exit a vehicle in order to diminish the possibility that the driver could make unobserved movements. The court said: "What is at most a mere inconvenience cannot prevail when balanced against legitimate concerns for the officer's safety." If officers have reason to believe a driver may be armed and dangerous, they can legally frisk the driver for weapons.

In addition, if police officers make a stop for a traffic violation and are reasonably suspicious that the situation is dangerous, they not only can order the driver out of the car and frisk her or him, but they also can order any passengers in the car out and frisk them as well, *(United States v. Tharpe [1976])*. In addition, if a frisk of at least one occupant of a car is permitted, the police may also check the passenger compartment for weapons *(Michigan v. Long [1983])*.

PRINCIPLES OF STOP AND FRISK

Wrobleski and Hess (1986, pp. 394–95) cite seven specific principles from *Terry* v. *Ohio* that apply to most stop-and-frisk situations:

1. *Police officers have the right and duty to approach and interrogate persons in order to investigate crimes.*
2. *Police officers may stop and make a limited search of a suspect if they observe unusual conduct that leads them to reasonably conclude, in light of their experience, that criminal activity may be afoot and that the individual whose suspicious behavior the officers are investigating at close range is armed and probably dangerous.*

3. The test of the officers' action is whether a "reasonably prudent man in the same circumstances would be warranted in the belief that his safety or that of others was in danger."

4. Officers may proceed to stop and frisk if nothing occurs to change the officers' theory that criminal activity may occur or that the suspect is armed.

5. The type of search in stop and frisk must be limited. It is a "protective seizure and search for weapons and must be confined to an intrusion which is reasonably designed to discover guns, knives, clubs, or other hidden instruments of assault."

6. If these conditions (principles 1–5) are met, the stop and frisk does not constitute an arrest.

7. Since stop and frisk actually involves a search and seizure, it must be governed by the intent of the Fourth Amendment of the Constitution, which forbids indiscriminate searches and seizures.

The Terry case established that the authority to stop and frisk is independent of the power to arrest. A stop is not an arrest, but it is a seizure within the meaning of the Fourth Amendment and therefore requires reasonableness.

In the case of *United States* v. *Mendenhall* (1980), Justice Stewart wrote: "We conclude that a person has been 'seized' within the meaning of the Fourth Amendment only if, in view of all of the circumstances surrounding the incident, a reasonable person would have believed that he was not free to leave."

To fully understand the *Terry* decision and cases following it regarding stop and frisk, look next at the Fourth Amendment, at the controversial exclusionary rule, and at its underlying requirement for stop and frisk: reasonable suspicion.

THE FOURTH AMENDMENT

The Fourth Amendment of our Constitution states: "The right of the people to be secure in their persons, houses, papers, and effects, against unreasonable searches and seizures, shall not be violated, and no warrants shall issue but upon probable cause, supported by oath or affirmation, and particularly describing the place to be searched, and the persons or things to be seized."

The Fourth Amendment forbids unreasonable searches and seizures and requires that any search or arrest warrant be based on probable cause.

You have seen that stop and frisk are forms of search and seizure, but that they fall far short of being a full-blown search or arrest. They are, nonetheless, bound by the Fourth Amendment. As stated in the first half of that amendment, they must be *reasonable*.

Reasonable

How would you define *reasonable*? Most people have a general idea of what would be reasonable—in their opinion. Reasonable means sensible, logical, fair, showing good judgment. Oran's *Law Dictionary for Nonlawyers* (1985, p. 254) defines reasonable as

> A broad, flexible word used to make sure that a decision is based on the facts of a particular situation rather than on abstract legal principles. It has no exact definition, but can mean *fair, appropriate, moderate, rational*, etc. Its definition tends to be circular. For example, *reasonable care* has been defined as "that degree of care a person of ordinary prudence [the so-called *reasonable person discussed in the last chapter*] would exercise in similar circumstances."

Reasonable means sensible, rational, justifiable.

The *Terry* case considered the "competing interests" in the stop-and-frisk situation. On the one hand is the individual's constitutional right to be free from unreasonable searches and seizures. According to the Supreme Court: "Even a limited search of the outer clothing for weapons constitutes a severe, though brief, intrusion upon cherished personal security, and it must surely be an annoying, frightening, and perhaps humiliating experience."

On the other hand, however, it is the duty of the police to detect and prevent crime and to do so without endangering their lives. The Court noted that "American criminals have a long tradition of armed violence, and every year in this country many law enforcement officers are killed in the line of duty, and thousands more are wounded." If officers reasonably suspect the person they are stopping might be armed and dangerous, it is their obligation to pat them down for weapons.

The right established in the *Terry* decision to stop and frisk someone based on articulable, reasonable suspicion only was confirmed four years later when the Court stated (Adams v. Williams [1972]):

> The Fourth Amendment does not require a policeman who lacks the precise level of information necessary for probable cause to arrest to simply shrug his shoulders and allow a crime to occur or a criminal to

escape. On the contrary, Terry *recognizes that it may be the essence of good police work to adopt an intermediate response. . . . A brief stop of a suspicious individual, in order to determine his identity or to maintain the status quo momentarily while obtaining more information, may be most reasonable in light of the facts known to the officer at the time.*

The facts known to the officer at the time may be provided by an informant, as was the case in *Adams v. Williams.* In this case, police were tipped off that Williams had a gun and was carrying drugs. Acting on this tip, a police officer stopped Williams's car and asked him to open the car door. When Williams lowered his car window, the officer reached into the car and retrieved a loaded handgun from Williams's waistband, precisely where the informant said it would be. This protective search for weapons WAS legal with the evidence able to be admitted in court against him.

The facts known to the officer at the time may also have been obtained from police in another area. The U.S. Supreme Court ruled unanimously on January 8, 1965, that police can act without a warrant to stop and briefly detain someone they know is wanted by police in another city. The stop-and-frisk rules established in *Terry* were further extended in *United States v. Hensley* (1958). In this case police officers stopped a suspect in his car based on information from a wanted flyer received from a neighboring police department, a very common situation. The flyer described the crime (an armed robbery) and the suspects wanted for questioning. When the officers approached the car, they saw a revolver sticking out from under the passenger's seat and arrested the driver and the passenger. The U.S. Supreme Court ruled that seizure of the handgun was legal, noting that

The ability to briefly stop that person, ask questions, or check identification in the absence of probable cause promotes the strong government interest in solving crimes and bringing offenders to justice. It also held that if a wanted flyer is issued on articulable facts supporting reasonable suspicion that the person wanted has committed an offense, the other police officers can rely on the flyer as a basis for stopping a person answering the description, for checking identification, and for posing questions about the offense, and may detain the person briefly while attempting to obtain further information from the department issuing the flyer.

In addition, the Court stressed the need for law enforcement agencies to cooperate and to communicate rapidly with each other:

In an era when criminal suspects are increasingly mobile and increasingly likely to flee across jurisdictional boundaries, this rule is a matter of common sense: it minimizes the volume of information concerning suspects that must be transmitted to other jurisdictions and enables police in one jurisdiction to act promptly in reliance on information from another jurisdiction.

Bennett and Hess (1987, p. 115) describe the criteria California has established for actions making a stop-and-frisk situation "reasonable": (1) furtive movements, (2) inappropriate attire, (3) carrying suspicious objects such as a TV or pillowcase, (4) vague, nonspecific answers to routine questions, (5) refusal to identify oneself, and (6) appearing to be out of place.

These criteria are similar to the partial listing of "possible indicators of criminal behavior" that officers might use in deciding to make a stop (Ferdico, 1985, p. 288): (1) the suspect is known to have a felony record; (2) the suspect fits a "wanted" notice; (3) the suspect's actions are unusual for the time of day or night; (5) the suspect's clothing is peculiar or inappropriate, e.g., a coat on a hot day; (6) the suspect's vehicle is peculiar in some respect, e.g., a clean license on a dirty car; and (7) the suspect is in an unusual place or is acting strangely.

Any one of the preceding factors may not be sufficient to establish articulable reasonable suspicion, but a combination of two or three along with the officer's experience may be justification for a stop.

Police officers must rely on their own discretion as to what is reasonable in a given situation. They are expected to *act* if they are reasonably suspicious of someone's actions. In a stop-and-frisk-situation, reasonable suspicion is all that is required. A full-blown search or arrest requires more than reasonable suspicion; it requires probable cause, a concept discussed in the next chapter.

THE EXCLUSIONARY RULE

Reference has already been made to the fact that evidence obtained illegally is not admissible in court. This was established by the exclusionary rule, which protects the right to be free from unreasonable search and seizure guaranteed by the Fourth Amendment.

Courts uphold the Fourth Amendment by the exclusionary rule that demands that no evidence can be admitted in a trial unless it was obtained legally—that is, within the constitutional standards set forth in the Fourth Amendment.

One well-known case illustrating the limits on stop and frisk is the *Sibron* case, decided on the same day as *Terry* v. *Ohio*.

Sibron v. New York

In this case, a uniformed patrol officer watched Sibron fraternizing with several known drug addicts during an eight-hour time span. He did not hear what they said, and he did not see anything being passed between them. When Sibron and a few known drug addicts went into a restaurant, the officer followed them, still not hearing their conversation or seeing anything passed between them. When the police officer approached Sibron, Sibron began to reach into his pocket. The officer grabbed his arm and reached into the same pocket, finding envelopes of heroin.

Sibron was convicted on a narcotics charge, which was appealed on the basis that his Fourth Amendment rights had been violated. The Supreme Court agreed, noting that since the officer had not seen or heard anything to make him *reasonably* suspicious that a crime involving a dangerous weapon was about to be committed, he had no justification for the stop: "The inference that persons who talk to narcotics addicts are engaged in criminal traffic in narcotics is simply not the sort of reasonable inference required to support an intrusion by the police upon an individual's personal security."

Some important exceptions to this rule exist, however. You'll look more closely at this rule and the exceptions to it in the next chapter.

In suppressing the evidence, the Court said that the officer's intent obviously was to search for narcotics and, as such, exceeded the scope of the *Terry* decision. There was not probable cause to arrest Sibron, nor was there reasonable suspicion that Sibron was armed and dangerous so as to justify a frisk.

Another case related to stop and frisk was also decided the same day as *Terry*, that is, *Peters v. New York.*

Peters v. New York

In the case of Peters v. New York (1968) the Court affirmed the conviction of a defendant who had been convicted on the basis of possessing burglar tools that were discovered during a patdown frisk by the officer.

In this case, an off-duty police officer responded to noises outside his apartment door by chasing the suspicious individuals. Upon catching Peters, the officer patted down his clothing, discovering a hard object that he suspected could be a knife. In fact, it turned out to be an envelope containing burglar's tools. The suspect was charged with possessing burglary tools.

The Court did not decide the *Peters* case by using a *Terry v. Ohio* stop-and-frisk analysis. Rather, they held that the officer had sufficient probable cause to arrest Peters for the attempted burglary, justifying the search as reasonable for Fourth Amendment purposes as a search incident to arrest.

The Significance of Sibron and Peters to the Law of Stop and Frisk

As noted by Whitebread and Slobogin (1986, p. 200):

The Sibron decision is important because it makes clear that Terry is intended to establish only a narrowly circumscribed power to search on less than probable cause to arrest, and that the right to frisk is not an automatic concomitant to a lawful stop. It also establishes proper motive as a prerequisite to a proper frisk: a search motivated by a desire to discover evidence of a crime, rather than weapons, is constitutionally impermissible unless there is an adequate basis for arrest. Finally, the Court indicated that contraband discovered in the course of a proper protective frisk can be lawfully seized.

The *Peters* case is not a crucial elaboration of the "stop and frisk" doctrine of *Terry* simply because it is not treated as a "stop and frisk" case by the Court's majority. It is significant, however, because it highlights the Supreme Court's decision to carve out two tiers when viewing the Fourth Amendment in the context of a street encounter. When there is a stop justified by less than probable cause, the *Terry-Sibron* set of restrictions binds the search. When the justification for the stop reaches the threshold level of probable cause to arrest, the entirely distinct jurisprudence of "search incident to a lawful arrest" governs the nature of a permissible search, including motive and scope." The law of arrest is the focus of the next chapter.

SUMMARY

The law of stop and frisk deals with that time frame during which officers follow up on their suspicions, but before the time that the requisite probable cause is established to justify an arrest.

The *Terry* decision established that police officers who have reasonable suspicion that someone is about to commit a crime may stop the person and possibly "frisk" them for weapons—the precedent for the stop-and-frisk procedure.

A *stop* is a brief detention of a person based on "specific and articulable facts" for the purpose of investigating suspicious activity. The *Miranda* warning need not be given during a stop. A *frisk* is a reasonable search for weapons for the protection of the police officers and others when the officer suspects the person may be presently armed and dangerous.

Police officers may stop motorists who violate traffic laws, who appear to be driving under the influence of alcohol or drugs, or who they suspect do not have a valid driver's license or vehicle registration. Merely stopping to inquire is not permitted.

The *Terry* decision established that the authority to stop and frisk is independent of the power to arrest. A stop is not an arrest, but it *is* a seizure within the meaning of the Fourth Amendment and therefore requires reasonableness.

The Fourth Amendment forbids unreasonable searches and seizures and requires that any search or arrest warrant be based on probable cause. In this context reasonable means sensible, rational, justifiable. Courts uphold the Fourth Amendment by the exclusionary rule, which demands that evidence may not be admitted in a trial unless it was obtained legally—that is, within the constitutional standards set forth in the Fourth Amendment.

Discussion Questions

1. How does a "stop and frisk" differ from an "arrest"?
2. How does the law of stop and frisk seek to serve the "competing interests" of society?
3. What factors may an officer consider in determining reasonable suspicion?
4. How does the exclusionary rule uphold the Fourth Amendment?
5. How might a stop-and-frisk contact escalate into an arrest situation?
6. Have you ever been stopped by police officers and questioned? Frisked?
7. How is the stop-and-frisk procedure frequently portrayed in TV shows?
8. What lawsuits might police officers be opening themselves up to during a stop and frisk?

References

Bennett, Wayne W., and Hess, Kären M. *Criminal Investigation.* 2d ed. St. Paul, Minn.: West Publishing Company, 1987.

del Carmen, Rolando V. *Criminal Procedure for Law Enforcement Personnel.* Monterey, Calif.: Brooks/Cole Publishing Company, 1987.

Ferdico, J. N. *Criminal Procedure for the Criminal Justice Professional.* 3d ed. St. Paul, Minn.: West Publishing Company, 1985.

Frase, Richard S.; Haugen, Phebe; and Costello, Martin J. *Minnesota Misdemeanors and Moving Traffic Violations.* St. Paul, Minn.: Butterworth Legal Publishers, 1986.

LaFave, Wayne R. and Israel, Jerold. *Criminal Procedure.* St. Paul, Minn.: West Publishing Company, 1985.

Oran, Daniel. *Law Dictionary for Nonlawyers.* 2d ed. St. Paul, Minn.: West Publishing Company, 1985.

Whitebread, Charles H., and Slobogin, Christopher. *Criminal Procedure. An Analysis of Cases and Concepts.* 2d ed. Mineola, N.Y.: The Foundation Press, Inc., 1986.

Wrobleski, Henry M., and Hess, Kären M. *Introduction to Law Enforcement and Criminal Justice.* 2d ed. St. Paul, Minn.: West Publishing Company, 1986

SHOULD ILLEGAL EVIDENCE BE EXCLUDED FROM COURT?

You have been briefly introduced to the exclusionary rule and the fact that it forbids illegally obtained evidence to be introduced at a trial. Opinion is divided over whether this is important to our criminal justice system or not.

Illegal Evidence Should Be Excluded

The principal argument made by opponents of the rule is that it frees the guilty. . . . But raising the specter of prisons across America being emptied by the exclusionary rule is just scaremongering. A General Accounting Office study found that only 0.4 percent of federal cases were not prosecuted because of problems with illegal searches, and only 1.3 percent of those that went to trial lacked some evidence because of the rule (half of the defendants in these cases were convicted anyway). . . .

Indeed, the politicians and law-enforcement officials are simply pandering to the public perception that criminals are being set free: *New York Times* columnist Tom Wicker reports that a member of President Reagan's Task Force on Violent Crime told him that the rule had to be changed not because it prevented many criminals from going to jail, but because people thought that it did. . . .

Few violent crimes are involved in such cases. . . . And what of the few violent criminals who do go free because illegal evidence against them is thrown out of court? They do not go free because "the constable blundered," for there would have been no evidence to convict the defendant had not the constable blundered in the first place. In virtually every case, the evidence was collected only because the constitutional rules were broken.

The exclusionary rule performs two particularly valuable functions. The first is to deter unconstitutional police conduct. . . . The second purpose of the rule—indeed, the original basis for it—is to help protect peoples' right to privacy. Justice Joseph P. Bradley wrote that "the essence" of an illegal search "is the invasion of [a person's] indefeasible right of personal security, personal liberty, and private property." It would be inconsistent to provide constitutional protection against certain searches and seizures because they violate fundamental individual rights, but then to allow the fruit of such illegal actions to be used against a defendant.

Excerpted from Doug Bandow, "Save the Exclusionary Rule," *Inquiry*, July 1983.

Illegal Evidence Should Not Be Excluded

As interpreted by the Supreme Court, the Constitution absolutely prohibits a judge from looking at the [illegally obtained] evidence to determine whether it would have any value for the jury. If the means used
to obtain the evidence breached any constitutional rule, then the evidence must be treated as if it had never existed. Obviously guilty defendants have gone free in cases such as these:

> Stopping a speeder, the trooper notices something suspicious
> about the driver's behavior, and demands that the trunk be
> opened. Inside, he finds a gun with the driver's fingerprints on it.
> The gun turns out to have been used to murder a bank teller. The
> court suppressed the gun, keeping its very existence from the jury,
> because the Constitution, as the Supreme Court reads it,
> demanded that the officer have more than a "suspicion" to justify
> searching the trunk.

There is nothing in the Constitution that says that improperly obtained evidence must not be used. The exclusionary rule has been developed by the courts in response to the complete failure of the government to prosecute policemen who violate the law in the course of
their duties. There are and always have been laws prohibiting the police from using illegal methods of gathering evidence. Occasionally,
overzealous police violated these laws in their desire to catch and
convict criminals. Such police violations rarely were punished.

The exclusionary rule has been the judge's answer to the prosecutor's failure to discipline errant police. The courts are saying, "We're
going to make it *pointless* for you to break the law; if you do something illegal to get the evidence, we won't let you use it. Period." Prosecutors don't indict wayward police because prosecutors have to work
with the police day-in and day-out. And there are some prosecutors
whose crusading enthusiasm sometimes leads them to condone or
even encourage improper police tactics. Because no one else has
taken on the task of making the police obey the law, the judges have
imposed the exclusionary rule.

Excerpted from an editorial in *The Washington Times*, "Abolish the Exclusionary Rule," December 8, 1982.
Reprinted with permission of the *Washington Times*.

CHAPTER 6

Lawful Arrests

The Constitution does not guarantee that only the guilty will be arrested. If it did, § 1983 would provide a cause of action for every defendant acquitted—indeed, for every suspect released.
—U.S. Supreme Court

DO YOU KNOW

How to define the term arrest?

What a citation is? A summons?

When an arrest is legal?

What the requirements are for arrest without a warrant?

What probable cause is?

What the major sources of probable cause are?

What the essential elements of an arrest are?

How much force can be used in making an arrest?

What the only justification for use of deadly force is?

What rights an arrested person has?

How an arrest differs from a stop?

Who has immunity from arrests?

What the possible results of an illegal arrest are?

Introduction   The power of arrest is described by Ferdico (1985, p. 67):

Chapter 6

> *The power of arrest is the most important power that law enforcement officers possess. It enables them to deprive a person of the freedom to carry out daily personal and business affairs, and it initiates against a person the processes of criminal justice, which may ultimately result in that person being fined or imprisoned. Since an arrest has a potentially great detrimental effect upon a person's life, the law provides severe limitations and restrictions on the law enforcement officer's exercise of the power of arrest.*

In addition to providing great power to law enforcement, the authority to arrest can also place the law enforcement officer in great danger. Some individuals would kill rather than face arrest. In dealing with the actual physical arrest, law enforcement officers should always be aware of the great danger in which they have placed themselves, as discussed in chapter 1.

ARREST DEFINED

Definitions of arrest vary from state to state. According to Bennett and Hess (1987, p. 214), "Most state laws define an *arrest* in general terms as: 'The taking of a person into custody, in the manner authorized by law for the purpose of presenting that person before a magistrate to answer for the commission of a crime.' "

Oran's *Law Dictionary* (1985, p. 26) defines arrest as follows:

An arrest is "the official taking of a person to answer criminal charges. This involves at least temporarily depriving the person of liberty and may involve the use of force."

The Maine Supreme Court has said: "An arrest in criminal law signifies the apprehension or detention of the person of another in order that he may be forthcoming to answer for an alleged or supposed crime" (State v. MacKenzie [1965]).

Citations and Summons

Before looking at arrests in detail, it is important to distinguish two alternatives to arrest: the citation and the summons.

STATE
COUNTY
CITY OF _____

VEHICLE DESCRIPTION:
Lic. No_____ Year_____ State_____
Make_____ Model_____ Color_____

CRIME OR VIOLATION:
Date: Month_____ Day_____ Year_____ Time_____
Place_____
City_____
Statute or Ordinance Violated:
County or Municipality:_____
Offense:_____
Description:_____
(see reverse also) _____
_____
_____

ISSSUING OFFICER:
Dept. _____ Number _____

_____
Signature of Isssuing Officer

CITATION OF OFFENSE

DEFENDANT'S NAME _____
                    First   Middle   Last
ADDRESS _____

CITY _____ STATE _____ ZIP _____

Birth Date _____ Ht. _____ Wt. _____ Sex _____
Operating License or
other I.D. _____ State _____

YES   NO   Was the violation, otherwise a petty misdemeanor, commited in a manner
☐   ☐   or under circumstances, so as to endanger or be likely to endanger any
            person or property?

YOU ARE HEREBY SUMMONED TO APPEAR BEFORE:
☐ County Court   ☐ Juvenile Court   ☐ Traffic Violations Bureau
                        (you will be notified)

On the_____ day of _____, 19___ at _____ A.M./P.M.
to answer to the alleged offense herein. YOUR REQUESTED signature hereunder is
a promise to appear as summoned herein. Failure to so appear will result in a
warrant issued for your arrest.

_____
Signature

Figure 6–1 **Sample Citation**

Police officers who charge traffic violators do not usually arrest them. Rather they give them a ticket—a *citation*. The individual usually has a choice of simply paying the fine, or appearing in court and pleading not guilty and letting the judge decide if the ticket was justified. Citations may also be written for violating city ordinances such as fire codes and building codes.

A second alternative is a *summons*. A magistrate can choose to issue a summons to an individual. The summons directs that person to appear in court at a specific time on a specific date for a specific purpose. Like the arrest warrant, the summons is based on a complaint filed against an individual. The summons eliminates the need for arresting the person and is often used when it is assumed the accused will appear in court to answer the charges filed against him or her.

A citation is a ticket. A summons is an order to appear in court.

WHEN ARRESTS MAY BE LAWFULLY MADE

Lawful arrests can usually be made in three ways.

Police officers can usually make a lawful arrest:

- *For any crime committed in their presence*
- *For any felony if they have probable cause*
- *With an arrest warrant*

In the first two instances a warrant is not required. In fact, according to del Carmen (1987, p. 103):

> *Although arrest warrants are preferred by the courts and desirable for purposes of police protection from liability lawsuits, they are in fact seldom used in police work and are not constitutionally required, except in home arrests. About 95 percent of all arrests are made without a warrant.*

WARRANTLESS ARRESTS FOR CRIMES COMMITTED IN THE PRESENCE OF AN OFFICER

If police officers observe a crime being committed, they have the authority to arrest the individual(s) involved in committing the crime. As noted in *State* v. *Pluth* (1923), the officers must know that a crime is being committed before making the arrest. They cannot merely suspect that someone is about to commit a crime. It must actually take place in the officers' presence.

The arrest must take place without delay. According to the Supreme Court of Mississippi:

> *The arrest for misdemeanors committed or attempted in the presence of officers must be made as quickly after the commission of the offense as the circumstances will permit. After an officer has witnessed a misdemeanor, it is his duty to then and there arrest the offender. Under some circumstances, there may be justification for delay, as for instance, when the interval between the commission of the offense and the actual arrest is spent by the officer in pursuing the offender, or in summoning assistance where such may reasonably appear to be necessary.* (Smith v. State 1956).

Police officers who come to the crime scene of a misdemeanor after it has been committed usually *cannot* make an arrest even though the suspect is still at the scene. In many states officers must obtain an arrest warrant to make an arrest for a misdemeanor not committed in their presence.

In some states, however, exceptions exist. For example, officers may arrest for misdemeanors not committed in their presence if the suspect might flee or might conceal or destroy evidence or if the incident involves a traffic accident. In other states, such as Minnesota, officers may arrest for unwitnessed misdemeanors, such as domestic assault, driving under the influence of drugs or alcohol, and shoplifting.

WARRANTLESS ARRESTS BASED ON PROBABLE CAUSE

The second type of lawful warrantless arrest is an arrest based on probable cause that the suspect has committed a *felony*.

According to Creamer (1980, p. 9), "Probable cause for an arrest is defined as a combination of facts or apparent facts, viewed through the eyes of an experienced police officer, which would lead a man of reasonable caution to believe that a crime is being or has been committed."

The United States Supreme Court has defined probable cause this way: "Probable cause exists where the facts and circumstances within their [the arresting police officers'] knowledge and of which they had reasonably trustworthy information [are] sufficient in themselves to warrant a man of reasonable caution in the belief that an offense has been or is being committed [by the one about to be arrested]" Brinegar v. United States [1949].

Oran (1985, pp. 239–40) defines probable cause as follows:

Probable cause—"The fact that it is more likely than not that a crime has been committed by the person whom a law enforcement officer seeks to arrest."

Probable cause must be established BEFORE a lawful arrest can be made.

Facts and evidence obtained *after* an arrest cannot be used to establish probable cause. They *can* be used, however, to strengthen the case IF probable cause was established before the arrest, making the arrest legal.

In contrast to warrantless arrests for misdemeanors, which must be made as soon as practical, warrantless arrests for felonies based on probable cause do *not* need to be made immediately.

Sources of Probable Cause

Probable cause is based on a "totality of circumstances."

The two main sources of probable cause are (1) what police officers see, hear, and smell and (2) on information given to them by other agencies, victims, or informants.

Observational Probable Cause

Observational probable cause includes anything police officers become aware of through their senses. Often their interpretation of what they see, hear, or smell is grounded in their past experiences, training, and their knowledge of criminal behavior.

Suspicious Conduct   Officers are trained to recognize actions/behaviors that are out of the ordinary. Individuals who are constantly peering over their shoulders, individuals who appear to be making cash transactions for goods on the streets, individuals who become nervous at the appearance of a police officer—any of these might arouse suspicion. Suspicious conduct alone, however, is seldom enough to establish probable cause. And it should be remembered that many people become nervous in the presence of authority figures, particularly those in uniform.

Being High on Drugs   Officers are trained to recognize the person who is under the influence of drugs. Common indicators include extreme perspiration, lack of balance, slurred speech, needle marks on the arms or legs, pupils that do not dilate or pupils that are extremely dilated, pupils that do not respond to light, heavy eyelids, and extreme nervousness. People who are on drugs often commit crimes to support their habit. Consequently, police treat them with suspicion.

Associating with Known Criminals   Just as being on drugs makes it more likely that the person may be involved with crimes, so people who associate with known criminals are regarded suspiciously. This association in itself, however, will not produce probable cause to arrest. Recall the *Sibron* decision discussed in the last chapter.

Criminal Record   The simple fact that a person has a criminal record is not sufficient to produce probable cause, but it can contribute to the "totality of circumstances." The Supreme Court said in *Beck v. Ohio* (1964) that the officer's knowledge of the suspect and his past record was "not entirely irrelevant upon the issue of probable cause." Nonetheless, the Court continued: "[T]o hold that knowledge of either or both of these facts [the suspect's physical appearance and previous record] constituted probable cause would be to hold that anyone with a previous criminal record could be arrested at will."

Running Away   One particularly suspicious behavior is running away at the sight of police officers. It cannot by itself, however, establish probable cause for an arrest, as established in *Wong Sun v. United States* (1963). In this case federal agents went to a laundry at six in the morning on a tip that the operator of the laundry, James Wah Toy, was selling heroin. One agent rang the bell, and when Toy answered, the agent said he'd come for his laundry. Toy replied that they weren't open yet and tried to close the door. The agent then identified himself. At this, Toy slammed the door and ran down the hall to his living quarters in the back of the laundry. The agents broke in the door and followed Toy to his bedroom. Toy reached into a nightstand drawer, so one agent drew his gun, pulled Toy's hand from the drawer, and placed him under arrest.

When Toy's case was appealed, the Supreme Court said the arrest was not made with probable cause: "Toy's refusal to admit the officers and his flight down the hallway thus signified a guilty knowledge no more clearly than it did a natural desire to repel an apparently unauthorized intrusion."

Presence in an Unusual Place or at an Unusual Time   Often just the presence of someone at a particular place such as a hotel rooftop or at an unusual time such as in a parking lot of a store that has been closed for several hours is enough to arouse suspicion.

Presence in a High Crime Area   Police know where crime is most likely to occur. They are, therefore, more suspicious when they observe individuals acting secretively or appearing at a suspicious place or time.

Presence at a Crime Scene   If police respond to a burglary call and arrive to find a window broken, the house dark, and a man prowling around with a flashlight, they can reasonably stop and frisk that individual when he comes out. Based on what they find, they might have probable cause to arrest the individual. Sometimes, however, innocent individuals are present at crime scenes. Mere presence at the scene is generally not sufficient to establish probable cause.

Failure to Answer Questions, to Provide Identification, or Providing False Information to Police   Most people will answer questions asked of them by the police and are willing to provide personal identification. Individuals who are unwilling to answer, who answer evasively, or who answer untruthfully are suspect. Especially suspicious is anyone who uses a false ID.

Physical Evidence   A broken window in an expensive, well-kept home; a car with its backseat loaded with televisions, VCRs, and videocameras; a person running down the street with bloodstained clothing; burglary tools in an individual's possession, and the like, can also help to establish probable cause.

The Totality   Any of the preceding may add to officers' belief that they have probable cause, and recall that reasonable suspicion is enough to make a stop. If the suspicion remains, officers may conduct a frisk. And, if the questioning of the individual or the pat-down produces more information to increase the officers' suspicion, probable cause can be established. At that point a warrantless arrest can be made. A mere investigatory stop may develop into a probable cause arrest.

Informational Probable Cause

Most crimes are not committed in the presence of a police officer. Officers must rely on information provided by others and then act accordingly. They may or may not need an arrest warrant.

Informational probable cause includes all information provided to police officers by others. This can include official sources, victims of crimes, and informants. Generally, the most reliable information is provided by official sources. Information from victims and from informants must be substantiated.

Official Sources   Official sources include information received at roll call, from dispatch, from police bulletins, and from wanted posters. The leading case on the legality of stopping a person on the basis of a "wanted" notice is *U.S.* v. *Hensley* (1985) discussed in the last chapter.

Police may also make arrests on the basis of official information, but the prosecution must be able to prove that the *original source* of the information was reliable. The original source is often a victim of a crime or an informant.

Victims   Victims can provide valuable information about crimes committed against them. They are usually reliable and can help police establish probable cause. In certain types of crimes, however, the victim may also be the perpetrator of the crime, for example, in arson and computer crimes. In such cases, the credibility of the victim may not be as high.

Informants   Information may also be provided by people who see a crime committed, the so-called "eyewitness." In most instances, these informants are credible. Recognize, however, that they often have something to gain by providing the information, and that they may be out for revenge of some type. Informant reliability becomes an important issue (see chapter 12).

Information can also be provided by people who did not actually see the crime committed but who have information about it. In addition, information may be provided by individuals who routinely aid the police department. The difficulty with such information is that unless the identity of the informant is made known, the information may not be used during a trial. It CAN, however, be used to further the investigation.

It is the police officers' responsibility to establish the reliability of the information they receive from victims and informants. As Ferdico (1985, p. 175) notes:

> When the information about criminal activity comes from an informant, the officer must satisfy the "totality of circumstances" test set out in the case of Illinois v. Gates. That test simply requires the officer to provide underlying facts and circumstances indicating a substantial basis for a magistrate to determine that probable cause to arrest or search exists.

The information from an informant plays one part in the "totality of the circumstances" test, and what that informant knows, and how he or she knows it, serves only as a part of the total picture considered by the magistrate (Illinois v. Gates, 1983). What is required is that the affidavit permits a magistrate to make a "common sense evaluation of probable cause."

ARRESTS WITH A WARRANT

Technically the Fourth Amendment requires that to be reasonable all arrests be made with a warrant based on probable cause. The warrant must name the person making the complaint, the specific offense being charged, the name of the accused, and the basis for the probable cause. If the name of the person is not known, the warrant may contain a detailed description of the suspect. Such a warrant is known as a John or Jane Doe warrant.

The person making the complaint must swear the facts given are true and sign the complaint. The complaint is then signed by a magistrate.

The Requirements of the Warrant

Ferdico (185, p. 77) lists six requirements for an arrest warrant:

1. *The warrant must bear the caption of the court or division of the court from which it issues.*
2. *The person to be arrested must be named in the warrant if the name is known. If not known, the warrant should contain any name or description by which the person can be identified with reasonable certainty. In other words, the warrant must show on its face that it is directed toward a particular individual.*
3. *The warrant should describe the offense charged in the complaint. This description should be in the language of the appropriate statute or ordinance. The important consideration, however, is that the description be in words definite enough for the accused to readily understand the charge. Stating that the accused is charged merely with "a felony" or "a misdemeanor" is insufficient and will invalidate the warrant.*
4. *The time of issuance of the warrant should be stated.*
5. *The warrant should be directed to an appropriate officer or officers and should command that the defendant be brought before the proper judicial official.*
6. *The warrant must be signed by the issuing magistrate and must state the magistrate's official title.*

These requirements may vary from state to state. Officers who are making an arrest under the authority of an arrest warrant should read it carefully to make certain it meets the requirements of their state.

State of _____   **County of** _____   _____ **Court**

CCT	SECTION/Subdivision	U.O.C.	GOC
	~~ADMINISTRATIVE~~		
	~~INFORMATION~~		

CTY. ATTY. FILE NO.	CONTROLLING AGENCY	CONTROL NO.
COURT CASE NO.		DATE FILED

☐ ✓ if more than 6 counts (see attached)

Complaint   ☐ SUMMONS
☐ WARRANT
☐ ORDER OF DETENTION

State of _____
PLAINTIFF,
VS.

☐ FELONY
☐ GROSS MISDEMEANOR

Name: first, middle, last	Date of Birth	SJIS COMPLAINT NUMBER
DEFENDANT.		

COMPLAINT

The Complainant, being duly sworn, makes complaint to the above-named Court and states that there is probable cause to believe that the defendant committed the following offense(s). The complainant states that the following facts establish PROBABLE CAUSE.

THEREFORE, Complainant requests that said Defendant, subject to bail or conditions of release be:
    (1) arrested or that other lawful steps be taken to obtain defendant's appearance in court; or
    (2) detained, if already in custody, pending further proceedings;
and that the said Defendant otherwise be dealt with according to law.

COMPLAINANT'S NAME:	COMPLAINANT'S SIGNATURE:

Being duly authorized to prosecute the offense(s) charged, I hereby approve this Complaint.

DATE:	PROSECUTING ATTORNEY'S SIGNATURE

PROSECUTING ATTORNEY:

NAME/TITLE:	ADDRESS/TELEPHONE:

FORM B.1

Figure 6–2   **Sample Complaint**

Serving the Warrant

Warrants for felonies can usually be served at any time in most states. Arrests for misdemeanors, however, must usually be served during the day. Police officers can request that the warrant be served at night, a warrant commonly referred to as being nightcapped or as a *nightcapped* warrant.

WHAT CONSTITUTES AN ARREST?

At what point does an arrest actually occur? Ferdico (1985, p. 68) lists four basic elements necessary to constitute an arrest:

1. *A purpose or intention to effect an arrest under real or pretended authority [not always true].*
2. *An actual or constructive seizure or detention of the person to be arrested by one having the present power to control the person.*
3. *A communication by the arresting officer to the person to be arrested of the intention or purpose then and there to make the arrest.*
4. *An understanding by the person to be arrested that it is the intention of the arresting officer then and there to arrest and detain him or her [the fundamental element].*

The elements of an arrest are (1) an intent to arrest, (2) a seizure or detention of the person arrested, (3) a statement of the authority for making the arrest and what the crime is, and (4) an understanding of what is happening by the arrestee.

Intention to Arrest   This element is what sets an arrest apart from other situations when an officer might stop or detain someone. For example, a police officer might stop a vehicle with expired license plates to warn the driver of the violation. Or he might stop a person who is acting suspiciously, but with no intention *at the moment* to arrest the person. He might restrain someone who is threatening to "punch out" a buddy in a bar. In none of these cases, does the officer intend to make an arrest.

A Seizure   The physical act of arresting has been portrayed thousands of times on television shows. The arresting officers may spread-eagle suspects up against the wall—a very visible kind of seizure. Or they may simply confront them. What must be clear is that the person being arrested is not free to leave. Technically two types of seizure are possible. The first, is known as an *actual* seizure, that is, the arrest is made using physical force. The second type of seizure, and the more common, is a

Minnesota State Trooper Robert Meyerson takes a person into physical custody, affecting the arrest. The Trooper's vehicle is a mustang bearing only the State Patrol shield. It is otherwise unidentifiable as a patrol vehicle and is one of twenty such units currently patrolling Minnesota's highways.

simple confrontation, with no resistance offered by the person being arrested. This type of seizure is known as a *constructive* seizure.

The Arrest Statement   The words spoken by arresting officers are familiar: "This is the police. You are under arrest for the murder of John Doe." To communicate that an arrest is being made, officers:

- State their authority as a law enforcement officers
- State what the person is being arrested for

An Understanding by the Arrestee   Most people will understand the simple statement "You are under arrest for . . . ," especially if it is accompanied by any degree of touching by the police officer. Exceptions to the individual understanding that an arrest is occurring include those persons who are drunk or under the influence of drugs, retarded, insane, or unconscious when being arrested. In these cases, the arrest is still legal even though the person arrested does not at the time understand what is happening.

Search Incidental to Arrest

The *Chimel* case provides that it is legal for police officers to search an arrested person and the area within his immediate control (reach) for weapons and destructible evidence, as will be discussed in the next chapter. This search should normally be done as soon as possible for the officers' safety and to locate any contraband.

CIRCUMSTANCES INVOLVED IN AN ARREST

Time   As noted previously, arrest for a misdemeanor committed in the presence of police officers must be made as soon as practical. Arrests with an arrest warrant should usually be made during the daytime unless the element of surprise is necessary for safety reasons. Common sense dictates that arrests should seldom be made during religious ceremonies or while the individual is engaged in some public function.

Place   In most states the city police have the authority to arrest only within their city limits. The sheriff and county police are usually limited to their own county, and state troopers are usually limited to their state.

Limited jurisdiction traditionally posed a problem for law enforcement officers as offenders sought to outrun them to outside the city limits, county border, or the state line. To eliminate this problem, the "hot pursuit" rule was developed. This rule allowed police officers, sheriffs, or state troopers to go outside their jurisdiction to make an arrest IF they were in "hot pursuit," meaning in actual pursuit of the individual.

Fresh Pursuit

Stuckey (1986, p. 44) states that "Today most states have adopted what is known as the Uniform Act of Fresh Pursuit. This act provides that a peace officer of one state may enter another state in fresh pursuit to arrest one who has committed a felony in the state from which the offender fled."

He goes on to explain what constitutes "fresh pursuit": "[I]t is generally held today that if a pursuit is uninterrupted and continuous, it is a fresh pursuit."

Some states require that anyone so arrested be brought before the nearest court. Other states allow the arresting officers to return with their prisoner to their own state.

Assistance from Others

Police officers may call upon private citizens to help make an arrest if needed. States vary greatly in regard to who *must* respond to an officer's request for assistance in making an arrest. Some states specify any male eighteen years or older. Other states specify any able-bodied person eighteen years or older. Failure to assist when asked to do so is a misdemeanor in many states, even if helping the police presents some danger to the citizen.

USE OF FORCE IN MAKING AN ARREST

The amount of force used in making an arrest must be "reasonable."

When making an arrest, police officers can use only as much force as is needed to overcome resistance. If the suspect does not resist arrest, NO force can be used.

Officers can break down a door or break in a car window to make an arrest if necessary. This can be done only after officers have announced themselves, stating the purpose of entry and demanding to be let in. Exceptions may be made. If the officers fear the suspect may harm them or others or may destroy evidence, they may request a "no-knock arrest warrant."

A warrant with a "no knock" provision authorizes the police to enter premises unannounced. They can, for example, break down a door, enter through a window, or use a front end loader tractor to force entry into fortified "crack houses" which have barricaded doors and windows, alarms, and other protection. A "no knock" warrant affords officers the element of surprise and is justified when either officer or citizen safety or the destruction of evidence is a concern. A safety trend is the development of specially trained "entry teams" to assist in executing such dangerous warrant services.

Handcuffing

Whether handcuffs are used depends on the situation and on department policy. Certainly if those arrested are seen as a threat to the police officer, others, or themselves, or as persons who may try to escape, handcuffs should be used. Some departments have as a policy that anyone taken into custody is to be handcuffed.

Use of Deadly Force

Ferdico (1985, p. 91) asserts that "Except in cases of self-defense, the officer is *never* justified in using firearms or other deadly force to effect an arrest for a misdemeanor. *The rule is that it is better that a misdemeanant escape rather than a human life be taken.*"

In the past, this was not the case for someone suspected of committing a felony. The "fleeing felon" rule allowed police officers to shoot to kill any felon who fled to escape arrest. This is no longer true. Recall that in *Tennessee v. Garner* (1985), the Court ruled that law enforcement officers cannot shoot "fleeing felons" unless they present an "imminent danger to life." In other words, police officers cannot shoot someone suspected of a felony if they run.

Not only does the use of handcuffs clearly indicate an arrest situation, it also reflects a critical step to assure officer safety.

The only justification for use of a deadly weapon is self-defense or protecting the lives of others.

DISPOSITION OF PRISONERS

Once a person is arrested, the police must assume responsibility for that person's safety and well-being. If the person is injured, medical care must be provided. Sometimes the person is taken directly before a judge and bail is set. Frequently, however, the person is booked and then either released on bail or jailed.

Booking

After the police arrest someone, they usually take the suspect to the police station for *booking*. This consists of entering the arrest in the official law enforcement records, fingerprinting and photographing the suspect, and sometimes posting bail.

Inventory Searching

Prisoners who are to be jailed will usually be subjected to a search. This serves two purposes. First, it protects the prisoner's personal property in that it is all listed and then placed in a safe place until the prisoner is released. Second, it protects the officers and other prisoners and helps assure that no weapons or illegal drugs will be taken into the jail. Similarly, an impounded vehicle can be inventory searched for the same reasons.

Sheriff's Department

Arrest Report

A R R E S T E E	Person Arrested: (Last)		(First)		(Middle)		Sex M/F	Race	DOB	Age
							Hgt	Wgt	Hair	Eyes
	Address: No:	St:					S/M/T			
	Apt:	City:		ST:	Zip:		DL No:			
	Phone:	(H)	Phone:		(B)		ST:	Type:	Exp:	

O F F E N S E	Offense Suspected/Charged:		Felony	Arrest Made: On View Call Warrant
			Gr. Misd.	Warrant No.
			Misd.	Circle: Drunk Drinking Cursed Resisted
	Arrest Date:	Time:	Petty Misd.	Armed: Y/N Type:

A S S O C I A T E S	Associates in Offense: (Last)	(First)	(Middle)	DOB	MV Involved: Y/N
					MV Yr.
					Make
					Model

C O M P L A I N A N T	Complainant's Name (Last)		(First)		(Middle)		DOB	Style
								Color
	Address: No:	St:						Lic ST
	Apt:	City:			ST:	Zip:		Lic. No.
	Phone:		(H)	Phone:		(B)		VIN No.

Relationship of Complainant to Suspect, if any:

					Vehicle Impounded: Y/N
A ☐ Stranger	D ☐ Spouse	G ☐ Girlfriend	J ☐ Neighbor	M☐ Customer	1 ☐ Unknown
B ☐ Relative	E ☐ X-Spouse	H ☐ Landlord	K ☐ Employer	N ☐ Merchant	9 ☐ Other
C ☐ Acquaintance	F ☐ Boyfriend	I ☐ Tenant	L ☐ Employee	0 ☐ Officer	Where:

W I T N E S S	Witness' Name (Last)		(First)		(Middle)		DOB	
								Key Disposition:
	Address: No:	St:						
	Apt:	City:			ST:	Zip:		
	Phone:		(H)	Phone:		(B)		Property Placed in Property Room: Y/N

R I G H T S	Arrestees Rights Given By:	Date:	Time:	Location:
	Comments:			

Reporting Officer Rank Name		ID	Division	Reviewing Supervisor Rank Name		ID
Assisting Officer Rank Name		ID	Division	Page 1 of ____ Pages		

Figure 6—3 **Sample Arrest Report**

Because there are no "secret" arrests in the United States, prisoners must be "booked," including taking photographs. Such identifying information can be obtained in a police station or in the field.

Rights of Prisoners

Even though they are accused of breaking the law, prisoners have certain rights. One of these basic rights is to know the charges brought against them.

In many states, the prisoner also has the right to make a phone call. States vary considerably in their laws governing who can be called, how many calls can be made, and who pays for them. In most states prisoners can make at least one local phone call at no cost. Some states allow several. Typically prisoners call family members, lawyers, bail bondspeople, or friends. States also vary in regard to whether they must inform prisoners of their right to make a call and whether they must tell them if the call is monitored. If the prisoner is physically disabled, some states require that the police help in making the call. The bottom line is that prisoners are not to be held incommunicado.

Prisoners also have a right to be brought before a magistrate without "undue delay." This will depend on local situations. In large cities, it should be within a few hours since magistrates are typically available. In small, rural areas, however, the magistrate may be out of town for the weekend. In such cases the delay will be much longer.

People who are arrested usually have the right to

- *Know the charges against them*
- *Make a phone call*
- *Appear before a magistrate without "undue delay"*

AN ARREST AND A STOP COMPARED

Law enforcement involves decisions and discretion. Police officers are charged with investigating suspicious circumstances. What begins as a simple stop may progress to a frisk and then to an arrest and full-body search. The reasonableness of this progression was established in the landmark *Terry* case. The basic differences between a stop and an arrest is summarized in table 6-1.

Table 6–1 Stop vs. Arrest

	Stop	Arrest
Justification	Reasonable suspicion	Probable cause
Warrant	None	Maybe
Officer's Intent	To investigate suspicious activity	To make a formal charge
Search	"Pat-down'" for weapons	Full search for weapons and evidence
Scope	Outer clothing	Area within suspect's immediate control
Record	Minimal—field notes	Fingerprints, photographs, and booking

AN ARREST OR NOT?

You've seen how a simple stop can escalate to become an arrest. There is a middle ground that is technically short of an arrest, but much more than a simple stop. Ferdico (1985, p. 71) notes:

> At a still higher level of intensity [than a stop] are police contacts with members of the public involving a detention or temporary seizure of a person that is more intrusive on a person's freedom of action than a brief investigatory "stop," but that does not satisfy the four elements of a technical arrest discussed earlier. In such instances, courts often hold that, despite the lack of a technical arrest, the seizure is so similar to an arrest in important respects that it should be allowed only if supported by probable cause to believe a crime has been or is being committed.

Ferdico cites the leading case in this area as *Dunaway v. New York* (1979). In this case police picked up the defendant at a friend's home and took him to the police station for questioning. He was never told that he was under arrest, but he was not free to leave. Even though he was not booked and, therefore, would have no arrest record, the Supreme Court ruled that the seizure was illegal because the defendant was not free to leave. The "seizure" was much more than a simple stop and frisk and, as such, should have been based on probable cause.

"It does not matter," asserts del Carmen (1987, p. 94), "whether the act is termed an 'arrest' or a mere 'stop' or 'detention' under state law. When a person has been taken into custody against his or her will for purposes of criminal prosecution or interrogation, there is an arrest under the Fourth Amendment, regardless of what state law says."

This contention is echoed in *Cupp v. Murphy* (1973): "The detention of the respondent against his will constituted a seizure of his person, and the Fourth Amendment guarantee of freedom from unreasonable searches and seizures is clearly implicated."

CITIZEN'S ARREST

Not all arrests are made by police officers. Individuals not associated with law enforcement may also make arrests if they see a crime being committed. This includes ordinary people who witness a crime as well as private security officers. They must then immediately turn the arrested person over to law enforcement officers.

Stuckey (1986, p. 42) clarifies:

The arrest by a private person is sometimes referred to as a "citizen's arrest," but the private person does not have to be a citizen to make an arrest. The private person may make arrests under certain conditions. These conditions are restrictive to discourage the private person from making arrests. . . . A private person arrest generally requires that the crime for which the arrest is made must have been committed, or attempted, in the presence of the arresting person.

Most state statutes do not specify if a private person making an arrest can use force. Nor do most state statutes specify if a private person making an arrest can call for assistance from others as the police can.

IMMUNITY FROM ARREST

Certain classifications of people have immunity from arrest because of federal or state statutes.

Foreign diplomats, including ambassadors, ministers, their assistants, and attaches, and their families and servants have complete immunity from arrest. Foreign consuls and their deputies as well as some legislators and out-of-state witnesses also have limited immunity.

According to international law and numerous treaties and agreements with other nations, the United States has granted total immunity

---

CERTIFICATE AND DECLARATION OF ARREST BY PRIVATE PERSON
AND DELIVERY OF PERSON SO ARRESTED TO PEACE OFFICER

DATE _____

TIME _____

PLACE _____

I, _____, hereby declare and certify that I have

arrested (Name) _____

for the following reasons: _____

_____

_____

_____

_____

_____

and I do hereby request and demand that you _____,
a peace officer, take and conduct this person whom I have arrested to the nearest
magistrate, to be dealt with according to law; and if no magistrte can be contacted
before tomorrow morning, then to conduct this person to jail for safe keeping until the
required appearance can be arranged before such magistrate, at which time I shall be
present, and I will then and there sign, under oath, the appropriate complaint against this
person for the offense which this person has committed, and for which I made this arrest;
and I will then and there, or thereafter as soon as this criminal action or cause can be
heard, testify under oath of and concerning the facts and circumstances involved
herein. I will save said officer harmless from any and all claim for damage of any kind,
nature, and description arising out of his acts at my direction.

Name of private person
making this arrest _____

Address _____

Peace Officer Witnesses to this statement:

_____

_____

Figure 6—4 **Sample Citizen's Arrest Form**

to foreign ministers and ambassadors, their families, their staffs, and
their servants. They cannot be detained or arrested for any offense
unless they are United States citizens or they become permanent
residents. They may, however, be sent out of the country if it is
perceived that they are breaking our laws.

Foreign consuls and their deputies have immunity from arrest for
any act committed while performing their assigned duties. Even this
immunity may be waived if a serious felony is involved.

Many states have granted their legislators immunity from civil lawsuits. There is no immunity for a legislator facing criminal charges.

Finally, out-of-state witnesses are also often granted immunity, as noted by Stuckey (1986, p. 51):

> The Uniform Act to Secure the Attendance of Witnesses from Without the State in Criminal Cases *has been adopted by most of the states. This act provides that if a person goes into a state in obedience of a subpoena to testify in that state, he shall not be subject to arrest in connection with any crime committed in the state prior to his entrance into the state to testify. He is also granted a reasonable time to leave the state after testifying without being subject to such an arrest. He is not, however, granted any immunity from arrest for a crime that he may commit while in the state to testify.*

The reason for such immunity is to permit individuals carrying out important legal functions to be free to do so.

EFFECT OF ILLEGAL ARRESTS

If an illegal arrest is made, this does *not* provide grounds for dropping the charges against the illegally arrested person. It does not eliminate a trial, and it does not affect the validity of the judicial proceedings in any way. As noted in *State* v. *Boynton* (1948), "The fact that one is illegally arrested is not grounds for quashing the indictment, information, or complaint brought against the person and does not preclude a trial on the charges, or affect the validity of the proceedings in any way."

This does not mean that an illegal arrest does not often ruin the prosecution's case. What frequently happens is that the evidence in the case will be excluded per the exclusionary rule if it was obtained in violation of the defendant's constitutional rights or was in any way "fruit of the poisonous tree."

If an arrest is illegal, so is any search incidental to that arrest. Therefore, any evidence seized during the search is, under the exclusionary rule, inadmissible in court.

Often this is the only evidence there is. In like manner, any confession made under the duress of an illegal arrest will also be ruled inadmissible in court. Further, a witness's identification of a suspect may also be ruled inadmissible if it was in any way associated with an illegal arrest.

Another outcome of an illegal arrest is that the police officers involved can be sued for false arrest or false imprisonment.

SUMMARY

An arrest is the official taking of a person to answer criminal charges. This involves at least temporarily depriving the person of liberty and may involve the use of force (Oran). Alternatives to an arrest are a citation (a ticket) and a summons (an order to appear in court).

Police officers can usually make a lawful arrest (1) for any crime committed in their presence, (2) for any felony if they have probable cause, and (3) with an arrest warrant.

Probable cause refers to the fact that it is more likely than not that a crime has been committed by the person whom a law enforcement officer seeks to arrest. It is a necessary prerequisite for an arrest, that is, it must be established *before* an arrest can be made—with or without a warrant. The two main sources of probable cause are what police officers see, hear, and smell (observational probable cause) and information given to them by other agencies, victims, or informants.

The elements of an arrest are (1) an intent to arrest, (2) a seizure or detention of the person arrested, (3) a statement of the authority for making the arrest and what the crime is, and (4) an understanding of what is happening by the arrestee. When making an arrest, police officers can use only as much force as is needed to overcome resistance. If the suspect does not resist arrest, NO force can be used. The only justification for use of deadly force is self-defense or protecting the lives of others.

People who are arrested usually have the right to know the charges, to make a phone call, and to appear before a magistrate without "undue delay."

An arrest differs from a stop in important ways. A stop is justified by reasonable suspicion, an arrest by probable cause. A stop does not involve a warrant, an arrest may. The officer's intent in a stop is to investigate suspicious activity; in an arrest it is to make a formal charge and detain a person. The frisk in a stop is limited to a "pat-down" of the suspect's outer clothing for weapons. The search in an arrest is limited to the area within the suspect's immediate control but is intended to find either weapons or evidence. The record made in a stop is minimal, usually just field notes. The record made in an arrest is more extensive, usually including fingerprints, photographs, and a formal booking.

Foreign diplomats, including ambassadors, ministers, their assistants, and attaches, and their families and servants have complete immunity from arrest. Foreign consuls and their deputies as well as some legislators and out-of-state witnesses also have limited immunity.

If an arrest is illegal, so is any search incidental to that arrest. Therefore, any evidence seized during the search is, under the exclusionary rule, inadmissible in court, as will be discussed in detail in the next chapter and in chapter 10.

Discussion Questions

1. What benefits could there be of arrests with or without a warrant?
2. What factors can be used to formulate probable cause?
3. Why is the power of arrest important to law enforcement officers?
4. How does a "citizen's arrest" differ from an arrest by a police officer?
5. What benefit could possibly result from permitting immunity from arrest for certain political figures, both foreign and domestic?
6. Must a person be under physical control to be "under arrest"?
7. Do you know anyone who has been arrested?
8. What feelings do you think you would experience if you were arrested and had done nothing illegal?

References

Bennett Wayne W., and Hess, Kären M. *Criminal Investigation.* 2d ed. St. Paul, Minn.: West Publishing Company, 1987.

Creamer, J. S. *The Law of Arrest, Search, and Seizure.* 3d ed. New York: Holt, Rinehart, and Winston, 1980.

del Carmen, Rolando V. *Criminal Procedure for Law Enforcement Personnel.* Monterey, Calif.: Brooks/Cole Publishing Company, 1987.

Ferdico, J. N. *Criminal Procedure for the Criminal Justice Professional.* 3d ed. St. Paul, Minn.: West Publishing Company, 1985.

Oran, Daniel. *Law Dictionary for Nonlawyers.* 2d ed. St. Paul, Minn.: West Publishing Company, 1985.

Stuckey, Gilbert B. *Procedures in the Justice System.* 3d ed. Columbus, Ohio: Charles E. Merrill Publishing Company, 1986.

Wrobleski, Henry M., and Hess, Kären M. *Introduction to Law Enforcement and Criminal Justice.* 2d ed. St. Paul, MN: West Publishing Company, 1986.

IS POLICE MISCONDUCT SOMETIMES JUSTIFIED?

Because police officers have such "awesome power," does this sometimes justify misconduct on their part?

Police Misconduct Is Often Justified

In times of danger, it is the policeman, the highway patrolman, the sheriff's deputy or the federal agent who offers innocent citizens their only protection. It is these law enforcement officers who risk their own lives—and sometimes lose them—for the sake of others.

In one Mississippi home a mother and four children began the year 1982 in bleak despair, their policeman-husband-father having been shot and stabbed to death on New Year's Eve while carrying out his duties as a highway patrolman. Four black males, one convicted of a previous murder and all with criminal records, are charged with the slaying.

[There are countless] tragedies created by criminals turned loose on society by too-lenient judges, plea-bargaining prosecuting attorneys and soft-headed parole boards.

When a patrolman stops a speeding automobile he never knows whether the driver is an upstanding citizen who absent-mindedly stepped too heavily on the accelerator or a criminal who has just robbed a bank or committed murder. A law-abiding citizen will understand the officer's caution.

When a policeman or sheriff's deputy sets out to apprehend a murderer or an armed robber, he knows that he himself may be fired upon or perhaps killed.

The next time you read about a policeman being sued or suspended from duty because someone has accused him of "brutality'" in making an arrest, think about these two cases [cases in which officers were killed]. All too often, if a policeman has used force of any kind in making an arrest, it is because he has been attacked or threatened, or knows that he is confronting imminent danger.

Excerpted from George Shannon. "Police Officer Might Be the Best Friend You Ever Had," *Union Leader,* March 4, 1982. Reprinted with permission.

Police Misconduct Is Never Justified

Police misconduct is a concept that comfortable suburban dwellers, or those fortunate enough to live in more affluent parts of the central city, have difficulty relating to. In part, that's because the allegations often are made by people who live a different style of life. . . .

As middle-class citizens we tend to give little attention to police misconduct. We know that it probably happens from time to time. Our inclination is to believe that when it does, it is to some streetwise tough who knows no other language, or "has it coming to him."

Police officers hold the awesome power to arrest, detain, and even to kill with legal authority. The responsibility attendant upon that power is equally awesome. When it is misused it must be dealt with severely.

Police officers who demonstrate an inability to function in a professional manner should not be permitted to continue in that capacity. . . .

Excerpted from David LaFontaine, "Police Guilty of Misconduct Ought to Be Relieved of Duties," *Minneapolis Star and Tribune*, December 23, 1981.

CHAPTER 7

Searches and the

Fourth Amendment

It is unreasonable for a police officer to look for an elephant in a matchbox. —Legal maxim.

DO YOU KNOW

Why warrantless arrests are presumed unreasonable?

What probable cause to search means?

What special conditions may be specified in a search warrant?

What limitations are placed on searches with a warrant? Incident to an arrest? With consent?

In what instances a search warrant is not required?

What plain-view evidence is?

How the search in a "frisk" situation is limited?

When a vehicle can be legally searched?

What precedents were established by the Carroll, Chimel, Terry, and Weeks decisions?

What emergency situations might justify a warrantless search?

How "expectation of privacy" affects searches?

If border searches and searches at international airports are legal?

What limitation is placed on ALL searches, with or without a warrant?

When general searches are legal?

What the exclusionary rule is and does?

Introduction

Chapter 7

Several years ago, police officers went to Ted Chimel's home with an arrest warrant charging him with burglarizing a coin shop. The officers insisted they had the right to search Chimel's home because they had a warrant for his arrest. They made a thorough search despite Chimel's objections, and they found several coins during their extensive search. With the coins as evidence, Chimel was convicted in a California court. His lawyer appealed the decision, claiming the coins had been illegally seized, and in a historic decision (*Chimel v. California* [1969]) the United States Supreme Court agreed. This decision gave added strength to the exclusionary rule (established in *Weeks* v. *United States* in 1914).

Police officers must always be certain a search is legally justified. In the *Chimel* case, for example, the officers conducted a very thorough search, but the evidence was not admissible because the search itself was illegal. Officers who do not know when they have the legal authority to search not only lose valuable time, but they also lose cases and possibly leave themselves open to civil liability as well.

COMPLYING WITH THE FOURTH AMENDMENT

An analysis of search-and-seizure law begins with the presumption that ALL warrantless searches are unreasonable and, therefore, violative of the Fourth Amendment. Recall that the Fourth Amendment has been made applicable to the states through the Fourteenth Amendment. It is indeed "essential to liberty in the American scheme of justice." Recall, also, that every constitutional amendment that is directly applicable to law enforcement is applicable to state and local government via the due process clause of the Fourteenth Amendment. Consequently, if evidence seized during a search is to be admissible in court, it must be legally seized. The best way to assure this is by having a search warrant.

SEARCH WITH A SEARCH WARRANT

Interpreting the Fourth Amendment strictly, all searches conducted with a search warrant must be "based upon probable cause, supported by oath and affirmation, and particularly describing the place to be searched and the persons or things to be seized."

The Fourth Amendment requires that searches conducted under authority of a search warrant be based on probable cause. Searches with a warrant are presumed to be reasonable. All others searches are presumed to be unreasonable.

A key concept in the Fourth Amendment is PROBABLE CAUSE. You looked at probable cause as it relates to arrest in the last chapter. Consider now how it relates to searches.

Probable Cause

Probable cause is stronger than the reasonable suspicion required for a frisk. The question is, "Would a reasonable person believe that either the individual committed the offense, or that the contraband or evidence would be where it is said to be?" As Oran says,

Probable cause to search means it is more likely than not that the items sought are where the officers believe them to be.

Smith v. *United States* (1949) defined probable cause as "The sum total of layers of information and the synthesis of what the police have heard, what they know, and what they observe as trained officers. We [the court] weight not individual layers but the laminated total."

According to Creamer (1980, p. 9),

> *Probable cause for the issuance of a search warrant is defined as facts or apparent facts, viewed through the eyes of an experienced police officer, which would lead a man of reasonable caution to believe that there is something connected with a violation of law on the premises to be searched.*

Creamer notes that the concept of probable cause has existed for over two thousand years and is one of the oldest and most important concepts in criminal law. He suggests (p. 8) that "This concept of probable cause has acquired its legal potency in the United States because it has con-stitutional dimensions and because it is interpreted in the final analysis by impartial judges rather than by the police. The severe penalty that the courts impose on police who fail to abide by the spirit of the Fourth Amendment is to declare the evidence they gathered to be inadmissible."

Obtaining a Search Warrant

Officers who have probable cause to believe evidence of a crime is located at a specific place must go before a magistrate (judge) and swear under oath what they are looking for and where they think it can be found. In determining whether probable cause for the warrant exists, the reviewing judge must consider the "totality of the circumstances." In other words, all the factors submitted are viewed as a whole in considering whether a reasonable person would believe that the evidence will be found where the officer(s) claim.

The warrant must include the reasons for requesting the search warrant, the names of the officers who applied for it, names of others who have information to contribute, what specifically is being sought, and the signature of the judge issuing it.

Special Conditions

Sometimes officers ask for special conditions to be attached to the search warrant.

Special provisions of search warrants, including making an unannounced entrance and carrying out the search at night, must be approved by a magistrate as part of the search warrant.

If officers want to make an unannounced entrance because they are afraid the evidence might be destroyed or officer safety requires it, they can request a *no-knock* search warrant. The search warrants for drug busts using bulldozers to crash through the walls of suspected crack houses would have such a provision.

In other cases, the illicit activity occurs primarily at night, illegal gambling, for example. In such cases, the officers can ask the judge to include a provision allowing them to execute the warrant at night.

Carrying Out the Search Warrant

Once signed by a judge, the warrant becomes an order for the police to carry out the search. Police officers must usually carry out the warrant during daylight hours. They must also usually identify themselves as officers, state their purpose, and show the search warrant to the person in authority. The officers may use reasonable force to execute the warrant if they are denied entrance or if no one is home.

Once the officers have gained entrance, they may conduct their search, limiting it to the specific locations listed in the warrant and for the specific evidence described. That is, they can only search areas where it is reasonable to believe the specified items might be found.

SEARCH WARRANT

STATE OF _____, COUNTY OF _____ _____ COURT

TO: _____

_____ (A) PEACE OFFICER (S) OF THE STATE OF _____ .

WHEREAS, _____ has this day on oath, made application to the said Court applying for issuance of a search warrant to search the following described (premises) (motor vehicle) (person):

_____

_____

located in the _____ of _____ , county of _____ STATE OF _____

for the following described property and things: (attach and identify additional sheet if necessary)

WHEREAS, the application and supporting affidavit of _____

(was) (were) duly presented and read by the Court, and being fully advised in the premises.

NOW, THEREFORE, the Court finds that probable cause exists for the issuance of a search warrant upon the following grounds: (Strike inapplicable paragraphs)

1. The property above-described was stolen or embezzled.

2. The property above-described was used as a means of committing a crime.

3. The possession of the property above-described constitutes a crime.

4. The property above-described is in the possession of a person with intent to use such property as a means of committing a crime.

5. The property above-described constitutes evidence which tends to show a crime has been committed, or tends to show that a particular person has committed a crime.

The Court further finds that probable cause exists to believe that the above-described property and things (are) (will be) (at the above-described premises) (in the above described motor vehicle) (on the person of _____).

The Court further finds that a nighttime search is necessary to prevent the loss, destruction, or removal of the objects of said search.

The Court further finds that entry without announcement of the authority or purpose is necessary (to prevent the loss, destruction, or removal of the objects of said search) (and) (to protect the safety of the peace officers).

NOW, THEREFORE, YOU _____

_____

THE PEACE OFFICER (S) AFORESAID, ARE HEREBY COMMANDED (TO ENTER WITHOUT ANNOUNCEMENT OF AUTHORITY AND PURPOSE) (IN THE DAYTIME ONLY) (IN THE DAYTIME OR NIGHTTIME) TO SEARCH (THE DESCRIBED PREMISES) (THE DESCRIBED MOTOR VEHICLE) (THE PERSON OF _____) FOR THE ABOVE-DESCRIBED PROPERTY AND THINGS, AND TO SEIZE SAID PROPERTY AND THINGS AND (TO RETAIN THEM IN CUSTODY SUBJECT TO COURT ORDER AND ACCORDING TO LAW) (DELIVER CUSTODY OF SAID PROPERTY AND THINGS TO _____).

BY THE COURT:

_____

Dated_____, 19___.   JUDGE OF   COURT

Figure 7–1 Sample Search Warrant

Searches conducted with a search warrant must be limited to the specific area and specific items described in the warrant.

Sometimes, however, officers come across items that are not named in the warrant but are very similar to the items described. For example, officers were searching for property stolen in a burglary of an Audio King store, and the warrant specified television sets, VCRs, and stereos. When the officers executed the warrant, they came across a room filled with television sets, VCRs, stereos, and videocameras. They could seize the videocameras as evidence, even though they were not specified in the warrant. They were similar to the other items.

Officers can also seize any *contraband* they find during a search with a warrant, even though it was not specified. Contraband includes anything it is illegal for people to own or have in their possession, such as illegal drugs or illegal weapons. The contraband does not need to be related to the crime described in the search warrant. This is discussed further under the "Plain-View Doctrine."

To reiterate, the Fourth Amendment requires that when possible, police officers should obtain a search warrant. Our high-tech age is making this more and more of a possibility. Car phones, for instance, can make obtaining warrants almost instantaneous. Because an independent magistrate decides that probable cause to search exists, the defendant has to prove that the warrant was invalid. Police discretion has been removed and thus the search with a warrant is presumed legal. So remember, good police work dictates getting a warrant whenever practical.

SEARCHES WITHOUT A WARRANT

Although the presumption is that a warrantless search is unreasonable, the law does recognize six exceptions. Through the development of case law, the United States Supreme Court has defined the following searches without a warrant to be reasonable.

Six exceptions to the warrant requirement are

- *Search incident to a lawful arrest*
- *Consent search*
- *Plain-view doctrine*
- *Stop and frisk*
- *Automobile exceptions*
- *Exigent (emergency) circumstances*

Because the preceding have been recognized as legitimate exceptions to the warrant requirement, evidence obtained in these circumstances is admissible in court (*Marshall v. Barlow's Inc.* [1978];
Michigan v. Tyler [1978]).

SEARCHES INCIDENT TO LAWFUL ARREST

Once a person has lawfully been taken into custody by a police
officer, our law recognizes the necessity of permitting a complete search
to be carried out. The reasons are twofold. First, officer safety requires
that any weapon on or near the defendant be located. Second, any
evidence or other contraband should be recovered.

Assume during this discussion that all arrests are legal; if not, the
exclusionary rule would prevent any evidence obtained during the
search from being used in court. If an arrest is legal, what kind of search
can be conducted? The police had an arrest warrant for Ted Chimel
before they searched his home. Why wasn't the evidence found during
this search admissible?

As the Supreme Court studied the *Chimel* case, they looked at the
principle of searches incidental to an arrest. It is the leading case in this
situation. The Court said:

> When an arrest is made, it is reasonable for the arresting officer to
> search the person arrested to remove any weapons that the latter
> might seek to use to resist arrest or effect an escape.
>
> It is entirely reasonable for the arresting officer to search for and
> seize any evidence on the arrestee's person in order to prevent its con-
> cealment or destruction and the area from within which the arrestee
> might gain possession of a weapon or destructible evidence.

The key phrases in this statement are *on the arrestee's person* and
the area from within which the arrestee might gain possession. The
Court described this as WITHIN THE PERSON'S IMMEDIATE
CONTROL—meaning within the person's reach. This has also been
defined as the person's "wing span." The fact that the defendant is
handcuffed does *not* restrict the scope of the search. The area remains
as if the defendant was not cuffed. How far? That would have to depend
on what the Court found to be "reasonable."

---

*Searches following an arrest must be immediate and must be limited
to the area within the person's reach (Chimel).*

This was not true in the *Chimel* case. Officers made an extensive,
hour-long search of the entire house. They should have had a search
warrant as well as an arrest warrant if they wanted to look for coins any

place other than in Chimel's pockets or the area immediately near him when arrested.

Following the *Chimel* decision, courts generally insisted that officers making a search incidental to an arrest have a definite idea of what they were searching for, as is required by a search warrant. This knowledge should dictate how far the search of the person went.

In 1973, however, the U.S. Supreme Court expanded the scope of searches allowed following arrests in *United States v. Robinson*. This case involved a full-scale search of an individual arrested for a minor traffic violation. The officer inspected the contents of a cigarette package found on Robinson and discovered illegal drugs. The drugs were admitted as evidence, with the Court stating:

> It is the fact of the lawful arrest which establishes the authority to search, and we hold that in the case of a lawful custodial arrest a full search of the person is not only an exception to the warrant requirement of the Fourth Amendment, but is also a "reasonable" search under that Amendment.
>
> Not all states follow this ruling, however. The Hawaiian Supreme Court, for example, limits the warrantless search following a custodial arrest to disarming the person if the officers believe him to be dangerous and searching for evidence related to the crime for which the person was arrested (State v. Kaluna, [1974]).

Also note that in 1977 the Supreme Court severely limited the searching of luggage, briefcases, or other personal property seized during an arrest. In *United States v. Chadwick* (1977) the Court said:

> Warrantless searches of luggage or other property seized at the time of an arrest cannot be justified as incident to that arrest either if the search is remote in time or place from the arrest or no exigency exists. Once law enforcement officers have reduced luggage or other personal property not immediately associated with the person of the arrestee to their exclusive control, and there is no longer any danger that the arrestee might gain access to the property to seize a weapon or destroy evidence, a search of that property is no longer an incident of the arrest.

Use of Force in Searching an Arrested Person

Ferdico (1985, p. 186) notes that

> When making a search of a person incident to arrest, law enforcement officers may use the degree of force reasonably necessary to protect themselves, prevent escape, and prevent the destruction or concealment of evidence.
>
> Courts have upheld seizures of drugs when the arrested person attempted to swallow them and an officer put a "choke hold" on the defendant, forcing him to spit out the drugs. (Salas v. State, 1971). A search incident to arrest to prevent the concealment of evidence may even extend to pumping the stomach or probing body cavities. How-

ever, the following conditions should be met before such a search is conducted: (1) There must be good reason to believe that the person's body contains evidence that should be removed. . . . (2) The search must be made by a doctor working under sanitary conditions and in a medically approved way. (3) Force may be used only to the extent necessary to make the person submit to the examination.

Searching People Other than the Arrested Person

The courts have ruled that if the person who is arrested is with other people, it is reasonable for the officers to search them for weapons. In *United States v. Vigo,* (1973) for example, officers arrested a man in the company of a woman. The officers searched the woman's purse. The court said the search was reasonable because a purse is a likely place to hide a weapon. It would not be reasonable, however, to search anyone not named in a search warrant if no one was actually arrested. To do so would require that they be named in the search warrant.

Searching the Vehicle of an Arrested Person

The landmark case for the warrantless search of a vehicle incident to an arrest is *New York v. Belton* (1981). In this case the United States Supreme Court said:

When a policeman has made a lawful custodial arrest of the occupant of an automobile, he may, as a contemporaneous incident of that arrest, search the passenger compartment of that automobile.

It follows from this conclusion that the police may also examine the contents of any containers found within the passenger compartment, for if the passenger compartment is within reach of the arrestee, so also will containers in it be within his reach.

SEARCH WITH CONSENT

Officers may conduct a search if they are given permission by someone who has the authority to do so. Ted Chimel could have given the officers permission to search his home, but he did not. Ferdico (1985, p. 210–11) cautions that

In general, the only person who is able to give a valid consent to search is the person whose constitutional protection against unreasonable searches and seizures would be invaded by the search if it were conducted without consent. This means, for example, that when the search of an individual's body or clothing is contemplated, the only person who can consent to such a search is the individual involved. The same rule applies to searches of premises except that when several people have varying degrees of interest in the same premises, more than one person may be qualified to give consent to search. . . . It is well settled that when two or more persons have substantially equal rights of ownership, occupancy, or other possessory interest in premises to be searched and property to be seized, any one of the persons may legally authorize a search and seizure, and thereby bind the others and waive their right to object.

Thus, if two people share an apartment, all that is required is the consent from one of them. In *Wright v. United States* (1968) the Court held:

This court and other courts have held that where there are multiple lawful residents of a premises, any one of such persons may give permission to enter and that if incriminating evidence is found, it may be used against all.

According to Ferdico, other individuals who may give consent include the following:

Host—Guest—The host or primary occupant of the premises may give a valid consent to a search of the premises and any evidence found would be admissible against the guest.

Employer—Employee—In general, an employer may consent to a search of any part of the employer's premises that is used by an employee [e.g., employees' lockers can be searched with the employer's consent].

School Official—Student—Courts have held that the search of a high school student's locker, when authorized by a school official, is valid because of the relationship between the school authorities and the students. [This does not apply to students' dormatory rooms, however.] This law is the subject of current litigation.

Parent—Child—A parent's consent to search premises owned by the parent will usually be effective against a child who lives on those premises. A parent may not consent to a search of an area of the parent's home occupied by the child, however, if the child uses the room exclusively, has sectioned it off, has furnished it with his own furniture, pays rent, or otherwise establishes an expectation of privacy.

Ferdico cites several instances of when individuals can *not* give consent:

Landlord—Tenant—A landlord has no implied authority to consent to a search of a tenant's premises or a seizure of the tenant's property during the period of the tenancy.

Hotel Employee—Hotel Guest—The U.S. Supreme Court held that the principles governing a landlord's consent to a search of tenant's premises apply with equal force to consent searches of hotel (and motel) rooms allowed by hotel employees. [Only the hotel guest can give consent.]

The consent must be *free and voluntary.* The Maine Supreme Court ruling in *State v. Barlow, Jr.* (1974) stated: "It is a well established rule in the federal courts that a consent search is unreasonable under the Fourth Amendment if the consent was induced by deceit, trickery or misrepresentation of the officials making the search."

CONSENT TO SEARCH

Before we search your premises _____
_____, it is my duty to advise you of your rights under the fourth amendment to the constitution. You have the right to refuse to permit us to search your property. If you voluntarily permit us to enter and search your premises as described above, any incriminating evidence that we find may be used against you in court or other proceedings. Prior to permitting us to search, you have the right to require us to secure a search warrant.

I understand my rights and voluntarily waive my rights to a search warrant and consent to a search of _____.

Date _____ Time _____ _____
                                                    Requested from

Witness _____ Date _____

Witness _____ Date _____

Figure 7–2   Sample Consent to Search Form

The request for permission to search must not be stated in a threatening way. It must not imply that anyone who doesn't give consent will be considered as having something to hide. No display of weapons or force should accompany a request to search. In *Weed* v. *United States* (1965), police confronted the defendant with drawn guns and a riot pistol and said they would get a warrant if they needed to. The court said consent given under these conditions was *not* free and voluntary. Likewise, in *People* v. *Loria* (1961), the police threatened to kick down the door of the defendant's apartment if he did not let them in. The court said consent was *not* free and voluntary.

Usually, officers should not request to search at night. In *Monroe v. Pape* (1961) Justice Frankfurter stated: "Modern totalitarianisms have been a stark reminder, but did not newly teach, that the kicked-in door is the symbol of a rule of fear and violence fatal to institutions founded on respect for the integrity of man. . . . Searches of the dwelling house were the special object of this universal condemnation of official intrusion. Nighttime search was the evil in its most obnoxious form." Again, unusual circumstances may require such a search.

If the request to search is granted, it must be limited to the area specified by the person granting the permission. The consent may be limited or withdrawn at any time. Herein lies a primary reason that a search with a warrant is much better for the officer than merely relying on consent.

Consent to search must be voluntary. The search must be limited to the area specified by the person granting the permission. The person may revoke the consent at any time.

THE PLAIN-VIEW DOCTRINE

The court recognizes that it would be ridiculously unreasonable to expect police officers to either ignore or to delay acting on something illegal that they see. Similar to not requiring an arrest warrant to allow officers to arrest someone they actually see committing a crime, a search warrant is not required for officers to seize contraband or other evidence that is in plain sight.

Plain-view evidence, unconcealed evidence that officers accidentally see while engaged in a lawful activity, is admissible in court.

Evidence qualifies as plain-view evidence if the officers are engaged in a lawful activity when they find the evidence; if the evidence is not hidden; and if the discovery of the evidence is accidental.

For instance, if an officer is invited into a person's home and the officer sees illegal drugs on the table, the drugs can be seized. Likewise, an officer carrying out a legal act such as executing a traffic stop or search warrant may seize any contraband discovered. Similarly, contraband such as marijuana fields can be legally observed from an airplane over private property without a search warrant.

A frisk is less intrusive than a full search; however properly obtained evidence will be admitted into court, while illegally obtained evidence will be excluded.

STOP AND FRISK

The elements of stop-and-frisk law have been discussed but are important to include here as a critical exception to the warrant requirement for a legal search. Recall that if officers have an articulable, reasonable suspicion that an individual is involved in criminal activity, the officers may make a brief investigatory stop. If the officers reasonably suspect that the person is presently armed and dangerous, a frisk may be conducted without a warrant (*Terry v. Ohio*, [1964]).

If a frisk is authorized by the circumstances of an investigative stop, only a limited pat-down of the detainee's outer clothing for the safety of the officer is authorized.

Anything that reasonably feels like a weapon may then be removed and used as evidence against the person if it is contraband or other evidence. If an officer has specific information about where a weapon is on a person, the officer may reach directly for it. (Adams v. Williams [1972]).

Similarly, the passenger compartment of a car can be searched if that vehicle is stopped and the person(s) are detained but not arrested. Such a search would have to remain limited to the area where a weapon could be, and it would have to be done with the belief that, as in a frisk situation, the person is presently armed and dangerous.

THE AUTOMOBILE EXCEPTION

Because of their mobility, automobiles and other similar conveyances may need to be searched without a warrant. The precedent for a warrantless search of automobiles came from *Carroll v. United States* (1925). *The incidents involved in this case were described by Wrobleski and Hess (1986, pp. 285–386) like this:*

> During Prohibition in the 1920s, some 1,500 agents pursued bootleggers, many of whom brought liquor down from Canada. In addition to the imports, there was so much local production that the 9,500 stills raided in the first six months of prohibition were known to be only a small fraction of the total.
>
> Visualize a scene in a Michigan "honky-tonk" during the 1920s. Four men were sitting at a table holding a meeting; two were supposed buyers, and two were bootleggers. The "buyers" were actually federal prohibition agents. Although the meeting seemed to go well, the two bootleggers, George Carroll and John Kiro, were somewhat suspicious. They indicated that the liquor had to come from the east end of Grand Rapids, Michigan. They would get it and return in about an hour. Later that day, Carroll called and said delivery could not be made until the next day. But the two did not return the next day.
>
> The agents returned to their normal duty of watching a section of road between Grand Rapids and Detroit known to be used by bootleggers. Within a week after their unsuccessful attempt to make the "buy," the agents recognized Carroll and Kiro driving by. They gave chase but lost the car near East Lansing.
>
> Two months later they again recognized Carroll's car coming from the direction of Detroit. They pursued the car and this time were successful in overtaking it. The agents were familiar with Carroll's car, they recognized Carroll and Kiro in the automobile, and they had reason to believe the automobile would contain bootleg liquor. A search of the car revealed sixty-eight bottles of whiskey and gin, most of it behind the upholstery of the seats where the padding had been removed. The contraband was seized, and the two men were arrested.
>
> George Carroll and John Kiro were charged with transporting intoxicating liquor and were convicted in federal court. Carroll's appeal, taken to the United States Supreme Court, resulted in a landmark decision defining the rights and limitations for warrantless searches of vehicles

---

Carroll v. United States *establishes that automobiles can be searched without a warrant provided (1) there is probable cause to believe the contents of the vehicle violate the law, and (2) the vehicle would be gone before a search warrant could be obtained.*

Justifications for acting without a warrant were further specified in *Robbins v. California* (1981):

- The mobility of motor vehicles often produces exigent circumstances.
- A diminished expectation of privacy surrounds the automobile.
- A car is used for transportation and not as a residence or repository of personal belongings.
- The car's occupants and contents are in plain view.
- Automobiles are necessarily highly regulated by the government.

According to del Carmen (1987, p. 171): "The general rule is that a *seizure occurs every time a motor vehicle is stopped;* the provisions of the Fourth Amendment against unreasonable searches and seizures therefore apply. . . . There must be at least a reasonable suspicion to justify an investigatory stop of a motor vehicle. The leading case on this issue is *United States v. Cortez (1981)* in which the Court said:

> Based upon that whole picture, the detaining officers must have a particularized and objective basis for suspecting the particular person stopped of criminal activity.

If police have legally stopped a vehicle and have probable cause to believe the vehicle contains contraband, they can conduct a thorough search of the vehicle, including the trunk and any closed packages or containers found in the car or the trunk. The Court said in *United States v. Ross* (1982): "If probable cause justifies the search of a lawfully stopped vehicle, it justifies the search of every part of the vehicle and its contents that may conceal the object of the search."

Limitations on warrantless searches of automobiles were set in *United States v. Henry* (1958), with the Court stating: "Once these items [for which a search warrant would be sought] are located, the search must terminate. If, however, while legitimately looking for such articles, the officer unexpectedly discovers evidence of another crime, he can seize that evidence as well." This is where the *plain-view doctrine* would come into play.

Inventory Searches of Impounded Vehicles

Police officers can legally tow and impound vehicles for many reasons, including vehicles parked in tow-away zones or abandoned on a highway. When police impound a vehicle, they may legally conduct an inventory search. This search protects both them and the owner of the vehicle.

According to del Carmen (1987, p. 182):

> The leading case on inventory search is South Dakota v. Opperman (1976). In that case, the defendant's illegally parked car was taken to the city impound lot, where an officer, observing articles of personal property in the car, proceeded to inventory it.

Because of their mobility, automobiles present an exception to the general requirements for searches. Here police conduct a warrantless search of a vehicle, including its trunk.

In the process, he found a bag of marijuana in the unlocked glove compartment. The Court concluded that in following standard police procedures prevailing throughout the country and approved by the overwhelming majority of courts, the conduct of the police was not "unreasonable" under the Fourth Amendment. It is generally accepted that such an inventory search must be a standard procedure of the particular department. An officer from a department that usually does not conduct inventory searches cannot decide to do it on one particular vehicle.

EXIGENT CIRCUMSTANCES

The sixth circumstance in which lawful warrantless searches can be made is if an exigent (emergency) situation exists. The courts have recognized that sometimes situations will arise that reasonably require immediate action or evidence may be destroyed. Police officers who have established probable cause that evidence is likely to be at a certain place and who do not have time to get a search warrant, may conduct a warrantless search. But there MUST be *extenuating circumstances* (exigent circumstances).

Warrantless searches are almost always challenged by defense attorneys—and they frequently are successful in their challenges. The two most common challenges are obvious: (1) the police officers did not establish probable cause, and (2) they had sufficient time to obtain a search warrant.

del Carmen (1987, pp. 150–52) describes four commonly encountered "exigent circumstances":

1. Danger of physical harm to the officer or destruction of evidence.
   *The court has implied that a warrantless search may be justified if
   there is reasonable ground to believe that delaying the search until
   the warrant is obtained would endanger the physical safety of the
   officer or would allow the destruction or removal of the evidence
   (Vale v. Louisiana, 1970).*

2. Danger to a third person. *An officer may enter a dwelling without a
   warrant in response to screams for help. In one case the Court said:
   "The Fourth Amendment does not require police officers to delay in
   the course of an investigation if to do so would gravely endanger
   their lives or the lives of others"* (Warden v. Hayden, 1967).

3. Driving while intoxicated (DWI). *The police may, without a search
   warrant and by force if necessary, take a blood sample from a person arrested for drunk driving, as long as the setting and procedures are reasonable (as when the blood is drawn by a medical doctor in a hospital) (Schmerber v. California, 1966) and other legal
   requirements exist (often serious injury or death, etc.).*

4. Searches in "hot pursuit" (or "fresh pursuit") of dangerous suspects. *The police may enter a house without warrant to search for a
   dangerous suspect who is being pursued and who they have reason
   to believe is within the premises if they are in immediate pursuit of
   the individual.*

---

*Emergency situations include danger of physical harm to the officer,
danger of destruction of evidence, danger to a third person, driving
while intoxicated, hot-pursuit situations, and individuals requiring
"rescuing," for example, unconscious individuals.*

Sauls (1988, p. 24) suggests that "Courts commonly recognize
three threats as providing justification for emergency warrantless
action—danger to life, danger of escape, and danger of destruction or
removal of evidence. . . . an awareness of the threat present in a
particular situation is the key to correct on-the-spot decisions that
avoid violations of citizens' fourth amendment rights."

Included in the "danger to life" category are persons suspected of
being armed and dangerous (discussed in the last chapter) and people
who are unconscious. If police officers come across an unconscious
person, they have an obligation to search the person's pockets or purse
for identification and for any possible medical information. If they
discover evidence of criminal activity or contraband during this search,
they may seize it. For example, in *Vause v. United States* (1966) two
police came upon an unconscious man on a public street. They were

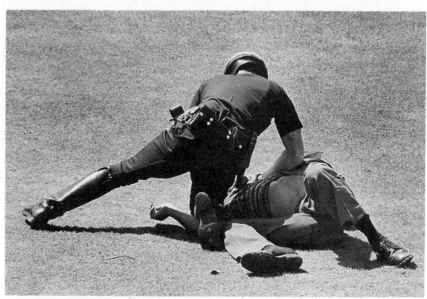

Officers who reasonably suspect that a person is armed and dangerous and who might pose a threat to self, the officer, or others, can take immediate steps to subdue that individual and conduct a search for weapons.

unable to rouse him, so they called for an ambulance and then searched his pockets for identification. During this search they found fifteen cellophane packets containing narcotics. The Court affirmed the reasonableness of the search: " . . . the search of one found in an unconscious condition is both legally permissible and highly necessary."

OPEN FIELDS AND ABANDONED PROPERTY

This is an area of search and seizure that does not neatly fit in any of the six exceptions to needing a search warrant. It might be considered a natural extension of the plain-view doctrine. In effect, however, the courts have dealt with this area by extending the doctrine that anything held out to the public is not protected by the Fourth Amendment because there is no reasonable expectation of privacy.

If there is no expectation of privacy, the protection of the Fourth Amendment does not apply.

The case establishing the principles of search and seizure of abandoned property and open fields was *Hester v. U.S. (1924)*. In this case the police were investigating bootlegging operations and went to the home of Hester's father. As they came up to the house, they saw a man identified as Henderson drive up to the house. The police officers hid and saw Hester come out and give Henderson a bottle. The police sounded an alarm, and Hester ran to a car parked nearby, removed a gallon jug, and he and Henderson ran across an open field.

One officer chased them. Hester dropped his jug, breaking it, but retaining about half its contents. Henderson threw his bottle away. Officers found another broken jar still containing some liquid outside the house. The officers determined the jars contained illegal whiskey. They seized the evidence even though they had no search or arrest warrants. Hester was convicted of concealing "distilled spirits," but on appeal said the officers conducted an illegal search and seizure. The Court disagreed, stating:

> It is obvious that even if there had been a trespass, the above testimony was not obtained by an illegal search or seizure. The defendant's own acts, and those of his associates, disclosed the jug, the jar and the bottle—and there was no seizure in the sense of the law when the officers examined the contents of each after it had been abandoned.

The Court went on to clearly state: "The special protection accorded by the Fourth Amendment to the people in their 'persons, houses, papers, and effects,' is not extended to the open fields." This includes property disposed of in such a manner as to relinquish ordinary property rights.

The "open-fields" doctrine holds that land beyond that normally associated with use of that land, that is, undeveloped land, can be searched without a warrant.

"Curtilege" is the term used to describe that portion of property generally associated with the common use of land, e.g., buildings, sheds, fenced-in areas, and the like. Inside such areas the "open-fields" doctrine does not apply. A warrant would be needed to search within the curtilege.

Similarly, once a person has discarded or abandoned property, he or she maintains no reasonable expectation of privacy. Thus, something thrown from a car, discarded during a chase, or even garbage that is disposed of (once off the curtilege) becomes abandoned property that police may inspect without a warrant.

BORDER SEARCHES AND SEIZURES

According to Meshbesher, at our international borders (1986, p. 23): "Generally all routine searches of persons, belongings, effects, and vehicles are presumptively reasonable under the Fourth Amendment. The Constitution does not require even a suspicion of criminal activity" (*United States v. Ramsey* [1977]; *Carroll v. United States* [1925]; *Boyd v. United States* [1886]). Meshbesher (p. 34) also states

The importance of security at our borders makes warrantless searches "reasonable," thus complying with the Fourth Amendment requirements.

that "the Supreme Court has recognized that routine border searches may be carried out not only at the border itself but at its 'functional equivalents,' as well," including airports receiving nonstop flights from foreign countries.

Routine border searches and searches at international airports are legal.

He further notes (p. 41) that increasingly people at airports are being "subject to investigative detention" because they fit a drug courier profile. This profile, developed by Drug Enforcement Agency Agent Markonnis, includes the following characteristics: (1) arrival from a source city; (2) little or no luggage or large quantity of empty suitcases; (3) rapid turnaround on airplane trip; (4) use of assumed name; (5) possession of large amount of cash; (6) cash purchase of ticket; (7) nervous appearance.

The policy for such broad powers to search is clearly international security. With increasing incidents of international terrorism and drug trafficking, the Court will probably continue to find such sweeping searches at our international borders sufficiently reasonable.

The farther a person gets from the border, however, the more traditional search-and-seizure requirements come back into play. Roving border patrol agents may stop individuals or cars away from the actual border only if they have the traditional "reasonable suspicion." Similar to the authorized use of roadblocks elsewhere, border agents can establish roadblocks that stop cars in a certain pattern (every car, every other car, every fifth car, etc.). But searches may only be conducted following the traditional rules applying to motor vehicles, such as probable cause to believe contraband exists and the like.

SCOPE OF SEARCHES

No matter under what authority a search is conducted, one general principle is critical. The search must be limited in scope. Anything beyond is unreasonable and, thus, unconstitutional as regulated by the Fourth Amendment.

All searches must be limited. General searches are unconstitutional. They are never legal.

The legal maxim at the beginning of this chapter refers to narrowing the scope of a search. Looking for "an elephant in a matchbox" suggests that it would be unreasonable to look for a stolen twenty-four-inch television set in a dresser drawer.

RESULTS OF ILLEGAL SEARCH AND SEIZURE

It is important to remember, as stressed by Ferdico (1985, p. 138):

The most important effect of an illegal search or seizure is the exclusion of the evidence obtained from being used in court against the person whose rights were violated by the search. . . . application of the exclusionary rule in a particular case will usually result in a lost case for the prosecution and the release of the person charged with the crime. From the law enforcement officer's standpoint, the suppression of crucial evidence may represent a total waste of weeks or months of investigation, evidence-gathering and case evaluation. It should be clear, then, that strict compliance with all statutes, court rules, and court decisions dealing with search and seizure procedures is of the utmost importance from the first report of a possible crime through the ultimate disposition of the case.

Any evidence obtained by an illegal search will be inadmissible in court under the exclusionary rule.

Legal search must conform to the Fourth Amendment
(made applicable to the states by the Fourteenth Amendment).

For a search to be "reasonable", it must fit within one of the following:

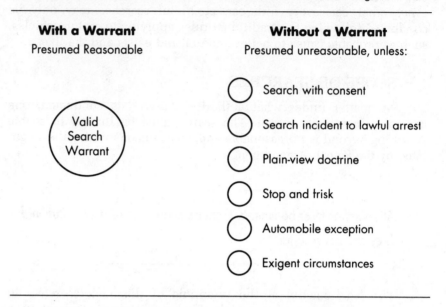

Figure 7–3   **Constitutional Analysis of Search and Seizure**

It is critical to understand that while the Fourth Amendment generally does not restrict the actions of private citizens, it *does* apply to *all* government workers. This includes federal, state, county, and local governmental bodies. Just as the FBI, state police, county sheriff, and local police are bound by the Fourth Amendment, so are the IRS, the postal service, fire inspectors, local building officials, and code enforcement officials.

SUMMARY

The Fourth Amendment requires that, to be reasonable, all searches conducted with a warrant be based on probable cause. Probable cause to search means it is more likely than not that the items sought are where the officers believe them to be. Special provisions of search warrants, including making an unannounced entrance and carrying out the search at night, must be approved by a magistrate as part of the search warrant. Searches conducted with a search warrant must be limited to the specific area and specific items described in the warrant.

Six exceptions to the search warrant requirement have been established by case law:

- Search incident to a lawful arrest
- Consent search

- Plain-view doctrine
- Stop and frisk
- Automobile exceptions
- Exigent circumstances

Searches incidental to a lawful arrest must be immediate and must be limited to the area within the person's reach (*Chimel*).

In searches with consent, the consent must be voluntary. The search must be limited to the area specified by the person granting the permission, and the person may revoke the consent at any time.

The plain-view doctrine establishes that unconcealed evidence that officers accidentally see while engaged in lawful activity is admissible in court.

In a stop-and-frisk situation, the frisk must be limited to a pat-down of the outer clothing for the safety of the officer.

Carroll v. *United States* established that automobiles can be searched without a warrant provided (1) there is probable cause to believe the contents of the vehicle violate the law, and (2) the vehicle would be gone before a search warrant could be obtained.

Searches also may be conducted without a warrant in exigent (emergency) situations such as danger of physical harm to the officer, danger of destruction of evidence, danger to a third person, encountering a person who is driving while intoxicated and serious injury results, following "hot pursuit," or dealing with an unconscious person.

The Court has said that if there is no reasonable expectation of privacy, no warrant is required to search. In addition, our national security dictates that routine border searches and searches at international airports are reasonable and thus legal.

All searches, with or without a warrant, must be limited. General searches are unconstitutional and never legal. Any illegally obtained evidence is inadmissible in court under the exclusionary rule, with two important exceptions to be discussed in chapter 10.

Discussion Questions

1. What are the advantages and disadvantages of a consent search?
2. How does a search incident to a lawful arrest differ from a frisk?
3. What is the importance of the Fourth Amendment as it relates to searches?
4. What determines an "unreasonable" search?
5. Can you think of other emergency situations when it might not be possible to obtain a search warrant?
6. Why are automobile searches different from searches of homes?
7. Even if a search seems to be authorized by law, might it turn "unreasonable"?
8. What are the most common reasons for warrantless searches of people?

References

Bennett, Wayne W., and Hess, Kären M. *Criminal Investigation.* 2d ed. St. Paul, Minn.: West Publishing Company, 1987.

Creamer, J. S. *The Law of Arrest, Search, and Seizure,* 3d ed. New York: Holt, Rinehart, and Winston, 1980.

del Carmen, Rolando V. *Criminal Procedure for Law Enforcement Personnel.* Monterey, Calif.: Brooks/Cole Publishing Company, 1987.

Ferdico, John N. *Criminal Procedure for the Criminal Justice Professional.* 3d ed. St. Paul, Minn.: West Publishing Company, 1985.

Meshbesher, Ronald I. *Minnesota Search & Seizure: What's Left of the Right to Privacy?* Eau Claire, Wisc.: Professional Education Systems, Inc., 1986.

Oran, Daniel. *Law Dictionary for Nonlawyers.* 2d ed. St. Paul, Minn.: West Publishing Company, 1985.

Sauls, John Gales "Emergency Searches of Persons" *FBI Law Enforcement Bulletin* 57, no. 1, (January 1988): 24–30.

Wrobleski, Henry M., and Hess, Kären M. *Introduction to Law Enforcement and Criminal Justice* 2d ed. St. Paul, Minn.: West Publishing Company, 1986.

BASIC ISSUE

IS THE SEARCH LEGAL?

You know the importance of conducting legal searches. Unless the search is legal, the evidence is inadmissible in court. The following cases all involve some sort of search. Decide if each search is legal.

Three on-the-Street Encounters

Shortly after an armed bank robbery, a police officer approaches a man who matches a description of the robber. He orders the man, at gunpoint, against a wall and pats down his clothing, discovering a handgun. Another officer encounters a well-dressed businessman collapsed on a downtown street. Searching the man's pockets, he locates cocaine. A third officer interviewing a juvenile suspect in the investigation of a recent homicide spots what appears to be blood on the shoes of the youth. Without arresting the youth, he seizes the shoes. [Which of these searches is legal?]

From John Gales Sauls, "Emergency Searches of Persons," *FBI Law Enforcement Bulletin*, January, 1988.

A Narcotics Possession Charge

Colton, California, narcotics detectives, in December of 1970, arrested a man and a woman for possession of narcotics. The suspects had a nine-month-old baby girl with them and the detectives found contraband, heroin, in the infant's diapers. [Was the search legal?]

People v. Padilla & Corona, Cal. Municipal Ct., Dec. 29, 1970.

A Murderer

On January 13, 1964, Pamela Mason, a fourteen-year-old school girl, left her house on a babysitting assignment. Eight days later her frozen body was discovered in a snowdrift just a few miles from her home. Her throat had been slashed, and she had been shot in the head.

The defendant's car matched the description of a car that had been seen on the night Pamela disappeared and at the spot where her body had been found. The defendant, by his own admission, frequently visited a launderette where she posted her babysitting notice, and a knife belonging to the defendant was found there. The defendant's wife voluntarily produced two shotguns and two rifles that belonged to the defendant and offered them to the police. A subsequent examination of the guns revealed that one of the rifles had fired the bullet that was found in the murdered girl's brain.

Upon the basis of this evidence, the state attorney general, who was authorized under New Hampshire law to issue warrants, used an arrest warrant for the defendant and a search warrant for his automobile. Sweepings of dirt and other fine particles taken from the car matched like particles taken from the clothes of the murdered girl. [Was the search of the car legal?]

Coolidge v. New Hampshire, 403 U.S. 443 (1971).

The preceding two cases are extracted from Frank Carrington, *Neither Cruel Nor Unusual*, New York: Crown Publishers, 1978. Reprinted by permission.

A Body Search

In *United States* v. *Cameron*, agents had sufficient articulable facts justifying further inquiry and ultimately a search of a person crossing a border. Without a warrant, the agents took the suspect to a doctor who performed two digital examinations of his rectum while agents held his legs up against his chest. Then, the suspect was to undergo two enemas that did not produce any contraband. Next, the suspect was forced to drink a laxative after several agents held him down and pried his mouth open. [Was this search legal?]

United States v. *Hernandez* 473 U.S. (1985) is the leading Supreme Court case on seizures of persons at the border on reasonable suspicion. Montoya Hernandez arrived in the Los Angeles Airport on a ten-hour direct flight from Bogota, Colombia. A customs inspector noted that her passport showed she had traveled eight times to either Miami or Los Angeles. Questioning revealed that she did not speak English and did not know anyone in the United States.

Further, she had $5,000 in cash, which she told customs inspectors she was going to spend at K-Mart and J. C. Penney's to buy goods for her husband's store. Finally, she had no hotel reservations and only light luggage.

Based on these facts, the customs agents suspected that she was a "balloon swallower," so the customs agents strip-searched her. No contraband was found, but the strip search revealed she was wearing two pairs of plastic underpants with a paper towel lining in the crotch.

Based on these facts, the customs agents detained Ms. Hernandez until she would submit to an X ray or produce a monitored bowel movement. She was not permitted to call her husband or a lawyer. About twenty-four hours after her initial detention, the customs agents made a telephone application for a warrant to conduct an X ray and rectal examination and the magistrate issued the warrant. The rectal exam revealed a balloon containing cocaine. Eventually, eighty-eight balloons containing 528 grams of cocaine were recovered. [Was the search legal?]

Extracted from Ronald I. Meshbeshter, *Minnesota Search & Seizure: What's Left of the Right to Privacy?* Reprinted by permission.

Danger of Destruction of Evidence Emergency

The U.S. Supreme Court was presented with a warrantless search of a person in response to a perceived danger of destruction of evidence in *Cupp* v. *Murphy*. Police officers took fingernail scrapings from Murphy after he voluntarily came to the police station after having been told of the death of his wife. The body of Mrs. Murphy, who had been strangled and whose neck bore bruises and lacerations, had been discovered in her house about twelve hours earlier. . . . In *Murphy*, the police officers possessed facts amounting to probable cause that Murphy had evidence of the homicide on his hands. His wife's residence had shown no signs of forced entry or theft when her body was discovered, suggesting that her assailant was someone she knew. She and her husband had experienced a stormy marriage and fought often. Mr. Murphy had volunteered his whereabouts on the evening of the killing without being asked and had expressed no concern or curiosity about his wife's fate. Murphy had a dark spot on a finger that appeared to be dried blood and rubbed his hands behind his back and in his pockets after being asked to submit to fingernail scraping. The fact that his wife's neck bore lacerations and the fact of her strangulation made it probable that trace evidence existed on the hands of the killer. The recent occurrence of the crime, coupled with the spot on Murphy's finger and the facts pointing to him as the killer, made it probable that evidence of the crime was presently on his hands. [Were the scrapings legal?]

Extracted from John Gales Sauls, "Emergency Searches of Persons," *FBI Bulletin.*

Answers for Basic Issue Seven Section

Three on-the-Street Encounters—All are legal.

A Narcotics Possession Charge—At a preliminary hearing the judge threw out the evidence on the grounds that "A baby has the rights of a person, and therefore must be afforded the protections of the Constitution." Since the nine-month-old was too young to consent to the search, the evidence must be suppressed, the judge said, as he dismissed the case.

A Murderer—After studying the case for more than five months, the Supreme Court held (5-4) that the search of the automobile was unreasonable. Although five justices in the majority could not agree on why the search was illegal, they did find that the search warrant was invalid on the basis that the attorney general was not a neutral and detached magistrate. Conviction reversed.

A Body Search—In *United States* v. *Cameron*, the Ninth Circuit, after weighing various factors including the lack of a warrant, the intrusiveness of the procedure, and the availability of less intrusive alternatives held the search and seizure to be unreasonable. *United States* v. *Hernandez* search was legal.

Danger of Destruction of Evidence Emergency—Search was legal.

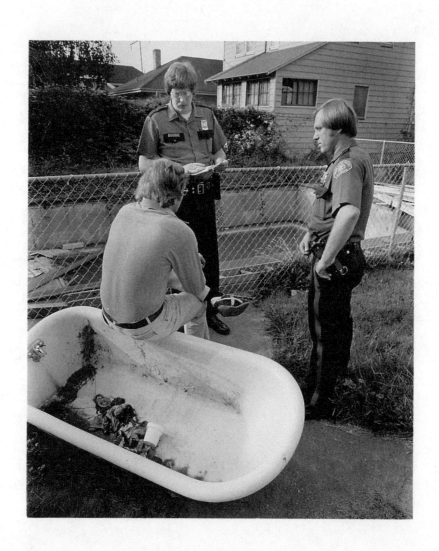

CHAPTER 8

The Law of Confessions

You have the right to remain silent. Anything you say can and will be used against you in a court of law—*Miranda* decision

DO YOU KNOW

What is protected by the Fifth Amendment? How this relates to the Fourteenth Amendment?

How the voluntariness of a confession is determined?

What the "totality of circumstances" includes?

What was established by the Escobedo decision?

What the primary case used for analyzing confessions is?

What was established by Miranda?

When the Miranda warning must be given? When it should be given?

What the public safety exception is?

How the Fourth Amendment affects admissibility of confessions?

If silence constitutes a waiver of the Miranda?

How to assure that a waiver of the Miranda is valid?

Introduction

Chapter 8

The vast majority of police work involves talking to people. From the moment police dispatch receives a call through the final disposition of the case, law enforcement relies on conversations to deal with every matter that comes its way.

Communicating, in and of itself, is an important skill developed throughout a career. The abilities to listen, to talk, and to communicate both verbally and nonverbally are abilities that help every officer far more than guns ever do. These abilities help calm the injured, assist the victimized, and control the frightened. They also help solve crimes.

The law enforcement officer, however, has much more to be concerned with than just *how* to communicate effectively. An important, complex body of law has developed concerning what information obtained by an officer through conversation, by whatever name, can be used in court.

Yeschke (1987, p. 25) notes: "While the roles of interviewer and interrogator are currently looked upon as synonymous, they are distinctly different in many ways. Through both, truthful information is sought; however, the motive, unique directives used, and the potential use of the final results of each are major differences."

This chapter introduces you to the different forms of communication that can occur between officers and others, as well as the laws that apply to such interactions. This area of law is not to be taken lightly. Because a confession by the accused provides the prosecution with powerful evidence, it can be devastating when such an admission is rejected by the court for failing to meet the necessary legal requirements. While this area of law is admittedly complex, the basic guidelines must be mastered.

THE FIFTH AMENDMENT AND DUE PROCESS OF LAW

The Fifth Amendment to the United States Constitution states that "No person shall . . . be compelled in any criminal case to be a witness against himself, nor be deprived of life, liberty, or property, without due process of law." Even the lay person usually knows what a person on the witness stand means when he "takes the fifth." This translates into "I refuse to answer on the grounds that it may incriminate me." The guarantees in the Fifth Amendment were incorporated under the Fourteenth Amendment and held applicable to the states in *Malloy* v. *Hogan* (1964) because it is, indeed, one of those amendments determined to be fundamental to our concept of ordered liberty.

The Fifth Amendment provides for protection against self-incrimination and guarantees citizens "due process of law." The Fourteenth Amendment made this applicable to the states.

Perhaps no other area of criminal procedure has produced more controversy. While the U.S. Supreme Court has taken several paths to reach an answer over the years, questions remain. The primary question that concerns police officers, however, is when will confessions be admissible as evidence in court? Justice Frankfurter, in *Culombe v. Connecticut* (1961), stated:

Despite modern advances in the technology of crime detection, offenses frequently occur about which things cannot be made to speak. And where there cannot be found innocent human witnesses to such offenses, nothing remains—if police investigation is not to be balked before it has fairly begun—but to seek out possibly guilty witnesses and ask them questions, witnesses, that is, who are suspected of knowing something about the offense precisely because they are suspected of implication in it.

NEED FOR INTERROGATION

No one has ever seriously questioned the need for interrogation by the police. It is seen as a necessary aspect of solving crimes. Inbau (1961) sets forth the following three points:

1. *Many criminal cases, even when investigated by the best-qualified police departments, are capable of solution only by means of an admission or confession from the guilty individual or upon the basis of information obtained from the questioning of other criminal suspects.*
2. *Criminal offenders, except, of course, those caught in the commission of their crimes, ordinarily will not admit their guilt unless questioned under conditions of privacy, and for a period of perhaps several hours.*
3. *In dealing with criminal offenders, and consequently also with criminal suspects who may actually be innocent, the interrogator must, of necessity, employ less-refined methods than are considered appropriate for the transaction of ordinary, everyday affairs by and between law-abiding citizens.*

Early common law permitted confessions to be obtained by any manner, including force or the threat of force. For obvious reasons, the reliability of such admissions is to be questioned. Indeed, by the middle of the eighteenth century, English courts began to limit the admissibility of confessions. The courts increasingly questioned whether the confession was "voluntary" and not provided under improper pressure by the authorities.

And so, while the need for interrogations by law enforcement is acknowledged, not all confessions will be admissible in court. According to Whitebread and Slobogin (1986, p. 357): "The Supreme Court has excluded confessions which are considered the product of 'compulsion' by the state, in part because it may not be reliable as evidence, but primarily because society should not sanction coercive techniques, regardless of the importance of the information they may produce."

VOLUNTARINESS OF CONFESSIONS

The exclusionary rule prohibits using confessions obtained in violation of a person's constitutional rights.

The first confession case decided by the United States Supreme Court was *Brown* v. *Mississippi* (1936). Convictions against the black defendant in a murder case were based solely on confessions obtained by the police using such abhorrent methods as hanging, horrible whippings, and other brutal methods. The Court held the confessions inadmissible, finding the convictions void for violating the Fourteenth Amendment due process rights of the defendants.

In the case of *Fikes* v. *Alabama* (1957), the Supreme Court summarized the standard of that time as "Whether the totality of the circumstances that preceded the confessions deprived the defendant of his power of resistance." This has been termed the "Due Process Voluntariness Test." A coerced confession, obviously, has little credibility.

Whitebread and Slobogin (1986, p. 358) state that "Determining such a standard required a specific case-by-case analysis. But the factors that the courts have identified in assessing the voluntariness of a confession can be broken down into three broad categories."

Voluntariness of a confession is determined by (1) the police conduct involved, (2) the characteristics of the accused, and (3) the timing of the confession.

Police Conduct   Police conduct refers to specific behavior police use while trying to obtain a confession.

In the case of *Rogers* v. *Richmond* (1961), Justice Frankfurter stated that involuntary confessions are "excluded not because such confessions are unlikely to be true, but because the methods used to extract them offend an underlying principle in the enforcement of our criminal law; that ours is an accusatorial and not an inquisitorial system—a system in which the state must establish guilt by evidence independently and freely secured and may not by coercion prove its charge against an accused out of his own mouth."

Police conduct that has been found to extract confessions in ways that are inconsistent with due process include

- Physical force or the threat of force
- Falsely aroused sympathy from the defendant
- Promises of leniency
- Unfair and manipulative questioning by a state-employed psychiatrist
- Confinement in a small place

- Isolation from family, friends, or lawyer
- Deprivation of basic needs such as food, drink, and sleep
- Unreasonably long interrogations

Characteristics of the Accused   In this area the court needs to ask whether any special characteristics of the accused might cause the reliability of the information to be questioned. Factors considered here include

- Age of the accused
- Level of intelligence and education
- Mental illness or other emotional problems
- Physical condition
- Drug or alcohol influence

Each of the preceding must be considered when an admission or confession is obtained.

Timing of the Confession   This refers to the stage of the legal action at which the confession is obtained. If the accused has, in fact, already been indicted for a crime, criminal procedure dictates that at such a critical stage in the process the lawyer for the accused must be in attendance. This may prohibit certain attempts by law enforcement to obtain admissions unless this right is properly waived by the defendant.

TOTALITY OF CIRCUMSTANCES

The court considers all the preceding factors as part of the "totality of the circumstances" that determine if the confession was, in fact, voluntary.

The totality of circumstances includes police conduct, characteristics of the accused, and timing of the confession.

The difficulty with such an approach is that it requires case-by-case analysis.

THE SIXTH AMENDMENT RIGHT TO COUNSEL

The first step away from the case-by-case voluntariness analysis occurred in *Massiah v. United States* (1964). Here the Supreme Court emphasized the defendant's Sixth Amendment right to counsel. The Court held that incriminating statements obtained by the government from a radio transmitter voluntarily installed in a car belonging to a friend of the defendant's violated the defendant's Sixth Amendment rights. Government agents had deliberately elicited the statements after he had been indicted and in the absence of retained counsel.

The case of *Escobedo v. Illinois* (1964) was decided in the same year as *Massiah* and also dealt with the defendant's Sixth Amendment right to counsel. After being arrested, Escobedo was released on a writ of habeas corpus. He was re-arrested ten days later and questioned. His requests to see his lawyer were ignored. Eventually Escobedo provided a statement and was subsequently convicted of murder.

In holding the statement inadmissible, Justice Goldberg stated:

> We hold . . . that whereas here the investigation is no longer a general inquiry into an unsolved crime but has begun to focus on a particular suspect, the suspect has been taken into police custody, the police carry out a process of interrogations that leads itself to eliciting incriminating statements, the suspect has requested and been denied an opportunity to consult with his lawyer, and the police have not effectively warned him of his constitutional right to remain silent, the accused has been denied the assistance of counsel in violation of the Sixth Amendment . . . and that no statements elicited by the police during the interrogation may be used against him at a criminal trial.

Escobedo established the Sixth Amendment right of a defendant to have a lawyer present during interrogation.

Whitebread and Slobogin 86, (19 p. 365) expand on this case:

> Escobedo held that once an individual is the focus of investigation by the police, he may not be denied access to his attorney—if he has one and if he asks for him. But it still did not define precisely when a suspect becomes the accused. More importantly, the decision did not state what rights accrue to a person who does not have, and cannot afford, an attorney, or to a person who has an attorney and does not ask to see him. In Miranda, the Court took a significant step toward resolving those questions, effectively limiting the Escobedo holding to its facts.

MIRANDA

Two years after *Massiah* and *Escobedo*, the United States Supreme Court decided the case of *Miranda v. Arizona* (1966). The case is perhaps the best-known case to the public and has been said to be the most significant law enforcement case ever decided. *Miranda* served to extend the *Escobedo* decision and to shift the area of inquiry to the Fifth Amendment.

The Miranda case is the primary modern case used for analyzing confession cases.

The Case

Ernesto Miranda was a poor twenty-three-year-old with only a ninth-grade education. He was arrested at his home for rape and was then taken to the police station where he was identified by the complaining witness. Within two hours he signed a written confession. Miranda was never informed of his right to consult with an attorney, to have an attorney present during questioning, or of his right not to be compelled to incriminate himself.

The legal issue in the *Miranda* case was whether the police must inform a suspect who is the subject of custodial interrogation of his constitutional rights concerning self-incrimination and counsel before questioning.

The Court stated:

> We hold that when an individual is taken into custody or otherwise deprived of his freedom by the authorities and is subject to questioning, the privilege against self-incrimination is jeopardized. Procedural safeguards must be employed. . . . He must be warned prior to any questioning that he has a right to remain silent, that anything he says can be used against him in a court of law, that he has the right to the presence of an attorney, and that if he cannot afford an attorney one will be appointed for him prior to any questioning if he so desires.
>
> Opportunities to exercise those rights must be offered to him throughout the interrogation.

According to del Carmen (1987, pp. 256–57):

> Miranda v. Arizona has had the deepest impact on the day-to-day crime investigation phase of police work. Miranda is significant in that seldom does the Court tell police exactly what do do. The Court literally told the police what warnings ought to be given if the evidence attained from the interrogation will be admitted in court. Miranda also clarified some of the ambiguous terms used in Escobedo. ''By custodial interrogation,'' said the court, ''we mean questioning initiated by law enforcement officers after a person has been taken into custody or otherwise deprived of his freedom of action in any significant way.'' It added, ''This is what we meant in Escobedo when we spoke of an investigation which had focused on an accused.'' The Escobedo case brought the right to counsel to the police station prior to trial; the Miranda case went beyond the police station and brought the right to counsel out into the street if an interrogation is to take place.

Peace Officers
Constitutional Pre-Interrogation Requirements

The following warnings must be given prior to questioning a person who is in custody or is deprived of his freedom of action in any significant way:

THE CONSTITUTION REQUIRES I INFORM YOU THAT:
1) YOU HAVE THE RIGHT TO REMAIN SILENT.
2) ANYTHING YOU SAY CAN AND WILL BE USED AGAINST YOU IN COURT.
3) YOU HAVE THE RIGHT TO TALK TO A LAWYER NOW AND HAVE HIM PRESENT NOW OR AT ANY TIME DURING QUESTIONING.
4) IF YOU CANNOT AFFORD A LAWYER, ONE WILL BE APPOINTED FOR YOU WITHOUT COST.

Waiver of Rights
The suspect may waive his rights but the burden is on the officer to show the wavier is made voluntarily, knowingly, and intelligently.
He must affirmatively respond to the following questions:
1) DO YOU UNDERSTAND EACH OF THESE RIGHTS I HAVE EXPLAINED TO YOU?
2) DO YOU WISH TO TALK TO US AT THIS TIME?

Election of Rights
A subject can avail himself of his rights at any time and interrogation must then cease.
If a subject will not waive his rights, or during questioning elects to assert his rights, no testimony of that fact may ever be used against him at trial.

Figure 8–1   A *Miranda* Warning Card

LaFave and Israel (1985, pp. 284–85) stress that

Miranda thus represents a striking contrast to both Escobedo v. Illinois, decided two years earlier, and the Court's usual "totality of circumstances" approach to the due process voluntariness issue. While the holding in Escobedo had been cautiously limited to the facts of the particular case before the Court, the Miranda holding most certainly was not, for it contained a set of rules to be followed by police in all future custodial interrogations. And while "totality of circumstances" holdings were not easily applied to other cases with somewhat different pressures or defendants of somewhat different susceptibilities, the nature of the Miranda rules was such that this was not true of this landmark decision.

LaFave and Israel summarize the rules as follows:

1. These rules are required to safeguard the privilege against self-incrimination and thus must be followed in the absence of "other procedures which are at least as effective in appraising accused persons of the right of silence and in assuring a continuous opportunity to exercise it."

2. These rules apply "when the individual is first subjected to police interrogation while in custody at the station or otherwise deprived of his freedom of action in any significant way," and to "[g]eneral on-the-scene questioning as to facts surrounding a crime or other general questioning of citizens in

the fact-finding process" or to "[v]oluntary statements of any kind."

3. Without regard to his prior awareness of his rights, if a person in custody is to be subjected to questioning, "he must first be informed in clear and unequivocal terms that he has the right to remain silent," so that the ignorant may learn of his right and so that the pressures of the interrogation atmosphere will be overcome for those previously aware of the right.

4. The above warning "must be accompanied by the explanation that anything said can and will be used against the individual in court," so as to ensure that the suspect fully understands the consequences of foregoing the privilege.

5. Because this is indispensable to protection of the privilege, the individual also "must be clearly informed that he has the right to consult with a lawyer and to have the lawyer with him during interrogation," without regard to whether it appears that he is already aware of this right.

6. The individual must also be warned that "if he is indigent a lawyer will be appointed to represent him," for otherwise the above warning would be understood as meaning only that an individual may consult a lawyer if he has the funds to obtain one.

7. The individual is always free to exercise the privilege, and thus if he "indicates in any manner, at anytime prior to or during questioning, that he wishes to remain silent, the interrogation must cease"; and likewise, if he "states that he wants an attorney, the interrogation must cease until an attorney is present."

8. If a statement is obtained without the presence of an attorney, "a heavy burden rests on the Government to demonstrate that the defendant knowingly and intelligently waives his privilege against self-incrimination and his right to have retained or appointed counsel," and such waiver may not be presumed from the individual's silence after warnings or from the fact that a confession was eventually obtained.

9. Any statement obtained in violation of these rules may not be admitted into evidence, without regard to whether it is a confession or only an admission of part of an offense or whether it is inculpatory or allegedly exculpatory.

10. Likewise, exercise of the privilege may not be penalized, and thus the prosecution may not "use at trial the fact that [the defendant] stood mute or claimed his privilege in the face of accusation."

LaFave and Israel (p. 285) stress that

Although these rules sound inflexible and unbending, neither the Supreme Court nor the lower courts have generally taken a rigid approach in the application of Miranda. Indeed, the Supreme Court asserted in Michigan v. Tucker *(1974) that the Miranda decision "recognized that these procedural safeguards were not themselves rights protected by the Constitution but were instead measures to insure that the right against compulsory self-incrimination was protected. . . . The suggested safeguards were not intended to 'create a constitutional straitjacket,' . . . but rather to provide practical reinforcement for the right against compulsory self-incrimination."*

This is not, however, an area allowing great creativity by police officers. They should generally adhere to the developed rule.

WHEN THE *MIRANDA* WARNING MUST BE GIVEN

It is imperative for law enforcement officers to know when they must give the *Miranda* warning, when they probably should give it, and when they do not need to give it. As noted by Yeschke (1987, p. 32): "In 1976 the Supreme Court held that the focus of suspicion was not the test of when the Miranda warnings are to be given to a suspect. It held that the warnings were required only in police *custodial situations*. At that time the Supreme Court removed the misconception that the warnings are to be given to anyone upon whom suspicion is 'focused,' as held in *Beckwith v. United States* (1976). *Police custody* is the test, not focus."

The Miranda warning must be given to a suspect who is interrogated in the custody of the police, that is, when the suspect is not free to leave.

Circumstances surrounding an interrogation and whether the situation requires a *Miranda* warning were expanded on in *Oregon v. Mathiason* (1977) when the court said:

Any interview of one suspected of a crime by a police officer will have coercive aspects to it, simply by virtue of the fact that the police officer is part of a law enforcement system which may ultimately cause the suspect to be charged with a crime. But police officers are not required to administer Miranda warnings to everyone whom they question. Nor is the requirement of warnings to be imposed simply because the questioning takes place in the station house, or because the questioned person is one whom the police suspect. Miranda warnings are required only where there has been such a restriction on a person's freedom as to render him "in custody." It was that sort of coercive environment which Miranda by its terms was made applicable, and to which it is limited.

According to Ferdico (1985, p. 314): "Law enforcement officers often have difficulty determining when a person is in 'custody' or is 'deprived of his freedom of action in any significant way' so as to entitle the person to the *Miranda* warnings. One of the reasons for this difficulty is that the meaning of the word custody depends upon a consideration of a variety of circumstances. A safe policy to follow is to give the warnings whenever there is any doubt whether or not they apply."

And del Carmen (1987, p. 263) gives this advice: "A lot of confusion can be avoided if the officer simply remembers that 'custodial interrogation' takes place in two general situations: (1) when the suspect is under arrest and (2) when the suspect is not under arrest, but is 'deprived of his freedom in a significant way.'"

This echoes the statement of the court in *California* v. *Bakeler* (1983) that, for the purposes of *Miranda* the ultimate determinant of whether a person is "in custody" is "whether the suspect has been subjected to a formal arrest or to equivalent restraints on his freedom of movement."

Suspect under Arrest

Clearly, a person who is arrested is "in custody" and must be given the *Miranda* warning IF the police are going to ask the suspect questions. Mere detention does not by itself require the *Miranda* warning.

Suspect at the Police Station

If police direct a suspect to come to the police station for questioning or take the suspect there, this is a coercive atmosphere and the *Miranda* warning is required. If, however, the suspect voluntarily comes to the station, no warning is required. As noted in *Miranda* (1966): "There is no requirement that police stop a person who enters a police station and states that he wishes to confess to a crime, or a person who calls the police to offer a confession or any other statement he desires to make. Volunteered statements of any kind are not barred by the Fifth Amendment and their admissibility is not affected by our holding today."

The same is usually true of questioning a suspect in a police car. If the suspect is asked to get into the car, it is usually a custodial situation. If, on the other hand, someone flags down a police car and makes a voluntary confession of a crime just committed, no *Miranda* warning is required.

Suspect Is in Custody for Another Offense

Since the suspect is obviously in custody, it is imperative that the *Miranda* warning be given before any questioning begins. All that is required is that a custodial situation exist. It does not matter what the person is in custody for.

Other Factors Indicating a Custodial Situation

Questioning someone in his or her home in the middle of the night with a number of police officers present has been considered "coercive" by the court (Orozco v. Texas [1969]). Clearly, the time the questioning occurs and the number of police officers present can affect whether *Miranda* is required.

Any kind of physical restraint places the situation within the *Miranda* requirement. As found in *People* v. *Shivers* (1967), if a police officer holds a gun on a person, that person is "in custody" and not free to leave. If, however, the suspect also has a gun, it is unlikely he would be considered "in custody" (Yates v. United States [1967]). Ferdico (1985, p. 320) stresses that "This is a potentially important situation because armed offenders often make damaging admission while holding off the police."

WHEN *MIRANDA* WARNINGS GENERALLY ARE NOT REQUIRED

del Carmen (1987, pp. 266–68) lists nine instances when *Miranda* warnings are not normally required.

- No questions asked [This is not interrogation]
- General questioning at the crime scene
- Questioning witnesses
- Volunteered statements
- Statements made to private persons, e.g., friends, cellmates
- Questioning in an office or place of business [If the person is free to go]
- "Stop-and-frisk" cases
- Before a grand jury
- Noncustodial interrogations by a probation officer.

Brief questioning in stores, restaurants, parks, hospitals, and other public places is generally considered noncustodial unless the subject is not free to leave and, thus, is "in custody." In fact, a person could be detained sufficiently to be "in custody" in a variety of settings.

Likewise, very brief questioning such as in the "stop-and-frisk" cases and general questioning at a crime scene mentioned above are *not custodial* situations. Ferdico (1985, p. 318) notes: "It is likely that a law enforcement officer would be allowed to briefly detain all potential witnesses at the scene of a crime for questioning without triggering *Miranda*. Innocent citizen witnesses directed by an officer not to leave the scene of a crime are not likely to consider themselves in custody or under arrest and it is unlikely that a court would so consider them (*Arnold v. United States,* 1967)." The same is true of traffic stops; questioning a driver who has committed a traffic violation is not considered custodial. It is similar to the brief, on-the-street "stop-and-frisk" encounter.

Also, private security officers are *not* required to advise suspects of their Miranda rights. The rule from Miranda applies only to police officers. Case law continues to recognize the clear differentiation between public police and private security.

Other Factors Indicating a Noncustodial Situation

In addition to conducting the questioning in public and keeping it brief, conducting it during normal "business" hours tends to make it more noncustodial, as does questioning in the presence of family, friends, or of other individuals in the area. Again, the factors need to be considered in total.

Officers may also make it plain to people being questioned that they are not under arrest and that they are free to leave at any time (United States v. Manglona [1969]). However, just telling them that they are not under arrest does not automatically make it so.

And, as noted by Ferdico (1985, p. 320), "The absence of other incidents of arrest such as handcuffing, searching, fingerprinting, photographing, and other booking procedures tends to indicate a non-custodial interview *Hicks v. United States* (1967); *United States v. Thomas* (1968)." The totality of the circumstances will be considered in deciding.

Finally, statements made to undercover agents or informants do not require *Miranda*. Because the suspects do not know to whom they are speaking, and, in fact, are going about their own business, they could not have any reason to believe they are "in custody."

THE PUBLIC SAFETY EXCEPTION

An important exception to the *Miranda* requirement is when the safety of the public is involved, as described by Bennett and Hess (1987, pp. 196–98);

> On June 12, 1984, in New York v. Quarles, the Supreme Court ruled on the Public Safety Exception to the Miranda warning requirement. In 1980, two police officers were stopped by a young woman who told them she had been raped and gave them a description of her rapist who, she stated, had just entered a nearby supermarket and was armed with a gun. The suspect, Benjamin Quarles, was located, and the officer ordered him to stop. Quarles ran, and the officer momentarily lost sight of him. When he was apprehended and frisked, he was found to be wearing an empty shoulder holster. The officer asked Quarles where the gun was, and he nodded toward some cartons and said, "The gun is over there." The officer retrieved the gun, put Quarles under formal arrest, and read him his rights. Quarles waived his rights to an attorney and answered questions.
>
> At the trial, the court ruled pursuant to Miranda that the statement, "The gun is over there" and the subsequent discovery of the gun as a result of that statement were inadmissible at the defendant's trial.
>
> The U.S. Supreme Court, after reviewing the case, ruled that the procedural safeguards which deter a suspect from responding and increase the possibility of fewer convictions were deemed acceptable in Miranda to protect the Fifth Amendment privilege against self-

[handwritten margin note: Don't worry about]

incrimination. However, if Miranda warnings had deterred the response to the officer's question, the cost would have been more than
just the loss of evidence that might lead to a conviction. As long as the
gun remained concealed in the store, it posed a danger to the public
safety.

The Court ruled that in this case the need to have the suspect talk
took precedence over the requirement that the defendant be read his
rights. The Court ruled that the material factor applying this "public
safety" exception is whether a public threat could possibly be removed
by the suspect making a statement. In this case the officer only asked
the question to insure his and the public safety. He then gave the Miranda warning before continuing questioning.

---

*The public safety exception allows police officers to question
suspects without first giving the Miranda warning if the information
sought sufficiently affects the officer's and the public's safety.*

FOURTH AMENDMENT VIOLATIONS AND *MIRANDA*

Another important consideration in whether information obtained will be admitted in court is whether it violates a person's Fourth
Amendment right to a "reasonable expectation of privacy." As described by Bennett and Hess (1987, pp. 245–46):

> In a landmark case, Katz v. United States (1967), the U.S. Supreme
> Court considered an appeal by Charles Katz, who had been convicted
> in California of violating anti-gambling laws. Investigators had ob-
> served Katz for several days as he made phone calls from a phone
> booth at the same time each day. Suspecting that he was placing horse
> racing bets, they attached an electronic listening/recording device to
> the phone booth and recorded Katz's illegal activities. The evidence
> was used in obtaining his conviction. The Supreme Court reversed this
> decision saying " . . . 'the Fourth Amendment protects people not
> places'. . . . Wherever a man may be, he is entitled to know that he
> will remain free from unreasonable searches and seizures." The inves-
> tigators did have probable cause, but they erred in not presenting their
> information to a magistrate and obtaining prior approval for their ac-
> tions.

---

*Statements, including confessions, will not be admissible in court if
they were obtained while violating a person's Fourth Amendment
right to a reasonable expectation of privacy.*

WAIVING THE RIGHTS

A waiver is a purposeful, voluntary giving up of a known right. Suspects must know and understand their constitutional rights to legally waive them.

If after hearing a police officer read the Miranda warning, suspects remain silent, this is NOT a waiver. To waive their rights, suspects must state, orally or in writing, that (1) they understand their rights and (2) they will voluntarily answer questions (3) without a lawyer present.

It is best to obtain a written waiver when possible.

The competency of suspects to understand and waive their rights should always be considered. People who are under the influence of alcohol or other drugs, who are physically injured, who are in shock, or who are very young or very old may have difficulty understanding the situation. In the case of juveniles, it is also best to obtain a waiver from their parents or guardians.

Even if suspects waive their rights initially, they may rescind the waiver at any point in the interrogation. If they no longer want to answer questions, or if they want a lawyer present, their wishes must be respected immediately.

For juveniles and extremely elderly people or people having problems understanding for whatever reason, officers should take the time to explain and ask questions to determine if they understand *each* section of the waiver and feel comfortable that they in fact understand. The benefits of the extra effort will pay off in public relations, in court, and in other ways. It will help to firm up "voluntariness" in court to show that this was done and possibly influence the judge and jury favorably.

EFFECT OF *MIRANDA* ON LAW ENFORCEMENT

Many studies have assessed the effect of the *Miranda* decision on law enforcement investigations and convictions. According to LaFave and Israel (1985, pp. 285–86):

Various studies have indicated that defendants given the warnings seldom request counsel and that about as many confessions are obtained by giving the Miranda rights as were gotten before the Miranda decision. It also appears that Miranda has had little effect upon clearance and conviction rates. This apparently is because most suspects do not grasp the significance of the warnings and seem unable really to un-

STATEMENT

TIME_____DATE_____PLACE_____

_____

I, the undersigned, _____, being_____

years of age, state that I live at_____

in the _____ of_____, that I have been warned and

advised by _____, a person who has identified himself

as _____, that: (1) I have the right to remain silent; (2) I have the
right to refuse to answer any one or all of the questions put to me; (3) anything I say may be used against me in court; (4)
I have the right to talk to a lawyer of my own choice and ask his advice before being questioned, and to have him present
with me during the questioning; (5) if I cannot afford a lawyer and want one, a lawyer will be provided for me; (6) if I decide
to answer questions now without a lawyer present I still have the right to stop answering at any time; and (7) if I wish I may
stop answering at any time until I talk to a lawyer.

I further state that I am willing to answer questions and make a statement; that I do not want a lawyer; that I understand
and know what I am doing; that no promises or threats have been made to me and no pressure or coercion of any kind has
been used against me. I therefore make this statement of my own free will.

_____

Figure 8–2   **Statement and Waiver of Rights**

Statement of Miranda Rights

1. You have the right to remain silent.
2. Anything you say can and will be used against you in a court of law.
3. You have the right to talk to a lawyer and have him present with you while you are being questioned.
4. If you cannot afford to hire a lawyer, one will be appointed to represent you before any questioning, if you wish.
5. You can decide at any time to exercise these rights and not answer any questions or make any statements.

Waiver of Rights

I have read the above statement of my rights and I understand each of those rights, and having these rights in mind I waive them and willingly make a statement.

_____

Witnessed by:

_____
Officer's Name

_____
Officer's Department

Date: _____, 19____

Time: _____M.

Figure 8–3   Written Waiver of Rights in English

derstand that the object of the policeman's questions is to gather evidence which could be used to put them in jail.

Also, it is important to have available *Miranda* warnings in the languages most commonly encountered in the area, for example, Spanish, Korean, Hmong, and the like. Interpreters might be used, and *Miranda* warning cards in specific languages might be printed.

**ADVERTENCIA ANTES DE TOMAR CUALQUIER
CONFESION HABLADA O ESCRITA**

(1) Tiene el derecho de permanecer en silencio y no tiene que dar ninquna declaracion, y cualquier declarcion que haga puede ser usada encontra de usted en su juicio de ley.

(2) Cualquier declaracion que haga puede ser usada como evidencia encontra de usted en su corte de ley.

(3) Tiene el derecho de tener un abogado presente para aconsejarle antes y durante que le hagan preguntas.

(4) Si no puede emplear un abogado, tiene el derecho que le nombren un abogado para aconsejarle antes y durante que le hagan preguntas.

(5) Tiene el derecho de terminar la entrevista a cualquier hora.

Figure 8—4   *Miranda* **Warning in Spanish**

SUMMARY

The Fifth Amendment provides for protection against self-incrimination and guarantees citizens "due process of law." The Fourteenth Amendment makes this applicable to the states. Voluntariness of a confession is determined by the totality of circumstances including such factors as (1) the police conduct involved, (2) the characteristics of the accused, and (3) the timing of the confession.

Escobedo established the Sixth Amendment right of a defendant to have a lawyer present during interrogation. *Miranda*, the primary modern case used for analyzing confession cases, went much further. It established that the *Miranda* warning must be given to a suspect who is interrogated in the custody of the police, that is, the suspect is not free to leave.

The public safety exception allows police officers to question suspects without first giving the *Miranda* warning if the information sought sufficiently affects the officer's and the public's safety.

Statements, including confessions, will not be admissible in the court if they were obtained while violating a person's Fourth Amendment right to an expectation of privacy or as a result of any other constitutional violation.

If suspects remain silent after hearing a police officer read the *Miranda* warning, this is NOT a waiver. To waive their rights, suspects must state, orally or in writing, that (1) they understand their rights and (2) they will voluntarily answer questions (3) without a lawyer present.

Discussion Questions

1. Why does "voluntariness" play such an important role in the law of confessions?
2. What factors determine whether a statement is made "voluntarily"?
3. At exactly what point are police officers required to give the so-called "*Miranda* rights" to a suspect?
4. Are private security officers required to advise suspects of their rights per the *Miranda* decision?
5. Why does the "public safety exception" to the *Miranda* rule permit a custodial interrogation by the police without the reading and waiver of the rights normally required?
6. What constitutes a sufficient waiver of rights by a suspect?
7. Is there a need for a second-language *Miranda* warning card in your area?

References

Bennett, Wayne, and Hess, Kären M. *Criminal Investigation*. 2d ed. St. Paul, Minn.: West Publishing Company, 1987.

del Carmen, Rolando V. *Criminal Procedure for Law Enforcement Personnel*. Monterey, Calif.: Brooks/Cole Publishing Company, 1987.

Ferdico, John N. *Criminal Procedure for the Criminal Justice Professional*. 3d ed. St. Paul, Minn.: West Publishing Company, 1985.

Inbau. *Police Interrogation—A Practical Necessity*. S2 J. Crim L.C. & P.S. 16, 17, 19 (1961).

Inbau, Fred Edward, Reid, John E., and Buckley, Joseph P. *Criminal Interrogation and Confessions*. 3d ed. Baltimore, MD: Williams and Wilkins, 1986.

LaFave, Wayne R., and Israel, Jerold. *Criminal Procedure*. St. Paul, Minn.: West Publishing Company, 1985.

Whitebread, Charles H., and Slobogin, Christopher. *Criminal Procedure: An Analysis of Cases and Concepts*. 2d ed. Mineola, N.Y.: The Foundation Press, Inc., 1986.

Wrobleski, Henry, and Hess, Kären M. *Introduction to Law Enforcement and Criminal Justice*. 2d ed. St. Paul, Minn.: West Publishing Company, 1986.

Yeschke, Charles L. *Interviewing: An Introduction to Interrogation*. Springfield, Ill.: Charles C. Thomas, Publisher, 1987.

DOES THE MIRANDA WARNING HINDER INVESTIGATIONS?

Does the *Miranda* decision impede police investigations and make it harder for them to get confessions? Or is it a necessity to assure that defendant's rights are not violated? According to Patrick Malone (1986), "When issued twenty years ago, it [Miranda] quickly became—and remains to this day—the most reviled decision ever issued by the Supreme Court in a criminal case." The following discussions look at this volitile issue.

The Miranda Rule Does NOT Handcuff the Police

Next to the warning on cigarette packs, *Miranda* is the most widely ignored piece of official advice in our society. Even when *Miranda* is violated, it is rare that a confession will be ruled inadmissible or that a suspect will go free. Ernest Miranda himself was retried and reconvicted. A recent federally funded study in Illinois, Michigan, and Pennsylvania found that convictions were lost as a result of judges throwing out confessions in only five out of the 7,035 cases studied, or 0.07 percent. . . .

The rights of defendants, most of whom richly deserve a spell behind bars, have never been a popular cause, and police tactics have never excited much public curiosity. As the constitutional law scholar Yale Kamisar once observed, the typical police suspect and his interrogator are generally viewed "as garbage and garbage collector, respectively."

[Patrick Malone, "You Have the Right to Remain Silent: Miranda After Twenty Years." from *The American Scholar*, Volume 55, Number 3, Summer 1986.]

Whether suspects do not fully grasp the significance of the warnings, or whether conscience (and the desire to get the matter over with) override the impact of the warnings, it is plain that for the past 20 years suspects have continued to confess with great frequency. It is equally plain that this would not have been the case if Miranda really had projected counsel into the police station. . . .

[Yale Kamisar, *The New York Times*, June 11, 1986.]

In practice few suspects actually rely on their right of silence. Even when the caution that one need not answer is faithfully administered by the interrogating police officer, very few suspects have the strength of mind to say nothing.

[Michael Zander, *The New York Times*, January 27, 1986.]

The Miranda Rule DOES Handcuff the Police

Because of [Miranda], . . . convictions are lost when police officers trip up on the technicalities, even when there is no doubt that the confession they obtain is both voluntary and reliable. . . .

Anyone who doubts that this case affected the U.S. criminal-justice system need only check the casebooks. They are filled with examples of seemingly voluntary confessions thrown out on Miranda grounds. Several years ago the California Supreme Court, relying on Miranda, reversed the conviction of a confessed triple-murderer who had been given repeated warnings of his rights and had repeatedly signed statements waiving these rights and confessing to his crime.

[Edwin Meese III, *The Wall Street Journal*, June 13, 1986.]

The *Miranda* ruling addressed four cases. In none of the cases was there the slightest doubt about the individual's guilt or any reason to believe the confession had been coerced. Rather, the Court seemed to suggest the police erred by not protecting the accused sufficiently from his own poor judgment or desire to talk. . . .

Now, twenty years after *Miranda*, it is almost incontestable that the decision weakened law enforcement, especially during the late 1960s and early 1970s. It is also very likely that it contributed to the surge in crime rates during that period. . . .

Nearly as important as *Miranda's* effects on police and prosecutors were its effects on the public, which was severely demoralized by seeing confessed criminals go free on "improper warnings" in a number of highly visible cases.

[William Tucker. From *Vigilante*. Stein and Day Publishers, 1986.]

In a blazing dissent by Justice White, a four-justice minority protested that criminal defendants who previously would have been convicted on what the Court had always held to be the most satisfactory kind of evidence would henceforth escape trial altogether or be acquitted. . . . .

Their prophecy has come true. The impact of the *Miranda* decision has been devastating, according to Prof. Emeritus Fred Inbau of Northwestern University School of Law, a leading authority on police interrogation techniques. FBI statistics show that police used to solve more than 90 percent of the nation's murder cases. After Miranda, their effectiveness began to drop, and today the percentage of unsolved murders has tripled to an all-time high of 28 percent. In robberies, too, a crime in which interrogation is also crucial, police clearance rates dropped by 35 percent. Thus in 1985 alone, the Supreme Court's unreasonableness on reasonable interrogation cost America as many as 3600 additional unsolved murders and 64,700 unsolved robberies.

[Eugene H. Methvin. "The Case of Common Sense vs. Miranda." *Reader's Digest*, August, 1987.]

CHAPTER 9

The Law of Identification

Procedures

The greatest thing a human soul ever does in this world is to see something, and tell what it saw in a plain way. Hundreds of people can talk for one who can think, but thousands can think for one who can see. To see clearly is poetry, prophecy, and religion, all in one—John Ruskin

DO YOU KNOW

How reliable eyewitness identification of a suspect is?

What factors may account for mistaken identification?

What amendments to the Constitution are relevant to identification procedures?

What the common types of identification are?

If a suspect has the right to have counsel present during a lineup? The precedent case?

What the role of counsel is during a lineup?

What the Kirby limitation is?

How to assess the reliability of an eyewitness identification?

If a suspect has the right to counsel during a photographic identification? The precedent case?

If a suspect has the right to counsel when handwriting samples are being taken? The precedent case?

What actions do not constitute self-incrimination?

The factor most responsible for misidentification?

What the results of an unfair lineup are?

Introduction

Chapter 9

Can there ever be a more dramatic moment during a trial than when the witness turns to the accused and declares with finger pointing, "That's the man!"

Such an identification can obviously be extremely persuasive. It can also be, and frequently has been, inaccurate, inflicting very serious harm on the defendant. For these two reasons, the courts have expended great effort in determining the law of identification.

It is only natural to expect that a person who was an eyewitness to a particular incident would be the most accurate witness. After all, if a person was there and saw it, should that not be the strongest testimony of all? It seems so easy—too easy.

In the early phase of a trial during which prospective jurors are questioned to determine their fitness as jurors, known as *voir dire*, both the prosecutor and the defense counsel are permitted to ask questions that may start the jurors thinking about significant issues. When the prosecution's case centers on eyewitness identification, the effective defense lawyer can immediately start to plant the "seed of reasonable doubt."

For example, the defense lawyer may ask whether the jurors have ever approached someone they were certain they knew, maybe even spoken to him or her, only to discover it wasn't the individual they thought it was? Or the jurors may be asked if they can describe the clothing worn by their spouses that morning. Suddenly, the accuracy of what we see becomes questionable.

MISTAKEN IDENTITY: IT DOES HAPPEN

Legal history abounds with cases that clearly present the tragedies of wrongful convictions that were based on mistaken identification. Two separate cases illustrate the inherent problems in basing a conviction solely on eyewitness identification. The first case involved Adolph Beck, who served seven years in prison for crimes he did not commit. His conviction was based on the mistaken identifications of twenty-two witnesses! As noted by Watson (1924, p. 250), a committee that investigated the case of Beck concluded:

> *Evidence as to identity based on personal impressions, however bona fide, is perhaps of all classes of evidence the least to be relied upon, and therefore, unless supported by other facts, an unsafe basis for the verdict of a jury.*

Eyewitness identification can be the least reliable form of evidence.

In the second case, seven eyewitnesses testified that Father Bernard Pagano, a Roman Catholic priest, was the man who had held them up at gunpoint. It was only at the midway point of the trial that another man came forward and admitted to being the armed robber (LaFave and Israel, 1985 p. 321).

The probability of mistaken identify was graphically illustrated in a study by Dr. Robert Buckhout. In his study, viewers of the evening news aired by a New York City television station were shown a video of a mugging. They were then shown a lineup of six men and asked to phone in their identification of the mugger. More than 2,000 viewers phoned, but less than 15 percent (a percentage equal to random selection) correctly identified the mugger.

REASONS FOR MISIDENTIFICATION

The dynamics of eyewitness identification are complex. There would be no problem if humans could accurately perceive, recall, and communicate what they have seen. As noted by Whitebread and Slobogin (1986, p. 414), "Extensive research indicates that both our ability to observe what someone looks like under the circumstances likely to be present during a crime and our capacity to recall what we observe is surprisingly deficient."

LaFave and Israel (1985, pp. 321–22) state that

> *Identification testimony has at least three components. First, witnessing a crime, whether as a victim or a bystander, involves perception of an event actually occurring. Second, the witness must memorize details of the event. Third, the witness must be able to recall and communicate accurately. Dangers of unreliability in eyewitness testimony arise at each of these three stages, for whenever people attempt to acquire, retain, and retrieve information accurately they are limited by normal human fallibilities and suggestive influences. . . .*
>
> *In the first place, perception is not a mere passive recording of an event but instead is a constructive process by which people consciously or unconsciously use decisional strategies to attend selectively to only a minimal number of environmental stimuli. . . . Many identification errors are due to circumstances of the observation such as a brief observation period, poor lighting conditions or a stress-inducing situation. Psychological research has demonstrated that anxiety and fear produce significant perceptual distortion. Furthermore, personal expectations, needs and biases may distort perception. Evidence indicates that people are poorer at identifying members of another race than of their own. Perception is both incomplete and inaccurate.*
>
> *Furthermore, memories are not indelibly preserved . . . Considerable memory loss occurs during the many days—and often months—that typically elapse between the offense and an eyewitness identification of the suspect. Memory is a constructive process to which details may be added which were not present in the initial representation or in the event itself. The mere wording of a question put to an eyewitness during a deposition, interview or trial may affect not only the immediate answer but also the witness' memory of the original event. . . .*

Another source of errors in identification is the process by which information is retrieved from memory for purposes of making an identification. . . . Lineups and photo arrays are structured recognition tests. Witnesses are likely to perceive them as multiple-choice tests that lack a "none of the above" option. Thus, the witness may view the task as one of identifying the individual who best matches the witness' recollection of the culprit, even if that match is not perfect.

Mistaken identification can be made because a person didn't see the suspect clearly due to distance, poor lighting, poor eyesight, fear, or plain lack of attention; to lack of recall; to inaccurate recall; or to the inability to communicate what was seen.

Obviously, perception can be influenced by many factors. The stress of a traumatic situation has a tremendous effect on how accurately a person perceives a situation, causing both physiological and emotional factors to come into play. The setting itself may influence perception, for instance, distance and lighting will be factors. Even seemingly little things can draw attention from the total picture. Most people, for example, have seen police thrillers in which the assailant uses a false scar or mole, or a flamboyant article of clothing, perhaps dark glasses, to draw the attention of that witness away from the "whole" of the scenario. One such armed robber was never identified, even though all of his robberies were committed while he was totally nude.

In addition, the ability to accurately recall a situation observed can begin to deteriorate within moments of the actual event. Every good investigator knows the importance of obtaining complete witness statements as soon after the event as possible. This is, in fact, the basis for the majority of laws having a statute of limitations, a time limit by which a legal action must be initiated. The law realizes that after a reasonable period of time, recollection becomes stale, and that, in the interest of justice, a limitation must be set.

In addition, such factors as age, trauma, and intelligence all play a part in determining *what* is recalled, for *how long*. Even if recall itself does not present a problem, witnesses must have the ability to communicate their observations in a way that can be understood, an ability not everyone has to the same degree.

Whitebread and Slobogin (1986, p. 415) suggest: "These and other problems with eyewitness identification cannot be fully rectified by the legal system. In particular, the law cannot have much of an effect on witness' perceptual and recall capabilities. But it can try to control any conscious or unconscious attempt by the police or the prosecution to supply what perception and memory cannot." While a court cannot go back to provide adequate lighting, a better vantage point, or a clearer mind at the moment of the observation, laws can be established to ensure fairness in the methods used to obtain eyewitness identification and testimony.

LEGAL HISTORY

It was not until 1967 that the United States Supreme Court seriously evaluated the system of eyewitness identification. The Court sought to clarify this body of law by confronting the cases of *United States* v. *Wade* (1967), *Gilbert* v. *California* (1967), and *Stovall* v. *Denno* (1967).

Before looking at these landmark cases, however, a review of the Fifth and Sixth Amendments of the Constitution is important, because the United States Supreme Court has used both amendments in deciding cases involving identification of suspects.

The Fifth and Sixth Amendments

The Fifth Amendment states:

No person . . . shall be compelled in any criminal case to be a witness against himself; nor be deprived of life, liberty, or property, without due process of law; . . .

This amendment guarantees *due process of law* and protects against *self-incrimination*.

The Sixth Amendment states:

In all criminal prosecutions, the accused shall enjoy the right to a speedy and public trial, by an impartial jury of the state and district wherein the crime shall have been committed, which districts shall have been previously ascertained by law, and to be informed of the nature and cause of the accusation; to be confronted with the witnesses against him; to have compulsory process for obtaining witnesses in his favor, and to have the assistance of counsel for his defense.

The most relevant segments of this amendment are the right of suspects to confront witnesses against them and to have the assistance of counsel for their defense. Both these rights have important bearing on eyewitness identification.

The Fifth and Sixth Amendments have relevance to the admissibility of various types of identification.

The court has sought to balance the defendant's right to a fair trial with the need to admit relevant, crucial evidence. In some states, admission of expert testimony on the unreliability of eyewitness identification is within the trial court's discretion (*State v. Helterbridle*, Minn. [1980]).

TYPES OF PERSONAL IDENTIFICATION

Identifying a suspect is sometimes referred to in legal jargon as the *corporeal identification procedure*. *Corporeal* simply means "relating to the body or personal." Four types of personal identification are commonly used in criminal investigations.

Personal identification may be made using a lineup, a showup, photographs, or in-court identification.

Lineup Identification

In a lineup identification a witness to or victim of a crime is shown several persons for the purpose of identifying the perpetrator of the crime. Lineups are usually conducted at the jail or police station.

Bennett and Hess (1986, p. 232) suggest the following requirements for a fair lineup:

The lineup, often portrayed on TV, provides an opportunity for a witness to identify a suspect in comparison to others. Participants in a lineup may be required to state a certain phrase, assume a particular stance, or otherwise act as the perpetrator did at the time of the crime.

Lineups can have from five to ten persons. The suspect cannot be of a different race, exceptionally taller or shorter, have longer or shorter hair, or be dressed differently from the other persons in the lineup. The suspect cannot be handcuffed unless all persons in the lineup are handcuffed. Nor can the suspect be asked to step forward, turn a certain direction, or speak certain words unless every participant in the lineup is asked to do the same. Suspects can refuse to participate in a lineup, but such refusals can be used against them in court (Schmerber v. California 1966).

It is important that people viewing the lineup are instructed that they do not need to identify anyone.

LaFave and Israel (1985, p. 340) contend: "It may generally be said that lineups are the most useful and least questionable witness identification procedure. They are obviously less suggestive than one-man showups, and are also more reliable than photographic identifications."

Many police departments photograph their lineups to demonstrate their fairness. Other departments use a form describing the lineup as shown in Figure 9-1.

Showup Identification

In a showup identification a witness to or victim of a crime is shown *one* suspect for the purpose of identifying the perpetrator of the crime. This is usually conducted at the scene immediately following the crime and the detaining of a suspect. It may also take place at a hospital if a witness is in critical condition. Showup identification is also called *field-identification*.

The critical factor in a showup identification is *time*. There must be a reasonable basis for believing the immediate identification is required before showup identification is used.

Photographic Identification

In photographic identification a witness to or victim of a crime is shown a series of pictures from which to identify the perpetrator of a crime. Photographic identification should meet the same general requirements of a lineup, that is, five to ten pictures of individuals of similar appearance should be used. They should be of comparable race, height, weight, and general description. Clothing should also be similar. As with a lineup, witnesses should be told that they do not need to identify anyone from the group of pictures.

The pictures can be kept separately or mounted on a board. They can be numbered for identification, but they should contain no other information.

In specific instances, a single photograph can be shown, analogous to a showup, but sufficient reason must exist.

In other instances, witnesses may be asked to go through mug-shot books if it is believed that the suspect has a record.

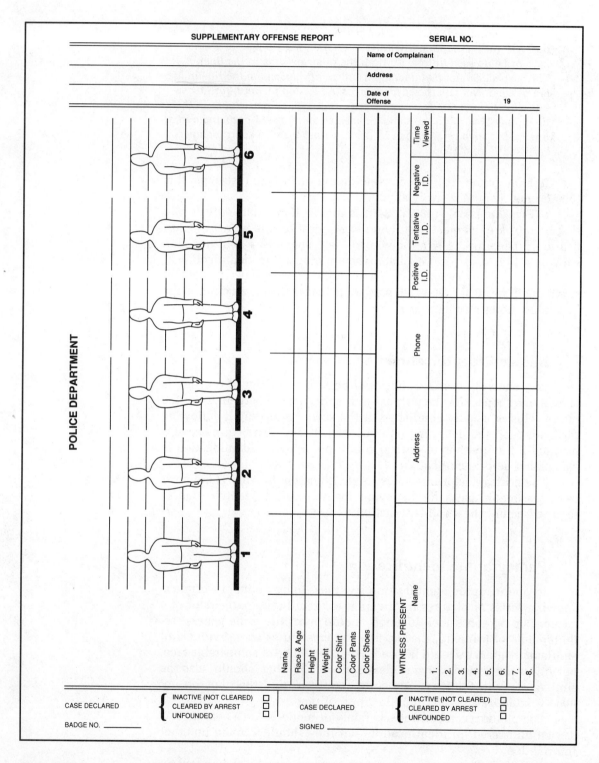

Figure 9–1   **Sample Lineup Form**

A victim or other witness may be asked to look through "mug books" if the investigating officer believes the suspect may have a prior record, or even if the police have no specific leads.

In-Court Identification

In-court identification occurs during the trial, when the prosecuting attorney asks his or her witness, "Is the person who robbed you present in the court today?" It's a safe bet the eyewitness will identify the person sitting with the defense attorney. In fact, some defense lawyers have switched seats with the defendant for just such purpose.

Each of these types of identification presents specific legal issues. Several important court cases have dealt with "due process" and when a suspect has the right to counsel during the identification process.

RIGHT TO AN ATTORNEY DURING LINEUP IDENTIFICATION

In *United States* v. *Wade* (1967), the Court sought to answer the question "whether courtroom identifications of an accused are to be excluded from evidence because the accused was exhibited to the witnesses before trial at a post-indictment lineup conducted for identification purposes without notice to and in the absence of the accused's appointed counsel."

In *Wade*, the defendant was placed in a lineup made up of himself and a number of other prisoners. Each one had to wear strips of tape on his face, as the robber in the case had done, and say, "Put the money in the bag." This lineup was conducted after the defendant had been indicted and after he had a defense attorney appointed. His lawyer, however, was not notified of this lineup.

The United States Supreme Court held that such procedures violated the defendant's constitutional rights under the Sixth Amendment and concluded that for Wade, the postindictment lineup was a *critical stage* of the prosecution at which he was "as much entitled to such aid [of counsel] as at the trial itself." Thus, both Wade and his counsel should have been notified of the impending lineup, and counsel's presence should have been a requisite to conduct the lineup, absent an "intelligent waiver."

Suspects have a right to have an attorney present during a lineup (Wade).

The Supreme Court held that Wade's postindictment lineup was a critical stage in the criminal process and that the presence of the accused's attorney was necessary to assure the defendant's basic right to a fair trial.

Waiver

Suspects may waive the right to have an attorney present. This waiver, however, must be made *knowingly* and *voluntarily*. It is generally best to use a release form.

The Role of the Attorney during Lineup

Although the *Wade* decision specifies that a suspect has a right to have an attorney present during a lineup, the decision does not indicate what the attorney is to do. del Carmen (1987, p. 236) suggests that "The main role of a lawyer is to make sure that the procedure is fair. . . . Lawyers should be accorded all professional courtesies, but must not be allowed to control the proceedings; neither should an attorney's disruptive presence be tolerated. . . . Counsel should not be allowed to question the witness before, during, or after the line-up. . . ."

Police officers, especially rookies, should pay particular attention to the statement that lawyers "*must not be allowed to control the proceedings.*" The attorney is there only as an observer to insure that his client's due process rights are not infringed upon. Frase (1985, p. 160) notes that more than one role might be possible:

> The Court seems to envision the attorney's presence as largely preventive: "presence of counsel itself can often avert prejudice"; counsel may assist law enforcement "by preventing the infiltration of taint." Justice Black, while agreeing that counsel was necessary, believed that an attorney could also advise the suspect "not to participate in the lineup or to participate only under certain conditions." In his dissent,

---

Pre-Trial Identification Warning and Waiver

Name _____   Address _____

Age _____   Place _____

Date _____   Time _____

Warning

Before appearing at any confrontation with any witnesses being conducted by (Name of Police Department) in relation to (Description of Offense), you must understand your legal rights.

The results of the confrontation can and will be used against you in court.

You have the right to the presence and advice of an attorney of your choice at any such confrontation.

If you cannot afford an attorney and you want one, an attorney will be appointed for you at no expense, before any confrontation is held.

Waiver

I have been advised of my right to the advice of an attorney and to have an attorney present at any confrontation with witnesses, and that if I cannot afford a lawyer, one will be appointed for me before any such confrontation occurs. I understand these rights.

I do not want a lawyer and I understand and know what I am doing.

No promises have been made to me and no pressures of any kind have been used against me.

_____

Signature of Suspect

Certification

I, (Name of Officer), hereby certify that I read the above warning to (Name of Suspect) on (Date), that he indicated that he understood his rights, and signed the WAIVER form in my presence.

_____

Signature of Officer

_____

Witness

Figure 9–2   Waiver of Right to Counsel during Lineup

Justice White imagined a more menacing role for attorneys. They might "hover over witnesses and begin their cross-examination then" or "suggest rules for the lineup and . . . manage and produce it."

In practice, the role of the attorney has been almost entirely that of observer. Indeed, it is uncertain whether an attorney has any legal authority to object to proceedings during the course of the lineup itself.

LaFave and Israel (1985, p. 334) make the interesting point that

> *If the lawyer is to serve as an observer because . . . he is better able than the defendant and others present to recognize suggestive influences, then this would suggest that it may well be necessary for him to take the stand himself to testify as to what went on at the lineup. This places the defense attorney in a dilemma. Under the Model Rules of Professional Conduct, if a lawyer learns he will be required to be a witness at trial for his client, except as to an uncontested issue, he should withdraw from the case unless doing so "would work a substantial hardship on the client."*

The Model Code of Pre-Arraignment Procedure (1975) suggests that a second position to take is to view a lineup as "a fully adversary proceeding in which the counsel for the suspect may make objections and proposals, which if they are proper or even reasonable must be respected."

Lawyers may take an active role to correct any suggestiveness occurring or simply observe and then use this information at the trial, perhaps to the defendant's advantage.

NO RIGHT TO AN ATTORNEY DURING SHOWUP IDENTIFICATION

In *Kirby v. Illinois* (1972) two Chicago police officers stopped Kirby and a companion for questioning. When the police officers asked for identification, Kirby presented a social security card and traveler's checks with the name Willie Shard. When the officers checked the records, they found that Shard had reported his billfold stolen the previous day. Shard was asked to come to the police station.

When he came in, he immediately identified Kirby and his companion as the pair who had stolen his billfold. Neither suspect was advised of the right to have a lawyer present. According to the United States Supreme Court, this was not necessary; no such right existed. The *Wade* decision applied only "at or after the initiation of adversary judicial criminal proceedings—whether by way of formal charge, preliminary hearing, indictment, information or arraignment."

The Kirby limitation is that a suspect does not have the right to a lawyer in showup identification, that is, preindictment identification.

Frase (1985, p. 162) suggests that "Perhaps the major reason for the *Kirby* limitation on *Wade* was the desire to avoid interference with the conduct of immediate, on-the-street identification procedures. The Court in *Kirby* may have felt that such "alley confrontations" are essential to effective law enforcement and that because of their proximity in time and place to the crime, they are also more reliable than the later, more staged lineup."

A similar sentiment was expressed in *United States* v. *Kinnard* (1968):

> *Many different situations occur on our streets daily which, as a practical matter, warrant if not require the police to present a suspect to a complaining witness shortly following detention or arrest. Indeed, such confrontations often occur even without any special police effort to bring them about. Defense counsel cannot always be riding in police cruisers. If police are no longer able to get identification confrontation promptly while the complainant's recollection is fresh, a drastic change in police procedures must take place. The police need greater flexibility than an absolute application of the Wade ruling as presently drawn appears to portend.*

This sentiment was echoed in *Bates* v. *United States* (1968):

> *There is no prohibition against a viewing of a suspect alone in what is called a "one-man showup" when this occurs near the time of the alleged criminal act; such a course does not tend to bring about misidentification but rather in some circumstances to insure accuracy. The rationale underlying this is in some respects not unlike that which the law relies on to make an exception to the hearsay rule, allowing spontaneous utterances a standing which they would not be given if uttered at a later point in time. An early identification is not error. Of course, proof of infirmities and subjective factors, such as hysteria of a witness, can be explored on cross-examination and in argument. Prudent police work would confine these on-the-spot identifications to situations in which possible doubts as to identification needed to be resolved promptly; absent such need the conventional lineup viewing is the appropriate procedure.*

Neil v. *Biggers* (1972) also involved a one-man showup. Ferdico (1985, pp. 352–53) describes this case:

> *Neil* v. *Biggers* involved a defendant who had been convicted of rape on evidence consisting in part of the victim's visual and voice identification of him at a station-house showup seven months after the crime. At the time of the crime, the victim was in her assailant's presence for nearly one-half hour and directly observed him indoors and under a full moon outdoors. She testified at trial that she had no doubt that the defendant was her assailant. She gave the police a thorough description of the assailant immediately after the crime that matched the description of the defendant. And she had made no identification of others presented at previous showups or lineups, or through photographs. The Court, despite its concern about the seven-month delay

between the crime and the confrontation, held that the central question was "whether under the 'totality of the circumstances' the identification was reliable even though the confrontation procedure was suggestive."

The Court listed five factors to consider in evaluating the likelihood of misidentification:

"Factors to assess eyewitness reliability include

- *the witness's opportunity to see the criminal at the time of the offense,*
- *witness's degree of attention,*
- *accuracy of the witness's prior description of the criminal,*
- *level of certainty demonstrated at the identification confrontation,*
- *—and time between the crime and the identification confrontation"* (Neil v. Biggers [1972]).

Emergency Showup Identifications

Stovall v. Denno (1967) involved a man accused of killing another man and injuring his wife. The wife was hospitalized, and the police brought Stovall, in handcuffs, to her bedside and asked her if he was "the man." Although this was certainly "suggestive," the Court upheld the admissibility of the identification because of the emergency situation:

> Here was the only person in the world who could possibly exonerate Stovall. Her words, and only her words, "He is not the man" could have resulted in freedom for Stovall. The hospital was not far distant from the courthouse and jail. No one knew how long Mrs. Behrendt might live. Faced with the responsibility of identifying the attacker, with the need for immediate action and with the knowledge that Mrs. Behrendt could not visit the jail, the police followed the only feasible procedure and took Stovall to the hospital room. Under these circumstances, the usual police station lineup, which Stovall now argues he should have had, was out of the question.

NO RIGHT TO AN ATTORNEY DURING PHOTOGRAPHIC IDENTIFICATION

In the case of *United States v. Ash* (1973), the Court held that there is no right to counsel when a series of photos are displayed to a witness, as opposed to having a witness actually view a lineup.

A primary reason for this holding was that the defense lawyer will be able to view the photos as shown, and that the critical stage analysis should apply only to "trial-like confrontations." Whitebread and Slobogin (1986, p. 417) state: "Since, unlike at a lineup, the defendant is not present during a photographic display, he is not confronted by the prosecutor or the intricacies of the adversary system and thus is not entitled to counsel." Again, such photos could not be so unfair as to violate the defendant's due process rights.

A suspect is not entitled to counsel during a photographic identification (Ash).

Thus, the cases of Wade, Gilbert, and Ash would suggest that the only pretrial identification procedure that would involve the Sixth Amendment right to counsel would be an actual lineup and confrontational one-on-one settings.

NO RIGHT TO AN ATTORNEY DURING TAKING OF HANDWRITING SAMPLES

Gilbert v. California (1967) addressed whether identification procedures other than a lineup would require the accused's lawyer being present, as specified by the Sixth Amendment. In this case the Court held that the taking of handwriting samples (exemplars) would not be a "critical stage" of the criminal proceedings because the taking of such a sample could be done in the very same way during the trial.

A suspect does not have the right to have counsel present when handwriting samples are being taken.

The Supreme Court, in *Wade*, stated that "a lineup was different from certain other identification procedures, such as analyzing fingerprints, blood samples, clothing, hair, etc." The court in *Wade* explained that counsel would not be required because:

> knowledge of the techniques of science and technology is sufficiently available, and the variables in techniques few enough, that the accused has the opportunity for a meaningful confrontation of the Government's case at trial through the ordinary processes of cross-examination of the Government's expert witnesses and the presentation of the evidence of his own experts.

PROTECTING THE PRIVILEGE AGAINST SELF-INCRIMINATION

Schmerber v. *California* (1966) established that taking a blood sample from a suspect was not a violation of his privilege against self-incrimination. In its decision the Court said the Fifth Amendment privilege offered "No protection against compulsion to submit to fingerprinting, photography or measurements, to write or speak for identification, to appear in court, to stand, to assume a stance, to talk, or to make a particular gesture." For example, taking a blood sample from a driver suspected of being drunk at the scene of a serious accident would be permitted. Of course, the taking of such evidence would have to be done in a reasonable, legal manner, which may include the requirement of obtaining a warrant.

Fingerprinting, photographing, submitting to blood tests, being asked to write or speak, appearing in court, assuming a stance, or making a gesture do not constitute self-incrimination but may require a warrant to obtain (Schmerber).

IN-COURT IDENTIFICATION

Wade also dealt with in-court identification. In this case the Court stated that in-court identification will be admitted if the prosecution can prove by "clear and convincing evidence that the in-court identifications were based upon observations of the suspect other than the lineup identification."

In other words, even if a lineup identification by a witness is disallowed, an in-court identification can still be made IF the identification is made based on an *independent source*. Factors to be considered include

- The prior opportunity to observe the alleged criminal act
- The existence of any discrepancy between any prelineup description and the defendant's actual description
- Any identification prior to lineup of another person
- The identification by picture of the defendant prior to the lineup
- Failure to identify the defendant on a prior occasion
- The lapse of time between the alleged act and the lineup identification
- The conduct of the lineup

For in-court identification, unfair suggestiveness can be avoided by having the defendant sit in the spectator section of the courtroom until the eyewitness identification has been made.

WHAT CONSTITUTES AN "UNFAIR" IDENTIFICATION SITUATION?

In addition to clarifying the Sixth Amendment safeguards, the Supreme Court also made clear in *Stovall v. Denno* (1967) that the accused is "entitled to protection under the Fifth Amendment against an identification procedure that is so unnecessarily suggestive and conducive to irreparable mistaken identification as to amount to denial of due process of law. Unlike the Sixth Amendment right to Counsel, this due process standard applies to identification procedures without regard to whether adversary judicial criminal proceedings have begun."

The *Wade* decision included examples of common suggestive procedures that should not be allowed:

> that all in the lineup but the suspect were known to the identifying witness, that the other participants in a lineup were grossly dissimilar in appearance to the suspect, that only the suspect was required to wear distinctive clothing which the culprit allegedly wore, that the witness is told by the police that they have caught the culprit after which the defendant is brought before the witness alone or is viewed in jail, that the suspect is pointed out before or during a lineup, and that the participants in a lineup are asked to try on an article of clothing that fits only the suspect.

Other examples of lineups that have been found to be in violation of due process include

- The suspect is obviously larger than others in the lineup.
- The suspect is the only person wearing glasses.
- The suspect is the only person in jail clothing.
- The suspect is the only person of his race in the lineup.

Frase (1985, p. 158) states:

> The facts of Wade, Gilbert, and Stovall provide further examples of ordinary police procedures which are clearly suggestive. In Wade, the witnesses were able to see the lineup participants before the lineup began and one witness saw Wade in the custody of an FBI agent before the lineup. In Gilbert, one hundred witnesses made "wholesale identifications" of Gilbert in each other's presence, a procedure said to be "fraught with dangers of suggestion." The Stovall lineup was simply a one-man showup where the suspect, handcuffed to a police officer, was taken to the victim's hospital room where he was the only black person present. The victim was then asked if he was the guilty person.

Foster v. California (1969) illustrated a blatant violation of due process. The police conducted a very suggestive lineup, but the witness was not able to identify Foster. They then conducted a showup, but the witness could only tentatively identify Foster. So the police arranged a third lineup at which the witness made a positive identification. The Court disallowed the identification, saying it was "inevitable" that the witness would ultimately identify Foster, even if the identification was mistaken.

Identification procedures consisting of a photographic identification and a lineup identification in which only the suspect appears in both are also unnecessarily suggestive.

Basic Premises of the Supreme Court

The basic premises under which the *Wade* court was functioning are noted by Frase (1985, p. 158):

> First, eyewitness testimony is inherently unreliable. Faulty memories, untrained observers, awkward descriptions, the desire to help capture a criminal—these and many other factors make the witness's testimony untrustworthy. Second, the police rightly or wrongly believe they have apprehended the guilty person and cannot be expected to conduct flawless lineups at the expense of their own self-interest. Third, eyewitness evidence is an essential and irreplaceable aspect of crime control. Finally, suggestiveness is the vice most responsible for misidentification.

Suggestiveness *is most responsible for misidentification.*

Suggestiveness in Identification

Showups are often accused of being "suggestive," as is showing a single photograph to a witness for identification. *Manson v. Brathwaite* (1977) established that *in some instances* identification can be made from a single photograph.

In this case, an undercover police officer bought heroin from a man in an apartment. He described the seller to a fellow officer who, from the description, suspected the seller was Newell Brathwaite. This officer got a mugshot of Brathwaite and showed it to the undercover officer who identified the man in the photo as the person he had bought the heroin from. The police went to Brathwaite's apartment, the same apartment described by the undercover officer as being the place of sale, and arrested Brathwaite.

Brathwaite was convicted of selling narcotics, but on appeal to the U.S. Court of Appeals for the Second Circuit, the conviction was reversed. When the Supreme Court reviewed the case, they ruled that the appeals court was wrong. The majority (7 to 2) stated that any rule excluding the evidence " . . . goes too far since its application automatically and peremptorily, and without consideration of alleviating factors, keeps evidence from the jury that is reliable and relevant."

This decision was very unpopular with Justices Thurgood Marshall and William J. Brennan Jr. Justice Marshall wrote, in the dissenting opinion:

> *"The use of a single picture (or display of a single live suspect, for that matter) is a grave error, of course, because it dramatically suggests to the witness that the person shown must be the culprit. Why else would the police choose the person?"*

RESULTS OF AN UNFAIR IDENTIFICATION

Gilbert v. *California* (1967) established that if a postindictment lineup failed to meet *Wade* standards, any testimony about identification made at that lineup would be inadmissible at trial.

Jones (1981, p. 199) notes that *Stovall* v. *Denno* (1967) further established that

> *Regardless of whether an attorney for the accused was present at the identification procedure, if the identification procedure was unnecessarily suggestive and conducive to irreparable mistaken identification and therefore a denial of due process, evidence of the identification procedure and also any in-court identification by an identification procedure witness may be excluded unless despite the suggestive and unnecessary procedure the state can show by clear and convincing evidence that under the totality of the circumstances the in-court identification would be reliable.*

An unfair lineup will lead to exclusion of evidence of the lineup and of related in-court identification (Gilbert v. California and Stovall v. Denno).

Recall, however, that if the prosecution can establish that a witness had a source of identification independent from the unconstitutional identification, the court may allow that in-court identification.

SUMMARY

Eyewitness identification can be the least reliable form of evidence. It should be supported by other facts. Mistaken identification can be made because a person didn't see the suspect clearly due to distance, poor lighting, poor eyesight, fear, or plain lack of attention; to lack of recall; to inaccurate recall; or to the inability to communicate what was seen.

The Fifth and Sixth Amendments have relevance to the admissibility of various types of identification. Personal identification may be made using a lineup, a showup, photographs, or an in-court identification.

Suspects have a right to have an attorney present during a lineup (*Wade*). Lawyers may take an active role to correct any suggestiveness occurring or simply observe and then use this information at the trial, perhaps to the defendant's advantage.

The *Kirby* limitation is that a suspect does not have the right to a lawyer in showup identification, that is, preindictment identification.

Factors to assess eyewitness reliability include (1) the witness's opportunity to see the criminal at the time of the offense, (2) witness's degree of attention, (3) accuracy of the witness's prior description of the criminal, (4) level of certainty demonstrated at the identification confrontation, and (5) time between the crime and the identification confrontation (Neil v. Biggers [1972]).

A suspect is *not* entitled to counsel during a photographic identification or when handwriting samples are being taken. Fingerprinting, photographing, submitting to blood tests, being asked to write or speak, appearing in court, assuming a stance, or making a gesture do *not* constitute self-incrimination (*Schmerber*), but may require a warrant to obtain.

Suggestiveness is most responsible for misidentification. An unfair lineup will lead to exclusion of evidence of the lineup and of in-court identification.

Discussion Questions

1. How could an identification by a witness be questionable?
2. What is the difference between a lineup and a showup?
3. When is a suspect entitled to the presence of an attorney during the identification process?
4. Why is there no right to have an attorney present during the taking of handwriting samples, fingerprints, blood samples, hair, etc.?
5. May a suspect refuse to provide a blood sample, fingerprints, or writing samples on the basis of his right not to incriminate himself? What are the precedent cases?
6. What effect does unfair suggestiveness have during any identification procedures?

References

ABA Model Rules of Professional Conduct, rule 3.7.

Bennett, Wayne M. and Hess, Kären M. *Criminal Investigation*, 2d ed. St. Paul, Minn.: West Publishing Company, 1987.

Buckhout, Robert. "Nearly 2,000 Witnesses Can Be Wrong." *Soc. Act. & L.* at 7 May, 1975.

del Carmen, Rolando V. *Criminal Procedure for Law Enforcement Personnel*. Monterey, Calif.: Brooks/Cole Publishing Company, 1987.

Ferdico, John N. *Criminal Procedure for the Criminal Justice Professional*. 3d ed. St. Paul, Minn.: West Publishing Company, 1985.

Frase, Richard S. *Criminal Evidence: Constitutional, Statutory, & Rules Limitations*. St. Paul, Minn.: Butterworth Legal Publishers, 1985.

Jones, C. Paul and staff. *Criminal Procedure from Police Detention to Final Disposition*. 1981.

LaFave, Wayne R., and Israel, Jerold. *Criminal Procedure*. St. Paul, Minn.: West Publishing Company, 1985.

Model Code of Pre-Arraignment Procedure 429, 1975.

Watson, E. *The Trial of Adolph Beck*. 1924.

Whitebread, Charles H., and Slobogin, Christopher. *Criminal Procedure: An Analysis of Cases and Concepts*. 2d ed. Mineola, N.Y.: The Foundation Press, Inc., 1986.

BASIC ISSUE

CAN YOU ALWAYS BELIEVE YOUR EYES?

No two people will see the same situation exactly the same way. In fact, the same person may view a situation differently on different occasions. For example, consider the following illustration:

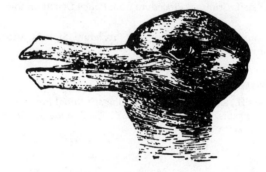

You may see a duck, a rabbit, or both. The same will be true of other people.

Several factors account for how people perceive objects and situations. *Context* is one important factor. For example, how would you interpret the following: 13

Now how do you interpret it? A 13 C

Another important factor affecting perception is how much attention the person is paying. For example, do you remember what the last person you saw today was wearing?

Other obvious influences are physical, for example, the acuity of the person's vision, the lighting, the distance.

Optical illusions such as those that follow show how you and others may see things differently depending on you perspective. Can you always believe your eyes?—See for yourself.

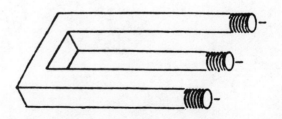

WHERE DID THE MIDDLE PEG COME FROM?

WHICH MAN IS THE TALLEST?

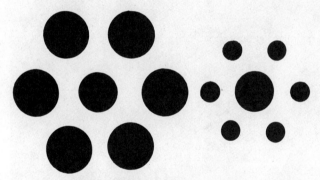

WHICH CENTER CIRCLE IS LARGER?

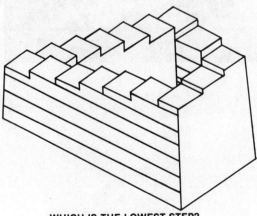

WHICH IS THE LOWEST STEP?

CHAPTER 10

The Laws

of Evidence

I come from a State that raises corn and cotton and cockleburs and Democrats, and frothy eloquence neither convinces nor satisfies me. I am from Missouri. You have got to show me.—Willard D. Vandiver, 1899

DO YOU KNOW

What evidence is?

What the law of evidence is?

What the most common type of evidence is?

What syndrome evidence is?

What the exclusionary rule is? What precedent cases are important at the federal and state levels?

What purpose the exclusionary rule is intended to serve?

What "fruit of the poisonous tree" refers to?

What hearsay evidence is and what exceptions exist to the hearsay rule?

What exceptions are made to the exclusionary rule?

In what sequence evidence for each side is presented at a trial?

Introduction

Chapter 10

Throughout this text you have been learning the rules of criminal procedure. You may be surprised at the complexity of the laws you are expected to understand and work with as a law enforcement professional.

The days of an individual just strapping on a gun and going to work are over. *Professionalism* and *law enforcement* are at last considered to co-exist. Education is an integral part of this professionalism. A word of encouragement is needed here, however. While you may feel as though the preparatory requirements for becoming a police officer are never-ending, the vast majority of students accomplish this phase of the process. They find that the solid educational base they have acquired not only brings them more enjoyment from their chosen career, but also makes them truly professionals.

In abridging the numerous reasons for learning all the rules, the bottom line is that officers need to know how to identify and gather the necessary evidence properly in order to have the court accept it. Simply obtaining evidence does not assure that a jury will ever get to actually examine it or consider its relevance.

Evidence is anything that helps to prove or disprove the truth of the point at issue. The law of evidence is the body of rules that regulates the admission of proof in court.

Studying evidentiary law can become complex because, in a sense, it covers the *entire* law of criminal procedure. This is so because the end purpose for having rules of criminal procedures is to determine what evidence the court decides is both fair and just.

The reason for the complexity of evidence law is that it seeks to achieve the extremely delicate balance reflected in the scales of justice. The police and the victim would like to see all evidence admitted used to convict the person *they* see as guilty. The accused wants to be certain that the evidence that may be used to send him/her to prison was obtained fairly, justly, and *legally*. Here is one point where the tension in our legal system is apparent. Should ALL evidence be admissible? Or only that determined to be reliable? How reliable? Should evidence that is very reliable still be admitted even if illegally obtained?

VIEWS OF THE LAW

To the uninformed, the law of evidence appears to be most unworkable, torn with loopholes that work against all but the guilty. A German proverb states: "There is no law without a loophole for him who can find it." The law has been likened to webs:

"Blind justice" exemplifies our American legal system. While seemingly complex, the rules of criminal procedure seek to balance only the information that will produce a fair result by including relevant facts and excluding irrelevant, prejudicial, or illegally obtained material.

> *Laws are spiders' webs, which stand firm when any light and yielding object falls upon them, while a larger thing breaks through them and escapes.*—Solon, sec. 14

> *Laws like to cobwebs, catch small flies, great ones break them before your eyes.*—Benjamin Franklin, Poor Richard, (1706–1790) 1734

The law has also been likened to firmer nets, but with the same outcome:

> Laws are generally found to be nets of such a texture, as the little
> creep through, the great break through, and the middle-sized alone are
> entangled in.—William Shenstone, On Politics (1714—1763)

> The net of law is spread so wide,
> No sinner from its sweep may hide.
> Its meshes are so fine and strong,
> They take in every child of wrong.
> O wondrous web of mystery!
> Big fish alone escape from thee!

Although each of the preceding has a somewhat different perspective on who is able to escape the law, each suggests that the law is imperfect, that many do escape it. Often they escape because evidence against them is not admitted into the trial. Perhaps nowhere else is the push and pull of the adversary system more evident than in this area of our law. Yet, as aptly stated by William Blackstone, (1723–1780) "It is better that ten guilty persons escape than one innocent suffer" (Commentaries on the Laws of England).

EXCLUDED EVIDENCE

Sloppy police work or inadequate knowledge of the legal rules all too frequently results in judges sustaining defense objections based on a variety of grounds. Whatever the grounds, the result is usually the same: evidence is excluded. Whether it was one crucial piece of evidence (e.g., the murder weapon or the body of the murder victim) or a series of less dramatic, circumstantial evidence obtained by the investigating officer over months, perhaps years, it is always devastating to hear an evidentiary objection sustained.

The case of *Brewer* v. *Williams* (1977) illustrates what can result from improper police investigation. This case is well known in the legal profession as the "Christian Burial Speech" case. In this case a crucial admission from the suspect was excluded because it was obtained in violation of the defendant's constitutional rights. The case began on Christmas Eve of 1968 when 10-year-old Pamela Powers disappeared while visiting a YMCA with her family in Des Moines, Iowa. Shortly after she was reported missing, a 14-year-old boy reported having been asked by a YMCA resident to hold several doors open for him while the man loaded a bundle from the building into a car. Within the bundle the boy reported seeing two "skinny and white" legs.

An arrest warrant was subsequently issued for Robert Williams, a resident at the YMCA and an escapee from a mental hospital. Williams eventually turned himself in to police in Davenport, Iowa. An agreement was reached with Williams' lawyer that the defendant would be returned by police to Des Moines.

All agreed that Williams would not be interrogated in any way during the 160-mile trip. However during the drive, knowing that

Williams was a mental patient and that he possessed a strong religious faith, one officer said the following to Williams. (In subsequent legal proceedings this became known as the "Christian Burial Speech.")

> *I want to give you something to think about while we're travelling down the road. . . . Number one, I want you to observe the weather-conditions, it's raining, it's sleeting, it's freezing, driving is very treacherous, visibility is poor, it's going to be dark early this evening. They are predicting several inches of snow for tonight, and I feel that you yourself are the only person that knows where this little girl's body is, that you yourself have only been there once, and if you get a snow on top of it you yourself may be unable to find it. And since we will be going right past the area on the way to Des Moines, I feel that we could stop and locate the body, that the parents of this little girl should be entitled to a Christian burial for the little girl who was snatched away from them on Christmas Eve and murdered. And I feel we should stop and locate it on the way rather than waiting until morning and trying to come back out after a snow storm and possibly not being able to find it at all.*

The detective told Williams that he did not want an answer, but that he just wanted Williams to think about it as they drove. Williams eventually directed the officers to the little girl's body.

While the lower courts admitted Williams's damaging statements into evidence, the United States Supreme Court affirmed the Court of Appeals' decision that any statements made by Williams could not be admitted against him because the way they were elicited violated his constitutional rights. Specifically, Williams was unconstitutionally deprived of his right to counsel. The Court said:

> *The pressures on state executive and judicial officers charged with the administration of the criminal law are great, especially when the crime is murder and the victim a small child. But it is precisely the predictability of those pressures that makes imperative a resolute loyalty to the guarantees that the Constitution extends to us all.*

The dramatic and devastating effect of disallowed evidence is painfully clear from this particular case. Law libraries across our nation are filled with many other examples of why it is critical that police officers understand the law of evidence. (Note: Williams was eventually found guilty, with the evidence being admitted for reasons to be discussed shortly.)

EVIDENCE DEFINED

To begin the study of this important area of criminal procedure, consider the following definition of evidence (Ballentine, 1969, p. 424):

> *The means by which any matter of fact, the truth of which is submitted to investigation, may be established or disproved. That which*

demonstrates, makes clear, or ascertains the truth of the very fact or point in issue, either on the one side or the other (Lynch v Rosenberger).

Oran (1985, pp. 114–15) offers a narrower definition of evidence:

All types of information (observations, recollections, documents, concrete objects, etc.) presented at a trial or other hearing.

KINDS OF EVIDENCE

Evidence can be classified in several different ways. One common classification is that of *physical* or *informational*. Physical evidence is anything that is real—can be seen, touched, smelled, or tasted—and helps establish the facts of a case. In fact, physical evidence is sometimes called "real evidence." Informational evidence, as the name implies, is any statement provided by victims, witnesses, and suspects.

Evidence can also be classified according to whether it is *corpus delicti evidence* or *associate evidence*. Corpus delicti evidence establishes that a crime has been committed; associative evidence links a suspect with a crime.

The most common form of evidence is testimony of a witness based on personal knowledge.

Another type of evidence is *demonstrative evidence*. According to Graham (1983, p. 426): "Demonstrative evidence, including such items as a model, map, chart, or demonstration, is distinguished from real evidence in that it has no probative value itself, but serves merely as a visual aid to the jury in comprehending the verbal testimony of a witness or other evidence." Graham also notes that "under prescribed circumstances, the result of an experiment may be admissible, or it may be proper to transport the trier of facts from the courtroom to conduct a view of real property or of an item that took part in the incident forming the subject of the litigation."

Still another type of evidence is *syndrome evidence. Syndrome evidence has been receiving more attention and acceptance recently.*

Syndrome evidence consists of facts presented by expert testimony that indicate existence of a specific condition, e.g., child abuse.

Just as a group of specific physical symptoms may suggest a specific disease to a physician, a group of specific behaviors may indicate a specific disorder to a judge and jury.

Syndrome evidence usually relates to a person's character and how that person might be expected to act. Common types of syndromes introduced in court include the battered-child syndrome (child abuse), the battering-parent syndrome, the battered-woman syndrome, familial–child sex-abuse syndrome, and posttraumatic stress syndrome (e.g., cases involving Vietnam veterans).

Each syndrome has clearly specified elements that need to be established. In the case of the battered-child syndrome, for example, three elements must be proven (Frase, 1985, p. 254):

Don't worry about

1. The child's injuries are of a type not associated with accidents.
2. The adult in custody cannot adequately explain the injuries.
3. There is more than one instance of nonaccidental harm or a pattern of abuse.

Each of the other syndromes have specific elements that must be proven. According to Frase (1985, pp. 252–53), syndrome evidence must meet four requirements:

First, the expert testimony on the syndrome must be helpful to the jury. Second the expert testifying about the syndrome must be qualified to do so. Third, the expert's findings must be scientifically accurate and reliable, as determined under the applicable standard. Finally, the probative value of the syndrome evidence must not be substantially outweighed by its potential prejudicial effect.

Evidence may take on a seemingly infinite variety of forms. Every case, whether civil or criminal, is built upon the evidence admitted into court in which a judge or jury will decide the final outcome. Because of this, evidence is clearly one of the most important aspects of the law.

Among the variety of duties of today's law enforcement professionals, investigating cases remains an important responsibility. According to Bennett and Hess (1987, p. 5): "A criminal investigation seeks all facts associated with a crime to determine the truth, what happened, and who is responsible."

DEALING WITH PHYSICAL EVIDENCE

Commonly found physical evidence includes fingerprints, palm prints, shoe and tire impressions, tools and toolmarks, weapons and ammunition, glass, soil, hairs and fibers, body fluids including blood, documents, safe insulation, rope and tape, drugs, explosives, and laundry marks.

Any physical evidence that is discovered during an investigation must be properly collected, marked, packaged, and stored until the trial.

The processing of a major crime scene is a complex task most often left to trained investigators. A simple error could ruin hours of police work. Here the scene of a sniper attack is investigated.

Collecting Physical Evidence

As noted by Bennett and Hess (1987, p. 36):

Collecting evidence requires judgment and care. Put liquids in bottles. Protect cartridges and spent bullets with cotton and put them in small

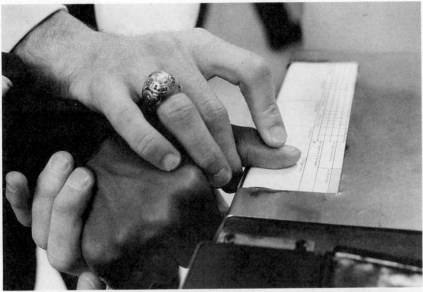

Permanent fingerprint files maintained by state agencies and the FBI provide an effective resource for law enforcement agencies nationwide. Computerization of these files has greatly simplified the process of matching suspect prints with those on file.

containers. Put other items in appropriate containers to preserve them for later packaging and transportation. . . .

To simplify testimony in court, one officer usually collects evidence. Another officer takes notes on the location, description, and condition of each item. The officer collecting evidence enters this information in personal notes or witnesses and initials the notes of the officer assigned to record information.

All evidence is identified by the officer who collects it and by any other officer who takes initial custody of it.

The most common errors in collecting evidence are not taking enough of a specific sample, not getting a standard of comparison, and not maintaining the integrity of the evidence. In any of these areas a defense attorney may seek to point out any possibility of "reasonable doubt."

A standard of comparison is a measure, model, or object to which evidence is compared to see if both came from the same source. For example, insulation from a safe that was broken into may be collected and later compared with safe insulation found in the cuff of a suspect's pants. The most common example of standards of comparison are fingerprints. Fingerprints by themselves are worthless without another set to compare them with.

Many departments have specially trained evidence technicians. Many others rely on crime laboratories from larger agencies.

To document the necessary chain of custody, physical evidence must be properly marked, preserved, and secured by the police. Any possible tampering with the evidence could cast doubt on its authenticity, preventing it from being admitted into trial.

Marking Physical Evidence

Evidence should be marked using a personal, easily recognized identification that is as small as possible. Care must be taken not to alter, change, or destroy the evidence. Where and how to mark the

items depend on what the evidence is. Common sense usually determines what can be directly marked with a pen or stylus and what
should be tagged.

Packaging Physical Evidence

Careful packaging is required to maintain the evidence in its
original state. Each item should be packaged separately to maintain the
integrity of that evidence. If evidence is not packaged separately, it is
said to be contaminated. Table 10–1 at the end of this chapter
summarizes how to package the most common types of evidence for
submittal to the laboratory.

Storing Physical Evidence

According to Bennett and Hess (1987, p. 174):

*Evidence is stored in vaults, property rooms, evidence rooms, evidence
lockers, garages, morgues, or under special conditions such as refriger-
ation. At the crime scene, the officer's vehicle trunk can provide temporary storage.*

*A proper storage area has ample space and is kept at 60 to 80 de-
grees Fahrenheit. A responsible person is in charge to ensure that established procedures are followed and that the area is secure at all
times.*

*All evidence received is recorded in a register, properly marked,
and put in the appropriate place. An evidence custodian checks each
piece of evidence received to ensure that all forms are properly completed and that the evidence is the same as described in the forms.*

The Chain of Custody

Custody of all physical evidence must be documented. The name
of any person having possession of the evidence, from the time it is
found and collected to the time it is presented in court, must be
recorded. Strict check-out procedures help assure that the chain of
custody is not questioned at trial. An evidence form such as that shown
in figure 10-1 can be used.

This is also referred to as maintaining the *continuity* of the
evidence. This provides the necessary proof that the evidence has not
been tampered with and is, in fact, the *same* evidence.

Beyond Collecting, Marking, Packaging, and Storing

It is important to understand that your purpose is primarily
centered on learning the *law* of evidence rather than the "how to" of
collecting and perserving it. While *how* evidence is physically obtained

CITY	EVIDENCE		POLICE DEPT.
DATE		DR. NUMBER	
SUSPECT			JUV ☐ ADULT ☐
CHARGE			
LOCATION			
BOOKED BY (FINDING OFFICER'S SIGNATURE)		DATE AND TIME	
INITIALS & P. NUMBER OF BOOKING OFFICER			

ARTICLES BOOKED

ITEM		ITEM NO.
ITEM		ITEM NO.
ITEM		ITEM NO.

INITIALS USED ON ITEMS BOOKED	THIS PACKAGE NO.	TOTAL NO. PACKAGES
CO-DEFENDANT		JUV ☐ ADULT ☐
CO-DEFENDANT		JUV ☐ ADULT ☐

CHAIN OF CUSTODY

SIGNATURE	DATE	TIME
SIGNATURE	DATE	TIME
SIGNATURE	DATE	TIME
SIGNATURE	DATE	TIME
SIGNATURE	DATE	TIME
SIGNATURE	DATE	TIME

Figure 10–1   Sample Evidence Form

does play an important role in its admissibility, the actual skills of such procedures as lifting fingerprints, obtaining tool impressions, or taking photographs are better left to other specialized texts.

THE EXCLUSIONARY RULE

While volumes have been written on the technicalities of rules of evidence for lawyers, little has been provided for working police officers. Perhaps the most important of the evidentiary rules pertaining to the law enforcement profession is the *exclusionary rule*. This rule was discussed briefly in the chapter on search and seizure. The following, more detailed discussion includes the rule itself, its history, the underlying rationale, how it has been applied, exceptions to the rule, and the current controversy over the rule.

Introduction to the Rule

Whitebread and Slobogin (1986, p. 16) state that

The exclusionary evidence rule is the result of an effort on the part of the judiciary to ensure that constitutional limitations on law enforcement are safeguarded. Simply stated, the rule prohibits the use of evidence or testimony obtained by government officials through means violative of the Fourth, Fifth, or Sixth Amendments. The rationale for the rule is that government officials, and in particular, the police, will be deterred from using illegal means to obtain evidence if such evidence may not be employed to support a conviction. A further rationale for the rule . . . is found in the sentiment that the judiciary should not be a partner to or otherwise sanction the lawlessness of a coordinate branch of government.

According to Frase (1985, p. 1):

Most motions to exclude evidence in criminal cases are based on alleged violations of the United States Constitution, particularly the fourth amendment (unreasonable searches and seizures), fifth amendment (privilege against compelled self-incrimination), or sixth amendment (right to counsel and right of confrontation). It is also possible to argue that the use of particular evidence would violate due process rights, even if it does not violate a particular provision of the bill of rights. Thus, conduct which "shocks the conscience" of the court may be excluded (Rochin v. California [1952]), and any evidence— particularly confessions or identification testimony—may be excluded if it is found to be unreliable (Stovall v. Denno [1967]).

History of the Rule

The beginnings of the exclusionary rule can be found in 1886 in *Boyd v. United States.* In this case the United States Supreme Court held that forcing disclosure of papers amounting to evidence of a crime violated the suspect's constitutional rights. The Court held that the Fourth Amendment applied "to all invasions on the part of the government and its employees of the sanctity of a man's home and the privacies of life. It is not the breaking of his doors, and the rummaging of his drawers, that constitutes the essense of the offense; but it is the invasion of his indefensible right of personal security, personal liberty and private property." This was a precursor to the landmark case that established the exclusionary rule, *Weeks v. United States* (1914).

Weeks v. United States *established the exclusionary rule at the federal level.*

In *Weeks* v. *United States*, the Court stated:

> *If letters and private documents can thus be seized [unconstitution-*
> *ally] and held and used in evidence against a citizen accused of an*
> *offense, the protection of the Fourth Amendment declaring his right to*
> *be secure against such searches and seizures is of no value, and, so far*
> *as those thus placed are concerned, might as well be stricken from the*
> *Constitution. The efforts of the courts and their officials to bring the*
> *guilty to punishment, praiseworthy as they are, are not to be aided by*
> *the sacrifice of those great principles established by years of endeavor*
> *and suffering which have resulted in their embodiment in the funda-*
> *mental law of the land.*

The Bill of Rights, remember, was written to limit the power of the federal government, so initially the exclusionary rule did not apply to the states. As a result, evidence that was illegally obtained at the state level was often admitted at the federal level—figuratively, handed to the federal prosecutor "on a silver platter."

When the Fourteenth Amendment was passed, however, forbidding states to "deprive any person of life, liberty, or property, without due process of law," the question arose whether the exclusionary rule should be applied at the state level. *Wolf* v. *Colorado* (1949) established that the exclusionary rule was not applicable at the state level. This precedent was followed for over a decade. Some evidence was excluded for other reasons, however. For example, in *Rochin* v. *California* (1952) police administered an emetic by force to make a suspect vomit drugs he had swallowed. The court disallowed the evidence saying that it was obtained by "conduct that shocks the conscience."

Another case disregarding the *Wolf* precedent was *Ellkins* v. *United States* (1960), which disallowed the admission of evidence illegally obtained by state officials into federal trials (the silver platter doctrine).

In 1961, the *Wolf* precedent was reversed in *Mapp* v. *Ohio*.

Mapp v. Ohio *made the exclusionary rule applicable at the state level.*

The Supreme Court, overruling *Wolf*, held that "all evidence obtained by searches and seizures in violation of the Constitution, is, by that same authority, inadmissible in a state court." The Court gave the following reasons:

> *Since the Fourth Amendment's right of privacy has been declared en-*
> *forceable against the States through the Due Process Clause of the*
> *Fourteenth, it is enforceable against them by the same sanction of ex-*
> *clusion as is used against the Federal Government. Were it otherwise*
> *then just as without the Weeks rule the assurance against unreason-*

able federal searches and seizures would be "a form of words," value-less and undeserving of mention in a perpetual charter of inestimable human liberties, so too, without that rule the freedom from state invasions of privacy would be so ephemeral and so neatly severed from its conceptual nexus with the freedom from all brutish means of coercing evidence as not to merit this Court's high regard as a freedom "implicit in the concept of ordered liberty."

Underlying Rationale of the Exclusionary Rule

del Carmen (1987, p. 53) asserts that "The exclusionary rule has rested primarily on the judgment that the importance of deterring police conduct that may violate the constitutional rights of individuals throughout the community outweighs the importance of securing the conviction of the specific defendant on trial *(United States v. Caceres* 1979)."

The purpose of the exclusionary rule is to deter police from obtaining evidence illegally and to make it clear that the court will not tolerate such illegality. This is sometimes referred to as the "judicial integrity" rationale (Mapp v. Ohio [1962]). Deterring police from obtaining evidence illegally is seen as one means to help protect specific constitutional rights.

As noted by LaFave and Israel (1985, p. 80):

The deterrence of unreasonable searches and seizures is a major purpose of the exclusionary rule. This was acknowledged by the Court in Wolf ("the exclusion of evidence may be an effective way of deterring unreasonable searches"), Eikins ("Its purpose is to deter—to compel respect for the constitutional guarantee in the only effectively available way—by removing the incentive to disregard it"), and Mapp (rule a "deterrent safeguard without insistence upon which the Fourth Amendment would have been reduced to 'a form of words' "). Later, in Linkletter v. Walker, 1965, the rule was characterized as "an effective deterrent to illegal police action," while in Terry v. Ohio the Court stressed that the rule's "major thrust is a deterrent one." But the rule serves other purposes as well. There is, for example, what the Elkins Court referred to as "the imperative of judicial integrity," namely, that the courts not become "accomplices in the willful disobedience of a Constitution they are sworn to uphold." This language was later relied upon in Mapp and Terry. A third purpose of the exclusionary rule, as recently stated most clearly by some members of the Court, is that "of assuring the people—all potential victims of unlawful government conduct—that the government would not profit from its lawless behavior, thus minimizing the risk of seriously undermining popular trust in government" (United States v. Calandra, 1974).

The primary purpose underlying the exclusionary rule is deterring police misconduct.

The exclusionary rule is not statutory law, but is a judge-made rule of evidence, as noted in *United States* v. *Leon* (1984):

> *The Fourth Amendment contains no provision expressly precluding the use of evidence obtained in violation of its commands. . . . This rule thus operates as a judicially created remedy designed to safeguard Fourth Amendment rights generally through its deterrent effect, rather than a personal constitutional right of the person aggrieved.*

Applications of the Rule

The Supreme Court has held that constitutional guarantees apply to state or federal action, not action by private citizens. In other words, if a private citizen comes by evidence illegally, for example, breaking into someone's home or car to obtain the evidence, the evidence can be used in court. This does not hold true, however, if the citizen was acting under the direction or encouragement of the police, that is, as the agent of the police. An inference can be made to the cases which have steadfastly held that private citizens, including private security officers, need not read a person their Miranda rights before questioning. To date, the courts have been unwilling to extend the exclusionary rule to private citizens. It is reasonable, however, to anticipate a judicial extension of the exclusionary rule to private security if the private sector abuses this privilege.

Fruit of the Poisonous Tree

The exclusionary rule may affect not only specific evidence that was illegally obtained, but will also extend well beyond that, involving any other evidence obtained as a result of the originally illegally obtained evidence. Such evidence is referred to as *fruit of the poisonous tree.*

The precedent case for this extension of the exclusionary rule is *Silverthorne Lumber Co.* v. *United States* (1920). In this case a United States Marshal unlawfully entered and searched the Silverthorne Lumber Company's offices and illegally took some books and documents. When the company demanded their return, the government did so, but not before making copies of the documents. These copies were later impounded by the district court and became the basis for a grand jury indictment. A subpoena was then served on the company to produce the originals. When the company refused, it was convicted of contempt of court. The Supreme Court, however, reversed the conviction saying that: "[T]he essence of a provision forbidding the acquisition of evidence in a certain way is that not merely evidence so acquired shall not be used before the Court but that it shall not be used at all. In other words, once the primary source (the "tree") is proven to have been obtained unlawfully, any secondary evidence derived from it (the "fruit") is also inadmissible.

The doctrine of fruit of the poisonous tree states that evidence obtained as a result of an earlier illegality must be excluded from trial.

This extension of the exclusionary rule is based on the same rationale as the exclusionary rule, that is, to deter illegal police activity and to preserve the integrity of the court.

The Supreme Court has ruled, however, that the doctrine does not apply in civil deportation proceedings or in grand jury proceedings. In *United States v. Calandra* (1974) the Court ruled that "fruits of illegally seized evidence" can be used as a basis for questions to a witness before a grand jury. In addition, some lower courts have allowed such evidence to be used in sentencing and in probation or parole revocation hearings.

Exceptions to the Rule

The exclusionary rule applies only in cases where a constitutional right has been violated.

Important exceptions to the exclusionary rule exist.

Valid Independent Source   If similar evidence is obtained from a valid, independent source, that evidence can be admitted. Whitebread and Slobogin (1986, p. 37) explain that "[I]n *Segura v. United States*, the Court held that while evidence discovered as a direct result of an illegal entry into an apartment must be excluded, evidence subsequently found in the apartment pursuant to a valid search warrant is admissible if the warrant is based on information wholly unconnected with the initial entry and known to the police before their entry."

The "Inevitable Discovery" Doctrine   This exception was established in *Nix v. Williams* (1984), the case referred to earlier, where Detective Nix's well-known "Christian Burial Speech" caused Williams to disclose where he had hidden his victim's body. The rationale underlying the exception was that the body would "inevitably" have been discovered anyway, even without Williams's assistance. This has also been called the "hypothetical independent source" exception because, given time, an independent source would emerge with the same evidence. In the *Nix* case, the Supreme Court upheld Williams's conviction

What frequently occurs in judicial interpretation is that the court may not want the result that will occur if a direct, literal interpretation of a law is used. Therefore, rationales are stretched (sometimes to their breaking point) so as to permit the finding the court wants. In this instance the Supreme Court appears to be "chipping away" at the exclusionary rule, and the pendulum seems to be swinging, although slowly, toward favoring the prosecution.

Attenuation   The word *attenuate* means "to make thin." Sometimes the link between the original illegal evidence and the related evidence is so weak that the evidence is allowed in court. As noted by Whitebread and Slobogin (1986, p. 38), "[T]he weaker the link between the initial unlawful conduct and the subsequent lawful discovery of evidence that results from the initial conduct, the less likely the poisonous tree doctrine will be invoked." Attenuation is illustrated in *Wong Sun v. United States* (1963), described by Frase (1985, p. 7):

> Agents illegally searched Toy's laundry and obtained statements incriminating one Yee. A search of Yee uncovered heroin and further incriminating statements by Yee against Toy and a third man, Wong Sun, who was then arrested and released on recognizance. Several days later, Wong Sun made an unsigned confession after returning voluntarily to discuss the case with an agent. As to Toy, both his statements and the narcotics seized from Yee were held suppressible as direct fruits of the illegal search of Toy's laundry; but the connection between Wong Sun's confession and his prior illegal arrest was considered to be sufficiently attenuated given the break in custody.

Attenuation is also referred to as the "purged taint" exception if the "fruit of the poisonous tree" doctrine is involved as it was in *Wong Sun v. United States*. According to del Carmen (1987, p. 57): "Purged *taint* refers specifically to the 'fruit of the poisonous tree' doctrine and applies when the defendant's subsequent voluntary act dissipates the taint of the initial illegality. A defendant's intervening act of free will is sufficient to break the causal chain between the tainted evidence and the illegal police conduct; hence the evidence becomes admissible."

Harmless Error   The harmless error exception refers to instances where the preponderance of evidence suggests the defendant's guilt and the "tainted" or illegal evidence is not critical to proving the case against the defendant. In *Harrington v. California* (1969) the Court ruled that the evidence should be examined as a whole, and that if overwhelming untainted evidence supported the conviction, or if the error involved an element of the crime that was well established, then the error would be considered "harmless."

Good Faith   The good-faith exception involves instances where police officers are not aware that they are violating Fourth Amendment principles. In such instances, note Whitebread and Slobogin (1986, p. 24): "[T]he exclusionary rule can have no deterrent effect and therefore, in light of the 'enormous cost' associated with exclusion, should not operate to exclude evidence at trial."

This same reasoning was put forth by Justice White in a dissenting opinion in *Stone v. Powell* (1976), as he argued that the exclusionary rule should not disqualify evidence *seized by an officer acting in the good-faith belief that his conduct comported with existing law and having reasonable grounds for his belief. . . . for it is painfully apparent that in each of them [situations] the officer is acting as a reasonable officer would and should act in similar circumstances. Excluding the evidence can in no way affect his future conduct unless it is to make him less willing to do his duty.*

The good-faith exception often comes into play when officers are executing arrest or search warrants. If such warrants are later found to be invalid, the evidence obtained while executing the warrants is still admissible because the officers were acting in "good faith." Two important cases are significant here: *Sheppard* and *Leon*.

In *Massachusetts* v. *Sheppard* (1984) police sought a search warrant on a Sunday. The detective could not find the appropriate form and instead, took a warrant form used previously to search for controlled substances. The detective made some needed changes in the form and presented it to the magistrate, warning him that some other changes in the form might be necessary. The magistrate believed probable cause had been established and granted the warrant, assuring the detective that all changes needed in the form would be made. Although the judge made some changes, he did not make all the needed changes. The evidence seized during the search authorized by the warrant was ruled to be admissible because the detective had acted on the reasonable belief that the warrant was valid, even though it was later found to be invalid.

Another case decided on the same day, *United States* v. *Leon* (1984), established that "[i]n the ordinary case, an officer cannot be expected to question the magistrate's probable cause determination or his judgement that the form of the warrant is technically sufficient." In this case a search warrant was issued based on information from an informant. It was later determined that the reliability of the informant had not been established and that the information was old ("stale"); therefore, there was no probable cause and the warrant was invalid. The trial court excluded the evidence, and the decision was affirmed by the Court of Appeals. The government then sent the case to the Supreme Court, asking that it look at the case in terms of the good-faith exception. The Supreme Court overturned the decision saying "The exclusionary rule is designed to deter police misconduct rather than to punish the errors of judges and magistrates."

Standing to Raise Exclusionary Rule

An interesting exception to the exclusionary rule is that defendants cannot ask to have excluded evidence that was obtained through the violation of the constitutional rights of someone other than themselves. If, for example, Defendant A is interrogated without having been given the *Miranda* warning, and even if force is used against Defendant A during such an interrogation, if Defendant A provides information that incriminates Defendant B, the evidence is admissible in the case against Defendant B but cannot be used in the case against Defendant A.

The trend is to expand the exclusionary rule to individuals not previously permitted to take advantage of this doctrine. Courts are showing a tendency to recognize the standing of individuals who did not have their own constitutional rights directly violated, but who were affected by someone else's rights being violated. This is an area of the law that is experiencing change.

EXCULSIONARY RULE

A judge-made doctrine to enforce constitutional requirements of search and seizure:

IF search/seizure violates suspect's constitutional rights,

THEN the resulting evidence may not be admitted into court against that suspect,

NOR can any evidence resulting indirectly from the unconstitutional search/seizure (Fruit of the Poisonous Tree)

UNLESS the evidence would inevitably have been discovered through lawful means

OR the Good Faith exception allowed an error by police.

Controversy regarding the Exclusionary Rule

As noted by Frase (1985, p. 3):

The application of these exclusionary rules has always been controversial. Particularly in the fourth amendment context, where the evidence itself is almost always highly reliable, the exclusion of the evidence appears to give clearly guilty persons an undeserved windfall with no guarantee that the exclusion will deter future illegalities. Similar dissatisfaction is felt with the deterrent purposes of exclusions under the Miranda and Wade-Gilbert rules. . . . These dissatisfactions have led to considerable pressure to limit the applicability of these exclusionary rules and to promote alternative remedies to prevent or redress constitutional violations.

LaFave and Israel (1985, p. 81) caution that "The exclusionary rule is like capital punishment in that it is easy to see when the deterrent effect has failed but not when it has succeeded." They go on to cite evidence suggesting that the rule does have a deterrent efffect:

That the suppression doctrine has had a deterrent effect is nonetheless suggested by various post-exclusionary rule events, such as the dra-

matic increase in use of search warrants where nearly none were used before, stepped up efforts to educate police on Fourth Amentment law where such training had before been virtually nonexistent, and creation and development of working relationships between police and prosecutors.

Arguments for the Rule

Several arguments supporting the exclusionary rule are outlined by del Carmen (1985, pp. 62–63):

1. It definitely deters violations of constitutional rights by police and prosecutor. A number of studies and testimonies by police officers support this contention.

2. It manifests society's refusal to convict lawbreakers by relying on official lawlessness, a clear demonstration of our commitment to the rule of law that states that no person, not even a law enforcement official, is above and beyond the law.

3. It results in the freeing of the guilty in a relatively small proportion of cases. A 1978 study by the General Auditing Office found that of 2,804 cases in which defendants were likely to file a motion to suppress evidence, exclusion succeeded in only 1.3 percent. Moreover, the same study reported that of the cases presented to federal prosecutors for prosecution, only 0.4 percent were declined by the prosecutors because of Fourth Amendment search-and-seizure problems.

4. It has led to more professionalism among the police and increased attention to training programs. Fear of exclusion of evidence has forced the police to develop greater expertise in their work.

5. It preserves the integrity of the judicial system. The admission of illegally seized evidence makes the court a party to violations of constitutional rights.

6. It prevents the government, whose agents have violated the Constitution, from profiting from its wrongdoing. Somebody has to pay for the mistake. Let the government absorb it, not the suspect who has already been wronged.

Arguments against the Exclusionary Rule

Opponents of the rule claim that it "handcuffs" the police. Other opponents say that it doesn't really deter police misconduct. Opponents further contend that the rule helps guilty individuals remain unpunished. As noted by del Carmen (1987, p. 63):

Opponents, including justices in the Supreme Court, have argued strongly in rejection of the exclusionary rule. Among their arguments are these:

1. The criminal goes free because the constable has blundered. It is wrong to make society pay for an officer's mistake. Punish the officer, not society.

2. It excludes the most credible, probative kinds of evidence—fingerprints, guns, narcotics, or dead bodies—and thereby impedes the truth-finding function of the courts.

3. It discourages internal disciplinary efforts by law enforcement agencies. Why discipline when the evidence will be excluded anyway? The police would suffer a double setback.

4. It encourages perjury by the police in an effort to admit the evidence, particularly in major cases, in which the police might feel that the end justifies the means. It is better to lie than to let a presumably guilty person go free.

5. It diminishes respect for the judicial process and generates disrespect for the law and the administration of justice.

6. There is no proof that the exclusionary rule deters police misconduct. In the words of former Chief Justice Berger: "There is no empirical evidence to support the claim that the rule actually deters illegal conduct of law enforcement officials."

7. Only the United States uses the exclusionary rule. No other civilized country does.

8. It has no effect on those large areas of police activity that do not result in criminal prosecutions. If the police make an arrest or search without any thought of subsequent prosecution (such as when they simply want to remove a person from the streets overnight or when they confiscate contraband so as to eliminate the supply), they do not have to worry about the exclusionary rule because that is effective only if the case gets to trial and the evidence is used.

OTHER TYPES OF EXCLUDED EVIDENCE

Sometimes evidence is excluded because of other reasons, notably, because the evidence is hearsay or because it involves a privileged communication.

The Hearsay Rule

Hearsay evidence is defined by Oran (1985, p. 142) as

Secondhand evidence. Facts not in the personal knowledge of the witness, but a repetition of what others said, that are used to prove the truth of what those others said. Oral or written evidence that depends on the believability of something or someone not available in court.

Hearsay evidence is a statement heard by someone else repeated by a witness during a trial.

One important reason hearsay evidence is not admissible is that there is no opportunity to cross-examine the person who made the original statement. Hearsay evidence is not admissible in a trial unless it fits specific exceptions. As noted by del Carmen (1987, pp. 337–43):

Exceptions to the hearsay rule include (1) confessions and admissions, (2) dying declarations, (3) spontaneous declarations, (4) previously recorded testimony, (5) past recollection recorded, (6) business records, and (7) official records.

Confessions and Admissions   These are hearsay because they are statements made by someone not on the witness stand and not available for cross-examination. They are an important exception to the hearsay rule because people do not readily make confessions and admissions. If they do so, they are probably telling the truth. The confession or admission must be made voluntarily or it is not admissible.

Dying Declarations   As the name implies, these are statements made by someone who is dying. To be admissible, the hearsay evidence must meet four criteria (del Carmen, 1987, p. 338): (1) The victim must have given up hope of surviving. (2) The declaration must concern the cause of death. (3) It must also be based on the victim's personal knowledge. Opinions are not admissible. (4) The victim must be dead. If the victim does survive, then live testimony rather than the dying declaration is required.

Spontaneous Declarations   Spontaneous declarations are made as the direct result of some exciting or shocking event. They are made immediately, without time for thought or reflection. They are testified to by the person *hearing the statement*, not the person who made it, thus qualifying as hearsay evidence. Spontaneous declarations, also called *res gestae statements,* are exceptions because they are very likely to be true. Spontaneous declarations must meet three requirements (del Carmen, 1987, p. 339): (1) A startling event must have occurred. (2) The declaration must be made contemporaneously. Time is critical. (3) The speaker must have personal knowledge of the acts observed.

Previously Recorded Testimony   Depositions or transcripts of statements made under oath at a hearing or trial can be admitted into evidence if there was a chance for cross-examination at the time the testimony was recorded, and if the person giving the testimony is not available for the current case.

Past Recollection Recorded   Sometimes a person does not remember having stated something, even after having been shown a record of it. If this happens, the record can be introduced as evidence. Five requirements must be met, however (del Carmen, 1987, p. 341): (1) The witness must have no present recollection of the facts in the record. (2) The record must have been made shortly after the event. (3) The recording must have been witnessed. (4) The witness must testify that the record was true when it was made. (5) The document must be authenticated as an accurate record of the statement.

This is the exception that allows police officers to actually read from their reports if they don't remember details in court—another reason for writing good reports.

Business Records and Other Official Records   These documents are generally considered to be accurate statements of fact and, therefore, are exceptions to the hearsay rule.

Privileged Communications

Don't worry about

A *privileged communication* is one that need not be told to anyone else, including a judge during a trial. Privileged communications are established by law and are necessary to protect specific individuals' "need to know" certain information. To obtain the needed information, confidentiality must be assured.

The most well-known privileged communication is probably that between lawyers and their clients. Our adversarial judicial system relies on defense attorneys having full disclosure by their clients of the facts in the case. The only way this is going to happen is if the client is certain the lawyer will not reveal what the client says. Only the client can allow the information to be released.

A second well-known type of privileged communication is between physicians and their patients. This includes psychiatrists because they are physicians. Some states also include psychologists, psychotherapists, and social workers in this category.

A third commonly accepted privileged communication is between the clergy and their parishioners.

Other privileged communications are not as clearly defined nor as firmly protected by the law. Among these are communications between journalists and their sources, between the state and its informants, and even between spouses.

It is of interest that in the past the spouse of a person on trial could not be called as a witness and could not testify against the spouse. Only adverse testimony is covered. The spouse can give testimony that would help the defendant. The privilege against "adverse spousal testimony" was claimed to exist to preserve the institution of marriage. In actuality, however, since the vast majority of defendants were male, it also served to protect men and to deny women the right to testify against their spouses if they so desired. In some states, the privilege may be claimed for events that occurred before the marriage. In effect, a person could marry someone who knew of his or her crime and make it impossible for that person to ever testify. This is changing.

In twenty-six states the witness spouse now holds the privilege; that is, the spouse of the defendant can testify. The accused spouse can no longer prohibit the testimony in these states. Twenty-four states, however, still grant the privilege to the accused spouse. Federal courts have asserted that the privilege against adverse spousal testimony is granted to the witness spouse. As stated in *Trammel v. U.S.* (1980):

> *The ancient foundations for so sweeping a privilege [that of adverse spousal testimony] have long since disappeared. Nowhere in the common-law world—indeed in any modern society—is a woman regarded as chattel or demeaned by denial of a separate legal identity and the dignity associated with recognition as a whole human being. Chip by chip, over the years those archaic notions have been cast aside so that "no longer is the female destined solely for the home and the rearing of the family, and only the male for the marketplace and the world of ideas."*

Before leaving the subject of evidence, a brief overview of how evidence is presented during the trial will round out the topic.

HOW EVIDENCE IS PRESENTED AT TRIAL

Evidence is presented in an established sequence during a trial. Usually the prosecution presents its case first. The first witness is questioned by the prosecution (called direct examination) and then questioned by the defense (called cross-examination). The prosecutor may again question this first witness (called redirect), and the defense attorney may do likewise (called re–cross-examination). Each prosecution witness is called and goes through this sequence. When all witnesses have been called, the prosecution "rests" and it is the defense's turn.

The defense attorney then calls its first witness for direct examination. The attorney will not only try to refute what the prosecution has claimed but will also begin to build a case for the defendant. After the first defense witness has undergone direct examination, it is the prosecution's opportunity for cross-examination. The sequence repeats itself just as during the prosecution's turn at presenting its evidence. When the defense has presented all its evidence, it "rests."

The sequence in presenting evidence for each side at a trial is (1) direct examination by the attorney who called the witness, (2) cross-examination by the opposing attorney, (3) redirect by the witness's attorney, and (4) re-cross by the opposing attorney.

At this point the prosecution has another chance to prove its case, called a rebuttal. As the name implies, however, the prosecution must confine itself to rebutting or refuting what the defense presented. At this stage, the same series of direct, cross-examination, redirect, and re–cross-examination can occur. When the prosecution is finished, it again "rests."

The "last word" is given by the defense in what is called a rejoinder if the prosecution presents evidence that the defense wants to refute.

In summary, the main stages of presenting evidence are as follows:

- The prosecution presents its evidence.
- The defense presents its evidence, including refuting the evidence presented by the prosecution.
- The prosecution refutes the defense's evidence (rebuttal).
- The defense refutes the prosecution's rebuttal (rejoinder).

After both sides have "rested," the counsels present their arguments and the court instructs the jury.

SUMMARY

Evidence is anything that helps to prove or disprove the truth of the point at issue. The law of evidence is the body of rules that regulates the admission of proof in court. The most common form of evidence is testimony of a witness based on personal knowledge.

Syndrome evidence consists of facts presented by expert testimony that indicate existence of a specific condition.

Weeks v. *United States* established the exclusionary rule at the federal level. *Mapp* v. *Ohio* made the exclusionary rule applicable at the state level. The primary purpose underlying the exclusionary rule is deterring police misconduct.

The doctrine of "fruit of the poisonous tree" states that evidence obtained as a result of an earlier illegality must be excluded from trial. Exceptions to the exclusionary rule include the following:

- Valid independent source *(Segura* v. *United States)*
- The "inevitable discovery" doctrine *(Nix* v. *Williams)*
- Attenuation *(Wong Sun* v. *United States)*
- Harmless error *(Harrington* v. *California)*
- Good Faith *(Stone* v. *Powell)*

Hearsay evidence is a statement heard by someone else and repeated by a witness during a trial. Hearsay evidence is generally not admissible. Exceptions to the hearsay rule include (1) confessions and admissions, (2) dying declarations, (3) spontaneous declarations, (4) previously recorded testimony, (5) past recollection recorded, (6) business records, and (7) official records.

The sequence in presenting evidence at a trial is (1) direct examination by the attorney who called the witness, (2) cross-examination by the opposing attorney, (3) redirect by the witness's attorney, and (4) re-cross by the opposing attorney.

Discussion Questions

1. Why is it important for law enforcement students to understand the legal rules of evidence?
2. Why does the layperson get the impression that the law is full of "loopholes" through which the guilty may escape?
3. What alternatives could be developed to replace the exclusionary rule?
4. Does the end justify the means for the exclusionary rule?
5. Why does the "hearsay rule" exist?
6. What arguments can you make for privileged communications?
7. Why is the law of evidence so complicated?
8. Why would the physical preservation of evidence provide a fertile area to create doubt for the jury?
9. What would be the easiest way to prevent doubt from being created?
10. What trends do you see regarding the exclusionary rule?

References

Ballentine, James A. *Ballentine's Law Dictionary*. 3d ed. Edited by William S. Anderson. Rochester, N.Y.: The Lawyers Co-Operative Publishing Company, 1969.

Bennett, Wayne W., and Hess, Kären M. *Criminal Investigation*. 2d ed. St. Paul, Minn.: West Publishing Company, 1987.

Cleary, Edward W. *McCormick on Evidence*. 3d ed. St. Paul, Minn.: West Publishing Company, 1984.

del Carmen, Rolando V. *Criminal Procedure for Law Enforcement Personnel*. Monterey, Calif.: Brooks/Cole Publishing Company, 1987.

Frase, Richard S. *Criminal Evidence: Constitutional, Statutory, & Rules Limitations*. St. Paul, Minn.: Butterworth Legal Publishers, 1985.

Graham, Michael H. *Evidence Text, Rules, Illustrations and Problems: The Commentary Method*. St. Paul, Minn.: National Institute for Trial Advocacy Administrator's Office, 1983.

LaFave, Wayne R., and Israel, Jerold H., *Criminal Procedure*. St. Paul, Minn.: West Publishing Company, 1985.

Oran, Daniel. *Law Dictionary for Nonlawyers*. 2d ed. St. Paul, Minn.: West Publishing Company, 1985.

Whitebread, Charles H., and Slobogin, Christopher. *Criminal Procedure: An Analysis of Cases and Concepts*. 2d ed. Mineola, N.Y.: The Foundation Press, Inc., 1966.

SHOULD "GOOD FAITH" OVERRIDE THE EXCLUSIONARY RULE?

Reference to the exclusionary rule has been frequent throughout this text because the rule is so critical to criminal procedure. You've looked at arguments for and against the rule. Perhaps a middle ground might be needed instead. See if you agree.

A Proposed Modification of the Exclusionary Rule

The fundamental and legitimate purpose of the exclusionary rule—to deter illegal police conduct and promote respect for the rule of law by preventing illegally obtained evidence from being used in a criminal trial—has been eroded by the action of the courts barring evidence of the truth, however important, if there is any investigative error, however unintended or trivial. We believe that any remedy for the violation of a constitutional right should be proportional to the magnitude of the violation. In general, evidence should not be excluded from a criminal proceeding if it has been obtained by an officer acting in the reasonable, good faith belief that it was in conformity to the Fourth Amendment to the Constitution. A showing that evidence was obtained pursuant to and within the scope of a warrant constitutes prima facie evidence of such a good faith belief. We recommend that the Attorney General instruct United States Attorneys and the Solicitor General to urge this rule in appropriate court proceedings, or support federal legislation establishing this rule, or both. If this rule can be established, it will restore the confidence of the public and of law enforcement officers in the integrity of criminal proceedings and the value of constitutional guarantees. . . .

Application of the rule has been carried to the point where it is applied to situations where police officers make reasonable, good faith efforts to comply with the law, but unwittingly fail to do so. In such circumstances, the rule necessarily fails in its deterrent purpose.

The present application of the exclusionary rule not only depresses police morale and allows criminals to go free when constables unwittingly blunder, but it diminishes public respect for the courts and our judicial process.

If the rule is redefined to limit its application to circumstances in which an officer did not act either reasonably, or in good faith, or both, it will have an important purpose that will be served by its application. Moreover, it will gain the support of the public and the respect of responsible law enforcement officials.

The Attorney General therefore should support legislatively and in court the position that evidence obtained in the course of a reasonable, good faith search should not be excluded from criminal trials.

The following statutory language would accomplish this purpose:

Except as specifically provided by statute, evidence which is obtained as a result of search or seizure and which is otherwise admissible shall not be excluded in a criminal proceeding brought by the United States unless:

1. the defendant makes a timely objection to the introduction of the evidence;

2. the defendant establishes by a preponderance of the evidence that the search or seizure was in violation of the Fourth Amendment to the Constitution of the United States; and,

3. the prosecution fails to show by a preponderance of the evidence that the search or seizure was undertaken in a reasonable, good faith belief that it was in conformity with the Fourth Amendment to the Constitution of the United States. A showing that evidence was obtained pursuant to and within the scope of a warrant constitutes prima facie evidence of such a good faith belief.

Extracted from *Attorney General's Task Force on Violent Crime, Final Report,* August 17, 1981.

Table 10—1   Submitting Evidence to the FBI Lab.

Specimen	Identification	Amount Desired		Preservation	Wrapping and Packing	Transmittal	Miscellaneous
		Standard	Evidence				
Abrasives, including carborundum, emery, sand, etc.	On outside of container. Type of material. Date obtained. Name or initials.	Not less than one ounce	All	None	Use containers, such as ice-cream box, pillbox, or plastic vial. Seal to prevent any loss.	Registered mail or UPS or air express	Avoid use of envelopes.
Acid	Same as above	One pint	All to one pint	None	Plastic or all-glass bottle. Tape in stopper. Pack in sawdust, glass, or rock wool. Use bakelite or paraffin-lined bottle for hydrofluoric acid.	UPS express only	Label acids, glass, corrosive.
Adhesive tape	Same as above	Recovered roll	All	None	Place on waxed paper or cellophane.	Registered mail	Do not cut, wad, or distort.
Alkaline—caustic soda, potash, ammonia, etc.	Same as above	One pint liquid. One pound solid	All to one pint. All to one pound	None	Plastic or glass bottle with rubber stopper held with adhesive tape.	UPS express only	Label alkali, glass, corrosive.
Ammunition (Cartridges)	Same as above	Two		None	Outside shipping container must be made of wood or fiberboard, per Department of Transportation regulations. Pack ammunition in cotton, soft paper, or cloth.	UPS or air express	Unless specific exam of cartridge is essential, do not submit. Shipping is costly.
Anonymous letters, extortion letters, bank robbery notes	Initial and date each document unless legal aspects or good		All	Do not handle with bare hands.	Place in proper enclosure envelope and seal with "Evidence" tape or transparent cello-	Registered mail	Advise if evidence should be treated for latent fingerprints.

(continued)

Specimen	Identification	Amount Desired Standard	Amount Desired Evidence	Preservation	Wrapping and Packing	Transmittal	Miscellaneous
	judgment dictates otherwise.				phane tape. Flap side of envelope should show (1) wording "Enclosure(s) to Bureau from (name of submitting office)," (2) title of case, (3) brief description of contents, and (4) file number, if known. Staple to original letter of transmittal.		
Blasting caps	On outside of container. Type of material, date obtained, and name or initials.		All	Should not be forwarded until advised to do so by the Laboratory. Packing instructions will be given at that time.			
Blood: 1. Liquid Known samples	Use adhesive tape on outside of test tube. Name of donor, date taken, doctor's name, name or initials of submitting Agent or officer	1/6 ounce (5cc) collected in sterile test tube	All	Sterile tube only. NO REFRIGERANT.	Wrap in cotton, soft paper. Place in mailing tube or suitably strong mailing carton.	Airmail, special delivery, registered	Submit immediately. Don't hold awaiting additional items for comparison.
2. Drowning cases	Same as above	Two specimens: one from each side of heart	All	Same as above	Same as above	Airmail, special delivery, registered	Same as above

(continued)

Specimen	Identification	Amount Desired		Preservation	Wrapping and Packing	Transmittal	Miscellaneous
		Standard	Evidence				
3. Small quantities:							
a. Liquid Questioned samples	Same as above as applicable		All to 1/6 ounce (5cc)	Allow to dry thoroughly on non-porous surface.	Same as above	Airmail, special delivery, registered	Collect by using eyedropper or clean spoon, transfer to non-porous surface. Allow to dry and submit in pillbox.
b. Dry stains not on fabrics	On outside of pillbox or plastic vial. Type of specimen, date secured, name or initials.		As much as possible	Keep dry.	Seal to prevent leakage.	Registered mail	
4. Stained clothing, fabric, etc.	Use tag or mark directly on clothes. Type of specimens, date secured, name or initials.		As found	If wet when found, dry by hanging. USE NO HEAT TO DRY. No preservative.	Each article wrapped separately and identified on outside of package. Place in strong box packed to prevent shifting of contents.	Registered mail or air or UPS express	
Bullets (not cartridges)	Initials on base, nose or mutilated area.		All found	None. Unnecessary handling obliterates marks.	Pack tightly in cotton or soft paper in pill-, match-, or powder box. Label outside of box as to contents.	Registered mail	
Cartridges (live ammunition)	Initials on outside of case near bullet end.		All found	None	Same as above.	UPS express or air express	Live ammunition cannot be sent through U.S. mails.
Cartridge cases (shells)	Initials preferably on inside near open end or on out-		All	None	Same as above.	Registered mail	

(continued)

Specimen	Identification	Standard	Amount Desired		Preservation	Wrapping and Packing	Transmittal	Miscellaneous
			Evidence					
Charred or burned	side near open end. On outside of container indicate fragile nature of evidence, date obtained, name or initials.		All		None	Pack in rigid container between layers of cotton.	Registered mail	Added moisture, with atomizer or otherwise, not recommended.
Checks (fraudulent)	See anonymous letters.		All		None	See anonymous letters.	Registered mail	Advise what parts questioned or known. Furnish physical description of subject.
Check protector, rubber stamp and dater stamp known standards. Note: Send actual device when possible.	Place name or initials, date, name of make and model, etc., on sample impressions.	Obtain several copies in full word-for-word order of each questioned checkwriter impression. If unable to forward rubber stamps, prepare numerous samples with different degrees of pressure.				See anonymous letters or bulky evidence wrapping instructions.	Registered mail	Do not disturb inking mechanisms on printing devices.
Clothing	Mark directly on garment or use string tag. Type of evidence, name or initials, date.		All		None	Each article individually wrapped with identification written on outside of package. Place in strong container.	Registered or UPS or air express	Leave clothing whole. Do not cut out stains. If wet, hang in room to dry before packing.

(continued)

Specimen	Identification	Amount Desired		Preservation	Wrapping and Packing	Transmittal	Miscellaneous
		Standard	Evidence				
Codes, ciphers, and foreign language material	As anonymous letters.		All	None	As anonymous letters.	As anonymous letters	Furnish all background and technical information pertinent to examination.
Drugs: 1. Liquids	Affix label to bottle in which found including name or initials and date.		All to one pint	None	If bottle has no stopper, transfer to glass-stoppered bottle and seal with adhesive tape.	Registered mail or UPS or air express	Mark "Fragile." Determine alleged normal use of drug and if prescription, check with druggist to determine supposed ingredients.
2. Powders, pills, and solids	On outside of pillbox. Name or initials and date.		All to 1/4 pound	None	Seal to prevent any loss by use of tape.	Registered mail or UPS or air express	
Dynamite and other explosives	Consult the FBI Laboratory and follow their telephonic or telegraphic instructions.						
Fibers	On outside of sealed container or on object to which fibers are adhering.	Entire garment or other cloth item.	All	None	Folded paper or pillbox. Seal edges and openings with tape.	Registered mail	Do not place loose in envelope.
Firearms	Mark inconspicuously as if it were your own. String tag gun, noting complete description on tag. Investigative notes should reflect how and where gun marked.		All	Keep from rusting.	Wrap in paper and identify contents of package. Place in cardboard box or wooden box.	Registered mail or UPS or air express	Unload all weapons before shipping.

(continued)

Specimen	Identification	Amount Desired Standard	Evidence	Preservation	Wrapping and Packing	Transmittal	Miscellaneous
Flash paper	Initials and date.	One sheet	All	Fireproof, vented location away from any other combustible materials. If feasible, immerse in water.	Individual polyethylene envelopes double-wrapped in manila envelopes. Inner wrapper sealed with paper tape.	Five sheets (8" X 101/2") surface mail parcel post. Over 5 sheets telephonically consult FBI Laboratory.	Mark inner wrapper "Flash Paper Flammable."
Fuse, safety	Attach string tag or gummed paper label, name or initials, and date.	One foot	All	None	Place in manila envelope, box, or suitable container.	Registered mail or UPS or air express	
Gasoline	On outside of all-metal container, label with type of material, name or initials, and date.	One quart	All to one gallon	Fireproof container	Metal container packed in wooden box.	UPS express only	
Glass fragments	Adhesive tape on each piece. Name or initials and date on tape. Separate questioned and known.		All	Avoid chipping.	Wrap each piece separately in cotton. Pack in strong box to prevent shifting and breakage. Identify contents.	Registered mail or UPS or air express	Mark "Fragile."
Glass particles	Name or initials, date on outside of sealed container.	3" piece of broken item	All	None	Place in pillbox, plastic or glass vial; seal and protect against breakage.	Registered mail	Do not use envelopes.

(continued)

Specimen	Identification	Amount Desired		Preservation	Wrapping and Packing	Transmittal	Miscellaneous
		Standard	Evidence				
Gunshot residue tests:. 1.Paraffin	On outside of container. Type of material, date, and name or initials.		All	Containers must be free of any nitrate-containing substance. Keep cool.	Wrap in waxed paper or place in sandwich bags. Lay on cotton in a substantial box. Place in a larger box packed with absorbent material.	Registered mail	Use "Fragile" label. Keep cool.
2. On cloth	Attach string tag or mark directly. Type of material, date, and name or initials.		All	None	Place fabric flat between layers of paper and then wrap, so that no residue will be transferred or lost.	Registered mail	Avoid shaking.
Hair	On outside of container. Type of material, date, and name or initials.	Dozen or more full length hairs from different parts of head and/or body.	All	None	Folded paper or pillbox. Seal edges and openings with tape.	Registered mail	Do not place loose in envelope.
Handwriting and hand printing, known standards	Name or initials, date, from whom obtained, and voluntary statement should be included in appropriate place.	See footnote.*		None	See anonymous letters.	Registered mail	

*Duplicate the original writing conditions as to text, speed, slant, size of paper, size of writing, type of writing instruments, etc. Do not allow suspect to see questioned writing. Give no instructions as to spelling, punctuation, etc. Remove each sample from sight as soon as completed. Suspect should fill out blank check forms in cases (FD–352). In hand printing cases, both upper- (capital) and lower-case (small) samples should be obtained. In forgery cases, obtain sample signatures of the person whose name is forged. Have writer prepare some specimens with hand not normally used. Obtain undictated handwriting when feasible.

(continued)

Specimen	Identification	Amount Desired		Preservation	Wrapping and Packing	Transmittal	Miscellaneous
		Standard	Evidence				
Matches	On outside of container. Type of material, date, and name or initials.	One to two books of paper. One full box of wood.	All	Keep away from fire.	Metal container and packed in larger package to prevent shifting. Matches in box or metal container packed to prevent friction between matches.	UPS express or registered mail	"Keep away from fire" label
Medicines (See drugs.)							
Metal	Same as above	One pound	All to one pound	Keep from rusting.	Use paper boxes or containers. Seal and use strong paper or wooden box.	Registered mail or UPS or air express	Melt number, heat treatment, and other specifications of foundry if available.
Oil	Same as above	One quart together with specifications	All to one quart	Keep away from fire.	Metal container with tight screw top. Pack in strongbox using excelsior or similar material.	UPS express only	DO NOT USE DIRT OR SAND FOR PACKING MATERIAL.
Obliterated, eradicated, or indented writing	See anonymous letters		All	None	See anonymous letters.	Registered mail	Advise whether bleaching or staining methods may be used. Avoid folding.
Organs of body	On outside of container. Victim's name, date of death, date of autopsy, name of doctor, name or initials.		All to one pound	None to evidence. Dry ice in package not touching glass jars.	Plastic or all-glass containers (glass jar with glass top).	UPS or air express	"Fragile" label. Keep cool. Metal top containers must not be used. Send autopsy report.

(continued)

| Specimen | Identification | Amount Desired | | Preservation | Wrapping and Packing | Transmittal | Miscellaneous |
		Standard	Evidence				
Paint: 1. Liquid	On outside of container. Type of material, origin if known, date, name or initials.	Original unopened container up to 1 gallon if possible.	All to 1/4 pint	None	Friction-top paint can or large-mouth, screw-top jars. If glass, pack to prevent breakage. Use heavy corrugated paper or wooden box.	Registered mail or UPS or air express	
2. Solid (paint chips or scrapings)	Same as above	At least 1/2 sq. inch of solid, with all layers represented	All. If on small object send object.	Wrap so as to protect smear.	If small amount, round pillbox or small glass vial with screw top. Seal to prevent leakage. Envelopes not satisfactory.	Registered mail or UPS or air express	Do not pack in cotton. Avoid contact with adhesive materials.
Plaster casts of tire treads and shoe prints	On back before plaster hardens. Location, date, and name or initials.	Send in shoes and tires of suspects. Photographs and sample impressions are usually not suitable for comparison.	All shoe prints; entire circumference of tires	Allow casts to cure (dry) before wrapping.	Wrap in paper and cover with suitable packing material to prevent breakage. Do not wrap in unventilated plastic bags.	Registered mail or UPS or air express	Use "Fragile" label. Mix approximately four pounds of plaster to quart of water.
Powder patterns (See gunpowder tests)							
Rope, twine, and cordage	On tag or container. Type of material, date, name or initials.	One yard	All		Wrap securely.	Registered mail	
Safe insulation or soil	On outside of container. Type of material, date, name or initials.	1/2 pound	All to one pound		Use containers, such as pillbox, or plastic vial. Seal to prevent any loss.	Registered mail or UPS or air express	Avoid use of glass containers and envelopes.

(continued)

Specimen	Identification	Amount Desired Standard	Amount Desired Evidence	Preservation	Wrapping and Packing	Transmittal	Miscellaneous
Shoe print lifts (impressions on hard surfaces)	On lifting tape or paper attached to tape. Name or initials and date.	Photograph before making lift of dust impression.	All	None	Prints in dust are easily damaged. Fasten print or lift to bottom of a box so that nothing will rub against it.	Registered mail	Always rope off crime scene area until shoe prints or tire treads are located and preserved.
Tools	On tools or use string tag. Type of tool, identifying number, date, name or initials.		All		Wrap each tool in paper. Use strong cardboard or wooden box with tools packed to prevent shifting.	Registered mail or UPS or air express	
Toolmarks	On object or on tag attached to or on opposite end from where toolmarks appear. Name or initials and date.	Send in the tool. If impractical, make several impressions on similar material as evidence using entire marking area of tool.	All	Cover ends bearing toolmarks with soft paper and wrap with strong paper to protect ends.	After marks have been protected, wrap in strong wrapping paper, place in strong box, and pack to prevent shifting.	Registered mail or UPS or air express	
Typewriting, known standards	Place name or initials, date, serial number, name of make and model, etc., on specimens.	Obtain at least one copy in full word-for-word order of questioned typewriting. Also include partial copies in light, medium, and heavy degrees of touch. Also carbon paper samples of every character on the keyboard.	All	None	See anonymous letters.	Registered mail	Examine ribbon for evidence of questioned message thereon. For carbon paper samples either remove ribbon or place in stencil position.

(continued)

Specimen	Identification	Amount Desired		Preservation	Wrapping and Packing	Transmittal	Miscellaneous
		Standard	Evidence				
Urine or water	On outside of container. Type of material, name of subject, date taken, name or initials.	Preferably all urine voided over a period of 24 hours.	All	None. Use any clean bottle with leakproof stopper.	Bottle surrounded with absorbent material to prevent breakage. Strong cardboard or wooden box.	Registered mail	
Wire (See also toolmarks.)	On label or tag. Type of material, date, name or initials.	Three feet (Do not kink.)	All	(Do not kink.)	Wrap securely.	Registered mail	Do not kink wire.
Wood	Same as above	One foot	All		Wrap securely.	Registered mail	

NOTE: This chart is not intended to be all-inclusive. If evidence to be submitted is not found herein, consult the specimen list for an item most similar in nature and submit accordingly.
SOURCE: The FBI

CHAPTER 11
Juvenile Justice

The children now love luxury. They have bad manners, contempt for authority, they show disrespect for adults and love to talk rather than work or exercise. They no longer rise when adults enter the room. They contradict their parents, chatter in front of company, gobble down food at the table, and intimidate their teachers.
—Socrates 469-399B.C.

DO YOU KNOW

What the doctrine of parens patriae refers to?

What four phases juvenile justice has gone through?

When and where the first juvenile reformatory was established?

What precedents were set in the cases of Kent, Gault, Winship, McKiever, and Breed?

What the components of the juvenile justice system are?

What unique factors are considered in the juvenile courts?

What three challenges face the juvenile justice system?

What four correction models exist?

Introduction

Chapter 11

You have already learned that our American legal system developed from old English law. In fact, many of our current laws, both civil and criminal, show little change from the original laws written on parchment by scribes in Medieval English Courts of Justice.

An area of law that *has* changed dramatically in the recent past, however, is juvenile justice. Professionals involved in the ever-growing field of juvenile justice continue to evaluate various ways of dealing with young people in an attempt to balance the needs of delinquent youth and the needs of the community.

Unlike today's juvenile courts that can provide treatment programs for virtually every problem, early legal systems failed to recognize sufficient differences between adults and children that would necessitate separate laws. Those early courts dealt with forbidden acts harshly, regardless of the offender's age.

BRIEF HISTORY OF JUVENILE JUSTICE

Ancient Rome granted fathers extraordinary authority in the treatment of their children. Punishment was often administered harshly, with children being brutalized in the name of discipline. Infanticide (the killing of children) was an accepted way to deal with difficult children. In England, the court operated on a principle known as *parens patriae.* The king was responsible for the general protection of all people in the realm, including the children. The king, by means of the chancery court, assumed guardianship over the persons and property of minors. McCreedy (1975, p. 1) notes that "In effect, the chancellor acted as a substitute father for those children who were abandoned, neglected, or destitute."

As defined by Oran (1985, p. 219):

The doctrine of parens patriae refers to the right of the government to take care of minors and others who cannot legally take care of themselves. This principle still prevails today.

The sixteenth and seventeenth centuries brought some slow signs of change. During this period the uniqueness of children began to be recognized. You can even see such changes in art. During the Middle Ages, for example, children were shown dressing and acting like small adults of the time. During the sixteenth and seventeenth centuries, however, they were depicted more like children. Children were perceived as being different, with different needs than adults.

Another English common law principle influencing our juvenile justice system was the belief that children under the age of seven were incapable of criminal intent. Between the ages of seven and fourteen

*While theories of delinquency have changed over time, the power of the government
has always been available to intervene in the life of a troubled youth.*

they were presumed incapable of criminal intent unless proven differently. After age fourteen, children were held responsible for their acts
and treated according to a strict interpretation of the law. In effect, age
had a direct bearing on how someone who broke the law was treated.
This concept remains in effect today.

According to Wrobleski and Hess (1986, p. 469), the juvenile
justice system has gone through four major phases.

---

*The four major phases of the juvenile justice system have been (1) a
Puritan emphasis, (2) an emphasis on providing a refuge for youth,
(3) development of the separate juvenile court, and (4) emphasis on
juvenile rights.*

The Puritan Emphasis (1646–1824)

The Puritan emphasis brought to America the concepts of *parens
patriae* and the belief that there was an age below which there could be
no criminal intent. However, from the time the colonists arrived until
the nineteenth century, the emphasis was on Puritan values. The
Puritans represented a drastic change in attitudes toward young people
in the English colonies in New England. Binder et al. (1988, p. 48) state:
"Under the influence of Puritanism, there existed a great deal of

concern and awareness about children and child rearing. The Puritans' views about childhood were not the same as those of contemporary Americans." Nonetheless, it was significant that society was finally recognizing the differences between children and adults. Childrearing and the treatment of children during this period would certainly be considered extremely harsh, perhaps even abusive, by today's standards.

Perhaps one of the first American "status offense" laws appeared on the law books of Massachusetts. It dealt with incorrigibility: Binder et al. (p. 50): "If a man have a stubborn or rebellious son of sufficient years of understanding, *viz.* sixteen, which will not obey the voice of his father or the voice of his mother, and that when they have chastened him will not harken unto them, then shall his father and mother, being his natural parents, lay hold on him and bring him to the magistrate assembled in Court, and testify to them by sufficient evidence that this their son is stubborn and rebellious and will not obey their voice and chastisement, but lives in sundry notorious crime. Such a son shall be put to death."

And children today think *their* parents are strict! Nonetheless, the Puritans believed that children were basically evil, and that whatever force was necessary to keep them under control was justified. McCreedy (1975, p. 2) points out that in 1828 in New Jersey, a boy of thirteen was hanged for an offense he committed when he was twelve. The Puritan emphasis lasted until the 1820s.

Providing a Refuge (1824–1899)

By the 1820s several states had passed laws protecting children from punishments associated with criminal laws. According to McCreedy (1975, p. 2): "The first change came in the area of institutional custody. Central to the reform effort in this area was a recognition of the brutality of confining children in the same institutions with adults convicted of crime. This awareness resulted in attempts to separate children from adult criminal offenders."

The first American institution to isolate children convicted of crimes from adult criminals was New York City's House of Refuge.

Established in 1825, the House of Refuge in New York City was the first juvenile reformatory.

As noted by Binder et al. (1988, pp. 228–29):

Although the development of a distinctive juvenile justice system started with the efforts of early-nineteenth-century reformers that led to the first house of refuge, some of the most significant practices and approaches to juvenile crime did not take shape until the latter part of the nineteenth century, during the period historians call the Progressive era. Extending roughly from the 1880s to the coming of World War I, the Progressive era represented a time of great turmoil in American social and intellectual life and in the establishment of the American juvenile justice system. . . . An unprecedented wave of immigration and a quickening pace of urbanization made many Americans aware of juvenile delinquency to a degree that had not been known before.

Other major changes are outlined in table 11-1.

Table 11–1   Antecedents of the Juvenile Court

1825	New York House of Refuge was opened, followed by houses in Boston (1826), Philadelphia (1828), and New Orleans (1845).
1831	Illinois passed a law that allowed penalties for certain offenses committed by minors to differ from the penalties imposed on adults.
1841	John Augustus inaugurated probation and became the nation's first probation officer.
1854	State industrial school for girls opened in Lancaster, Massachusetts (first cottage-type institution).
1858	State industrial school for boys in Lancaster, Ohio, adopted a cottage-type system.
1863	Children's Aid Society founded in Boston. Members of the organization attended police and superior court hearings, supervised youngsters selected for probation, and did the investigation on which probation selection was based.
1869	Law enacted in Massachusetts to direct State Board of Charities to send agents to court hearings that involved children. The agents made recommendations to the court that frequently involved probation and the placement of youngsters with suitable families.
1870	Separate hearings for juveniles were required in Suffolk County, Massachusetts. New York followed by requiring separate trials, dockets, and records for children; Rhode Island made similar provisions in 1891.
1899	In April, Illinois adopted legislation creating the first juvenile court in Cook County (Chicago). In May, Colorado established a juvenile court.

The Juvenile Court (1899–1960) and Early Procedure

"The juvenile court was founded in Cook County (Chicago) in 1899, when the Illinois legislature passed the Juvenile Court Act. The *parens patriae* doctrine provided the legal catalyst for the creation of the juvenile court [and the] use of informal procedures. . . . The kindly parent, the state, could thus justify relying on psychological and medical examinations rather than on trial by evidence" (Bartollas, 1988, p. 438).

The first juvenile court differed dramatically from adult court. According to Vetter and Territo (1984, p. 497): "The court's major objective was to help the wayward child become a productive member of the community. The determination of guilt or innocence, using standard rules of evidence, was not of primary importance. Instead, . . . court procedures were to be more diagnostic than legal in nature, giving major consideration to the information obtained on the youngster's environment, heredity, as well as his physical and mental condition.''

During this period the philosophy of *parens patriae* was in full effect. The Chicago legislation establishing the juvenile court was a reaction against the inhumane treatment of children confined in police stations and jails. It created many characteristics of our modern-day juvenile courts, including a separate court for juveniles, separate and confidential records, informal proceedings, and the possibility of probation. The major goal was to save the child.

Intellectual developments, including the "discovery" of adolescence, contributed to a growing awareness of delinquency. Most of those who examined the problem were convinced that existing approaches to it, including the long-established houses of refuge and state-sponsored reform schools, were not doing enough to combat juvenile crime. The Progressive era saw the development of new approaches to delinquency that have come down to our own time.

The chief focus of Progressive era reformers was the "decriminalization" of juvenile delinquency. These reformers sought to remove youngsters accused of crime from the ordeal of criminal proceedings. The reformers' effort ultimately succeeded, resulting in special juvenile courts to deal with young offenders. These courts focused on treatment rather than prosecution (Binder, et al., 1988, pp. 228–29).

According to Wrobleski and Hess (1986, p. 471), "The *parens patriae* doctrine made the state legally responsible for the children within that state, providing a legal foundation for state intervention in the family."

McCreedy goes on to note (1975, p. 7):

> The state, as the child's substitute parent, was not supposed to punish the child for his misconduct, but to help him. To reach this noble goal, many of the procedures used in adult criminal proceedings were abandoned or replaced with procedures commonly used in non-criminal (civil) court proceedings. A whole new legal vocabulary and new methods of operation were developed to reflect the new philosophy and procedures used in the juvenile justice system. Instead of a complaint being filed against the child, a petition was filed. No longer was the child to be arrested in the strict sense of the term. Instead, the child was given a summons. A preliminary inquiry or initial hearing replaced an arraignment on the charge. The child was not required to plead either guilty or not guilty to the alleged misconduct. Instead of being found guilty of a crime, the child was found delinquent. Moreover, adjudication of delinquency was not to be considered a conviction. None of the liabilities attached to a criminal conviction were to apply to a child found delinquent: for example, disqualification from future civil service appointments, the inability to be licensed by the state or the right to vote.

The differences in terminology are summarized in table 11-2.

Table 11–2.   The Language of Juvenile and Adult Courts

Juvenile court term	Adult court term
Adjudication	Conviction of guilt
Adjudicatory hearing	Trial
Adjustment	Plea bargaining
Aftercare	Parole
Commitment	Sentence to imprisonment
Delinquent act	Crime
Delinquent child	Criminal
Detention	Holding in jail
Dispositional hearing	Sentencing hearing
Hearing	Trial
Juvenile court	Court of record
Petition	Accusation or indictment
Probation	Probation
Residential child care facility	Halfway house
Shelter	Jail
Take into custody	Arrest

Reprinted with permission from Vetter and Territo, *Crime & Justice in America*. West Publishing Co., 1984. All Rights Reserved.

Although establishing juvenile courts was a tremendous advance in our juvenile justice system, it also presented some major problems. Since children were no longer considered "criminals," they lost many constitutional protections of due process, for example, not being given notice of the charge, not being provided with a lawyer, and not being given the chance to cross-examine witnesses.

Justification for the informal procedures in the juvenile justice system was set forth in *Commonwealth* v. *Fisher* (1905) soon after the establishment of juvenile courts:

> To save a child from becoming a criminal or from continuing in a career in crimes . . . the Legislature may surely provide for the salvation of such a child . . . by bringing it into one of the courts of the state without any process at all, for the purpose of subjecting it to the state's guardianship and protection. The natural parent needs no process to temporarily deprive his child of its liberty by confining it in his own home, to save it from the consequences of persistence in a career of waywardness; nor is the state, when compelled as parens patriae, to take the place of the father for the same purpose, required to adopt any process as a means of placing its hands upon the child to lead it to one of its courts.

Half a century later, the United States Supreme Court began to seriously question denying children the constitutional rights extended to adults charged with a crime. This lead to the fourth phase in the developing juvenile justice system—juvenile rights.

Juvenile Rights and Due Process (1960–Present)

The first of a series of landmark federal cases that drastically changed the juvenile justice system was *Shioutakon* v. *District of*

In many ways, juvenile court, laws, and procedures have become more like adult courts, laws, and procedures. The purpose of the juvenile system, however, remains rehabilitation.

Columbia (1956). The courts established that juveniles had the right to be represented by lawyers in court. If the parents could not afford a lawyer, the court was to appoint one.

A second case establishing juvenile rights was *Kent v. United States* (1966). Sixteen-year-old Morris Kent, who had a police record, was arrested for and charged with burglary, robbery, and rape, to which he confessed. After holding Kent for nearly a week at a juvenile detention facility, the judge decided to transfer the case to an adult criminal court without allowing Kent a hearing. The transfer, based on several reports by the probation staff, was entirely at the judge's discretion.

Even though Kent was examined by two psychiatrists and a psychologist, who concluded that Kent was "a victim of severe psychopathology" and needed psychiatric treatment, the judge waived Kent's case to the adult court. Kent was sentenced to thirty to ninety years in prison. Had Kent remained under the jurisdiction of the juvenile court, he would have been institutionalized for a maximum of five years.

The Supreme Court, in reviewing the case, decreed that "As a condition to a valid waiver order, petitioner (Kent) was entitled to a hearing, including access by his counsel to the social records and probation or similar reports which are presumably considered by the court, and to a statement of the reasons for Juvenile Court's decision."

Kent v. United States established that if a juvenile court transfers a case to adult criminal court, juveniles are entitled to a hearing, their counsel must be given access to probation records used by the court in reaching its decision, and the court must state its reasons for waiving jurisdiction over the case.

According to Arnold and Brungardt (1983, p. 24): "The impact of the Kent case went far beyond the relatively narrow legal issue—conditions of waiver to criminal court—that it addressed. It served as a warning to the juvenile justice system that the juvenile court's traditional laxity toward procedural and evidentiary standards would no longer be tolerated by the highest court in the land."

Justice Fortas, in the decision, stated: "There is evidence, in fact, that there may be grounds for concern that the child receives the worst of both worlds; that he neither gets the protection accorded to adults nor the solicitous care and regenerative treatment postulated for children." But things were about to change.

The following year (1967), another landmark Supreme Court ruling, *In re Gault*, resulted in additional major changes to our juvenile justice system. In this case, fifteen-year-old Gerald Gault received a six-year sentence for making lewd phone calls (an action for which an adult found guilty would receive a fine or a two-month sentence). The conviction was overruled because

- Neither Gault nor his parents had notice of the specific charges against him.
- No counsel was offered or provided to Gerald.
- No witnesses were present, thus denying Gerald the right of cross-examination and confrontation.
- No warning of Gerald's privilege against self-incrimination was given to him, thus no waiver of that right took place.

Justice Fortas summarized the opinion of the Court:

Where a person, infant or adult, can be seized by the State, charged and convicted of violating a state criminal law, and then ordered by the State to be confined for six years, I think the Constitution requires that he be tried in accordance with the guarantees of all provisions of the Bill of Rights made applicable to the States by the Fourteenth Amendment. Undoubtably this would be true of an adult defendant, and it would be a plain denial of equal protection of the laws—an invidious discrimination—to hold that others subject to heavier punishments could, because they are children, be denied these same constitutional safeguards. I consequently agree with the Court that the Arizona law as applied here denied to the parents and their son the right of notice, right to counsel, right against self-incrimination, and right to confront the witnesses against young Gault. Appellants are entitled to these rights, not because "fairness, impartiality, and orderliness—in short, the essentials of due process"—required them and not because they are "the procedural rules which have been fashioned from the generality of due process," but because they are specifically and un-equivocally granted by provisions of the Fifth and Sixth Amendments which the Fourteenth Amendment makes applicable to the States. . . .

"Under our Constitution," stated Justice Fortas, "the condition of being a boy does not justify a kangaroo court."

The Gault decision required that the due process clause of the Fourteenth Amendment apply to proceedings in state juvenile courts, including the right of notice, the right to counsel, the right against self-incrimination, and the right to confront witnesses.

As noted by Bartollas (1988, p. 443): "The *In re Gault* case of 1967 was influential because the U.S. Supreme Court reversed the conviction of a minor. This influential and far-reaching decision represented a new dawn in juvenile court history because it, in effect, brought the light of constitutional procedure into juvenile courts."

A dilemma for the court has been how to balance the informal and protective emphasis of the *parens patriae* doctrine with the constitutional rights of juveniles charged with crimes.

Just as a tension exists between the *parens patriae* philosophy and that of treating children like adults in the way we respond to their violations of the laws, which laws and rights apply to them creates a tension as well.

Society's perspective of juveniles and their needs continues to change. Having gone through a very liberal period during the 1960s and 1970s, every indication seems to be that our society is returning to more conservative, traditional values. This is very evident in the current trends of the juvenile justice system.

Not only is society at large expressing a desire to treat children more like adults as far as holding them accountable for their actions, ordering restitution, etc., but court cases are treating them more like adults as well.

We now know that juveniles enjoy the same constitutional rights as adults. Because of the unique nature of juvenile work in the law enforcement profession, it is important that law enforcement personnel know the specific laws pertaining to juveniles.

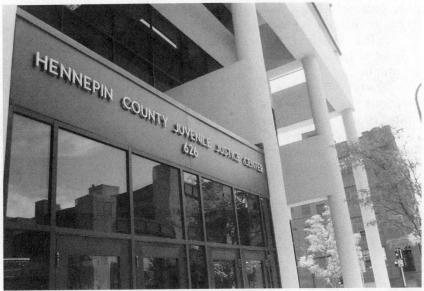

Modern juvenile justice centers have a variety of resources available to respond to the many problems affecting today's youth.

LAWS UNIQUE TO JUVENILES

Several laws are uniquely applicable to juveniles:

- Due process rights for children
- Rights of juveniles in custody
- Changes in the legal norms of juvenile court
- Rights of confined juveniles
- Rights of students

DUE PROCESS RIGHTS FOR CHILDREN

Due process is covered in the Fifth and Fourteenth Amendments. It pertains to rules and procedures designed to protect individual rights and to guarantee that every citizen receives fundamental fairness in the legal system.

For many years, the *parens patriae* philosophy dominated to the point that it excluded children from due process rights. The idea was that the state knew best and should, therefore, have carte blanche power to deal with its young people. Juveniles were denied such rights as having counsel and confronting their accusers.

Constitutionalists claim that juvenile courts were unconstitutional because they denied children the rights adults were given. They demanded that children have procedural rights as well as the rights of shelter, protection, and guardianship. Dependent and neglected children, because they are different from children who break the law, must be dealt with through separate court proceedings.

In the 1960s and 1970s, the United States Supreme Court handled a series of cases in which the constitutionalists' influence was very apparent.

The role of due process was initiated in the Warren Court by major decisions made in the 1960s. The first significant case was *Kent v. United States* (1966), a case previously discussed.

Several subsequent Supreme Court decisions demonstrated the Court's attempt to balance due process and the *parens patriae* philosophy.

The In re Winship *case (1970) decided juveniles were entitled to proof "beyond a reasonable doubt."*

This was a departure from the less strict "preponderance of evidence" basis used to that point. *In re Winship* (1970) involved a New York boy, committed to a state training school at age twelve for stealing $112 from a woman's purse. This sentence was based on a New York statute that allowed juvenile court decisions on the basis of "preponderance of evidence" instead of "beyond a reasonable doubt."

The Conservative Trend

The more conservative Supreme Court of the 1970s slowed the progress of comprehensive due process protection for juveniles.

In McKeiver v. Pennsylvania (1971), the Court denied juveniles the right to a jury trial in delinquency proceedings.

The Court shifted back to the *parens patriae* perspective and paternal protection of the juvenile court. At his adjudicatory hearing, Joseph McKeiver was found delinquent and placed on probation after his request for a jury trial was denied.

In *Breed v. Jones* (1975), the California juvenile court filed a petition against seventeen-year-old Jones for robbery. After hearing the testimony and finding the allegations true, the judge sustained the petition. Later, Jones was deemed unfit for juvenile court and ordered to be prosecuted as an adult. He was tried and again found guilty. His lawyer objected, claiming Jones was subjected to double jeopardy, but Jones was committed to the California Youth Authority (Breed v. Jones [1975].

The United States Supreme Court declared that Breed was subjected to double jeopardy:

---

*A juvenile court cannot adjudicate a case and then transfer the case
over to the criminal court for adult processing on the same offense;
this constitutes double jeopardy. (Breed v. Jones)*

Legal Rights in the Juvenile Justice System

During the 1960s and 1970s, the United States Supreme Court
dramatically increased adult constitutional safeguards. These changes
in the adult system directly affected rights in the juvenile system,
resulting in much litigation. Siegel and Senna (1988, p. 386–402)
reviewed siginficant decisions made in the lower court related to
juvenile rights during the pre-judicial, adjudicatory, and dispositional
stages of the juvenile justice system.

Arrest   Both adults and juveniles are subject to the same law of arrest. It
is significant to note, however, that this is an area of differences
between the adult and the juvenile systems. In the adult system the
taking into custody *is* an arrest, but in the juvenile system it is viewed
as "taking into protective custody." The major difference is that
juveniles can be taken into custody for more acts, such as status
offenses. The police officer must decide whether to release youths or
refer them to the juvenile court. This is great discretionary authority.

Custodial Interrogation   The *"Miranda warnings" are* applicable to children taken into custody. *In re Gault* helped establish that juveniles have
constitutional privileges. Youths can waive their rights without the
presence of a parent or attorney, but the circumstances of the case will
determine the waiver's validity. The *Miranda* requirement does not
apply if a youth is free to leave or is interrogated by a school principal
or anyone other than a police officer. Some states' requirements go
beyond *Miranda* and require a parent or guardian to be present during
interrogation. Practical problems may arise, however, when the parent
and child do not get along, or the parents cannot be reached or refuse
to respond. In such cases, a legal counselor (guardian ad litem) is often
appointed by the juvenile court.

Supreme Court Interpretations   In *Fare* v. *Michael C.* (1979), the Court ruled
that a juvenile asking to talk to his probation officer before custodial
interrogation by police was not the same as requesting a lawyer. The
Court also held that the totality of the circumstances were to be
considered to determine if a juvenile had given a valid waiver.

Search and Seizure   The Fourth Amendment ban against unreasonable search and seizure applies to juveniles. Two differences between adult and juvenile law make it easier for police to search suspected juvenile offenders. Juveniles can be taken into custody for status offenses and can be legally searched by police following such a seizure. Also, parents can permit police to search the rooms and possessions of children who are legal minors.

Identification from Lineups   Recall that in *United States* v. *Wade* (1967), an adult has the right to have a lawyer present during lineup procedures. Juveniles also have this right if charged with a delinquent act and placed in a lineup. In the case of *In re Holly*, the appellate court ruled that since Holly participated in a lineup without a lawyer present, his constitutional rights were abused and the trial unfair.

Fingerprinting   Fingerprinting juveniles is highly controversial. The Juvenile Justice and Delinquency Prevention Act of 1974 recommended that fingerprinting be done only on a judge's request, that juvenile fingerprints not be entered into the criminal section of the fingerprint registry, and that the fingerprints be destroyed after use. Various states have different rules regarding fingerprinting of juveniles, including authorizing the fingerprinting of any juvenile taken into custody for a felony level offense.

Pretrial Release and Detention   Specific requirements need to be met if a juvenile is to be detained. Juveniles also have the right to a lawyer during a detention hearing. And they have the right to confront and cross-examine witnesses and the privilege against self-incrimination. Three criteria to determine if juveniles should be detained are

1. Is there a need to protect the child?
2. Is the child a serious danger to the community?
3. Is it likely the child will return to court for adjudication?

Every state maintains great respect for the family unit, trying their best to maintain the child there rather than in detention any more than necessary.

In *Moss* v. *Weaver* (1981), the Court ruled that a probable cause hearing must be granted before a child can be detained for an extended time. States vary widely in regard to bail. Some release juveniles on bail; others do not.

Many states also use preventive detention if there is suspicion that juveniles may pose a threat to themselves or others. Preventive detention also removes the opportunity for offenders to intimidate witnesses or commit more crimes. Some believe preventive detention violates the "innocent until proven guilty" philosophy. In *Schall* v. *Martin* (1984), the Supreme Court ruled that juveniles can be placed in detention without bail before trial if they are deemed dangerous to themselves or society. Periodic detention hearings must be held during the detention period.

Plea Bargaining   While a majority of adult cases involve plea bargaining, substantially less plea bargaining occurs in juvenile courts. As the two systems become more similar, however, plea bargaining in juvenile courts has increased.

Transfer of Jurisdiction   Most jurisdictions allow for waiver or transfer of juvenile offenders to the criminal courts. *Kent* v. *United States* was the first step in establishing minimum requirements of due process in waiver proceedings. *Breed* v. *Jones* established that trial in an adult court *following* adjudication as a juvenile violated the Fifth Amendment's protection against double jeopardy.

Privacy of Records   Juvenile trials are usually closed to the press and names of offenders withheld. Juvenile records can, however, by court order, be seen by law enforcement officers and public officials if sufficient necessity exists. Even then, such records can be used only for limited purposes.

Adjudication   An adjudicatory, fact-finding hearing is held to review evidence. In *In re Gault*, the Supreme Court ruled that juveniles deserve the same fundamental fairness awarded adults, including the rights to counsel, to fair notice of charges, to confront and cross-examine witnesses, and protection against self-incrimination. Additionally, the prosecution must prove guilt beyond a reasonable doubt prior to the court adjudicating a youth delinquent. In the case of *McKeiver* v. *Pennsylvania* however, the Supreme Court ruled that the Fourteenth Amendment does not require that juveniles receive a jury trial. Clearly, the number of juveniles who are seeking to agressively defend their cases in court is increasing. No longer can police officers treat the rights of juveniles as any less important than those of adults.

Disposition   The court passes sentence based on the juvenile's offense, prior record, and family background. Some states have granted juveniles the right to due process during the dispositional hearing, but most states attempt to tailor court-ordered action to the child's needs.

Death Penalty for Children   Victor Streib, an expert on the subject, claims that 281 youths have been executed since 1642. As of 1989, 31 people on death row committed their crimes when they were teenagers. Twenty-five states allow the death penalty for juveniles convicted of murder. In 1989 the Supreme Court ruled that the death penalty for sixteen and seventeen year olds is not necessarily "cruel and unusual" punishment, and so, juveniles may be executed. Each state may now determine whether the death penalty will apply to juveniles.

Rights within Custody   Juvenile institutions are assumed to be less punitive and more therapeutic than adult prisons. To ensure that this is so, the courts have mandated two major rights: the right to treatment and the right to freedom from cruel and unusual punishment. Juveniles placed in institutions must also be free from arbitrary punishment, and

As due process rights of juveniles evolve, the only obvious differences between an adult and a juvenile hearing are the age of the accused and the lack of a jury. Some people are proposing the use of juries for juvenile hearings too.

assured of safety. *White v. Reid* (1954) established that juveniles could not be held in facilities that neglected their rehabilitation.

Right to Be Free from Cruel and Unusual Punishment   Pena v. New York State Division for Youth established that use of isolation, hand restraints, and tranquilizing drugs at Goshen Annex Center was punitive, antitherapeutic, and violated the Eighth and Fourteenth Amendments. Solitary confinement, strip-cells, and lack of educational opportunities were also condemned by the Court.

According to Bartollas (1988, p. 517):

> The charge that juvenile institutions are prohibitively expensive cannot be denied. Some states spend as much as $35,000 to $50,000 a year to confine a youth in a training school; few states spend less than $1,000 a month. Juvenile institutionalization is clearly a luxury that can be afforded only for violent and hard-core delinquents. The accusation that juvenile institutions are still inhumane also has considerable merit. Too many long-term institutions are violent and lawless, and only the strong survive in these predatory jungles. The high levels of stress in most training schools also make them inhumane. . . . However, the charge that juvenile institutions are schools of crime is open to debate.

Rights within the Family   Children have the right not to be abused or neglected within the family. While this is a broad area, courts have tried to avoid telling families how to raise their youngsters.

Rights within the School   The school's authority over students is derived from two sources: the doctrine of *in loco parentis* (in place of parents) and state statutes. Reutter describes *in loco parentis* as follows: "This doctrine holds that school authorities stand in the place of the parent while the child is at school. Thus, school personnel may establish rules for the educational welfare of the child and may inflict punishments for disobedience. The legal test is whether a reasonably knowledgeable and careful parent might so act"(Bartollas, "The School and Delinquency," p. 309, Source 75). Courts become involved in the schools in such matters as procedural due process, freedom of expression, hair and dress codes, and safety. The law pertaining to any physical punishment of children is changing, moving more toward *not* allowing it.

Procedural Due Process   A milestone case establishing due process for students was *Dixon* v. *Alabama State Board of Education* (1961). This case established that a student must receive notice and some opportunity for hearing before being expelled for misconduct. According to the doctrine of *in loco parentis*, the school system assumes parental duties while the youth is in school. Discipline is one responsibility traditionally placed in the school's hands. The Court in *Ingraham* v. *Wright* held that reasonable corporal punishment does *not* violate the Eighth Amendment guarantees against cruel and unusual punishment. Some states have prohibited any physical punishment by school personnel.

Search and Seizure in the Schools   In 1985, the landmark case of *New Jersey* v. *T.L.O.* established that school officials are NOT bound by the same search-and-seizure restrictions as law enforcement officers. In this case it was ruled that the search of a girl's purse was not a violation of her rights because the principal had probable cause to suspect the purse contained marijuana. (It, in fact, did.)

Warrentless Searchs of Students   The Supreme Court has ruled that:

> *While school children have a right to privacy, the school must also maintain a climate of learning and eased restrictions of search by school officials. School officials do not need a search warrant if they have probable cause to believe the subject of the search has violated or is violating the law. The key standard is reasonableness under all circumstances, meaning that if there is reason to believe the search will turn up evidence of breaking the law or school rules, and if the procedure followed is related to the purpose of the search and not excessively intrusive in view of the student's age and sex and the nature of the infraction, then the search is permissible (New Jersey v. T.L.O., (1985).*

Administrators may also conduct searches of student lockers, desks, and personal property without a warrant if they reasonably believe there is contraband within.

In *Re Guy Dumas* (1986) extended *New Jersey* v. *T.L.O.* to locker searches or other areas where students could store personal property while at school. Other cases have further articulated that school personnel do not need a search warrant to search lockers and the like, but at least "reasonable suspicion" is needed, with objective and articulable facts. It is not sufficient that a particular student is a "trouble maker" or "seems the type."

Drug sniffing dogs may be used to sniff lockers, desks, or cars on school property, but not students themselves.

The trend of cases is toward permitting locker searches without a warrant if officials have reasonable suspicion that the locker (or purse, etc.) contains contraband. This is an example of how the *parens patriae* philosophy is reconciled with constitutional law. Yes, juveniles have rights, but government has a responsibility to care for juveniles and to intervene when necessary for their welfare.

It is evident in this area of search and seizure that the courts are willing to weigh the needs of the community, the needs of the school, and the needs and rights of young people in developing law as it applies to juveniles.

Freedom of Expression   The United States Supreme Court ruled in *Tinker v. Des Moines Independent School District* (1969) that students do not lose their rights to freedom of speech when they enter the school building. Numerous cases have defined students' rights to freedom of religion and expression in school. Students have the right to free speech on school grounds as long as it does not interfere with school operations. What activities do and do not interfere continue to be argued.

Hair and Dress Codes   In the late 1960s and early 1970s, many court cases involved students suspended for hair and dress code violations. Several court decisions upheld the students' right to dress as they please and wear the hairstyle they chose. Hair and dress codes arguably violated students' constitutional rights to privacy and personal liberty. This continues to be an area of debate.

Safety   According to Bartollas (1988, p. 311): "Judicial intervention in the school has had both positive and negative impacts. Because the courts have made it clear students do not shed their constitutional rights at the schoolgates, students' rights are less likely to be abused than in the past. However, because school administrators often perceive themselves as handcuffed by the recent court decisions, they have become relunctant to take firm and forceful action against disruptive students, with the result that violence and delinquency in the schools has increased . . . thereby reducing the safety of students."

Cases have tended to support school officials acting out of concern for the safety of the student body. There are cases being decided that are giving school officials more power within their schools.

THE JUVENILE JUSTICE SYSTEM— THE TOTAL PICTURE

Laws related specifically to juveniles and juvenile courts are only one part of the juvenile justice system. The police, juvenile court, juvenile probation, residential and day treatment programs, detention facilities, long-term juvenile institutions, and aftercare are all interrelated.

The juvenile justice system has three basic parts: the police, the juvenile court, and corrections.

Thousands of public and private agencies also are involved in the juvenile justice system, with budgets totaling hundreds of millions of dollars.

The juvenile system is similar to the adult justice system in many ways. Both have interrelated agencies and can be divided into the three basic parts. In addition, both feel society's pressure to "get tough on crime," especially violent crime. Both systems are overloaded, financially constrained, and must constantly deal with staff recruiting, training, and burnout. Recidivism rates continue to concern the systems that genuinely try to serve their "clients."

The juvenile justice system does have significant differences from the adult system. The juvenile justice system emphasizes individual treatment and stresses rehabilitation more than the adult justice system. Juvenile offenders still have fewer rights than adult offenders, despite recent progress. Juvenile courts must also handle status offenses and have had to develop "hard" and "soft" policies toward juvenile justice, depending on the offense and the demands of society.

The Police and the Juvenile Justice System

According to Wrobleski and Hess (1986), pp. 478–80): "The police usually are the youth's initial contact with the juvenile justice system. They have broad discretion and may release juveniles to their parents, refer them to other agencies, place them in detention, or refer them to a juvenile court. The police may also temporarily detain juveniles, either for their own protection or to assure that they do appear in court."

Trojanowicz and Morash (1978, pp. 175–76) feel that

> The intake and screening process is an important aspect of the juvenile justice system. When used properly, it can effectively curtail or interrupt much delinquent behavior before it becomes serious. The intake process can also stimulate community agencies to help parents to better understand their children's behavior and the measures needed to prevent further delinquent acts.
>
> If the child is released at intake and no further processing takes place, there should still be a follow-up after any referral to a community agency by either the police or the intake unit. Follow-up facilitates not only the rendering of services to the child, but also promotes closer cooperation between the agencies involved.
>
> As noted by Eldefonso (1974, p. 3): "Generally juveniles are referred to local authorities after arrest. . . . In juvenile matters, probation departments provide most of the services for the court from initial

**Police
Responsibility**

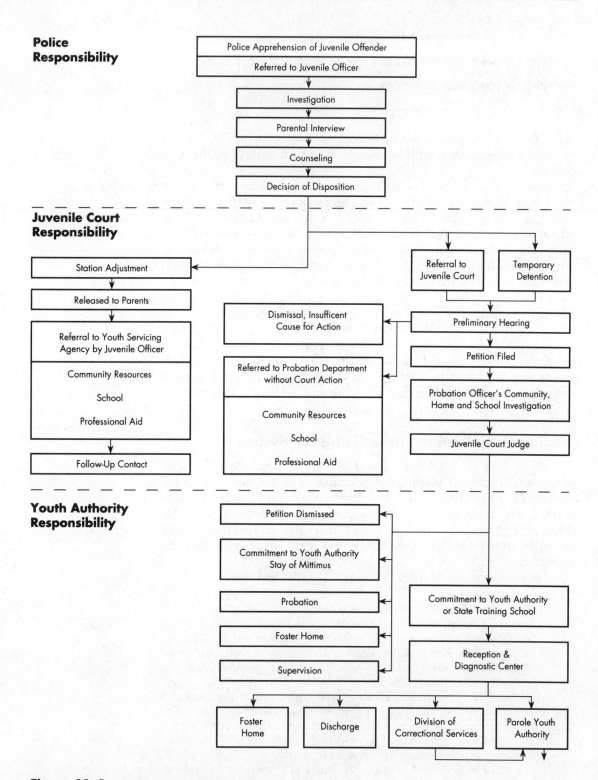

**Juvenile Court
Responsibility**

**Youth Authority
Responsibility**

Figure 11–1.   From Arrest to Disposition
International Association of Chiefs of Police

*screening and filing of a petition in behalf of the juvenile through ter-
mination of wardship (i.e., supervision and control)."*

*The probation department may or may not be part of a juvenile di-
vision. Carey et al. (1967, p. 26) have diagrammed the decision points
in police handling of juveniles. (See Figure 11–2.)*

Juvenile Courts

Juvenile courts of today are particularly specialized to handle
children's cases, keeping in mind the specialized goals and needs of the

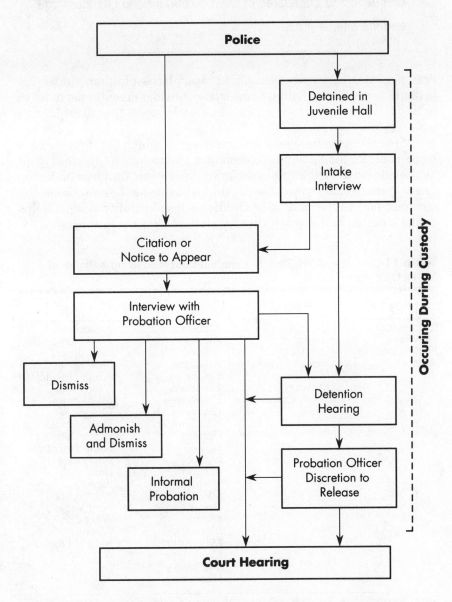

Figure 11–2   **Decision Points in Probation Handling of Juveniles**
Reprinted with permission from Carey, et. al.

juvenile justice system. Each state determines its own organizational structure, but all juvenile courts include a judge or referee, probation staff, government prosecutors and defense attorneys, and a number of social service programs. All courts aim at promoting rehabilitation. In the United States, most juvenile courts are established as lower courts of *limited jurisdiction*, to provide local attention to juvenile matters.

Unique factors considered in juvenile court include offender's age and the offense itself.

Age No one, nationally recognized age places children under the juvenile court's jurisdiction. Some states consider juvenile age to be 16 or under, but most include all children under age 18, as illustrated in table 11–3.

Several states have set a minimum age at which children are held responsible for their actions. For example, Massachusetts defines a child as a person between the ages of seven and seventeen. Children under the age of 7 are deemed incapable of criminal behavior. In most cases, the common-law understanding of children's responsibility is what helps define a child. And it may differ for civil or criminal purposes.

Table 11–3. Age at Which U.S. Criminal Courts Gain Jurisdiction of Young Offenders

Age 16	Age 17	Age 18	
Connecticut	Georgia	Alabama	Nevada
New York	Illinois	Alaska	New Hampshire
North Carolina	Louisiana	Arizona	New Jersey
Vermont	Massachusetts	Arkansas	New Mexico
	Michigan	California	North Dakota
	Missouri	Colorado	Ohio
	South Carolina	Delaware	Oklahoma
	Texas	District of Columbia	Oregon
		Florida	Pennsylvania
		Hawaii	Rhode Island
		Idaho	South Dakota
		Indiana	Tennessee
		Iowa	Utah
		Kansas	Virginia
		Kentucky	Washington
		Maine	West Virginia
		Maryland	Wisconsin
		Minnesota	Wyoming
		Mississippi	Federal Districts
		Montana	
		Nebraska	

Donna Hamperian et al., *Youth in Adult Courts* (Washington, D.C.: U.S. Government Printing Office, 1982; updated, 1987.

The Offense   Recently, states concerned about serious juvenile crimes are seeking to take these cases out of the juvenile court and place them into the adult system. Some courts give prosecutors the option of taking the case either to juvenile court or adult court with specific requirements needing to be met. These trends indicate a "toughening up" of juvenile justice policy and a recognition that juveniles do, indeed, cause a disproportinate amount of illegal activity.

Status offenses are also unique to juvenile court—these include truancy, running away from home, curfew, incorrigibility, liquor violations, and the like. In other words, status offenses are acts that are illegal only because of the person's age. The position of status offenders is very controversial. For example, some common behaviors— "unmanageable," "unruly," "dissolute," and "lewd" are arguably constitutionally vague and indefinite. One of the most successful policies has been to remove status offenders from secure lockups with delinquent youths. Further, nearly every state has legally prohibited incarcerating status offenders with delinquents. However, if a judge holds a status offender in contempt of court, the status offender may be placed in a secure detention facility. In the juvenile court, it is the intake division's duty to place the referral, either returning youths to the community or sending them to shelters or detention facilities. In more serious cases, juveniles commonly receive petitions to come before the juvenile court. The juvenile court judge (or referee) hears the case during an adjudicatory hearing, reviews the evidence, and determines if the youth is guilty.

The rights offered to juveniles in this court are guaranteed by the *In re Gault* case and consist of the right to have a lawyer, protection from self-incrimination, and the right to confront and cross-examine the witnesses. Recall that a disposition hearing is held after a youth has been found delinquent. (See Figure 11–3.)

Challenges to the Juvenile Justice Process

According to Bartollas (1988, pp. 390–97): "Today's juvenile justice system faces three major challenges: the "hard-line" mood of society, the conflicting multitude of attitudes and approaches regarding juvenile correction, and the limitations of the juvenile justice system."

Three challenges facing the juvenile justice system are

- *Society's current "hard-line" attitude.*
- *Conflicting approaches to correction.*
- *Limitations of the system.*

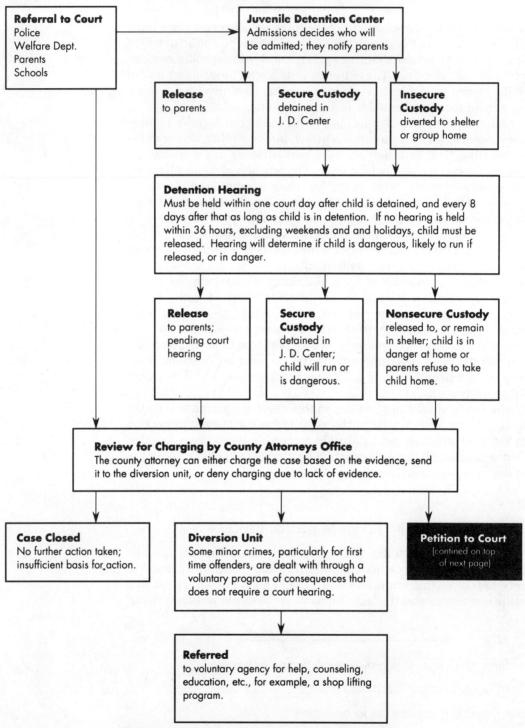

Referral to Court
Police
Welfare Dept.
Parents
Schools

Juvenile Detention Center
Admissions decides who will
be admitted; they notify parents

Release
to parents

Secure Custody
detained in
J. D. Center

Insecure Custody
diverted to shelter
or group home

Detention Hearing
Must be held within one court day after child is detained, and every 8
days after that as long as child is in detention. If no hearing is held
within 36 hours, excluding weekends and and holidays, child must be
released. Hearing will determine if child is dangerous, likely to run if
released, or in danger.

Release
to parents;
pending court
hearing

Secure Custody
detained in
J. D. Center;
child will run or
is dangerous.

Nonsecure Custody
released to, or remain
in shelter; child is in
danger at home or
parents refuse to take
child home.

Review for Charging by County Attorneys Office
The county attorney can either charge the case based on the evidence, send
it to the diversion unit, or deny charging due to lack of evidence.

Case Closed
No further action taken;
insufficient basis for action.

Diversion Unit
Some minor crimes, particularly for first
time offenders, are dealt with through a
voluntary program of consequences that
does not require a court hearing.

Petition to Court
(continued on top
of next page)

Referred
to voluntary agency for help, counseling,
education, etc., for example, a shop lifting
program.

Figure 11–3   Juvenile Justice System Flow Chart.
Source: Crystal, MN. Police Department. Reprinted with permission.

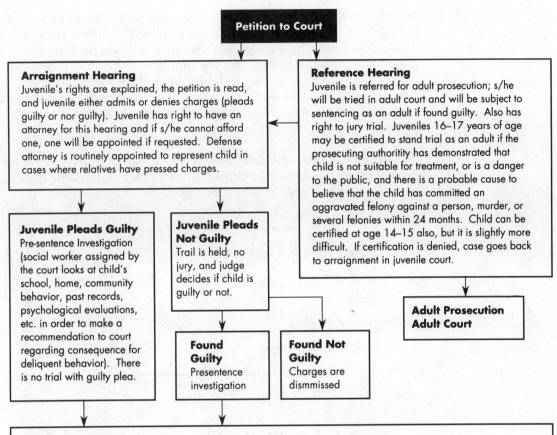

Petition to Court

Arraignment Hearing
Juvenile's rights are explained, the petition is read, and juvenile either admits or denies charges (pleads guilty or nor guilty). Juvenile has right to have an attorney for this hearing and if s/he cannot afford one, one will be appointed if requested. Defense attorney is routinely appointed to represent child in cases where relatives have pressed charges.

Reference Hearing
Juvenile is referred for adult prosecution; s/he will be tried in adult court and will be subject to sentencing as an adult if found guilty. Also has right to jury trial. Juveniles 16–17 years of age may be certified to stand trial as an adult if the prosecuting authoritity has demonstrated that child is not suitable for treatment, or is a danger to the public, and there is a probable cause to believe that the child has committed an aggravated felony against a person, murder, or several felonies within 24 months. Child can be certified at age 14–15 also, but it is slightly more difficult. If certification is denied, case goes back to arraignment in juvenile court.

Juvenile Pleads Guilty
Pre-sentence Investigation (social worker assigned by the court looks at child's school, home, community behavior, past records, psychological evaluations, etc. in order to make a recommendation to court regarding consequence for deliquent behavior). There is no trial with guilty plea.

Juvenile Pleads Not Guilty
Trail is held, no jury, and judge decides if child is guilty or not.

Found Guilty
Presentence investigation

Found Not Guilty
Charges are dismmissed

Adult Prosecution Adult Court

Dispostion Hearing
Judge looks at social worker's recommendation and makes a decision regarding consequences for the child's delinquent behavior. Dispositions can include any of the following:

1. Discontinued—no further action; case dropped.
2. Continued—case will be dropped if child does not get into further trouble within a certain specified time period.
3. Probation—child will be under the supervision of a probation officer for a period of time.
4. Restitution—child must pay for damages resulting from his/her delinquent behavior. May be put on weekend work program to "work off" amount owed.
5. Beta Program for boys—21 day work program; stay at County Home School; may be shortened for good behavior.
6. Psycholgical or chemical dependency evaluation, and treatment if indicated.
7. Out of home placement such as a group home or foster home.
8. Alpha Program—for repeat offenders who have serious attitude and behavior problems.
9. Committed to Commissioner of Corrections—s/he can sentence child to the state operated insitutions.

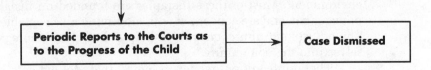

Periodic Reports to the Courts as to the Progress of the Child

Case Dismissed

The Hard-Line Mood of Society The public is currently becoming increasingly intolerant of serious youth crime. Dan Walker, former governor of Illinois, once said: "It is the people who are afraid; not the muggers, not the robbers, not the rapists, not the murderers, not the lawless. The people should not fear; the lawless should. That means we have to come up with a system that will make the lawless afraid. We need swift and sure punishment. And tougher punishment"(Bartollas, 1988, p. 391).

The Conflicting Multitude of Attitudes and Approaches Regarding Juvenile Correction Rehabilitation is the major model. It has three variations—justice, crime control, and logical consequences.

The basic correction models are

- *rehabilitation*
- *justice*
- *crime control*
- *logical consequences*

The Rehabilitation Model

The goal of *rehabilitation* is to change the offender's character, attitudes, or behavior. The medical model, the adjustment model, and the reintegration model all express variations of the rehabilitative philosophy.

The *medical model* holds that delinquency is generated by factors that can be isolated, identified, treated, and cured. This model supposes that the delinquent lacks free will or the ability to reason.

The *adjustment model* differs from the medical model in that its proponents believe delinquents can exercise free will and make responsible, law-abiding decisions. The adjustment model agrees with the medical model that delinquents do need treatment and uses reality therapy, transactional analysis, and positive peer culture to help juvenile offenders cope better with themselves, others, and their environment. Most of these therapies are founded on insight, not on punishment, and are concerned with modifying unacceptable behavior. The *adjustment approach* tries to help delinquents reintegrate themselves into the community.

The *reintegration model* assumes that delinquents' problems must be solved in the community where they began. This model stresses community-based corrections.

Many people believe the juvenile justice system is "too soft." Some facilities, however, do provide secure detention for particularly troubled youths.

The Justice Model

The justice model incorporates the due process and the least-restrictive philosophy. It challenges the *parens patriae* philosophy, which holds that states must justify interfering with a child's life. Children in need of help are not the same as children accused of crime. The justice model advocates accuracy and fairness in the juvenile justice system.

The justice model supports uniform sentencing and correctional programming. The least-restrictive philosophy claims that bad luck and chance are the only reasons many juveniles are caught, labeled, and processed. Once caught, the offenders begin living self-fulfilling prophecies. Supporters of the justice model stress that status offenders should be kept *out* of the juvenile justice system. This model supports the soft-line policy of decriminalization of status offenders and diverting minor juvenile offenders to voluntary services. However, it also assumes a hard-line policy when juvenile offenders commit serious crimes. In these instances, the punishment should be proportional to the crime—"just desserts."

The Crime Control Model

This model stresses punishment as a cure for juvenile misbehavior. The model became popular in the 1970s because it aimed at

Ray Nordine, Executive Director of Family Plus in Minneapolis, teaches parents the necessity of holding their children accountable for their actions. By explaining both the rules and the consequences of violating the rules, parents need only to enforce those rules to teach children responsibility.

protecting society and deterring crime while providing therapeutic accountability. Proponents of this model want more severity and certainty of punishment and greater use of incarceration for juvenile offenders. They believe the first priority of justice should be to protect the lives and property of the innocent. This model also promotes a "get-tough-with-drug-abusers" attitude.

The Logical Consequences Model

The logical consequences model is relatively new and still developing. It suggests that juvenile offenders should be made aware of how their socially unacceptable behavior affects society and what the costs and consequences are. This model is used extensively in probation, aftercare, and training schools. The model assumes juvenile offenders have free will and should be held accountable for their actions. The model also suggests that delinquents are so familiar with the justice system that they can take advantage of the permissiveness within it. Other assumptions made by this model are that delinquents will change their behavior only when the cost to themselves becomes too high and that mandatory community service is essential for juvenile corrections.

Although each model has a strong group of supporters, the presence and use of so many attitudes and approaches within a single juvenile justice system results in confusion and inefficiency.

Fragmentation of the Juvenile Justice System

Unfortunately, participants in the juvenile justice system seem to often disagree even among themselves as to what model is effective. This fragmented system is a result of the lack of agreement among the subsystems, the variety of agencies involved in the juvenile justice system, and the number of governmental agencies attempting to control the system from different perspectives and locations. Consequently, duplication of services and actual competition can result.

Juvenile courts continue to possess broad powers over youth who come under their jurisdiction.

In 1977, New York University's Institute of Judical Administration and the American Bar Association formed a joint committee and organized the *Standards for Juvenile Justice*, proposing a "recriminalization" of juvenile delinquency. For example, the committee thought sanctions should be "based on the seriousness of the offense committed," and that noncriminal offenses should be taken out of the juvenile court's jurisdiction. The committee also advised that judges seek to impose the "least restrictive alternative" during sentencing of juveniles and that they consider juvenile delinquency as juvenile crime. That same year, the state of Washington used the report by the committee to revise its juvenile code. During 1977 and 1978, New York also made refinements in its laws concerning juvenile sentencing based on the committee's report.

There is little doubt that society will continue to differentiate between juveniles and adults. In reality, this probably benefits everyone. Just *how* juveniles will be treated differently remains to be seen.

CONCLUSION

Having seen that the development of *juvenile* law has come about comparatively recently, it is worth noting the extent of law that has already been established. Let there be no mistake about it, our society places a great deal of importance on our youth, and the law reflects this fact.

An issue that remains in flux, however, is just how this law is going to deal with juveniles and what effect this will have on law enforcement. The beauty of our law is the fact that it is indeed a "living law" that can breathe, and develop, advance and retreat, solidify and alter itself. Nowhere in the entire body of American jurisprudence can this be seen more distinctly than in juvenile justice.

You have seen how the doctrine of *parens patriae* continues to permit the juvenile court to exercise broad discretion in its treatment of young people who find themselves within its system. The "classical theory" of delinquency tends to treat juveniles as adults, holding them more accountable for their actions by considering decisions to have been made via "free will," after weighing the pros and cons of such a decision.

Law enforcement has an opportunity to positively influence young people wherever children gather. Here an officer dressed as "McGruff—the crime fighting dog" passes out pencils imprinted with a safety message to children at a city picnic.

On the other hand, the "positivist theory" seeks to identify the *reason* a decision was made, proposing such factors as environmental, biological, or psychological influences as being at the root of the behavior.

These approaches continue to be accepted/rejected, molded, and adapted to respond to the way society chooses to perceive juvenile justice. There have been obvious trends in accepting the various approaches, often coinciding with the conservative or liberal trends evident throughout society. The fact is that all delinquent youth would fall within one of the many, many theories, but no one theory applies to *all* delinquent youth.

Without question, juvenile justice has come full circle from the ancient Roman times when children were viewed as an expendable commodity—worthy of little—to a time when we exuberantly declare our young people to be our most precious resource. It is in such an area as juvenile law that we see our American legal system doing what it does best—providing a firm basis from which to grow, overseeing the basic rights of all citizens, and remaining flexible enough to meet society's expectations.

ADULT AND JUVENILE JUSTICE SYSTEMS COMPARED

Table 11–4 summarizes the similarities and differences between the adult and the juvenile justice systems.

Table 11–4   Similarities and Differences between Adult and Juvenile Justice

Similarities between Juvenile and Adult Justice Systems	Differences between Juvenile and Adult Justice Systems
• Police officers, judges, and correctional personnel use discretion in decision-making in both the adult and the juvenile systems.	• The primary purpose of juvenile procedures is protection and treatment. With adults, the aim is to punish the guilty.
• The right to receive *Miranda* warnings applies to juveniles as well as adults.	• Age determines the jurisdiction of the juvenile court. The nature of the offense determines jurisdiction in the adult system.
• Juveniles and adults are protected from prejudical lineups or other identification procedures.	• Juveniles can be apprehended for acts that would not be criminal if they were committed by an adult (status offenses).
• Similar procedural safeguards protect juveniles and adults when they make an admission of guilt.	• Juvenile proceedings are not considered criminal; adult proceedings are.
• Prosecutors and defense attorneys play an equally critical role in juvenile and adult advocacy.	• Juvenile court procedures are generally informal and private. Those of adult courts are more formal and are open to the public.
• Juveniles and adults have the right to counsel at most key stages of the court process.	• Courts cannot release identifying information about a juvenile to the press, but they must release information about an adult.
• Pretrial motions are available in juvenile and criminal court proceedings.	• Parents are highly involved in the juvenile process but not in the adult process.
• Negotiations and the plea-bargain exist for children and adult offenders.	• The standard of arrest is more stringent for adults than for juveniles.
• Children and adults have a right to a hearing and an appeal.	• Juveniles are released into parental custody. Adults are generally given the opportunity for bail.
• The standard of evidence in juvenile delinquency adjudications, as in adult criminal trials, is proof beyond a reasonable doubt.	• Juveniles have no constitutional right to a jury trial. Adults have this right.
• Juveniles and adults can be placed on probation by the court.	• Juveniles can be searched in school without probable-cause or a warrant.
• Both juveniles and adults can be placed in pretrial detention facilities.	• A juvenile's record is sealed when the age of majority is reached. The record of an adult is permanent.
• Juveniles and adults can be kept in detention without bail if they are considered dangerous.	• A juvenile court cannot sentence juveniles to county jails or state prisons; these are reserved for adults.
• After trial, both can be placed in community treatment programs.	• There is no death penalty in the juvenile justice system.

Source: Larry J. Siegel and Joseph J. Senna. *Juvenile Delinquency,* 3rd ed., p. 340. West Publishing Company. Reprinted with permission.

SUMMARY

The doctrine of *parens patriae* refers to the right of the government to take care of minors and others who cannot legally take care of themselves. The four major phases of the juvenile justice system have been (1) a Puritan emphasis, (2) an emphasis on providing a refuge for youth, (3) development of the separate juvenile court, and (4) emphasis on juvenile rights.

Established in 1825 in New York City, the House of Refuge was the first juvenile reformatory. The first juvenile court was founded in

Chicago in 1899. The 1960s saw the change to an emphasis on juvenile rights. *Kent v. United States* established that if a juvenile court transfers a case to adult criminal court, juveniles are entitled to a hearing, their counsel must be given access to probation records used by the court in reaching its decision, and the court must state its reasons for waiving jurisdiction over the case. The *Gault* decision required that the due process clause of the Fourteenth Amendment apply to proceedings in state juvenile courts, including the right of notice, the right to counsel, the right against self-incrimination, and the right to confront witnesses.

A series of cases have continued to reinforce the trend extending more rights to juveniles, including *In re Winship* (1970) which decided that juveniles were entitled to proof "beyond a reasonable doubt" prior to being adjucated a delinquent. A more conservative trend was seen in *McKeiver v. Pennsylvania* (1971) when the Court denied juveniles the right to a jury trial in delinquency proceedings. *Breed v. Jones* established that a juvenile court cannot adjudicate a case and then transfer the case over to the criminal court for adult processing on the same offense; this constitutes double jeopardy.

The juvenile justice system has three basic parts: the police, the juvenile court, and corrections. Unique factors considered in juvenile court include the offender's age and the offense itself.

Three challenges facing the juvenile justice system are (1) society's "hard-line" attitude, (2) conflicting approaches to correction, and (3) limitations of the system.

The basic correction models are rehabilitation with its three variations of justice, crime control, and logical consequences.

Discussion Questions

1. What basic differences exist between adult and juvenile law?
2. Why do these differences exist?
3. Are juveniles any less protected by the Constitution than adults?
4. Do police use as much caution to insure the protection of constitutional rights when investigating juvenile-related matters?
5. In what direction do you see juvenile justice heading today—more liberal or conservative?
6. Why does juvenile work remain a "less favorite" area for most police officers to be involved in?

References

Arnold, W. R., and Brungardt, T. *Juvenile Misconduct and Delinquency*. Boston: Houghton Mifflin Company, 1983.

Bartollas, Clemens. *Juvenile Delinquency*. New York: John Wiley and Sons, 1988.

Binder, Arnold; Geis, Gilbert; and Dickson, Bruce. *Juvenile Delinquency: Historical, Cultural, Legal Perspectives*. New York: Macmillan Publishing Company, 1988.

Carey, J. T.; Goldfarb, J.; Rowe, M. H.; and Lohman, J. D. *The Handling of Juveniles from Offense to Disposition*. U.S. Department of Health, Education, and Welfare. Washington, D.C.: U.S. Government Printing Office, 1967.

Cox, Steven M., and Conrad, John J. *Juvenile Justice: A Guide to Practice and Theory*. 2d ed. Dubuque, Iowa: Wm. C. Brown Publishers, 1987.

Eldefenso, E., and Hartinger, W. *Control, Treatment, and Rehabilitation of Juvenile Offenders*. Beverly Hills, Calif.: Glencoe Press, 1976.

LaFave, Wayne R., and Israel, Jerold H. *Criminal Procedure*. St. Paul, Minn.: West Publishing Company, 1985.

McCreedy, K. R. *Juvenile Justice—System and Procedures*. Albany, N.Y.: Delmar Publishers, 1975.

Oran, Daniel. *Law Dictionary for Nonlawyers*. 2d ed. St. Paul, Minn.: West Publishing Company, 1985.

Senna, Joseph J. and Siegel, Larry J. *Introduction to Criminal Justice*. 4th ed. St. Paul, Minn.: West Publishing Company, 1987.

Siegel, Larry J., and Senna Joseph J. *Juvenile Delinquency*. 3d ed. St. Paul, Minn.: West Publishing Company, 1988.

Stuckey, Gilbert B. *Procedures in the Justice System*. 3d ed. Charles E. Merrill Publishing Co.

Trojanowicz, Robert C., and Morash, Merry. *Juvenile Delinquency: Concepts and Control*. 4th ed. Englewood Cliffs, N.J.: Prentice Hall, Inc., 1973.

Twentieth Century Fund Task Force on Sentencing Policy Toward Young Offenders. *Confronting Youth Crime*. New York: Holmes and Meier Publishers, Inc., 1978.

Vetter, Harold J., and Territo, Leonard. *Crime and Justice in America: A Human Perspective*. St. Paul, Minn.: West Publishing Company, 1984.

Wroblelski, Henry M., and Hess, Kären M. *Introduction to Law Enforcement and Criminal Justice*. 2d ed. St. Paul, Minn.: West Publishing Company, 1986.

A JUSTICE MODEL VS. A CHILD WELFARE MODEL

Justice for Juveniles (Charles E. Springer, 1987, U.S. Department of Justice, Office of Juvenile Justice and Delinquency Prevention) suggests that we abandon our traditional child welfare approach to juveniles and adopt instead a justice model. The following excerpts summarize the argument, how we came to our current model, and what is proposed in its place.

The first step in doing justice for juveniles is to revise juvenile court acts throughout the country so that when juvenile courts deal with delinquent children, they operate under a justice model rather than under the present treatment or the child welfare model. By a justice model is meant a judicial process wherein young people who come in conflict with the law are held responsible and accountable for their behavior.

The juvenile court should be maintained as a special tribunal for children, but when dealing with criminal misconduct, the emphasis and rationale of the court must be changed to reflect the following:

- Although young people who violate the law deserve special treatment because of their youth, they should be held morally and legally accountable for their transgressions and should be subject to prompt, certain, and fair punishment.
- Except for certain mentally disabled and incompetent individuals, young law violators should not be considered by the juvenile courts as being "sick" or as victims of their environments. Generally speaking, young criminals are more wrong than wronged, more the victimizers than the victims.
- Juvenile courts are primarily courts of justice and not social clinics; therefore emphasis in court proceedings should be on the public interest rather than on the welfare and treatment of the child. This does not mean that these ends cannot be successfully carried out by a justice-oriented juvenile court.
- Many environmental factors can contribute to the commission of a criminal act by a young person, but the major factor courts should deal with is the moral decision to violate rather than to obey the law. Law violators are best dealt with by doing justice—by reproval and punishment.
- To adopt a justice model is not to rule out or diminish the importance of rehabilitative measures employed by juvenile courts. Disapproval of, and punishment for, the wrongful act is probably the single-most important rehabilitative measure available to the

court. Additional counseling, education, and the like are easily incorporated into an accountability-punishment disposition for delinquents.

These ideas, however, are incompatible with the basic legal assumptions that ground the present juvenile court structure. What is proposed is a new structure, a model based on justice rather than on the questionable "alegal" social theories that underlie the present system.

Origins of Our Present System

The first juvenile court act was passed in Illinois in 1899. It adopted much of the practice and legislation that had resulted from the child-saving, house-of-refuge movement. It created a special court to deal exclusively with juveniles and incorporated a number of other special procedures for juveniles. Each of these special procedures had already been in practice in one or more jurisdictions—with the exception of one extremely important and radical departure from the past: the circuit and county courts of Illinois were given "original jurisdiction in *all* cases coming within the terms of this act." This important change divested the adult criminal courts of all criminal jurisdiction over children under age 16.

A second important feature of the act, as its title reveals, was that its purpose was to regulate the treatment and control of *dependent, neglected,* and *delinquent* children, thereby equating poor children with criminal children and insisting that they be treated in substantially the same manner. This became more significant when, in 1905, the Illinois act was amended so that the definition of "delinquent" included, in addition to criminal children, children who were incorrigible or who did any number of objectionable, noncriminal things such as knowingly associating with vicious persons, being absent from home without permission, growing up in idleness, visiting any public poolroom, habitually wandering about any railroad yard, and other such knavery.

The act does not mention punishment of a child for criminal conduct—only treatment and control of the kind a parent would give to a child.

Civil vs. Delinquency Jurisdiction

One of the major failings in the juvenile court system is what can be referred to as the "one-pot" jurisdictional approach—putting poor, rebellious, and criminal children in the same jurisdictional pot. The "pot" was called "wardship" and into it went dependent and neglected children, delinquent children, and rebellious and beyond-control (considered delinquent) children. All three kinds of children were thought to be the products or victims of bad family and social environments; consequently, it was thought, they should be subject, as wards of the court, to the same kind of solicitious, helpful care. Herein lies the major evidence of the complete positivistic-deterministic takeover of the theoretical and legislative base for the juvenile court system. Thus, the common declaration of status was that of wardship; and, as mentioned above, street dancers, grave robbers, and murders wind up, theoretically at least, in the same "pot" namely, as wards of the court, subject to being treated by the paternal court in the manner that loving parents would or should treat their child.

During the 1950's, a series of legislative reforms starting in New York and California recognized problems inherent in "one-pot" jurisdiction, and a three-part jurisdiction was provided for. Today, most States recognize basic jurisdictional differences among the three classes of juveniles: the poor, abused, and neglected; the delinquent; and the so-called status offenders. A graver distinction than this tripartite division is the more basic distinction between criminal and civil jurisdiction. This distinction is still blurred and needs clarification. The need for differentiation between criminal and civil was exquisitely expressed in 1926 by Professor John H. Wigmore in language which is extremely relevant to the issues under discussion.

We recognize the beneficient function of the juvenile court. We have always supported it, and we are proud that Illinois invented it. But its devoted advocates, in their zeal, have lost their balance. And, as usual in other fields of science that have been awakening to their interest in the crime problem, their error is due to their narrow and imperfect conception of the criminal law . . . .

They are ignoring . . . two functions of the criminal law (affirmation of moral law and deterrence), and they are virtually on the way to abolish criminal law and undermine social morality, by ignoring those other two functions . . . The courtroom is the only place in the community today where the moral law is laid down to the people with the voice of authority . . .

Law violators, young and old, should be punished for their crimes. . . . Even at a very early age, young people are not the guileless, plastic, and pliable people they are portrayed to be by those who would free them from all moral and legal responsibility. Children understand punishment and they understand fairness. Most of the juvenile justice system's faults can be improved by an honest return to undisguised punishments as the natural and just consequences of criminal behavior.

Of course, this does not mean that juvenile court action should be limited to the infliction of pain on children. What it means is that criminally active children should be held responsible and accountable for their crimes. After this is done, many other benefits can flow from a special court created and operated solely for young people. A punishment and accountability regimen promises enhanced expectations from rehabilitation programs and an added measure to deterrence.

It is time that we recognize the impossible double bind our juvenile judges are placed in when they, judical officers, are commanded to diagnose the "problem" of some young offender, when in most cases it is obvious that the criminal youth does not have a problem—he or she *is* the problem

CHAPTER 12

Other Issues

The law must be stable, but it must not stand still.—Roscoe Pound, *Introduction to the Philosophy of Law*

DO YOU KNOW

If electronic surveillance is governed by the Fourth Amendment?

What is needed for a warrant to undertake electronic surveillance?

When electronic surveillance infringes on a person's right to privacy?

How to define informant?

If people have to appear in court to testify?

How the credibility of hearsay evidence is determined?

What entrapment is?

What two approaches are used to defend against the charge of entrapment?

What consequences result from using an entrapment defense?

Introduction

Chapter 12

Reference has been made several times to our American legal system as the *living law*. Indeed, for over two centuries it has proven to be more than capable of forming and shaping itself to meet the changing needs of the society it serves.

Sometimes such adaptation is quick and obvious. For example, the Eighteenth Amendment of the United States Constitution initiating prohibition was ratified in 1919 and repealed by the Twenty-first Amendment in 1933. Other changes, such as administrative and procedural law, have come more slowly, drawing far less public attention.

Nonetheless, American law is continually under transition. Being torn down and built up again, not unlike the constant change in our earth's form, our law is shaped by the environment around it.

Some bodies of our law have proven more resistant to rapid change than has criminal law. Bodies of law such as real property (land) and contracts, with their roots firmly embedded in ancient English common law, have relied on precedent to resist any overly anxious transitions.

Criminal law, however, continues to be a body of law that shows rapid, dramatic change. After all, the founders of our Constitution wanted to build into our laws certainty that the tyranny they left behind would not reappear in the New World. The development of criminal

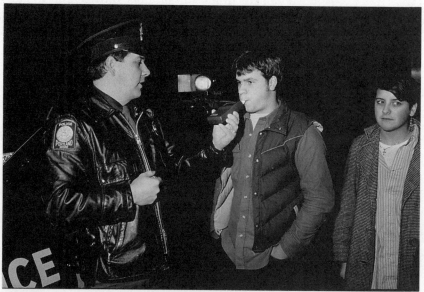

The framers of the United States Constitution could have had no way to foresee the advancements that technology would make. Their document has, however, withstood the test of time, continuing to establish the freedoms held dear to all Americans. Government officials today must comply with the same basic guidelines as officials did two hundred years ago.

The United States Supreme Court in 1989.

law in the United States remains in a transitional phase, shaping and molding into the form that serves its citizens best.

Recent rapid changes have clearly appeared in areas such as laws pertaining to child abuse and drunken driving, where the system has been modified to deal with offenders more rapidly and harshly. On the other hand, a number of states have lessened their laws dealing with marijuana in response to change in societal norms. The perceived needs of society dictate the law. Because of this, it becomes evident why political appointments to the judicial bench can raise such an uproar. The Reagan presidential administration had an unprecedented opportunity to appoint a number of federal judges, including United States Supreme Court justices. The effects of having a specifically picked judiciary to interpret laws are obvious and are but another reason why our laws are so very capable of change.

While land remains land, and contracts remain contracts, crime and the criminals who commit crime seem to be always on the move. Our increasingly sophisticated society itself has had a pronounced effect on law enforcement. A frighteningly serious debate exists over whether the professional criminal must strive to keep up with the police or the other way around.

New weapons, drugs, changes in moral values, new modes of rapid transportation, an increase in terroristic activity, and a society generally "on the move" have all resulted in rapid changes in the law enforcement profession. Henry Wrobleski, Director of Law Enforcement Education at Normandale Community College in Minnesota, states: "Want a different experience every day? Be a law enforcement officer!"

In turn, the study of criminal procedure remains in a state of flux. For many, this is what makes the study of our criminal justice system so entirely fascinating. It does not remain static.

This chapter is a direct response to these changes. Often, such changes do not fit neatly into the traditional chapter headings in most criminal procedure texts. Therefore, this chapter addresses timely issues important to the professional law enforcement officer.

Again, because of constant change in the law, the *professional* police officer maintains an updated knowledge of the law. Police officers whose departments do not have a system by which such changes are made known would be well advised to recommend this. The last chapter in this text offers some suggestions on how to keep current with our ever-changing law.

ELECTRONIC SURVEILLANCE

Electronic surveillance clearly illustrates our "living law" at work. The drafters of our Constitution in their wildest fantasies could hardly have foreseen the current technology. The general public has little understanding of the sophistication level existing in investigative equipment capable of intruding on their most intimate conversations.

The use of such investigative devices must comply with the Fourth Amendment rules as much as any activity conducted two hundred years ago. In other words, a balance must be struck between the necessity of law enforcement to incriminate the guilty, while assuring that such intrusiveness does not become unreasonable, disturbing our precious right to privacy. This is precisely the equitable balance the law of criminal procedure seeks to achieve.

Initially, the Supreme Court held in *Olmstead* v. *United States* (1928) that obtaining evidence by wiretapping a telephone did not violate the Fourth Amendment because the suspect's property was not physically invaded, and also because the Fourth Amendment was considered to apply to the seizure of *objects* (Ferdico, 1985 p. 362).

Subsequent cases invalidated such arguments, placing emphasis on "privacy" rather than "property."

A series of cases and legislation evolved that sought to come to grips with this complex, powerful new area of obtaining evidence. Presently, Title III of the Federal Omnibus Crime Control and Safe Streets Act of 1968 regulates the use of electronic surveillance.

The act carries on the concept that electronic surveillance is a "search and seizure" within the meaning of the Fourth Amendment (Ferdico, 1985 p. 362). During the 1960s, case law sought to define what uses of this technology would be considered "reasonable."

In *Osborn* v. *United States* (1966), a conversation was taped by a hidden recorder by undercover federal agents with a warrant in an attempt to prove that labor leader Jimmy Hoffa's lawyer was bribing a juror. The evidence was admitted on the basis that the electronic device was used in "precise and discriminate circumstances" set forth in the warrant.

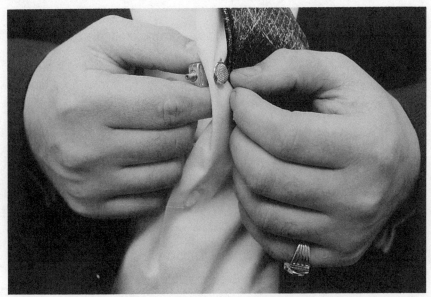

Like the increasing complexity of our high-tech age, the procedural concerns of such fourth amendment areas as electronic surveillance have become complex, yet essential for the law enforcement profession to understand.

Berger v. New York (1967) held that using such devices must be limited and that a "two month surveillance period was the equivalent of a series of intrusions, searches, and seizures pursuant to a single showing of probable cause" (Ferdico, 1985 p. 364). Warrants may be issued for such a time period, but beyond that they must be reviewed or extended.

Electronic surveillance is a form of search and seizure and as such is governed by the Fourth Amendment.

In *Katz v. United States* (1967) the Supreme Court held that obtaining evidence by attaching an electronic device to listen on a public phone booth (Ferdico 1985, p. 365) was an unlawful search and seizure because there was no warrant. In response, Congress enacted the Omnibus Crime Control and Safe Streets Act of 1968.

Other factors contributing to passage of this act included the social unrest caused by the assassinations of Martin Luther King, Jr. and Robert F. Kennedy as well as the "law and order" presidential campaign of Richard Nixon.

Title III called for judicial supervision of all aspects of electronic surveillance.

To obtain an electronic surveillance warrant, probable cause that a person is engaging in particular communications must be established by the court, and normal investigative procedures must have already been tried.

Title III established specific procedures to apply for, issue, and execute court orders to intercept wire or oral communications (Ferdico, 1985 p. 367).

Electronic surveillance is an infringement on one's privacy only when it intrudes on one's reasonable expectations of that privacy.

The Supreme Court has ruled that this expectation does not exist when someone voluntarily converses with someone else—the "unreliable ear" exception. The lower courts have held that this expectation does not exist when someone converses in public, because others *may* hear—the "uninvited ear" exception. For instance, a warrant is not required for an undercover officer to converse with suspects, using what they say in court.

Title III requires that "all nonconsensual surveillance for the purpose of investigating crime must take place pursuant to a warrant and establishes a detailed regulatory scheme for implementing this objective" (Whitebread and Slobogin, 1986, p. 320).

Police do not need a warrant to use an electronic beeper to monitor travel in public. *United States* v. *Knotts* (1983) held that a person traveling on a public thoroughfare has no reasonable expectation of privacy; therefore, using a beeper to track such a person cannot constitute a search. However, a warrant may be necessary to install a beeper to locate evidence or to track and monitor a person in a private residence.

Title III also regulates using electronic devices to tap or intercept wire communications. Such devices are legal under only two conditions: (1) a court order authorizes the wiretap, or (2) one person consents to the wiretap. *United States* v. *White* (1970) held that "the Constitution does not prohibit a government agent from using an electronic device to record a telephone conversation between two parties with the consent of one party to the conversation" (del Carmen, 1987 p. 211).

Title III also does not require a warrant for using a device to trace telephone calls or devices that record what phone numbers were called from a specific phone. The reason is that actual conversations are not being monitored. A warrant could be required, however, to install such devices.

USING INFORMANTS

Many crimes are solved not because officers stumble on crimes in progress, but because they get information from a number of sources that help them learn who may have been involved. Informants remain an important source of information.

An informant is any person who gives law enforcement officers

information on criminal activity.

Skilled police officers treat people with respect. One benefit of doing so is that individuals are more likely to approach officers with information. Even if they do not volunteer, they may *have* to divulge their information.

The judicial process can compel people to appear in court to testify.

The Sixth Amendment requires witnesses to give testimony in the defendant's favor. The basic way to compel attendance at trial proceedings is by a subpoena. The subpoena helps assure that witnesses will come to the trial. Once there, they must answer questions unless the answers might incriminate themselves.

One problem with using information from informants is that credibility is always an issue. While occasionally an "upstanding citizen" gives helpful information to the police, often such information comes from people associated with criminals. Perhaps they provide such information to get out of a present legal jam. Or perhaps they want to feel important to the "other side." It's difficult to speculate why, but the fact remains that such informers are easily discredited because they are often unreliable.

Again, our law seeks a balance between the inherent risk of using such potentially important and helpful information, and the very real possibility that it could be less than reliable or be easily made to appear so to the jury.

Officers who use informants to establish probable cause must follow specific legal procedures established by case law. And the law dealing with information obtained from informants is on the move.

Legal Requirements for Using Informants

Two United States Supreme court decisions, *Aguilar* v. *Texas* (1964) and *Spinelli* v. *United States* (1969), established specific requirements for law enforcement officers who use informants' information to prepare complaints or affidavits. These two "prongs" were considered separate and independent of each other.

The Aguilar case applied a two-pronged test to determine probable cause. The first prong tested the informant's basis of knowledge. Was the information accurate? Did the informant personally witness the information given? If not, did the information come from another source? Is there still reason to believe it?

The second prong tested the informant's credibility. Was the person reliable? Do you know the informant's identity? Is the informant an ordinary citizen or a criminal?

In other words, the historical two-pronged test for an informant's credibility looked at (1) the basis of knowledge and (2) the informant's credibility.

Ordinary citizens are presumed credible when they claim to be victims of or witnesses to a crime, or when they express concern for their own safety and do not expect anything in return for the information. It is also presumed that citizen informants would probably fear the consequences of committing perjury and would, therefore, be truthful.

When informants are criminals, they seldom will identify themselves. This poses a problem in determining credibility. One way to establish the credibility of criminal informants is to show that they have given accurate information in the past. Another way is to show that they made admissions or produced evidence against their own interest. A third way is to show they have been informants for a period of time. A fourth way to establish criminal informant credibility is to conduct the investigation with the informant supervised by a law enforcement officer.

Establishing Probable Cause through Secondhand Sources

Beck established that probable cause must come from "reasonably trustworthy information . . . within [the police officer's] knowledge." This knowledge need not be the officer's own firsthand observations. In *Whitely* v. *Warden* (1971), for example, police officers made a warrantless arrest based on information from a radio bulletin received from another jurisdiction.

According to Whitebread and Slobogin (1986, p. 81):

> The Supreme Court's leading case on the use of informants in the arrest context is Draper v. United States (1959). In that case, an informant advised police officers that the defendant was selling drugs, that he had gone to Chicago to secure a new supply and that he would be returning on a train carrying a tan bag that would contain the pur-

chased drugs. Further, the informant described what Draper would be wearing and said that he would "walk real fast." The officers observed a man fitting the description emerge from the train carrying a tan zipper bag and walking very quickly. They arrested Draper without a warrant, searched him, and found drugs. The Supreme Court, in upholding Draper's conviction, said the informant's tip, coupled with the corroboration of the information from the observation of the officers themselves, sufficed to establish probable cause to arrest.

In addition to holding that probable cause may be established by competent hearsay, the Draper *decision made it clear that an officer, acting without a warrant, need not postpone an arrest until competent evidence is adduced which at trial would prove the defendant's guilt.*

The landmark decision of *Illinois v. Gates* (1983), established that an arrest based on hearsay information, with or without a warrant, is valid if the *totality of circumstances* supports the credibility of the informant.

Illinois v.Gates established that the credibility of hearsay information from informants was to be based on the *totality of circumstances.*

The *Gates* decision turned away from the two-pronged requirements and toward a "totality of the circumstances" approach in determining probable cause. In other words, the judge will review *all* factors tending to establish probable cause, including that obtained from informants. This naturally would include such factors as basis of knowledge and credibility.

Revealing an Informant's Identity

Police officers are usually *not* required to reveal their informants' identities in their search warrant affidavits. Doing so often jeopardizes the informant's usefulness in future cases. If a name is not given, enough information must appear in the affidavit for the magistrate to believe the un-named informant is credible.

Information given by ordinary citizens is usually considered reliable by judges. They may not require the name of the informant to be revealed if it would put the informant in danger, but this may become an issue at trial.

Information provided by other police officers is usually considered highly reliable.

ENTRAPMENT

Entrapment, like the *Miranda* rule, is a subject that the public believes it is well versed on because of a heavy diet of television police shows. These "dramas" often depict officers setting up radar in obviously inconspicuous locations and then being assertively informed by the citizens tagged that the police method is a clear case of ENTRAPMENT. If only it were so easy . . .

According to LaFave and Israel (1985, p. 369):

> It is everywhere agreed that the agents of the government, in combatting crime, may properly employ some subterfuge and deception to obtain evidence of crime. A policeman may properly pretend to be drunk, lie in the gutter with his wallet protruding from his hip pocket and await the coming of the thief who is ready and willing to "roll" the drunk. . . . there is no entrapment if the policeman merely furnishes an opportunity for the commission of the crime by one ready and willing to commit it.

Entrapment is often used as a defense. Just what is entrapment? One definition was provided in *Sorrells* v. *United States* (1932): "Entrapment is the conception and planning of an offense by an officer, and his procurement of its commission by one who would not have perpetrated it except for the trickery, persuasion, or fraud of the officer." Indeed, when police officers encourage others to engage in criminal activity, this should not be viewed lightly. Such encouragement might, in fact, cause normally law-abiding citizens to commit crime.

Oran (1985, p. 111) says:

Entrapment is the act of government officials or agents (usually police) inducing a person to commit a crime that the person would not have otherwise committed.

According to Whitebread and Slobogin (1986, p. 443): "The defense of entrapment arises when a defendant, who has admittedly committed a crime, can prove that the actions of law enforcement authorities caused him to commit the crime . . . . The defense of entrapment is grounded in the belief that the government should not be able to accuse a person of a crime when the government itself is the instigator of the conduct."

Two approaches to define entrapment are the subjective approach and the objective approach.

The subjective approach, also called the *Sherman-Sorrells* approach uses a two-step test to determine if entrapment has occurred:

1. Was the offense induced by a government agent?

2. Was the defendant predisposed to commit this type of offense?

Most states use the subjective approach, focusing on the predisposition of the defendant to commit the offense charged. Only if the accused has no predisposition to commit such an offense does entrapment work as a defense.

This can be seen in the *DeLorean* case where the jury acquitted automobile manufacturer John DeLorean despite videotape evidence showing him selling narcotics. The jury concluded that such a well-respected businessman was not naturally predisposed to engaging in such activities and did so only as the result of the government's setting up the situation and trapping him.

In the subjective approach, the defendant usually has the burden of proof to establish that a government agent provided some inducement to commit the crime.

LaFave and Israel (1985, pp. 251–52) cite several objections to this approach to entrapment. First, the legislative intent is attacked as sheer fiction—is the conduct unquestionably criminal if the "temptor" is a private person rather than a government agent? Second, this approach creates an "anything goes" rule. Third, the defendant's past is used in a prejudicial way. The prosecutor can admit criminal records, reputation, previous acts of misconduct, and other kinds of information generally barred as hearsay.

The objective approach, also called the *Roberts-Frankfurter* approach, focuses on the inducements used rather than on whether they were government induced or whether the defendant was predisposed to committing such crime. That is, rather than looking at the defendant's predisposition to commit the crime, the focus is on the conduct of the government agent. Under this approach, the entire burden of proof is on the defendant who must clearly establish impropriety of police conduct. LaFave and Israel (1985, pp. 252) also note several objections to this approach. First, a defendant's predisposition IS important. Second, the "wrong" people can end up in jail. Third, it can promote inaccuracy in the fact-finding process. And fourth, it is questionable if the "purity" of the courts itself is sufficient justification to use this approach.

Entrapment is most often charged in drug arrests.

Sometimes "contingent fee" arrangements are involved in entrapment charges. This consists of paying another person to act on behalf of the police to induce someone else to commit a crime. According to LaFave and Israel (1985, p. 256):

> The landmark case on this subject is Williamson v. United States (1962) where federal agents told one Moye that they would give him $200 and $100, respectively, for legally admissible evidence that two specified persons were engaged in illicit liquor dealings. Moye made a purchase from one of them and produced evidence against both, for which he was paid the promised amount. Exercising its supervisory power over the administration of criminal justice in the federal courts,

*the court of appeals reversed the resulting conviction. The court ex-
plained:*

*"Without some . . . justification or explanation, we cannot sanction
a contingent fee agreement to produce evidence against particular
named defendants as to crimes not yet committed. Such an arrange-
ment might tend to a frame up, or to cause an informer to induce or
persuade innocent persons to commit crimes which they had no previous intent or purpose to commit. The opportunities for abuse are too
obvious to require elaboration."*

Anything held out to the public is not protected by the Fourth
Amendment because there is no reasonable expectation of privacy.

For example, you do not have a reasonable expectation of privacy
while moving about in public or talking to another person. The fact
always exists in such circumstances that it may be a police officer is
observing you, or that you are, in fact, talking to a police officer. This is
why undercover agents may conduct their investigations without a
warrant. If you invite someone into your home, you know that the
possibility exists that the person may be a police officer.

Procedural Concerns

If a defense of entrapment is claimed, several serious consequences result. As noted by LaFave and Israel (1985, p. 253), "Entrapment . . .is a 'dangerous and judicially unpopular defense that should
only be used in a few cases with ideal fact situation or in desperate
circumstances where no other defense is possible.' " This is because of
the changes in procedures that result. Once entrapment is used as a
defense, several evidentiary rules no longer apply, including inquiring
into the defendant's prior convictions, prior arrests, and "reputation."

In addition, such cases usually must be decided by a jury rather
than by a judge.

---

*If a defense of entrapment is used, the defendant's "reputation" and
any past record can be used in court. The trial must be by jury rather
than by a judge.*

Whitebread and Slobogin (1986, p. 453) suggest that entrapment
exists only if the defendant can show

1. that the offense was induced by the government (i.e., the
    government initiated the idea for the crime); and
2. that he was not predisposed to commit the type of offense . . .
3. that the governmental conduct was so outrageous that it
    violated concepts of fundamental fairness.

Abscam

Kamisar et al. (1986, pp. 474–75) describe the ABSCAM scandal that rocked the United States in the early 1980s:

> "Abscam" is an acronym combining the first two letters of Abdul Enterprises, a fictitious Middle Eastern corporation, and "scam," a slang term for swindle or confidence game. Abscam began as a standard "sting" operation, i.e., an FBI undercover scheme to recover stolen securities and paintings. In 1978, the operation shifted to political corruption in the New Jersey area. A year later, it had turned its attention to the "Asylum Scenario"; unsuspecting "middlemen" (private persons unaware that they were part of a government undercover operation) passed the word to various Congressmen, or to their aides and acquaintances, that wealthy Arabs were willing to bribe members of Congress in order to ensure that they would introduce private immigration bills on the Arabs' behalf if and when necessary. In early 1980, shortly before shutting down, the operation shifted to political corruption in Philadelphia.
>
> As a result of Abscam, a U.S. Senator, six U.S. Representatives and a number of other public officials and lawyers were convicted of various corrupt acts. Although many of the defendants (and many critics of the operation both in and out of Congress) charged that the FBI's methods constituted entrapment and/or violated the due process rights of the individuals caught in the operation, not a single Abscam defendant prevailed in the courts.

"Letters to the Editor" of *Newsweek* (March 1, 1980) showed the public's attitude toward the operation:

> Our national integrity has been on a downhill slide for seven years; we really don't need the FBI to grease the skids with Operation ABSCAM. Where no crime has been contemplated, the FBI has, through entrapment, induced to crime men who were previously involved in no wrongdoing. Aren't there enough naturally encouraging crime to keep the FBI busy? Must they spend astronomical sums creating crime?

Private Persons Inducing Someone to Commit a Crime

If a private person not connected with law enforcement induces someone to commit a crime, no defense of entrapment can be used.

SUMMARY

Electronic surveillance is a form of search and seizure and as such is governed by the Fourth Amendment. To obtain an electronic surveillance warrant, probable cause that a person was engaging in particular communications must be established by the court, and normal investigative procedures must have already been tried. Electronic surveillance is an infringement on one's privacy *only* when it intrudes on one's reasonable expectations of that privacy.

An informant is any person who gives law enforcement officers information on criminal activity. *Illinois* v. *Gates* established that the credibility of hearsay information from informants is to be based on the *totality of circumstances*. The government can compel people to appear in court to testify.

Entrapment is the act of government officials or agents (usually police) inducing a person to commit a crime that the person would not have otherwise committed. Two approaches to define entrapment are the subjective approach and the objective approach. If a defense of entrapment is used, the defendant's "reputation" and any past record can be used in court. The trial must be by jury rather than by a judge

Discussion Questions

1. What is meant by our "living law"?
2. Why does criminal law change more often than such areas as contract law and real property law?
3. Why does electronic surveillance create a new concern for constitutional law application?
4. What obvious problem arises from the use of informants?
5. Why is entrapment frequently a concept misunderstood by lay people?

References

del Carmen, Rolando V. *Criminal Procedure for Law Enforcement Personnel.* Monterey, Calif.: Brooks/Cole Publishing Company. 1987.

Ferdico, John N. *Criminal Procedure for the Criminal Justice Professional.* 3d ed. St. Paul, Minn.: West Publishing Company, 1985.

Kamisar, Yale; LaFave, Wayne R.; and Israel, Jerold H. *Criminal Procedure. Basic Comments and Questions,* 6th ed. St. Paul, Minn.: West Publishing Company, 1986.

LaFave, Wayne R., and Israel, Jerold. *Criminal Procedure.* St. Paul, Minn.: West Publishing Company, 1985.

Oran, Daniel. *Oran's Dictionary of the Law.* St. Paul, Minn.: West Publishing Company, 1983.

Senna, Joseph J., and Siegel, Larry J. *Introduction to Criminal Justice.* 4th ed. St. Paul, Minn.: West Publishing Company, 1987.

Whitebread, Charles H., and Slobogin, Christopher. *Criminal Procedure. An Analysis of Cases and Concepts.* 2d ed. Mineola, N.Y.: The Foundation Press, Inc. 1986.

WHAT ABOUT POLICE ETHICS AND VALUES?

A critical question relates to police officers and their ethics and values. The following, excerpted from "Learning Police Ethics," should provide much for the law enforcement officer to consider. Do values get learned this way and are the values suggested held by most veteran police officers?

Why They Become Police

Police applicants tend to see police work as an adventure, as a chance to do work out of doors without being cooped up in an office, as a chance to do work that is important for the good of society, and not as a chance to be the "toughest guy on the block." Nothing in the motivation to apply for a police position seems to predispose police officers towards unethical behavior.

How They Are Trained and "Socialized"

Police recruit training has changed substantially, but the central method of moral instruction does not appear to have changed. The "war story" still remains the most effective device for communicating the history and values of the department. The war stories not only introduce police work as it is experienced by police officers. They also introduce the ethics of police work as something different from what the public, or at least the law and the press, might expect. Van Maanen recounts one excerpt from a police academy criminal law lecture that, while not a "story," indicates the way in which the hidden values of police work are conveyed:

> I suppose you guys have heard of Lucky Baldwin? If not, you sure will when you hit the street. Baldwin happens to be the biggest burglar still operating in this town. Every guy in this department from patrolman to chief would love to get him and make it stick. We've busted him about ten times so far, but he's got an asshole lawyer and money so he always beats the rap . . . .If I ever get a chance to pinch the SOB, I'll do it my way with my thirty-eight and spare the city the cost of a trial.

ENCOUNTER: After they leave the academy, the rookies are usually handed over to Field Training Officers (FTOs). In the classic version of the first day on patrol with the rookie, the FTO says, "Forget everything they taught you in the academy, kid; I'll show you how police

320

work is really done." And show they do. The rookie becomes an observer of the FTO as he or she actually does police work. Suddenly the war stories come alive, and all the questions about how to handle tough situations get answered very quickly and clearly, as one police veteran recalls:

> On this job, your first partner is everything. He tells you how to survive on the job . . .how to walk, how to stand, and how to speak and how to think and what to say and see.

The Reality Shock

The encounter with the FTO is only part of the rookie's "reality shock" about police work. Perhaps even more important are the rookie's encounters with the public. By putting on the uniform, the rookie becomes part of a visible minority group. The self-consciousness about the new appearance is heightened by the nasty taunts and comments the uniform attracts from teenagers and others. The uniform and gun, as symbols of power, attract challenges to that power simply because they are there. Caught frequently in the cross-fire of equally unreasonable citizen demands, the rookie naturally reacts by blaming the public. The spontaneous reaction is reinforced by one of the central values of the police culture: the public as enemy. It is the public that transforms the rookie's self-conception, teaching him or her the pains of exercising power.

Finally, in the encounter stage, the rookie gets the major reality shock in the entire process of becoming a police officer. The rookie discovers that police work is more social work than crime fighting, more arbitration of minor disputes than investigations of major crimes, more patching of holes in the social fabric than weaving the webs to catch the big-time crooks. The rookie's usual response is to define most of the assignments received as "garbage calls," not *real* police work. Not quite sure whom to blame for the fact that he or she was hired to do police work but was assigned everything else, the rookie blames the police executive, the mayor and city council, and even previous U.S. presidents (for raising public expectations). But most of all the rookie blames the public, especially the poor, for being so stupid as to have all these problems, or so smart as to take advantage of welfare and other social programs.

METAMORPHOSIS: The result of those encounters is usually a complete change, a total adaptation of the new role and self-conception as a "cop." And with that transformation comes a stark awareness of the interdependence cops share with all other cops. This total change in perspective usually means that police accept several new assumptions about the nature of the world:

- loyalty to colleagues is essential for survival
- the public, or most of it, is the enemy

- police administrators are also the enemy
- any discrepancy between these views and the views of family and friends is due simply to the ignorance of those who have not actually done police work themselves.

The Values That Are Learned

Through the war stories of the academy instructor, the actions and stories of the FTO, the bull sessions with other rookies and veterans, the new officer's encounters with the public, a fairly consistent set of values emerges:

1. Discretion A: Decisions about whether to enforce the law, in any but the most serious cases, should be guided by both what the law says and who the suspect is.
2. Discretion B: Disrespect for police authority is a serious offense that should always be punished with an arrest or the use of force.
3. Force: Police officers should never hesitate to use physical or deadly force against people who "deserve it," or where it can be an effective way of solving a crime.
4. Due Process: Due process is only a means of protecting criminals at the expense of the law-abiding and should be ignored whenever it is safe to do so.
5. Truth: Lying and deception are an essential part of the police job, and even perjury should be used if it is necessary to protect yourself or get a conviction on a "bad guy."
6. Time: You cannot go fast enough to chase a car thief or traffic violator, nor slow enough to get a "garbage" call; and when there are no calls for service, your time is your own.
7. Rewards: Police do very dangerous work for low wages, so it is proper to take any extra rewards the public wants to give them, like free meals, Christmas gifts, or even regular monthly payments (in some cities) for special treatment.
8. Loyalty: The paramount duty is to protect your fellow officers at all costs, as they would protect you, even though you may have to risk your own career and own life to do it.

Extracted from Lawrence Sherman, "Learning Police Ethics," *Criminal Justice Ethics,* Vol. 1, No. 1, Winter/Spring 1982, pp. 10–19. Reprinted with permission.

SECTION THREE

The Officer's Involvement

You've looked at your own safety and at the total context in which law enforcement officers function. You've also seen that improper action could make you civilly liable. You've looked at the various responsibilities law enforcement officers have as they deal with crime and criminals. And, you've looked at how the law directly affects these responsibilities and the specific actions that might be taken in carrying them out.

This final section looks at the culmination of criminal investigation—what happens in the courtroom—in chapter 13. Everything that has been done up to this point can make a difference in whether justice is even served or not. How effective the police officers involved in the case are as witnesses can also make or break a case.

Then, since our law is constantly changing and evolving, the text concludes in chapter 14 with suggestions on how police officers can actually locate the law. This will be of help not only as you seek to learn what specific elements of a crime must be satisfied for a successful prosecution, but also as you try to keep current with the inevitable changes in criminal law and procedure.

CHAPTER 13

The Officer's View of
the Judicial Process

You are on trial, too—your credibility, your professionalism, your knowledge, your competence, your judgment, your conduct in the field, your use of force, your adherence to official policies, your observance of the defendant's rights—they're all on trial.—Devallis Rutledge

DO YOU KNOW

What the goals of our judicial process are?

What the critical stages in the criminal process are?

What the purpose of a preliminary hearing is?

What the discovery process requires?

When a coroner's jury is involved?

What pleas a defendant can make?

What direct examination and cross-examination are?

What strategies can help you excel as a witness?

Introduction

Chapter 13

Up to this point, you have sought to develop a working knowledge of both the practical and the legal aspects of doing a professional job on the street. You have explored the importance of safety, looked at some basic procedural concerns, and spent considerable time learning the law of criminal procedure.

In fact, it is a combination of all these areas that leads to the probable culmination of these efforts; that is, the point at which a final determination is made—in court.

It is common for officers, particularly new officers, to genuinely fear this part of their jobs. Granted, every officer is expected to prepare a case professionally for trial and to present that material professionally in a court of law. However, most officers are inadequately prepared for this area of their job.

As a result, due to lack of experience and confidence, most officers dread the time they will be subpoenaed into court to testify. It is common for officers to feel considerably more confident facing the unknown of a building search or a vehicle stop on a distant, abandoned road than to face being cross-examined in court!

Like so many other aspects of life, fear of the unknown is the most difficult fear to deal with. Officers learn from experience that testifying in court is just another part of the job, and they come to feel more comfortable dealing with it. Like other on-the-job learning, it is much easier if supplemented with basic materials to help officers know what to expect.

This chapter presents a basic working knowledge of the court process. By learning the process, the terminology, and the roles of the people involved, police officers will naturally be more comfortable in confronting this necessary, although initially intimidating, aspect of the law enforcement profession.

THE GOALS OF OUR CRIMINAL JUSTICE SYSTEM

To understand how the American criminal justice system operates, begin by looking at its purpose. Start from the premise that the purpose of the system is to provide a uniform, consistent way to ascertain truth and to establish justice nationwide.

LaFave and Israel (1985, pp. 22–31) set forth eight basic goals of the criminal justice process:

- *To establish an adversary system of adjudication—pitting one side against the other—accused against the accusor.*
- *To establish an accusatorial system requires a government that bears the burden of establishing the guilt of the accused— presumption of innocence and privilege against self-incrimination.*
- *To minimize erroneous convictions and protect the innocent. In In re Winship (1970) the court asserted that it is "far worse to convict an innocent person than to let a guilty man go free."*

- To minimize the burdens of accusation and litigation. The public remembers accusation even if a person is found innocent. Screening begins with the need for police officers to have probable cause to arrest, a provision for bail, a preliminary hearing, a right to a speedy trial, review requirements, and a prohibition against double jeopardy.
- To provide lay participation—to be tried by a jury of "peers" gives the process legitimacy.
- To respect the dignity of the individual. The adversary system places the state against the individual, elevating human dignity. The privilege against self-incrimination and the prohibitions against cruel and unusual punishment and against unreasonable search and seizure also show respect for the dignity of the individual.
- To maintain the appearance of fairness. The trial is open to public view and decisions are part of the public record.
- To achieve equality in applying the process. In other words, like defendants must be treated alike, based on the Fourteenth Amendment equal protection clause.

Eight goals of the criminal justice process are

- *To establish an adversary system of adjudication*

- *To establish an accusatorial system*

- *To minimize erroneous conviction*

- *To minimize the burdens of accusation and litigation*

- *To provide lay participation*

- *To respect the dignity of the individual*

- *To maintain the appearance of fairness*

- *To achieve equality in applying the process*

While this may appear simple, it is an undertaking so difficult that no single static set of rules has yet proven able to provide the means to accomplish this task.

In addition to serving these important goals, the criminal justice system in the United States embodies the idea of the "living law." No other body of law has grown, changed, developed, and literally reformed itself as much to meet the needs of a changing society.

The goal remains the same, but the rules by which the players involved in this system are required to abide continue to change. Why? Because the system itself attempts to meet the needs of the two, always diametrically opposed sides. Our system seeks to weigh each perspective, striving to strike a fair, equitable, unbiased balance. Obviously, such a goal is difficult to reach.

The system that has developed and continues to serve the criminal justice system most effectively is called the *adversary system*. In this system, only actual controversies between actual parties are adjudicated. As such, each side, as well as the system, expects, demands, and generally receives an aggressive pursuit of the facts, with the end result ideally being justice.

CRITICAL STAGES IN THE CRIMINAL JUSTICE SYSTEM

While the law of criminal procedure deals to a great degree with investigating cases, our system demands that officers adhere to the rules throughout the entire investigation. From the time police officers leave the police station to the time the matter arrives in court, rules must be followed. As on the street, an error during any of the subsequent phases could be fatal to the successful prosecution of the case. The following discussion is adapted from Wrobleski and Hess (1986, pp. 412–22):

The criminal justice system has several critical stages, that is, stages that are determined to be of such critical importance that specific legal rules must be satisfied: the complaint or charge, the arrest, booking, preliminary hearing, the arraignment, the trial, and sentencing.

The Complaint or Charge

The criminal justice process usually begins when a police officer or a citizen goes to a prosecutor to obtain a complaint. A *complaint* is a legal document that specifies an alleged crime and the supporting facts providing probable cause.

If the facts convince the prosecutor that a crime has been committed and adequate probable cause exists that the suspect accused of the offense is guilty, the prosecutor draws up a legal form specifying the facts in the case.

If, on the other hand, the prosecutor feels insufficient evidence has been presented, he will refuse to issue a complaint against the suspect. If the suspect is in custody, the prosecutor will order his release.

The formal complaint, called the *charge*, contains all necessary evidence and facts to allow a magistrate to determine independently that probable cause exists for believing the accused has committed the offense.

The Warrant

The police officer or citizen then presents the complaint to a magistrate, swears to its accuracy, and signs a statement to that effect. If the magistrate agrees with the charge, he orders an arrest *warrant*. If he does not agree, he dismisses the complaint.

An arrest warrant directs an officer to bring the suspect before the magistrate. The warrant is usually directed to the sheriff or constables of a county or to all police officers of the municipality within the court's jurisdiction. The officers then locate the suspect and arrest him if he is not already in custody.

A summons may be issued instead of a warrant. The summons sets the time and date the defendant must voluntarily appear in court.

The Arrest

Requirements for a legal arrest have been discussed. When making the arrest, officers must inform the suspect that they are acting on the authority of the warrant. The suspect is entitled to see it. If the officers do not have the warrant in their possession, they must show it to the suspect as soon as possible.

The arrest may occur at other points within the criminal justice process. In a misdemeanor case, it may have occurred without a complaint or warrant, provided the crime was committed in the presence of the arresting officer.

The Booking

After suspects are taken into custody, they are "booked." Suspects are formally put into the police records' system by the booking officer who records on the booking sheet the date, suspect's name, time of arrest, charge, physical description, and physical characteristics. Suspects are also photographed and fingerprinted. The prints are placed on file with the FBI in Washington, D.C., and the suspects have a police arrest record.

Bail and Writ of Habeas Corpus

One right of the accused is usually the right to be expeditiously released from custody. Not only is this essential for a person's immediate freedom, but it is also in keeping with the premise that a person is innocent until proven guilty. After the formal booking, suspects are usually entitled to be released on bail or their own personal recognizance ("R.P.R.d") if the crime is a misdemeanor, or released on bond if the crime is a felony.

The Eighth Amendment forbids excessive bail and implies the right to bail in most instances.

The amount of bail for each misdemeanor is determined by the judges of the courts. They decide how much money is "reasonable" as a deposit to bring defendants into court if they are released. However, some courts have a schedule for the amount of bail required for specific offenses such as violating municipal ordinances on shoplifting, driving under the influence of alcohol, and other violations.

In most cases, the judge sets bail when the prisoner comes before the court. The elapsed time between jailing suspects and their being brought to court to answer the charges is determined either by court policy or more frequently by statutory law. The Sixth Amendment guarantees suspects a speedy trial; therefore, following arrests, officers must take suspects before a magistrate without "unreasonable" delay. Periodically people in jail may be released on a *writ of habeas corpus*—a legal court order meaning literally "bring forth the body you have"—which commands that a prisoner be brought forth immediately rather than being held without benefit of the legal procedures all citizens are entitled to.

A writ of habeas corpus is often issued when a person is arrested without a formal arrest warrant and the police investigation is taking an unreasonable time. Most states have adopted guidelines about how long people may be jailed before being charged, released, or making an appearance in court. These rules generally range from thirty-six to seventy-two hours, taking into consideration weekends and holidays.

Misdemeanors vs. Felonies

Up to this point in the criminal justice process, it makes little difference what type of crime has been committed. The process is often the same for misdemeanors and felonies. But now misdemeanors and felonies are handled by different procedures. Because a misdemeanor is considered less serious than a felony, the procedures are less formal than for felonies. A misdemeanor may be handled by the officer merely issuing the defendant a citation and releasing him, possibly even without bail.

A felony, on the other hand, considered much more serious, with more serious consequences, requires more formal procedures. A formal complaint may be required, with a variety of procedural court appearances also required.

The Preliminary Hearing

The *preliminary hearing* provides the parties a chance to deal with initial issues, including determining if sufficient probable cause exists for the case to proceed. The magistrate first determines whether an offense has been committed and if sufficient evidence is present to believe that the accused committed it.

If the accused is being held, it is important to both the defendant and the prosecutor to hold the hearing within a reasonable time.

The preliminary hearing seeks to establish probable cause. This prevents people from being indiscriminately brought to trial.

In a preliminary hearing, the defendant is present, with or without counsel, and has a right to challenge what is stated against him in court. The defendant can waive the preliminary hearing and have the case sent directly to a higher court for disposition.

Preliminary hearings are generally held in a lower court or a court that has general jurisdiction.

The judge is not bound by the rules of evidence that ordinarily control a trial. A far broader range of evidence is usually admissible. The evidence need only show probable cause and reasonably and fairly tend to show the crime is as charged and the accused committed it.

The prosecutor has to show only probable cause.

The defense attorney can present evidence, cross-examine the prosecutor's witnesses, call defense witnesses, and present any type of defense.

In reality the preliminary hearing is often a mini-trial where the defense obtains as much information as possible to strengthen its case. Both prosecution and defense often use this stage of the criminal justice process for tactical purposes, with an eye on the possibility of plea bargaining.

The preliminary hearing is often a discovery tool for the defendants as they hear the evidence presented against them. This may also be true for the prosecution. If the case had gone to a grand jury, they may not be aware of the evidence against them. Most states have included the *discovery process* in their rules of criminal procedure. The discovery process requires that all pertinent facts on both sides be made available before the trial. The goal is to prevent surprises for either side and to allow both sides to adequately prepare for and respond to all facts.

Used properly, the discovery process encourages more final dispositions before trial, thereby saving court time. It also achieves mutually agreed on depositions rather than an all-or-nothing trial decision.

The discovery process requires that all pertinent facts on both sides be made available before the trial.

The preliminary hearing merely determines whether further action should be taken or whether justice demands that the defendant be released. At the preliminary hearing, the judge determines if probable cause exists and dismisses cases he feels the prosecutor should no longer pursue because of lack of sufficient evidence that the person committed the crime (probable cause).

The main intent of the preliminary hearing is to add to the checks and balances of the criminal justice system by preventing the police and prosecutor from indiscriminately bringing someone to trial. The preliminary hearing, one critical stage of due process, is a formal proceeding insuring that all accused persons are adequately informed and that all their constitutional rights are protected.

The outcome of a preliminary hearing may be to (1) dismiss the charges, (2) present an information and bind the defendant over to a higher court, (3) send the case to a grand jury or (4) set a trial date.

The Grand Jury

The United States Constitution requires an indictment by a federal grand jury before trial for most crimes against federal law. Although some states do not use grand juries, grand juries are frequently used to hear cases involving misconduct of public officials, violations of election laws, bankruptcy fraud, criminal conduct, and the like. This is another check within the system to insure that sufficient information exists for the government to proceed against the accused.

The consideration of a felony charge by a grand jury is in no sense of the word a trial. Only the prosecution's evidence is usually presented and considered. Contrary to the popular portrayal of grand juries on television and in movies, suspected offenders are usually not heard nor are their lawyers present to offer evidence in their behalf.

A grand jury is usually composed of twenty-three voting citizens of the county, selected by either the district or superior judges, jury commissioners, court officials, or some designated county supervisor. Grand juries meet in secret sessions and hear from witnesses and victims of crime. Because they meet in secret session, they are accusatory bodies and determine only whether enough evidence exists to accuse a person of a crime.

The prosecutor usually has considerable foundation for believing an offense has been committed before taking a case to the grand jury. The prosecutor is authorized to subpoena witnesses before the jury.

In some states, a grand jury can hear evidence from suspects. However, the persons being considered for indictment must sign a waiver of immunity and agree to answer all questions posed in the grand jury session even though their testimony might be incriminating and lead to an indictment. Their testimony also may be used against them in a criminal trial. Their lawyers are not allowed to be present in the grand jury room if they are testifying.

After the grand jury receives all testimonies and evidence, it begins its deliberations. If the majority of the grand jurors (or a specified number) agrees, they instruct the prosecutor to prepare an *indictment* that specifies all the facts of the case and the names of those who appeared before the jury.

The indictment is signed by the grand jury foreman and presented to the district or superior court judge. The judge then orders the issuance of a bench warrant for the arrest of the defendant if not already in custody. If the defendant is indicted, until he is arrested or brought before the court, the indictment must be kept secret; it is not public information. A summons may also be issued in lieu of a warrant.

If, after hearing all the evidence, the jurors believe there is no criminal violation, the grand jury issues a *no bill,* which means they find no basis for an indictment and will no longer consider the matter unless further evidence is presented.

In felony cases, prosecutors sometimes avoid the preliminary hearing by going directly to the grand jury for an indictment. This presents a tactical advantage for the prosecution because grand jury hearings are not public. If the prosecution can convince a grand jury to bring about an indictment based on probable cause, the prosecution does not need a preliminary hearing. An indictment eliminates the need for such a hearing because the defendant goes straight to trial.

The defense attorney or the defendant can demand a preliminary hearing if either feels a miscarriage of justice is occurring. In fact, even if not required by law, cases may be referred to a grand jury for political reasons, so that the prosecution has some "outside direction" as to whether to continue. For example, a case involving a police officer shooting and killing a suspect in the line of duty may well be sent to a grand jury. Thus, the prosecutor would not be accused of failing to act on the case against the police officer if no indictment was returned from the grand jury.

The Coroner's Jury

Coroners (sometimes called medical examiners) investigate violent deaths where suspicion of foul play exists. By law, coroners can conduct autopsies to determine the cause of death, and in many states they can conduct inquests. When used, the *coroner's jury* usually has six members. In some states the coroner's jury system has been abandoned and its functions performed by a professional medical examiner, usually a pathologist or a forensic expert.

The coroner's jury is involved in cases where the cause of death is in doubt.

The Arraignment

When defendants are charged with a felony, they must personally appear at an *arraignment*. As in the preliminary hearing, defendants are entitled to counsel. Arraignment procedures vary by state. Generally defendants appear before the court, are read the complaint, information, or indictment, and are given a copy, if they have not received one. They then enter a *plea*.

Defendants have several alternatives when they appear for the formal arraignment. *Standing mute*, that is, refusing to answer, is entered by the judge as a not guilty plea.

Nolo contendere means "no contest." By entering a plea of nolo contendere, defendants in effect throw themselves on the mercy of the court. This plea is often used when a person knows of some forthcoming civil action against him and does not want his plea to jeopardize his defense in the civil trial. (A guilty plea to any criminal offense could become a part of the civil trial.)

Guilty means the accused admits the actual charge or a lesser charge agreed to in a plea bargaining session. A guilty plea has many consequences: possible imprisonment, being labeled a criminal, a waiver of constitutional rights and of all defenses. Still, 90 percent of all criminal defendants in the United States plead guilty, but most plead guilty to offenses reduced from the original charges.

Not guilty means the accused denies the charges. He or she may have a valid defense for the charge such as intoxication, insanity, self-defense, or mistaken identity. Some states require defendants to plead not guilty automatically to capital crimes such as first-degree murder.

At the arraignment the defendant may stand mute or enter a plea of nolo contendere, guilty, or not guilty.

If defendants plead guilty or nolo contendere, a sentencing time is set. Usually a pre-sentence investigation is ordered to determine if probation is warranted. If defendants make no plea or plead not guilty, they may have the choice of a trial by a judge or by a jury. If they wish a jury trial, the case is assigned to the court docket and a date set. Sometimes, for tactical reasons, a defendant wants only a judge to hear the case rather than a jury.

Before looking at the trial itself, the court system within which it occurs, and the sentence that may result, consider first the "players."

THE PEOPLE INVOLVED

This section is entitled "The People Involved" because while it may at times seem like an independent machine, the justice system is

People comprise our criminal justice system. A rather incredible number of people, in addition to the victim and the suspect, play integral parts that make the system work.

people—professionals who know what the system requires and seek to provide it. A question often asked of law enforcement officers is, "How do you feel when the court lets the person you arrested off with just a slap on the wrist?" The answer reveals more than just the officer's emotion. It frequently demonstrates just how well officers understand the workings of the criminal justice system.

Newer, less-experienced police officers often respond with hostility, criticizing the ability of the judge or the jury. The defense attorney is seen as the enemy, out to "get" the officer, and to get the defendant "off" at any price. Experienced officers, however, understand that although the system does not always get the result that the particular officer perceives as *right*, the system is organized to be *fair*.

Rather than getting upset at a decision, blaming those involved, developing a festering anger towards those involved in the process, experienced, mature law enforcement professionals understand that the criminal justice system is like a game—with rules and players. In the end, there is a winner. Ideally it is, in fact, justice.

Usually, the side that plays the game most skillfully will win. In this case, skill involves understanding the rules of criminal procedure and developing the expertise to apply these legal rules to an infinite variety of police calls. The game includes other players too. It's a team concept. Any player might drop the ball and cause the entire team to lose. On the other hand, the entire team might work perfectly together, but with that matter of "luck" coming into play the result is an unanticipated outcome. You have undoubtedly heard of some "unbelievable" jury decisions.

Remembering that the prosecution has the entire burden to prove "beyond a reasonable doubt" that the defendant is guilty, it should be obvious that this is a difficult threshold to meet. Unlike the legal defense team that is literally handed the case in a neatly wrapped package to examine, dissect, and critique, police officers on the scene are thrown into a situation often hideous and extreme and expected to handle it as best they can. Frequently major pieces of the puzzle are missing: an eyewitness refuses to get involved; the weapon cannot be located; an alibi just cannot be contradicted; or an important piece of evidence will never see the courtroom because of the exclusionary rule.

Is it the officer's fault that an airtight case cannot be pieced together from what was found at the scene? Of course not. On the other hand, are defense attorneys to be blamed because they effectively seek to protect the rights of their clients, and in the end, the jury responded with an acquittal? Anyone accused of a crime would want an aggressive defense.

The system does not always provide the result that *everyone* believes is just. In this game, there is *always* a winner . . . and there is *always* a loser. Sometimes the loser will be the defendant, who will be looking at a lifetime in prison. But sometimes the loser is the state . . . the prosecution . . . the police officers. This is a fact of life.

Officers who let such results eat at them will find their careers to be long, frustrating, and unfulfilling. Most officers are convinced that their job is complete when their reports are turned in. From that point on, a myriad of other "players" takes the ball, and it is, in fact, out of the hands of the individual officer.

The majority of this text discusses the rules officers must deal with. This section looks at the role of the others involved in the entire process—the lawyers, judge, and witnesses.

The Prosecuting Attorney

The "chief" prosecuting attorney, sometimes called the district attorney (D.A.), is elected in most states. In smaller cities prosecution services may be contracted for from a private law firm.

Prosecuting attorneys have many responsibilities and a great deal of power. As the title implies, prosecuting attorneys decide who will be prosecuted, and aggressively pursue such prosecutions. If the prosecuting attorney decides to prosecute someone on serious charges, many decisions and duties must be performed. Once the charge is determined, the prosecuting attorney must decide whether to split the charge into separate trials. At the trial, the prosecuting attorney must prove the defendant guilty beyond a reasonable doubt, using all admissible evidence available. The prosecuting attorney also helps choose the jury members, decides which witnesses to call, and decides what physical evidence to introduce in court.

The State Attorney General

The attorney general, as chief law enforcement official at the state level, is given broad authority to coordinate prosecutions. The attorney general does not usually become involved in a trial unless called on by the local prosecutor. It is the attorney general's duty to present a case to the appellate court when it has been appealed. The attorney general also provides a variety of other legal services to state government.

The Defense Lawyer

A basic right of people charged with crimes is the right to counsel. When the accused cannot afford counsel, one may be provided for them free. If the accused can afford counsel, they may choose the attorney they want to represent them. Often the defense lawyer is the player police officers "love to hate." Defense lawyers are seen as true adversaries, helping the accused to avoid justice. In fact, the defense lawyer plays a critical role in our adversary system, not only advising clients, but keeping a watchful eye on the actions of the police and the prosecution.

Privileged Communication   Privileged communication places defense lawyers in awkward positions because the information given to attorneys in confidence by their clients cannot be used without the client's permission. Once the case is accepted, the counsel must remain until the case has reached a logical conclusion or is withdrawn with the permission of the court.

Defense attorneys have many duties to perform before and during the trial. One duty is to hold a private conference with the accused. The counsel will advise the defendant on a plea to enter, will file motions in the best interest of the client, and will conduct the defense at the trial. Defense attorneys also have the duty to cross-examine witnesses called by the prosecution and to present evidence on behalf of their clients.

Others

Other courtroom personnel include the clerk of court, the bailiff, and the court reporter.

The clerk of court maintains all records of a particular case, including copies of the accusatory pleas and motions. The clerk of court attends trials to swear in witnesses, mark exhibits, and maintain the evidence.

The bailiff helps the judge maintain order in the courtroom, calls witnesses to the stand, and ensures that the jurors have no contact with the public.

The clerk of court swears in the witness prior to questioning. Testimony on the record is preserved for potential review by appellate courts.

The court reporter records everything that is said during the trial, including testimonies, objections, rulings, and conferences.

The Judge

The judge has the important role of presiding over the trial. Judges have a great deal of power and authority. At some levels they are elected, and at others they are appointed.

The Function of the Trial Judge   The judge's primary responsibility during the trial is to see that justice is carried out. The judge must protect both the interests of the defendant and of the public. The judge controls the proceedings by limiting the introduction of evidence and arguments of counsel, controlling the conduct of the defendant and spectators, determining the admissibility of evidence, ruling on objections, protecting witnesses, and interpreting the laws for the jury. In many jurisdictions, the judge sentences the defendant following the conviction. In a court trial, the judge renders a verdict of guilty or innocent.

One important duty is keeping order in the court. To do so, judges have the authority to punish disruptive people by charging them with "contempt of court." Contempt is any act that embarrasses or obstructs the court, including insulting remarks or persistent arguments by the counsel, disorderly conduct by the defendant or spectators, and witnesses' refusals to be sworn in and testify.

Judges control their courtrooms. While judges are immune from civil liability, any errors in conducting a proceeding could result in a new trial being ordered by a higher court.

Witnesses

Ballentine's *Law Dictionary* defines a witness as "one who testifies in a cause or gives evidence before a judicial tribunal." Usually, one would immediately think of eyewitnesses, testifying about what they actually observed. However, "witnesses" can be others as well.

In fact, anyone called to testify in court is considered a witness, not just those who actually "saw" something the court is interested in. A witness can be anyone with information the court deems relevant.

Defendants, if they testify, would be witnesses. They might state under oath that they know nothing about a matter or never saw an alleged victim before. During sentencing, defendants may admit or deny having committed the crime they are accused of.

Victims who testify are also witnesses, providing possible eyewitness testimony or just information laying the foundation to help the prosecutor prove that a crime had been committed.

In addition, *expert witnesses* may testify about what they *know* about their field of expertise and apply this information to the case at hand. In criminal trials, for example, crime laboratory technicians may testify about what evidence was collected and how it was obtained. Analysts may testify about what percent of alcohol was found in a blood sample. A pathologist may testify about the entry/exit wounds from a bullet in a body or the effect of a blow to a victim's head. It is permissible for expert witnesses to provide conclusions based on a hypothetical situation similar to that believed to have occurred. And, the defense lawyer may call its own pathologist to provide a second, different opinion.

Jurors are subjected to and expected to comprehend, a great deal of information. Trials that continue for days, months, or even years, can generate an incredible amount of testimony, documents, and instructions from the judge.

Jurors

The Sixth Amendment requires a "public trial, by an impartial jury" for all defendants in serious criminal prosecutions. However, according to the "serious crime" requirements, persons charged with "petty" offenses are not entitled to trial by jury.

Jury size ranges from six to twelve members; the common law has traditionally used a twelve-member jury. The jury should be large enough to represent a cross-section of the community and to allow for group deliberation. Although some feel a twelve-member jury is necessary for adequate representation and deliberation, a six-member jury can successfully accomplish these duties as well. However, juries must consist of at least six people, and states may experiment with any number of jurors above six.

Jury selection consists of several steps. First, a list of names, called the "jury list," is compiled from voter registration lists, phone books, and the like. From this jury list, a random panel is selected, with some people being excused. People typically excused include aliens, those unable to speak English, those under eighteen, those charged with a felony or serving a felony sentence, people with mental or physical incapacities, or anyone with a substantial impairment to effectively carry out this important task.

The remaining people on the list then go through the *voir dire* process, which reduces the group to the desired size. This final step in the jury selection process is used to achieve an impartial jury, assuring that the chosen jury members are not biased toward either side. The term *voir dire* means "to see what is said," and this selection is conducted by the judge and the attorneys. Each side questions the prospective jurors and may excuse "for cause" anyone who appears biased. Each side also has a number of peremptories it can use to dismiss any potential jury member without a reason.

THE TRIAL PROCESS AND TESTIFYING IN COURT

Earlier in this chapter you looked at an overview of the trial process. It is evident that the American system of criminal justice is complex. This complexity is what causes most law enforcement officers to be apprehensive, if not downright frightened, of testifying in court. Most have no idea of what specifically will be expected of them in court. Therefore, many would prefer to face a physical confrontation on the street than a defense lawyer in a courtroom.

In fact, the only thing expected of police officers on the witness stand is that they simply tell the truth. Nothing more, nothing less. However, it is HOW officers testify that either helps or hinders the prosecutor.

The court expects officers to testify professionally. Officers are expected to be articulate—to be able to clearly communicate their answers. Officers are expected to appear professional—to look neat, sharp, believable. Officers are expected to be prepared—to have thoroughly reviewed their notes and reports, and to have brought to court any exhibits or other evidence needed for a complete testimony. Officers are expected to present a professional attitude—to present unbiased testimony, refraining from exhibiting inappropriate emotion or sarcasm. And last, but of vital importance, officers are expected to *know how the system operates*—to not have to be taken by the hand throughout the process.

Would you find doctors credible if they had to continually ask someone else what to do to complete a procedure, or to frequently consult a reference book, all the while appearing less than confident?

Likewise, would you find officers who appear unsure of themselves, not knowing what to do in the courtroom, always seeming to question their own testimony, as credible as officers who know their way around the courtroom, who appear confident, knowing what this aspect of the job requires, and carrying it out professionally?

Professionalism creates credibility in all aspects of law enforcement, including courtroom testimony.

While the jury and the attorney expect officers to present such a professional appearance before the judge, few officers are adequately prepared before the fact for this exciting part of the job.

As with so many other aspects of law enforcement they have learned in the not-too-distant-past, most officers have had to learn what is expected of them in court by experience. Almost every officer has a horror story of being humiliated on the stand. While it is always easiest to blame the defense lawyer or even the prosecutor, the fact is that such a negative experience is usually the result of the *officer's* not being prepared.

So let's get prepared . . .

Many police officers actually fear testifying in court more than other parts of their job. Preparation, combined with experience, can make this part of work enjoyable—even exciting.

Before Court ....

Prepare! Prepare! Prepare! It cannot be stressed enough that successful prosecutions are prepared for long before the judge calls the trial to order. In fact, the winning cases start being prepared from the earliest initiation of the enforcement action.

Developing sufficient *probable cause* is unquestionably the basis on which a successful case is built. It is far too easy for officers to "jump the gun" early in an investigation, leaving so many holes that even a merely adequate defense attorney can develop more than a reasonable doubt in the minds of the jury.

And here is where so many officers have difficulty— *slow down and wait until you have developed your case!*

At the very least, you will have enough information to provide complete testimony in a court of law. At best, you may discover far more information than you would have had you acted, or overreacted, too soon.

For example, when you observe a traffic offense, you may want to resist the desire to initiate the stop immediately. What may have at first appeared to have been only the failure to signal a turn could develop into a series of observed driving offenses, resulting in a successful prosecution for driving while intoxicated. Certainly, an officer's testimony in regard to a number of observed offenses substantiates a far better charge than a single offense.

Investigators also need to resist the impulse to make rapid arrests, resulting in simply forgetting to gather what the jury might consider as "obvious evidence" that should have been collected.

For example, consider the detective who responds to a sexual assault crime scene on a snowy Minnesota night. The victim got the license number of the vehicle in which she believed her assailant fled the scene, although she could not provide a positive identification of the man because he was wearing a nylon stocking over his face while he committed the rape. The suspect's vehicle was located at a nearby neighborhood bar, and an arrest was made. While the court determined that sufficient probable cause existed to justify the arrest of the suspect, a major problem developed during the trial. Why didn't the investigator document the footprints in the newly fallen snow at the scene where the suspect's vehicle was parked? The defense team gladly showed the jury the distinctive tread on the boots the suspect wore that night. When the detective testified that there was no reason for not photographing the footprints that could now be used to match the imprint with the suspect's boots, the jury could only question whether they never matched in the first place, or at least question the competency of the investigating officer.

If the situation allows it, take enough time to develop your case. Assure that every case will go the distance of a full trial by jury. Anticipate close scrutiny by the defense team.

Before Court ....PREPARE ADEQUATE REPORTS!   In 1987, a questionnaire was mailed to all eighty-seven Minnesota County Attorneys. Ninety-six percent of those responding believed police reports were either critically important or very important to the successful prosecution of criminal cases. According to these attorneys:

> *The police reports are often the first impression a judge or defense attorney has of an officer's competence, both generally and in regard to the specific elements of the offense charged. If the report is weak, defense attorneys and judges are inclined to require officers to testify and to scrutinize carefully the officer's testimony. A well-written report can often result in a settlement of the case without an Omnibus Hearing or trial.*
>
> *Good reports . . . serve later to refresh the officer's recollection.*
>
> *Poorly phrased reports or reports that are too brief have a tendency to blow up in your face at trial time.*
>
> *[Good reports] avoid unnecessary court proceedings when facts are fully set out in reports and give a strong professional image of the officer.*
>
> *If sloppy or incomplete, they will impeach the officer at trial.*
>
> *A well-written report alone can settle a case.*

Before Court ...   Prepare for the trial. Review your reports and notes thoroughly. Review any photographs taken at the scene. If needed, revisit the location of the incident. You can be sure that the defense attorney will be well prepared, and you need to be too.

You should also contact the prosecutor to discuss the case. More often than not, the attorney representing the government will be extremely busy and may or may not have called you. It is your responsibility to have let the prosecutor know of any problems with the case and to make yourself available to him or her to answer any questions beforehand. While many trials are routine for the prosecutor, the officer should make it a point to prepare thoroughly for every trial.

Before Trial ...   Know what to expect procedurally at the trial. If you have never been in that particular courtroom, arrive early enough to walk around it. See where the witness stand is, where you will take the oath, how to get in and out of the courtroom confidently.

You should also be familiar with the behavior expected of you in court. It is terribly embarrassing for an officer to be told to remove his hat or to spit out his gum. And don't think a judge would not do it! In addition, it is vitally important for officers to behave and testify professionally. Unprofessional, inappropriate responses, even though seemingly insignificant, can negatively sway the jury and possibly even affect the trial should the defense attorney's objections be sustained.

When Testifying in Court
DO:

- Confirm your court appearance.
- Arrive early.
- Dress appropriately.
- Act professionally and courteously to everyone—in and out of courtroom.
- On the witness stand, relax—take your time, THINK before you answer.
- Talk so everyone in the courtroom can hear you (loudly and clearly).
- Act naturally. Look at the jurors when you respond.
- Be prepared:
    - Discuss the case with the prosecutor beforehand.
    - Reveal ALL information to the prosecutor.
    - REVIEW REPORTS AND NOTES!
- Address people by appropriate titles (Your Honor, Sir, etc.).
- Give accurate, complete answers:
    - Answer only what is asked of you.
    - If you don't know, say so!
    - If you don't remember, say so!
    - "To the best of my recollection . . . "
- Maintain a professional attitude throughout the process.
- Ask whether you should wait outside the courtroom before/after your testimony.

DON'T:

- Take the process personally.
- Get angry at the defense attorney.
- Look at the prosecutor during questioning.
- Exhibit nervousness (sit still, don't stare at the ceiling or off into space).

- Smoke, chew gum, wear a hat.
- Whisper, roll your eyes, etc., while waiting to testify.

Throughout the Trial ....   Remember that this is an *adversarial* process. While officers may feel personally attacked, the final purpose is simply to determine the *truth*. Officers who understand the system, the goal, and the procedures do not take it personally. Keep in mind that if you, as an officer, think this is hard on you, imagine what it must feel like from the defendant's perspective.

A word of caution is appropriate here—do *not* lie. It sounds ridiculous to even say, but more than one officer has been put in a most uncomfortable spot, if not been charged with perjury for "manipulating the truth."

Your job as a law enforcement officer is to relay the facts as you received and perceived them, keeping in mind that they may not always be as clear and convincing as you would like. Yes, the role of the professional police officer is extremely important—but, it is not worth lying for. Being on the "side of the angels" absolutely *never* justifies fabricating evidence or lying on the stand. Accept the fact now that you will lose cases and that some guilty defendants will be acquitted. THIS IS NOT YOUR FAULT!

Professional police officers play the hands they are dealt, and if the game is won, fine. If not, they report for their next shift.

The majority of officers' activity in the courtroom is answering questions as witnesses during direct and cross-examination. *Direct examination* is generally a positive, supportive experience; *cross-examination* is generally an anxiety-provoking, stressful experience.

Direct examination *is the questioning of a witness by the attorney who called that particular witness to the stand.*

In your case, you will usually be called by the prosecutor. Questions during direct examination will be phrased in open-ended ways, providing you the opportunity to relate your story as you want. In fact, it is usually against court rules for attorneys to ask their own witnesses leading questions. As you become more experienced, you will learn increasingly more effective ways to tell your story—generally, clear, concise, and to the point.

Cross-examination, on the other hand, gives the opposing counsel the chance to test witnesses, seeking to verify the truthfulness of the witnesses' testimony.

Cross-examination *is questioning by the opposing attorney.*

Here, the attorney for the "other side" asks of the witness pointed, inquiring, specific questions pertaining to the direct questioning that just occurred. The purpose is clearly to "shoot holes" in the testimony of the witness. Again, this is not a personal attack. It is an important part of the process, and well-prepared officers need not fear it. In fact, it provides a great opportunity to reinforce the testimony provided on direct examination.

A tongue-in-cheek summary of what NOT to do, "How to Lose Your Court Case," has been compiled by the Minnesota Bureau of Criminal Apprehension.

How to Lose Your Court Case

1. Walk into court looking like a bum. This will confuse the judge and jury, for they may think you are the defendant. There is no valid reason for a jury giving less weight to the testimony of a witness who makes a poor appearance—but they do.

2. If your case has a weak point, don't tell your lawyer. Surprise your lawyer during trial. This always adds excitement and gives the defendant another chance to go free. Had you told your lawyer of the weakness, he might have prepared for it and avoided your little trap.

3. If the defendant pleads "not guilty," take this personally. How dare this ordinary civilian question your word. Let the judge and jury know that from this point it is a personal battle between you and the defendant and that you'll testify to whatever is necessary to obtain a conviction.

4. When opposing counsel wants you to become angry— cooperate. Answer "NO" to his sly little question, "Didn't you really arrest the defendant because you don't like him? After fifteen minutes of baiting by the attorney, get real mad and tell them what you really think of the lousy so-and-so you arrested.

5. Don't worry about the facts. Any misinformation you give on direct examination will be straightened out on cross-examination. The defendant's lawyer will be very happy to help the jury conclude that either you know nothing or you are trying to keep the truth from the jury.

6. Be absolutely positive about everything. Even if you don't know the exact distance, don't let the judge or jury think you're stupid. Tell them it was precisely 132 feet. This will make a good impression, unless the defendant's lawyer takes the trouble to prove you are wrong.

7. If you're positive that you don't know—guess. Such testimony is not admissible as evidence, but the judge might make an exception for you. If the judge won't even let you finish a sentence you started with "I guess," just sit there and pout.

8. Don't make notes at the time of arrest. See how much fun it is to test your memory. In criminal cases you often are called upon to testify at more than one trial. Without notes you can break the monotony by giving a different version of the incident at each trial.

9. If you do make notes, don't review them before trial. The judge will be very patient with you while you try to figure out what you wrote. The jury might feel that you are being picked on when you become confused over your own notes.

10. Appear to be very "cocky." Some people expect police officers to throw their weight around and you mustn't disappoint them. Often a juror studies the officer on the witness stand in hopes of detecting a similarity with the bully that once issued the juror a traffic ticket.

11. Act as though your job depends upon a conviction. This will remove the unbiased atmosphere that often prevails when a professional person is testifying. Members of the jury will pay less attention to your testimony, but as taxpayers will know you are trying.

12. Get rough with the defendant at time of arrest. In traffic cases this will often cause the defendant to plead "not guilty" and at least open the door to making the officer look like the culprit. Being courteous to motorists reduces the number of times an officer gets involved in courtroom battles.

13. Ignore the law of search and seizure. A motion to suppress may be sustained and you won't even have to testify at the trial. Why bother getting a search warrant, just to satisfy some constitutional requirements?

14. Tell more than the question calls for. The opposition may find out all sorts of things. If you ramble too far, the judge will keep reminding you to merely answer the question.

15. Argue with the judge and opposing counsel. Why be bound by silly rules of evidence and courtroom procedure? If you fail to heed the judge's warning, he may hold you in contempt of court and the jury will think he's a sorehead. The jury dislikes an argumentative witness, but you can leave the witness stand with all the glory of a martyr.

If an officer follows any one or more of these suggestions, he should have no trouble losing his case. When he does, he should throw a tantrum in the courtroom and blame one of the lawyers, or the judge, or jury, or even the Constitution of the United States. He should never blame himself.

If an officer prefers winning cases, he should walk into court and look like and act like a professional witness, proud to be a member of one of the most important professions in America. He will present his evidence in a professional and unbiased manner and the judge and jury can soon tell that he has properly prepared himself for trial. If he does lose his case, he will blame no one, but will leave the courtroom with the satisfaction of having performed his duty properly and proud to live in a nation where we would rather see ten guilty men go free than have one innocent man convicted.

Source: Minnesota Bureau of Criminal Apprehension Police Traffic Training Program

STRATEGIES FOR EXCELLING AS A WITNESS

The quotation at the beginning of this chapter is by Devallis Rutledge, a former police officer, presently a prosecutor. His book *Courtroom Survival: The Officer's Guide to Better Testimony* contains 180+ pages filled with practical, common sense, but vital advice for courtroom testimony, with many examples of courtroom dialogue. Some highlights from *Courtroom Survival* follow.

Set Yourself Up

—*Get into the habit of thinking ahead to the trial while you're still out in the field. What if they ask me this in court?*

—*The rules of court severely restrict you in answering questions. No defense attorney in his right mind is ever going to give you a chance to explain anything. So, if you're ever going to get the chance to explain yourself before the jury's impression of you gets set in their heads, you've got to know how to provoke the defense attorney into giving you a chance to explain. Some of these provokers are: definitely; certainly; certainly not; naturally; naturally not; and one that always does the trick: "Yes, and no."*

As a General Rule

—*Be Unconditional. Some cops seem to like the sound of the conditional word "would." When I'm prosecuting a case, I cringe at the sound of it. It's too indefinite:*

Example:
Q: Who was your partner?
A: That would be Officer Hill.

—*Don't Stall. Don't repeat the question back to the attorney.*
Example:
Q: Were you holding a flashlight?
A: Was I holding a flashlight? Yes, I was.

Strategies for testifying in court: (1) set yourself up, (2) be unconditional, and (3) don't stall.

Common Objections

—*There are at least 44 standard trial objections in most states. We're only going to talk about the 2 that account for upwards of 90% of the problems a testifying officer will have: that your answer is a conclusion, or that it is non-responsive.*

—*How to Avoid Conclusions. One way is to listen to the form of the question. You know the attorney is asking you to speculate when he starts his questions with these loaded phrases:*

Would you assume . . . ?

Do you suppose . . . ?

Don't you think that . . . ?

Couldn't it be that . . . ?

Do you imagine . . . ?

Wouldn't it be fair to presume . . . ?

Isn't it strange that . . . ?

And the one you're likely to hear most often:

Isn't it possible that . . . ?

—*Another major area of conclusionary testimony is what I call mindreading. You can't get inside someone else's brain. That means you don't know for a fact—so you can't testify—as to what someone else sees, hears, feels, thinks or wants; and you don't know for a fact what somebody is trying to do, or is able to do, or whether he is nervous, excited, angry, scared, happy, upset, disturbed, or in any of the other emotional states that can only be labeled with a conclusion.*

—*How to give "responsive" answers. You have to answer just the question that you're asked—no more, no less. That means you have to pay attention to how the question is framed. You answer a yes-or-no question with a "yes" or "no."*

Q: Did he perform the alphabet test?

A: Yes, twice—but he only went to "G."

Everything after the "yes" is non-responsive. The officer anticipated the next three questions and volunteered the answers. He should have limited each answer to one question:

Q: Did he perform the alphabet test?

A: Yes.

Q: How many times?

A: Twice.

Q: How far did he go correctly the first time?

A: To the letter "G."

Avoid conclusions and non-responsive answers. Answer yes-or-no questions with "yes" or "no."

Handling Cross-Examination

The defense lawyer's most important task is to destroy your credibility—to make you look like you're either an incompetent bun-

gler, or a liar, or both. How does he do that? He attacks you. He tricks you. He outsmarts you. He confuses you. He frustrates you. He annoys you. He probes for your must vulnerable characteristics.

Courtroom Excellence

Courtroom Survival is the name of the book, but that's not what it's about. Courtroom Excellence is the name of the game, and that's what this book is really about. It isn't enough for you to be able to get down off the stand, walk outside the courthouse, and say to yourself, "Whew! I made it through another one!" Get used to being just as good on the witness stand as you are on the streets.

SUMMARY

Eight goals of the criminal justice process are (1) to establish an adversary system of adjudication, (2) to establish an accusatorial system, (3) to minimize erroneous conviction, (4) to minimize the burdens of accusation and litigation, (5) to provide lay participation, (6) to respect the dignity of the individual, (7) to maintain the appearance of fairness, and (8) to achieve equality in applying the process.

The preliminary hearing seeks to establish probable cause to prevent people from being indiscriminately brought to trial. The discovery process requires that all pertinent facts on both sides be made available before the trial. The coroner's jury may be involved in cases where the cause of death is in doubt.

At the arraignment the defendant may stand mute or enter a plea of nolo contendere, guilty, or not guilty.

Direct examination is the questioning of a witness by the attorney who called that particular witness to the stand. Cross-examination is questioning by the opposing attorney.

Strategies for testifying in court include (1) setting yourself up, (2) being unconditional, and (3) not stalling. (4) Avoid conclusions and non-responsive answers. Answer yes-or-no questions with "yes" or "no."

DISCUSSION QUESTIONS

1. Why is the determination of whether an offense is a misdemeanor or a felony important?
2. What is the importance of the "burden of proof" in a criminal trial?
3. Why should defense lawyers be permitted not to tell the court when they know an accused is guilty?
4. Why is it important that an officer on the witness stand not take the proceedings personally?

5. What may an officer do to make the experience of testifying in court less frustrating and more likely to be successful?

6. What is meant by the statement that our system of criminal justice is an adversarial process?

REFERENCES

Ballentine, James A. *Ballentine's Law Dictionary*. Third Edition. Edited by William S. Anderson. Rochester, NY: The Lawyers Co-Operative Publishing Company, 1969.

LaFave, Wayne R., and Israel, Jerold H. *Criminal Procedure*. St. Paul: West Publishing Company, 1985.

Rutledge, Devallis. *Courtroom Survival: The Officer's Guide to Better Testimony*. Sacramento, Calif.: Custom Publishing Company, 1987.

Senna, Joseph J., and Siegel, Larry J. *Introduction to Criminal Justice*. 4th ed. St. Paul, Minn.: West Publishing Company, 1987.

Stuckey, Gilbert B. *Procedures in the Justice System*. 3rd ed. Columbus, Ohio: Charles E. Merrill Publishing Company, 1986.

Wrobleski, Henry M., and Hess, Kären M. *Introduction to Law Enforcement and Criminal Justice*. 2d ed. St. Paul, Minn.: West Publishing Company, 1986.

DOES THE ADVERSARY SYSTEM FOSTER JUSTICE?

Our criminal courts function under the adversary system: state vs. individual, prosecutor vs. defense attorney. Does this system produce justice? Excerpted from Opposing Viewpoints: "Is the Criminal Justice System Fair?"

The Adversary System Guarantees Justice

A number of reasons . . . warrant reliance on adversarial methods. The adversary process provides litigants with the means to control their lawsuits. The parties are preeminent in choosing the forum, designating the proofs, and running the process. The courts, as a general rule, pursue the questions the parties propound. Ultimately, the whole procedure yields results tailored to the litigants' needs and in this way reinforces individual rights. As already noted, this sort of procedure also enhances the economic efficiency of adjudication by sharply reducing impositional costs.

Party control yields other benefits as well. Perhaps most important, it promotes litigant and social acceptance of decisions rendered by the courts. Adversary theory holds that if a party is intimately involved in the adjudicatory process and feels that he has been given a fair opportunity to present his case, he is likely to accept the results whether favorable or not. Assuming this theory is correct, the adversary process will serve to reduce post-litigation friction and to increase compliance with judical mandates.

Almost every procedure in the adversary process moves at a measured pace rather than at maximum speed. Delay, or perhaps more accurately, deliberation, has been built into every aspect of the adversary system. If one adopts the view that any diminution in speed is a serious danger, then every part of the adversary process is open to challenge. The problem with this sort of challenge is that it fails to focus on the most important question, whether there is a need for a process that is careful, deliberative, and committed to airing the claims of each litigant fully rather than one that proceeds at maximum speed.

The proud history and constitutional status of the adversary system as well as the benefits to be derived from its individualizing effect are strong reasons for its retention. Adversary procedure has served as a guardian of individual liberty since its inception. It has facilitated the extension of personal rights to a wide range of minority groups. Given these facts and the absence of a clearly superior alternative, the American commitment to the adversary system ought to be maintained.

Excerpted from: Stephan Landsman, *The Adversary System: A Description and Defense* (Washington, D.C.: The American Enterprise Institute, 1984). Excerpts are reprinted with permission of the American Enterprise Institute for Public Policy Research.

The Adversary System Allows Injustice

It is obvious that litigators pride themselves on their won-lost record. The *National Law Journal* describes "the world's most successful criminal lawyer—229 murder acquittals without a loss!" . . . maybe each of these cases really had legal right on their side. And when a coin comes up heads 229 times in a row it may be fair, but there is another explanation. Lawyers themselves do not see the point of what they do as defending their clients' legal rights, but as using the law to get their clients what they want. My point is only that we have no reason at all to believe that when two overkillers slug it out the better case, rather than the better lawyer, wins.

From: David Luban, "The Adversary System Excuse," from David Luban, ed., THE GOOD LAWYER: LAWYERS' ROLES AND LAWYERS' ETHICS (Totowa, N.J.: Rowman & Allanheld, 1983), pp. 93-99, 117 & 118.

This sentiment is echoed by Anne Strick who argues that the adversary system hides the truth and fails to do justice. She views it as a "system in which truth is incidental; in which information is avoided or suppressed as eagerly as sought, and justice is largely accident."

It is a method of dispute settlement that requires all persons who go to law to settle differences to behave as enemies . . .

And Mr. Justice White, speaking from the height of the Supreme Court bench, noted: If defense counsel can "confuse a witness, even a truthful one, or make him appear at a disadvantage, unsure or indecisive, that will be his normal course." . . . .

Adversary ritual demands of all the same dance. For both the highest and lowest of ends, it provides the very same means. When he enters the lists, the lawyer must reach for the tools at hand. The most altruistic attorney on earth, limited to those means, must butcher truth—as the most virtuoso surgeon, required to operate with hammer and chisel, will produce a mangled patient.

From: *Injustice for All,* by Anne Strick.

CHAPTER 14

Keeping Current and

Researching the Law:

Strategies for Police Officers

The law does not generate justice. The law is nothing but a declaration and application of what is just.—Pierre-Joseph Proudhon, De la justice dans la revolution

DO YOU KNOW

What three audiences information can be written for?

What primary and secondary sources are?

What some of the most common secondary sources of information in law enforcement are?

What the primary sources of information in law enforcement are?

What the National Reporter System is?

What a key source of law enforcement statistics is?

Introduction

Chapter 14

Police work has not always been considered a profession. In times past all that was considered necessary was to hand officers a badge and a gun and let them "enforce the law." Today, however, law enforcement officers are expected to know and trained to know how to perform their duties and to know the law as it relates to these duties.

As already noted, the law is in a constant state of flux, changing to meet the needs of our society. No longer is the law "for the common man," or at least no longer is it understood by the common man. Even lawyers are finding it increasingly necessary to specialize to maintain a working knowledge of distinctive areas of law. Fewer attorneys are maintaining "general practices."

Yet today's law enforcement officers are expected, indeed required, to be aware of and know about the ever-changing criminal law. Failing to know the law could have disastrous effects, including having a case thrown out, or having the defendant acquitted, or being named as a defendant in a civil suit for acting improperly.

In addition, it is simply expected of a professional. If law enforcement is to be a profession and law enforcement officers are to be professionals, they must keep themselves apprised of updates in their field just like other professionals do.

Physicians are certainly expected to keep abreast of modern medical techniques. Bankers are expected to maintain an awareness of the changing aspects of the financial world. Airline pilots are expected to stay on top of improved safety methods and changing FAA rules. Businesses must keep abreast of and comply with OSHA requirements and IRS rules. Accountants must keep abreast of changing tax laws. Police officers, too, are expected to keep up on the changes occurring in laws related to their profession.

The key question is: How?

One answer is licensing. To maintain a license, some states require officers to obtain a specific number of continuing education credits (CEUs) per year. Some states require law enforcement officers to take periodic classes to get updates on the law. Many classes offered to police officers deal with reviewing present laws or becoming aware of new laws. Classes are one excellent way to keep up on the law.

Training continues to be somewhat of a luxury for many officers, however, particularly those in outstate areas or smaller departments where classes may not be readily available or where frequent time-off is just not practical. How, then, can an officer keep up on the law?

Being armed with a basic understanding of what is available and how these resources work makes researching the law a very obtainable goal. Remember, however, that like so many other things in life, legal research can be carried to an illogical extreme. No one would deny that any law library appears as a formidable foe. Viewing the literally thousands of books and hundreds of titles, you might wonder if ignorance of the law shouldn't be considered a defense. As noted in *The Living Law* (1982, p. 1):

One of the most striking features of the American legal system today is its sheer bulk. Congress and the administrative agencies generate tens of thousands of enactments and rulings each year. The nation's high courts add some 35,000 opinions annually. And the individual states contribute enough statutes and regulations to turn the tide into a flood.

Take heart. It IS manageable. The following pages describe the basic sources available to you.

POPULAR, SCHOLARLY, AND PROFESSIONAL SOURCES

A wealth of information at a variety of levels is available to you. It is important to recognize what audience the information is written for.

Information may be written at a popular level for the lay person, at a professional level for the practitioner, and at a scholarly level for the researcher.

Popular literature is written for the lay person. It is not necessarily less authoritative; it simply does not go into the depth that scholarly or professional literature does. Examples of popular literature would be articles dealing with criminal procedure found in *Time* or in *Newsweek*.

Scholarly literature, as the name implies, is written for people interested in theory, research, statistical analysis, and the like. Examples of scholarly literature would be articles in *Justice Quarterly*, an official publication of the Academy of Criminal Justice.

Professional literature is written for the practitioner in a given field. In law enforcement this would include articles in such publications as *Police Chief*, published by the International Association of Chiefs of Police or the *FBI Law Enforcement Bulletin*. It is from professional periodicals that you are most likely to keep yourself current on the ever-changing criminal law. These journals frequently have articles on newly enacted laws and their effects on law enforcement. If an officer's own department does not subscribe to such magazines, they are affordable enough for officers to subscribe personally.

PRIMARY AND SECONDARY SOURCES

Information may also be classified according to whether it is primary or secondary.

Primary information is raw data or the original information.

Sources of primary information for legal research include the United States Constitution, the constitutions of the fifty states, the statutes of the Unites States Congress and of the fifty state legislatures, and appellate court decisions of the federal and state courts.

Secondary information is information based on the raw data or original information.

Secondary information involves selecting, evaluating, analyzing, and synthesizing data or information. It is usually easier to understand by the nonlawyer than primary information.

You will rely on both primary and secondary resources if you need to research a specific aspect of the law. Look first at some of the more common secondary sources you might use. These can usually be found in a general library.

Among the important secondary information sources for legal research are periodicals, treatises/texts, encyclopedias, and dictionaries.

Legal Periodicals

Jacobstein and Mersky (1981, p. 268) describe the function of legal periodicals as "recording and critici[zing] of doings of legislators and judges, discussion of current case law, narration of lives of eminent lawyers, and the scientific study of . . . jurisprudence."

Three groups of legal periodicals can provide important information: law school publications such as the *Harvard Law Review*, bar association publications such as the *American Bar Association Journal*, and special subject and interest periodicals such as the *Black Law Journal* and the *Women Lawyers Journal*.

Treatises/Texts

Oran's Dictionary of the Law (1983, p. 427) defines a treatise as "a large, comprehensive book on a legal subject." Treatises or textbooks go into a specific subject in great depth.

Such works provide the backbone for a great deal of research by legal professionals. Specialized treatises exist in almost every area imaginable.

Although such works are an invaluable resource, they are frequently multivolume and always expensive. They make ideal additions to department libraries and are readily available at law libraries (e.g., law schools, county attorneys' offices, prosecutors' offices).

It is well worth an officer's time to become acquainted with the treatises/texts available. Stop in and browse. Because many of the sourcebooks deal with specific areas of the law, the particular source to use can be easily located.

Legal Encyclopedias

According to Jacobstein and Mersky (1981, p. 254):

> *Legal encyclopedias are written in narrative form, arranged [alphabetically] by subject and containing supporting footnote references to cases in point. In most instances, they are noncritical and do not attempt to be analytical or evaluative. Instead, they simply state the propositions of law, with introductory explanations of an elementary nature. A legal encyclopedia, because of these features, is a popular and useful research tool.*

They go on to identify three types of legal encyclopedias: those dealing with general law, those dealing with local or state law, and those dealing with special subjects. Within each, specific articles are arranged alphabetically for easy reference.

Corpus Juris Secondum (C .J. S.) is a general legal encyclopedia that tries to restate the entire body of American law in encyclopedic form. Published by West Publishing Company, it consists of approximately 150 volumes, including supplements and a 5-volume index.

American Jurisprudence 2d (AM. Jur. 2d) is another general legal encyclopedia that contains four hundred topics. Published by the Lawyers Co-operative Publishing Company and the Bancroft-Whitney Company, it contains approximately 90 volumes, including an 8-volume index.

Encyclopedia of Crime and Justice contains authoritative articles, often quite lengthy, on all areas of criminal justice. Published by Macmillan, this 4-volume set provides a good overview of the major areas of criminal justice.

Guide to American Law is another less voluminous encyclopedia on general topics.

Less comprehensive, but also informative, encyclopedias include *The Concise Encyclopedia of Crime and Criminals* (Hawthorne Books, 1961); and *The Encyclopedia of American Crime* (Facts on File, 1982).

Legal Dictionaries

Legal dictionaries help define words in their legal sense or use. Among the most popular American law dictionaries are *Ballentine's Law Dictionary* (Lawyers Cooperative Publishing Company, 1969); *Black's Law Dictionary*, 5th ed. (West Publishing Company, 1979); and Oran's *Law Dictionary for Nonlawyers*, 2d ed. (West Publishing Company, 1985). Whether hard bound or paperback, every officer's own library (if not briefcase) should contain a law dictionary.

PRIMARY INFORMATION SOURCES

Sometimes it is necessary to go to the actual constitutional provisions, statutes, or cases for more detailed information.

Primary sources are the federal Constitution, state constitutions, and federal and state laws, statutes, and actual cases.

As noted by Lutzker and Ferrall (1986, p. 100):

American law has four basic components, each of which exists on the federal and state levels:
1. *The Constitution;*
2. *Statute Law—the statutes, or laws, passed by the legislatures;*
3. *Regulatory Law—rules and regulations promulgated by government agencies that have the force of law;*
4. *Case Law—the interpretations of the other three made by the courts as a result of cases brought to them on appeal. . . .*
   [B]ecause it is essential for lawyers, politicians, and the public to have access to the most current additions and changes, all new and revised elements of the law appear fairly quickly in published form.

Reading Legal Citations

Although they look as if they were designed to bedevil the unwary, legal citations are actually simple to decipher. A legal citation is just a standardized way of referring to a specific element in the law. It has three basic parts: a volume number, an abbreviation for the title, and a page or section number. These are sometimes followed by the date.

The following are examples of legal citations.

- Supreme Court Case: 383 US 463 (1966). This means volume 383 of the *United States Reports, page 463*, decided in 1966. (The official reporter for United States Supreme Court opinions)
- Federal Law: 42 USC 1971 (1976). This means title (chapter) 42 of the *United States Code*, section 1971, passed in 1976.
- Federal Regulation: 28 CFR 42.6. This means title 28 of the *Code of Federal Regulations*, section 42.6.
- Journal: 131 U. Pa. L. Rev 353–387, Dec'82. This means volume 131 of the *University of Pennsylvania Law Review,*pages 353 to 387, from December 1982.

Researching provisions of federal and state constitutions does not present a problem. When it comes to case law, however, the situation is very different. According to Jacobstein and Mersky (1981, p. 13): "There are over three million judicial opinions in the United States, and over 47,000 American cases are published each year." Finding case law can be a real challenge.

CASE LAW

Court decisions are recorded as opinions that describe what the dispute was about, what the court decided, and why. The opinion is usually written by one member of the court. As Farnsworth (1983, p. 42) suggests: "The sheer number of decisions is an obvious obstacle to finding case law. Reported decisions of the Supreme Court of the United States and of most of the state appellate courts can be found in the official reports of those courts. Those decided from at least 1887 to date can also be found in a system of unofficial reports, the *National Reporter System*, which contains upwards of 7,000 volumes now running about 1,500 pages per volume."

The National Reporter System publishes seven regional sets of volumes as well as individual sets for California, Illinois, and New York courts.

Another system of unofficial reports, the American Law Reports, publishes only the cases thought to be significant and of special interest and discusses them in depth.

When referring to a case, both official and unofficial reports may be cited. Farnsworth (1983, p. 43) explains:

True, legal research is seldom depicted as part of the job in a police drama. The reality is, however, that the professional law enforcement officer must remain current on our ever changing and admittedly complex law.

Thus a correct citation would be Wangen v. Ford Motor Co., 97 Wis. 2d 260, 294 N. W. 2d 437, 13 A. L. R. 4th 1 (1980), meaning that the case was decided in 1980, is found at page 260 of volume 97 of the second series of official Wisconsin reports, at page 437 of volume 294 of the second series of the Northwestern set of the National Reporter System, and at page 1 of volume 13 of the fourth series of American Law Reports, where it is followed by an annotation.

Farnsworth (p. 43) goes on to note: "In this manner are collected the more than 40,000 reported court decisions that each year add to the existing total of roughly four million."

United States Supreme Court Reports are published in five current reports (Jacobstein and Mersky, 1981, p. 31):

- United States Reports (official edition), cited "U.S."
- United States Supreme Court Reports (Lawyers Co-operative Pub. Co.), cited "L. Ed." and "L Ed. 2d."
- Supreme Court Reporter (West Publishing Company), cited "Sup. Ct.," or "S. Ct."
- United States Law Week (Bureau of National Affairs), cited "U.S. L. W." or "U. W. L. Week."
- Commerce Clearing House, United States Supreme Court Bulletin.

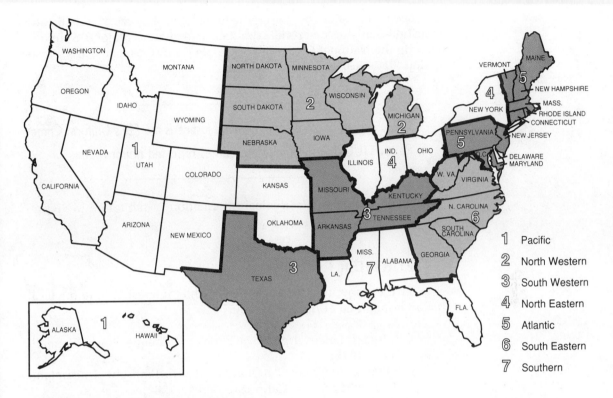

Fig. 14–1   **National Reporter System Map**
From West's Law Finder.

Briefing a Case.

Once you locate your case, you will want to make some notes to help you decipher it. Since cases are usually rather long, the best way to do this is to outline or "brief" the case. O'Block (1986, pp. 125–26) describes how to brief a case in a nonlawyer way. He suggests that six sections are important: (1) The case name and citation, including the year of the decision. (2) A summary of operable facts, beginning with a one-sentence statement on the type of case or offense involved. (3) Legal issues or questions of law involved in the case—the heart of the brief. (4) The court's decision—often phrased as an answer to the questions of law involved. (5) The court's reasoning—why they decided as they did. (6) Separate opinions or dissent—the decision need not be unanimous.

STATISTICAL DATA

Yet another kind of information you may need is statistical—numerical information on various aspects of police work. The Bureau of Justice Statistics (BJS), an agency of the U.S. Department of Justice, has been mandated by Congress to collect, analyze, publish, and distribute statistics on crime, criminals, and victims. Major BJS surveys include the National Crime Survey, State Court Caseloads, and Prosecution Statistics.

A key source of statistics in criminal justice is the FBI's Uniform Crime Reports (UCR) that summarizes crimes reported nationwide.

Another source of statistical information is that found in victimization reports.

FURTHER READING

Two texts written for the general public interested in doing legal research might be of interest to you:

- Alfred J. Lewis, *Using Law Books* (Dubuque, Iowa: Kendall/Hunt, 1976).
- Stephen Elias, *Legal Research: How to Find and Understand the Law* (Berkeley, Calif.: Nolo Press, 1982).

Another source of information that might be of value to you is Robert L. O'Block's *Criminal Justice Research Sources.*This Anderson Publishing Company reference (1986) is a comprehensive listing of various sources, including books, indexing services, journals, bibliographies, computerized literature searches, general reference sources (including reference books, career information guides, encyclopedias, dictionaries, newspapers, annuals and yearbooks), directories, government documents (including national commission reports), federal agencies, statistical data, and the National Criminal Justice Reference Service (NCJRS).

SUMMARY

Information may be written at a popular level for the lay person, at professional level for the practitioner, and at a scholarly level for the researcher.

Secondary information is information based on the raw data or original information. Among the important secondary information sources for legal research are periodicals, treatises/texts, encyclopedias, and dictionaries.

Primary information is raw data or the original information. Primary sources are the federal Constitution, state constitutions, and federal and state laws, statutes, and actual cases. The National Reporter

System publishes seven regional sets of volumes as well as individual sets for California, Illinois, and New York courts.

A key source of statistics in criminal justice is the FBI's *Uniform Crime Reports (UCR)* that summarizes crimes reported nationwide.

Discussion Questions

1. What benefits do police officers get from knowing basic legal research methods?
2. If you, as a police officer, had a question on basic law, where would you start looking?
3. What benefits would FBI statistical data provide a police department?
4. Why are primary sources themselves of only limited benefit?
5. What basic resources would benefit every professional law enforcement officer?

References

Dernbach, John C. and Singleton, Richard V II. *A Practical Guide to Legal Writing and Legal Method*. Littleton, Colo: Fred B. Rothman and Company, 1981.

Farnsworth, E. Allen. *An Introduction to the Legal System of the United States*. New York: Oceania Publications, Inc., 1983.

Jacobsten, J. Myron, and Mersky, Roy M. *Legal Research Illustrated*. 2d ed. New York: The Foundation Press, Inc., 1981.

The Living Law. A Guide to Modern Legal Research. The Lawyers Co-Operative Publishing Company (Bancroft-Whitney Company), 1982.

Lutzker, Marilyn, and Ferrall, Eleanor. *Criminal Justice Research in Libraries. Strategies and Resources*. New York: Greenwood Press, 1986.

O'Block, Robert. *Criminal Justice Research Sources*. Cincinnati: Anderson Publishing Company, 1986.

Oran, Daniel. *Law Dictionary for Nonlawyers*. 2d ed. St. Paul, Minn: West Publishing Company, 1985.

West's Law Finder. A Research Manual for Lawyers. St. Paul Minn.: West Publishing Company, 1980.

DO COPS NEED COLLEGE?

Throughout this text police officers have been referred to as professionals. Certainly, part of being a professional is a solid educational foundation. Just how much education does a police officer need to be effective? The following excerpt by Gerald W. Lynch, president of the John Jay College of Criminal Justice in New York City, presents interesting research findings related to the performance of police officers and their level of college education.

Cops and College

For the last 20 years, every national commission on violence and crime in America has concluded that college education can improve police performance. Police officers must be capable of grasping not only the legal issues of their work, but must have an understanding of human nature, of the social problems they confront daily and of the thinking of those whose attitudes towards the law are not their own. A college education, regardless of the area of study, can help crystallize raw experience, dispel prejudice and heighten tolerance for ambiguity.

In a Rand Corporation study of the New York City Police Department (1973), the level of education of an individual police officer was the most powerful predictor of civilian complaints about assaults on suspects, abuse of authority and religious or racial prejudice. Civilians complained three times more often about police officers who had not graduated from college than they did about officers who had graduated. College graduates violated the department's internal regulations concerning insubordination, negligent use of a revolver and absenteeism significantly less often than did officers who lacked a college education. The Rand study demonstrates that police discretion—including, most critically, the rare decision to use a gun—is improved when influenced by the broad understanding and maturity that college education can bring.

Before we allow a physician to set up shop, we require him to have had an average of 11,000 hours of training, and we require lawyers an average of 9,000. The number of training hours required of police officers has not increased dramatically since 1967, when officers nationwide were required to have an average of 200 hours of training before hitting the streets in uniform and armed. The New York City Police Academy puts recruits through a training program more rigorous than that of many cities, but the fact remains that it takes just six months to travel the path from civilian to officer.

APPENDIX

The Constitution of the

United States of America

We the People of the United States, in Order to form a more perfect Union, establish Justice, insure domestic Tranquility, provide for the common defence, promote the general Welfare, and secure the Blessings of Liberty to ourselves and our Posterity, do ordain and establish this Constitution for the United States of America.

Article I

Section 1 All legislative Powers herein granted shall be vested in a Congress of the United States, which shall consist of a Senate and House of Representatives.

Section 2 (1) The House of Representatives shall be composed of Members chosen every second Year by the People of the several States, and the Electors in each State shall have the Qualifications requisite for Electors of the most numerous Branch of the State Legislature.

(2) No Person shall be a Representative who shall not have attained to the age of twenty-five Years, and been seven Years a Citizen of the United States, and who shall not, when elected, be an Inhabitant of that State in which he shall be chosen.

(3) Representatives and direct Taxes shall be apportioned among the several States which may be included within this Union, according to their respective Numbers, which shall be determined by adding to the whole Number of free Persons, including those bound to Service for a Term of Years, and excluding Indians not taxed, three fifths of all other Persons. The actual Enumeration shall be made within three Years after the first Meeting of the Congress of the United States, and within every subsequent Term of ten Years, in such Manner as they shall by Law

direct. The Number of Representatives shall not exceed one for every thirty Thousand, but each State shall have at Least one Representative; and until such enumeration shall be made, the State of New Hampshire shall be entitled to chuse three, Massachusetts eight, Rhode Island and Providence Plantations one, Connecticut five, New York six, New Jersey four, Pennsylvania eight, Delaware one, Maryland six, Virginia ten, North Carolina five, South Carolina five, and Georgia three.

(4) When vacancies happen in the Representation from any State, the Executive Authority thereof shall issue Writs of Election to fill such Vacancies.

(5) The House of Representatives shall chuse their Speaker and other Officers; and shall have the sole Power of Impeachment.

Section 3   (1) The Senate of the United States shall be composed of two Senators from each State, chosen by the Legislature thereof, for six Years; and each Senator shall have one Vote.

(2) Immediately after they shall be assembled in Consequence of the first Election, they shall be divided as equally as may be into three Classes. The Seats of the Senators of the first Class shall be vacated at the Expiration of the second Year, of the second Class at the Expiration of the fourth Year, and of the third Class at the Expiration of the sixth Year, so that one third may be chosen every second Year; and if Vacancies happen by Resignation, or otherwise, during the Recess of the Legislature of any State, the Executive thereof may make temporary Appointments until the next Meeting of the Legislature, which shall then fill such Vacancies.

(3) No Person shall be a Senator who shall not have attained to the Age of thirty Years, and been nine Years a Citizen of the United States, and who shall not, when elected, be an Inhabitant of that State for which he shall be chosen.

(4) The Vice President of the United States shall be President of the Senate, but shall have no Vote, unless they be equally divided.

(5) The Senate shall chuse their other Officers, and also a President pro tempore, in the Absence of the Vice President, or when he shall exercise the Office of the President of the United States.

(6) The Senate shall have the sole Power to try all Impeachments. When sitting for that Purpose, they shall be on Oath or Affirmation. When the President of the United States is tried, the Chief Justice shall preside: And no Person shall be convicted without the Concurrence of two thirds of the Members present.

(7) Judgment in Cases of Impeachment shall not extend further than to removal from Office, and disqualification to hold and enjoy any Office of honor, Trust or Profit under the United States: but the Party convicted shall nevertheless be liable and subject to Indictment, Trial, Judgment and Punishment, according to Law.

Section 4   (1) The Times, Places and Manner of holding Elections for Senators and Representatives, shall be prescribed in each State by the

Legislature thereof; but the Congress may at any time by Law make or alter such Regulations, except as to the Places of chusing Senators.

(2) The Congress shall assemble at least once in every Year, and such Meeting shall be on the first Monday in December, unless they shall by Law appoint a different Day.

Section 5 (1) Each House shall be the Judge of the Elections, Returns and Qualifications of its own Members, and a Majority of each shall constitute a Quorum to do Business; but a small Number may adjourn from day to day, and may be authorized to compel the Attendance of absent Members, in such Manner, and under such Penalties as each House may provide.

(2) Each House may determine the Rules of its Proceedings, punish its Members for disorderly Behaviour, and, with the Concurrence of two thirds, expel a Member.

(3) Each House shall keep a Journal of its Proceedings, and from time to time publish the same, excepting such Parts as may in their Judgment require Secrecy; and the Yeas and Nays of the Members of either House on any question shall, at the Desire of one fifth of those Present, be entered on the Journal.

(4) Neither House, during the Session of Congress, shall, without the Consent of the other, adjourn for more than three days, not to any other Place than that in which the two Houses shall be sitting.

Section 6 (1) The Senators and Representatives shall receive a Compensation for their Services, to be ascertained by Law, and paid out of the Treasury of the United States. They shall in all Cases, except Treason, Felony and Breach of the Peace, be privileged from Arrest during their Attendance at the Session of their respective Houses, and in going to and returning from the same; and for any Speech or Debate in either House, they shall not be questioned in any other Place.

(2) No Senator or Representative shall, during the Time for which he was elected, be appointed to any civil Office under the Authority of the United States, which shall have been created, or the Emoluments whereof shall have been encreased during such time; and no Person holding any Office under the United States, shall be a Member of either House during his Continuance in Office.

Section 7 (1) All Bills for raising Revenue shall originate in the House of Representatives; but the Senate may propose or concur with Amendments as on other Bills.

(2) Every Bill which shall have passed the House of Representatives and the Senate, shall, before it become a Law, be presented to the President of the United States; If he approve he shall sign it, but if not he shall return it, with his Objections to that House in which it shall have originated, who shall enter the Objections at large on their Journal, and proceed to reconsider it. If after such Reconsideration two thirds of that House shall agree to pass the Bill, it shall be sent,

together with the Objections, to the other House, by which it shall likewise be reconsidered, and if approved by two thirds of that House, it shall become a Law. But in all such Cases the Votes of both Houses shall be determined by Yeas and Nays, and the Names of the Persons voting for and against the Bill shall be entered on the Journal of each House respectively. If any Bill shall not be returned by the President within ten Days (Sunday excepted) after it shall have been presented to him, the Same shall be a Law, in like Manner as if he had signed it, unless the Congress by their Adjournment prevent its Return, in which Case it shall not be a Law.

(3) Every Order, Resolution, or Vote to which the Concurrence of the Senate and House of Representatives may be necessary (except on a question of Adjournment) shall be presented to the President of the United States; and before the Same shall take Effect, shall be approved by him, or being disapproved by him, shall be repassed by two thirds of the Senate and House of Representatives, according to the Rules and Limitations prescribed in the Case of a Bill.

Section 8   (1) The Congress shall have Power To lay and collect Taxes, Duties, Imposts and Excises, to pay the Debts and provide for the common Defence and general Welfare of the United States; but all Duties, Imposts and Excises shall be uniform throughout the United States;

(2) To borrow Money on the credit of the United States;

(3) To regulate Commerce with foreign Nations, and among the several States, and with the Indian tribes;

(4) To establish an uniform Rule of Naturalization, and uniform Laws on the subject of Bankruptcies throughout the United States;

(5) To coin Money, regulate the Value thereof, and of foreign Coin, and to fix the Standard of Weights and Measures;

(6) To Provide for the Punishment of counterfeiting the Securities and current Coin of the United States;

(7) To establish Post Offices and post Roads;

(8) To promote the Progress of Science and useful Arts, by securing for limited Times to Authors and Inventors the exclusive Right to their respective Writings and Discoveries;

(9) To constitute Tribunals inferior to the supreme Court;

(10) To define and and punish Piracies and Felonies committed on the high Seas, and Offenses against the Law of Nations;

(11) To declare War, grant Letters or Marque and Reprisal, and make Rules concerning Captures on Land and Water;

(12) To raise and support Armies, but no Appropriation of Money to that Use shall be for a longer Term than two Years;

(13) To provide and maintain a Navy;

(14) To make Rules for the Government and Regulation of the land and naval Forces;

(15) To provide for calling forth the Militia to execute the Laws of the Union, suppress Insurrections and repel Invasions;

(16) To provide for organizing, arming, and disciplining, the Militia, and for governing such Part of them as may be employed in the Service of the Untied States, reserving to the States respectively, the Appointment of the Officers, and the Authority of training the Militia according to the discipline prescribed by Congress;

(17) To exercise exclusive Legislation in all Cases whatsoever, over such District (not exceeding ten Miles square) as may, by Cession of particular States, and the Acceptance of Congress, become the Seat of the Government of the United States, and to exercise like Authority over all Places purchased by the Consent of the Legislature of the State in which the Same shall be, for the Erection of Forts, Magazines, Arsenals, dock-Yards, and other needful Buildings;—And

(18) To make all Laws which shall be necessary and proper for carrying into Execution the foregoing Powers, and all other Powers vested by this Constitution in the Government of the United States, or in any Department or Officer thereof.

Section 9 (1) The Migration or Importation of such Persons as any of the States now existing shall think proper to admit, shall not be prohibited by the Congress prior to the Year one thousand eight hundred and eight, but a Tax or Duty may be imposed on such Importation, not exceeding ten dollars for each Person.

(2) The Privilege of the Writ of Habeas Corpus shall not be suspended unless when in Cases of Rebellion or Invasion the public Safety may require it.

(3) No Bill of Attainder or ex post facto Law shall be passed.

(4) No Capitation, or other direct, Tax shall be laid, unless in Proportion to the Census or Enumeration herein before directed to be taken.

(5) No Tax or Duty shall be laid on Articles exported from any State.

(6) No Preference shall be given by any Regulation of Commerce or Revenue to the Ports of one State over those of another; nor shall Vessels bound to, or from, one State, be obliged to enter, clear or pay Duties in another.

(7) No Money shall be drawn from the Treasury, but in Consequence of Appropriations made by Law; and a regular Statement and Account of the Receipts and Expenditures of all public Money shall be published from time to time.

(8) No title of Nobility shall be granted by the United States: And no Person holding any Office of Profit or Trust under them, shall, without the Consent of the Congress, accept of any present, Emolument, Office, or Title, of any kind whatever, from any King, Prince or foreign State.

Section 10 (1) No State shall enter into any Treaty, Alliance, or Confederation; grant Letters of Marque and Reprisal; coin Money; emit Bills of Credit; make any Thing but gold and silver Coin a Tender in

Payment of Debts; pass any Bill of Attainder, ex post facto Law, or Law impairing the Obligation of Contracts, or grant any Title of Nobility.

(2) No State shall, without the Consent of Congress, lay any Imposts or Duties on Imports or Exports, except what may be absolutely necessary for executing its inspection Laws: and the net Produce of all Duties and Imposts, laid by any State on Imports or Exports, shall be for the Use of the Treasury of the United States; and all such Laws shall be subject to the Revision and Controul of the Congress.

(3) No State shall, without the Consent of Congress, lay any Duty of Tonnage, keep Troops, or Ships of War in time of Peace, enter into any Agreement or Compact with another State, or with a foreign Power, or engage in War, unless actually invaded, or in such imminent Danger as will not admit of Delay.

Article II

Section 1   (1) The executive Power shall be vested in a President of the United States of America. He shall hold his Office during the Term of four Years, and, together with the Vice President, chosen for the same Term, be elected, as follows:

(2) Each State shall appoint, in such Manner as the Legislature thereof may direct, a Number of Electors, equal to the whole Number of Senators and Representatives to which the State may be entitled in the Congress: but no Senator or Representative, or Person holding an Office of Trust or Profit under the United States, shall be appointed an Elector.

The Electors shall meet in their respective States, and vote by Ballot for two Persons, of whom one at least shall not be an Inhabitant of the same State with themselves. And they shall make a List of all the Persons voted for, and of the Number of Votes for each; which List they shall sign and certify, and transmit sealed to the Seat of the Government of the United States, directed to the President of the Senate. The President of the Senate shall, in the presence of the Senate and House of Representatives, open all the Certificates, and the Votes shall then be counted. The Person having the greatest Number of Votes shall be the President, if such Number be a Majority of the whole Number of Electors appointed; and if there be more than one who have such Majority, and have an equal Number of Votes, then the House of Representatives shall immediately chuse by Ballot one of them for President; and if no Person have a Majority, then from the five highest on the List the said House shall in like Manner chuse the President. But in chusing the President, the Votes shall be taken by States, the Representation from each State having one Vote; a quorum for this Purpose shall consist of a Member or Members from two thirds of the States, and a Majority of all the States shall be necessary to a Choice. In every Case, after the Choice of the President, the Person having the greatest Number of Votes of the Electors shall be the Vice President. But if there should remain two or more who have equal Votes, the Senate shall chuse from them by Ballot the Vice President.

(3) The Congress may determine the Time of chusing the Electors, and the Day on which they shall give their Votes; which Day shall be the same throughout the United States.

(4) No Person except a natural born Citizen, or a Citizen of the United States, at the time of the Adoption of this Constitution, shall be eligible to the Office of President; neither shall any Person be eligible to that Office who shall not have attained to the Age of thirty five Years, and been fourteen Years a Resident within the United States.

(5) In Case of the Removal of the President from Office, or of his Death, Resignation, or Inability to discharge the Powers and Duties of the said Office, the Same shall devolve on the Vice President, and the Congress may by Law provide for the Case of Removal, Death, Resignation or Inability, both to the President and Vice President, declaring what Officer shall then act as President, and such Officer shall act accordingly, until the Disability be removed, or a President shall be elected.

(6) The President shall, at stated Times, receive for his Services, a Compensation, which shall neither be increased nor diminished during the Period for which he shall have been elected, and he shall not receive within that Period any other Emolument from the United States, or any of them.

(7) Before he enter on the Execution of his Office, he shall take the following Oath or Affirmation:—"I do solemnly swear (or affirm) that I will faithfully execute the Office of President of the United States, and will to the best of my Ability, preserve, protect and defend the Constitution of the United States."

Section 2 (1) The President shall be Commander in Chief of the Army and Navy of the United States, and of the Militia of the several States, when called into the actual Service of the United States; he may require the Opinion, in writing, of the principal Officer in each of the executive Departments, upon any Subject relating to the Duties of their respective Offices, and he shall have Power to grant Reprieves and Pardons for Offenses against the United States, except in Cases of Impeachment.

(2) He shall have Power, by and with the Advice and Consent of the Senate, to make Treaties, provided two thirds of the Senators present concur; and he shall nominate, and by and with the Advice and Consent of the Senate, shall appoint Ambassadors, other public Ministers and Consuls, Judges of the supreme Court, and all other Officers of the United States, whose Appointments are not herein otherwise provided for, and which shall be established by Law: but the Congress may by Law vest the Appointment of such inferior Officers, as they think proper, in the President alone, in the Courts of Law, or in the Heads of Departments.

(3) The President shall have Power to fill up all Vacancies that may happen during the Recess of the Senate, by granting Commissions which shall expire at the End of their next Session.

Section 3 He shall from time to time give to the Congress Information of the State of the Union, and recommend to their Consideration such Measures as he shall judge necessary and expedient; he may, on extraordinary Occasions, convene both Houses, or either of them, and in Case of Disagreement between them, with Respect to the Time of Adjournment, he may adjourn them to such Time as he shall think proper; he shall receive Ambassadors and other public Ministers; he shall take Care that the Laws be faithfully executed, and shall Commission all the Officers of the United States.·

Section 4 The President, Vice President and all Civil Officers of the United States, shall be removed from Office on Impeachment for, and Conviction of, Treason, Bribery, or other high Crimes and Misdemeanors.

Article III

Section 1 The judicial Power of the United States, shall be vested in one supreme Court, and in such inferior Courts as the Congress may from time to time ordain and establish. The Judges, both of the supreme and inferior Courts, shall hold their Offices during good Behaviour, and shall, at stated Times, receive for their Services, a Compensation, which shall not be diminished during their Continuance in Office.

Section 2 (1) The judicial Power shall extend to all Cases, in Law and Equity, arising under this Constitution, the Laws of the United States, and Treaties made, or which shall be made, under their Authority;—to all Cases affecting Ambassadors, other public Ministers and Consuls;—to all Cases of admiralty and maritime Jurisdiction;—to Controversies to which the United States shall be a party;—to Controversies between two or more States;—between a State and Citizens of another State;—between Citizens of different States;—between Citizens of the same State claiming Lands under Grants of different States, and between a State, or the Citizens thereof, and foreign States, Citizens or Subjects.

    (2) In all Cases affecting Ambassadors, other public Ministers and Consuls, and those in which a State shall be Party, the supreme Court shall have original Jurisdiction. In all the other Cases before mentioned, the supreme Court shall have appellate Jurisdiction, both as the Law and Fact, with such Exceptions, and under such Regulations as the Congress shall make.

    (3) The Trial of all Crimes, except in Cases of Impeachment, shall be by Jury; and such Trial shall be held in the State where the said Crimes shall have been committed; but when not committed within any State, the Trial shall be such Place or Places as the Congress may by Law have directed.

Section 3 (1) Treason against the United States, shall consist only in levying War against them, or in adhering to their Enemies, giving them Aid and Comfort. No Person shall be convicted of Treason unless on the

Testimony of two Witnesses to the same overt Act, or on Confession in open Court.

(2) The Congress shall have Power to declare the Punishment of Treason, but no Attainder of Treason shall work Corruption of Blood, or Forfeiture except during the Life of the Person attainted.

Article IV

Section 1 Full Faith and Credit shall be given in each State to the public Acts, Records, and judicial Proceedings of every other State. And the Congress may by general Laws prescribe the Manner in which such Acts, Records and Proceedings shall be proved, and the Effect thereof.

Section 2 (1) The Citizens of each State shall be entitled to all privileges and Immunities of Citizens in the several States.

(2) A Person charged in any State with Treason, Felony, or other Crime, who shall flee from Justice, and be found in another State, shall on Demand of the executive Authority of the State from which he fled, be delivered up, to be removed to the State having Jurisdiction of the Crime.

(3) No Person held to Service of Labour in one State, under the Laws thereof, escaping into another, shall, in Consequence of any Law or Regulation therein, be discharged from such Service or Labour, but shall be delivered up on Claim of the Party to whom such Service or Labour may be due.

Section 3 (1) New States may be admitted by the Congress into this Union; but no new State shall be formed or erected within the Jurisdiction of any other State; nor any State be formed by the Junction of two or more States, or Parts of States, without the Consent of the Legislatures of the States concerned as well as of the Congress.

(2) The Congress shall have power to dispose of and make all needful Rules and Regulations respecting the Territory or other Property belonging to the United States; and nothing in this Constitution shall be so construed as to Prejudice any Claims of the United States, or of any particular State.

Section 4 The United States shall guarantee to every State in this Union a Republican Form of Government, and shall protect each of them against Invasion; and on Application of the Legislature, or of the Executive (when the Legislature cannot be convened) against domestic Violence.

Article V

The Congress, whenever two thirds of both Houses shall deem it necessary, shall propose Amendments to this Constitution, or, on the

Application of the Legislatures of two thirds of the several States, shall call a Convention for proposing Amendments, which, in either Case, shall be valid to all Intents and Purposes, as Part of this Constitution, when ratified by the Legislatures of three fourths of the several States, or by Conventions in three fourths thereof, as the one or the other Mode of Ratification may be proposed by the Congress; Provided that no Amendment which may be made prior to the Year One thousand eight hundred and eight shall in any Manner affect the first and fourth Clauses in the Ninth Section of the first Article; and that no State, without its Consent, shall be deprived of its equal Suffrage in the Senate.

Article VI

(1) All Debts contracted and Engagements entered into, before the Adoption of this Constitution, shall be as valid against the United States under this Constitution, as under the Confederation.

(2) This Constitution, and the Laws of the United States which shall be made in Pursuance thereof; and all Treaties made, or which shall be made, under the Authority of the United States, shall be the supreme Law of the Land; and the Judges in every State shall be bound thereby, any Thing in the Constitution or Laws of any State to the Contrary notwithstanding.

(3) The Senators and Representatives before mentioned, and the Members of the several State Legislatures, and all executive and judicial Officers, both of the United States and of the several States, shall be bound by Oath or Affirmation, to support this Constitution; but no religious Test shall ever be required as a Qualification to any Office or public Trust under the United States.

Article VII

The Ratification of the Conventions of nine States, shall be sufficient for the Establishment of this Constitution between the States so ratifying the Same.

ARTICLES IN ADDITION TO, AND AMENDMENT OF, THE CONSTITUTION OF THE UNITED STATES OF AMERICA, PROPOSED BY CONGRESS, AND RATIFIED BY THE SEVERAL STATES, PURSUANT TO THE FIFTH ARTICLE OF THE ORIGINAL CONSTITUTION

Amendment I (1791)

Congress shall make no law respecting an establishment of religion, or prohibiting the free exercise thereof; or abridging the freedom of speech, or of the press; or the right of the people peaceably to assemble, and to petition the Government for a redress of grievances.

Amendment II (1791)

A well regulated Militia, being necessary to the security of a free state, the right of the people to keep and bear Arms, shall not be infringed.

Amendment III (1791)

No Soldier shall, in time of peace be quartered in any house, without the consent of the Owner, nor in time of war, but in a manner to be prescribed by law.

Amendment IV (1791)

The right of the people to be secure in their persons, houses, papers, and effects, against unreasonable searches and seizures, shall not be violated, and no Warrants shall issue, but upon probable cause, supported by Oath or affirmation, and particularly describing the place to be searched, and the persons or things to be seized.

Amendment V (1791)

No person shall be held to answer for a capital, or otherwise infamous crime, unless on a presentment or indictment of a Grand Jury, except in cases arising in the land or naval forces, or in the Militia, when in actual service in time of War or public danger; nor shall any person be subject for the same offence to be twice put in jeopardy of life or limb; nor shall be compelled in any criminal case to be a witness against himself, nor be deprived of life, liberty, or property, without due process of law; nor shall private property be taken for public use, without just compensation.

Amendment VI (1791)

In all criminal prosecutions, the accused shall enjoy the right to a speedy and public trial, by an impartial jury of the State and district wherein the crime shall have been committed, which district shall have been previously ascertained by law, and to be informed of the nature and cause of the accusation; to be confronted with the witnesses against him; to have compulsory process for obtaining witnesses in his favor, and to have the Assistance of Counsel for his defence.

Amendment VII (1791)

In Suits at common law, where the value in controversy shall exceed twenty dollars, the right of trial by jury shall be preserved, and no fact tried by a jury, shall be otherwise re-examined in any Court of the United States, than according to the rules of the common law.

Amendment VIII (1791)

Excessive bail shall not be required, nor excessive fines imposed, nor cruel and unusual punishments inflicted.

Amendment IX (1791)

The enumeration in the Constitution, of certain rights, shall not be construed to deny or disparage others retained by the people.

Amendment X (1791)

The powers not delegated to the United States by the Constitution, nor prohibited by it to the States, are reserved to the States respectively, or to the people.

Amendment XI (1798)

The Judicial power of the United States shall not be construed to extend to any suit in law or equity, commenced or prosecuted against one of the United States by Citizens of another State, or by Citizens or Subjects of any Foreign State.

Amendment XII (1804)

The Electors shall meet in their respective states and vote by ballot for President and Vice-President, one of whom, at least, shall not be an inhabitant of the same state with themselves; they shall name in their ballots the person voted for as President, and in distinct ballots the person voted for as Vice-President, and they shall make distinct lists of all persons voted for as President, and of all persons voted for as Vice-President, and of the number of votes for each, which lists they shall sign and certify, and transmit sealed to the seat of the government of the United States, directed to the President of the Senate;—The President of the Senate shall, in the presence of the Senate and House of Representatives, open all the certificates and the votes shall then be counted;—The person having the greatest number of votes for President, shall be the President, if such number be a majority of the whole number of Electors appointed; and if no person have such majority, then from the persons having the highest numbers not exceeding three on the list of those voted for as President, the House of Representatives shall choose immediately, by ballot, the President. But in choosing the President, the votes shall be taken by states, the representation from each state having one vote; a quorum for this purpose shall consist of a member or members from two-thirds of the states, and a majority of all the states shall be necessary to a choice. And if the House of Representatives shall not choose a President whenever the right of choice shall devolve upon them, before the fourth day of March next following, then the Vice-President shall act as President, as in the case of the death or other constitutional disability of the President—The person having the greatest number of votes as Vice-President, shall be the Vice-President, if such number be a majority of the whole number of Electors appointed, and if no person have a majority, then from the two highest numbers on the list, the Senate shall choose the Vice-President; A quorum for the purpose shall consist of two-thirds of the whole number of Senators, and a majority of the whole number shall be necessary to a choice. But no person constitutionally ineligible to the office of President shall be eligible to that of Vice-President of the United States.

Amendment XIII (1865)

Section 1 Neither slavery nor involuntary servitude, except as a punishment for crime whereof the party shall have been duly convicted, shall exist within the United States, or any place subject to their jurisdiction.

Section 2 Congress shall have power to enforce this article by appropriate legislation.

Amendment XIV (1868)

Section 1 All persons born or naturalized in the United States and subject to the jurisdiction thereof, are citizens of the United States and of the State wherein they reside. No State shall make or enforce any law which shall abridge the privileges or immunities of citizens of the United States; nor shall any State deprive any person of life, liberty, or property, without due process of law; nor deny to any person within its jurisdiction the equal protection of the laws.

Section 2 Representatives shall be apportioned among the several States according to their respective numbers, counting the whole number of persons in each State, excluding Indians not taxed. But when the right to vote at any election for the choice of electors for President and Vice-President of the United States, Representatives in Congress, the Executive and Judicial officers of a State, or the members of the Legislature thereof, is denied to any of the male inhabitants of such State, being twenty-one years of age, and citizens of the United States, or in any way abridged, except for participation in rebellion, or other crime, the basis of representation therein shall be reduced in the proportion which the number of such male citizens shall bear to the whole number of male citizens twenty-one years of age in such State.

Section 3 No person shall be a Senator or Representative in Congress, or elector of President and Vice-President, or hold any office, civil or military, under the United States, or under any State, who, having previously taken an oath, as a member of Congress, or as an officer of the United States, or as a member of any State legislature, or as an executive or judicial officer of any State, to support the Constitution of the United States, shall have engaged in insurrection or rebellion against the same, or given aid or comfort to the enemies thereof. But Congress may by a vote of two-thirds of each House, remove such disability.

Section 4 The validity of the public debt of the United States, authorized by law, including debts incurred for payment of pensions and bounties for services in suppressing insurrection or rebellion, shall not be questioned. But neither the United States nor any State shall assume or pay any debt or obligation incurred in aid of insurrection or rebellion against the United States, or any claim for the loss or emancipation of any slave; but all such debts, obligations and claims shell be held illegal and void.

Section 5 The Congress shall have power to enforce, by appropriate legislation, the provisions of this article.

Amendment XV (1870)

Section 1 The right of citizens of the United States to vote shall not be denied or abridged by the United States or by any State on account of race, color, or previous condition of servitude.

Section 2 The Congress shall have power to enforce this article by appropriate legislation.

Amendment XVI (1913)

The Congress shall have power to lay and collect taxes on incomes, from whatever source derived, with apportionment among the several States, and without regard to any census or enumeration.

Amendment XVII (1913)

The Senate of the United States shall be composed of two Senators from each State, elected by the people thereof, for six years; and each Senator shall have one vote. The electors in each State shall have the qualifications requisite for electors of the most numerous branch of the State legislatures.

When vacancies happen in the representation of any State in the Senate, the executive authority of such State shall issue writs of election to fill such vacancies: *Provided*, That the legislature of any State may empower the executive thereof to make temporary appointments until the people fill the vacancies by election as the legislature may direct.

This amendment shall not be so construed as to affect the election or term of any Senator chosen before it becomes valid as part of the Constitution.

Amendment XVIII (1919)

Section 1 After one year from the ratification of this article the manufacture, sale, or transportation of intoxicating liquors within, the importation thereof into, or the exportation thereof from the United States and all territory subject to the jurisdiction thereof for beverage purposes is hereby prohibited.

Section 2 The Congress and the several States shall have concurrent power to enforce this article by appropriate legislation.

Section 3 This article shall be inoperative unless it shall have been ratified as an amendment to the Constitution by the legislatures of the several States, as provided in the Constitution, within seven years from the date of the submission hereof to the States by the Congress.

Amendment XIX (1920)

The right of citizens of the United States to vote shall not be denied or abridged by the United States or by any State on account of sex.

Congress shall have power to enforce this article by appropriate legislation.

Amendment XX (1933)

Section 1 The terms of the President and Vice President shall end at noon on the 20th day of January, and the terms of Senators and Representatives at noon on the 3d day of January, of the years in which such terms would have ended if this article had not been ratified; and the terms of their successors shall then begin.

Section 2 The Congress shall assemble at least once in every year, and such meeting shall begin at noon on the 3d day of January, unless they shall by law appoint a different day.

Section 3 If, at the time fixed for the beginning of the term of the President, the President elect shall have died, the Vice President elect shall become President. If a President shall not have been chosen before the time fixed for the beginning of his term, or if the President elect shall have failed to qualify, then the Vice President elect shall act as President until a President shall have qualified; and the Congress may by law provide for the case wherein neither a President elect nor a Vice

President elect shall have qualified, declaring who shall then act as President, or the manner in which one who is to act shall be selected, and such person shall act accordingly until a President or Vice President shall have qualified.

Section 4   The Congress may by law provide for the case of the death of any of the persons from whom the House of Representatives may choose a President whenever the right of choice shall have devolved upon them, and for the case of the death of any of the persons from whom the Senate may choose a Vice President whenever the right of choice shall have devolved upon them.

Section 5   Sections 1 and 2 shall take effect on the 15th day of October following the ratification of this article.

Section 6   This article shall be inoperative unless it shall have been ratified as an amendment to the Constitution by the legislatures of three-fourths of the several States within seven years from the date of its submission.

Amendment XXI (1933)

Section 1   The eighteenth article of amendment to the Constitution of the United States is hereby repealed.

Section 2   The transportation or importation into any State, Territory or possession of the United States for delivery or use therein of intoxicating liquors, in violation of the laws thereof, is hereby prohibited.

Section 3   This article shall be inoperative unless it shall have been ratified as an amendment to the Constitution by conventions in the several States, as provided in the Constitution, within seven years from the date of the submission hereof to the States by the Congress.

Amendment XXII (1951)

Section 1   No person shall be elected to the office of the President more than twice, and no person who has held the office of President, or acted as President, for more than two years of a term to which some other person was elected President shall be elected to the office of the President more than once. But this Article shall not apply to any person holding the office of President when this Article was proposed by the Congress, and shall not prevent any person who may be holding the office of President, or acting as President, during the term within which this Article becomes operative from holding the office of President or acting as President during the remainder of such term.

Section 2 This Article shall be inoperative unless it shall have been ratified as an amendment to the Constitution by the legislatures of three-fourths of the several States within seven years from the date of its submission to the States by the Congress.

Amendment XXIII (1961)

Section 1 The District constituting the seat of Government of the United States shall appoint in such manner as the Congress may direct:

A number of electors of President and Vice President equal to the whole number of Senators and Representatives in Congress to which the District would be entitled if it were a State, but in no event more than the least populous State; they shall be in addition to those appointed by the States, but they shall be considered, for the purposes of the election of President and Vice President, to be electors appointed by a State; and they shall meet in the District and perform such duties as provided by the twelfth article of amendment.

Section 2 The Congress shall have power to enforce this article by appropriate legislation.

Amendment XXIV (1964)

Section 1 The right of citizens of the United States to vote in any primary or other election for President or Vice President, for electors for President or Vice President, or for Senator or Representative in Congress, shall not be denied or abridged by the United States or any State by reason of failure to pay any poll tax or other tax.

Section 2 The Congress shall have power to enforce this article by appropriate legislation.

Amendment XXV (1967)

Section 1 In case of the removal of the President from office or of his death or resignation, the Vice President shall become President.

Section 2 Whenever there is a vacancy in the office of the Vice President, the President shall nominate a Vice President who shall take office upon confirmation by a majority vote of both Houses of Congress.

Section 3 Whenever the President transmits to the President pro tempore of the Senate and the Speaker of the House of Representatives his written declaration that he is unable to discharge the powers and duties of his office, and until he transmits to them a written declaration to the contrary, such powers and duties shall be discharged by the Vice President as Acting President.

Section 4   Whenever the Vice President and a majority of either the principal officers of the executive departments or of such other body as Congress may by law provide, transmit to the President pro tempore of the Senate and the Speaker of the House of Representatives their written declaration that the President is unable to discharge the powers and duties of his office, the Vice President shall immediately assume the powers and duties of the office as Acting President.

Thereafter, when the President transmits to the President pro tempore of the Senate and the Speaker of the House of Representatives his written declaration that no inability exists, he shall resume the powers and duties of his office unless the Vice President and a majority of either the principal officers of the executive department or of such other body as Congress may by law provide, transmit within four days to the President pro tempore of the Senate and the Speaker of the House of Representatives their written declaration that the President is unable to discharge the powers and duties of his office. Thereupon Congress shall decide the issue, assembling within forty-eight hours for that purpose if not in session. If the Congress, within twenty-one days after receipt of the latter written declaration, or, if Congress is not in session, within twenty-one days after Congress is required to assemble, determines by two-thirds vote of both Houses that the President is unable to discharge the powers and duties of his office, the Vice President shall continue to discharge the same as Acting President; otherwise, the President shall resume the powers and duties of his office.

Amendment XXVI (1971)

Section 1   The right of citizens of the United States, who are eighteen years of age or older, to vote shall not be denied or abridged by the United States or by any State on account of age.

Section 2   The Congress shall have power to enforce this article by appropriate legislation.

Glossary

Acquit: Judicially to set free or discharge from an accusation of guilt of a crime or even a civil liability.

Acquittal: A verdict of not guilty.

Adjudication: A judicial determination or decree, a fact-finding hearing to review evidence in a juvenile case.

Adversary system: The placing of contesting parties against one another, each having standing to make their claim, with one being found in favor of.

Affidavit: A statement reduced to writing, sworn to before an officer or notary having authority to administer an oath.

Affirmation: A statement or declaration.

Appeal: Proceeding to have a case reheard in a higher court.

Appellate jurisdiction: Means the court has the authority to review and affirm or reverse the actions of a lower court.

Arraignment: A court procedure whereby the accused is read the charges against him and is then asked how he pleads.

Arrest: The official taking of a person into custody to answer criminal charges. This involves at least temporarily depriving the person of liberty and may involve the use of force.

Assault: An action creating reasonable apprehension of immediate harmful or offensive contact to another and intent to cause such apprehension (tort). Also refers to criminal body contact (crime).

Associative evidence: Links a suspect with a crime.

Attenuation: The link between the original illegal evidence and the related evidence is so weak that the evidence is allowed in court. Also referred to as the "purged taint" exception.

Attorney general: Chief law enforcement officer of a state or of the country.

Awareness spectrum: A measure of an officer's alertness to the surroundings.

Bail: Money or other financial security given to the court by a defendant to assure appearance in court, to be forfeited if the appearance is not made as ordered.

Bailiff: Individual responsible for keeping courtroom proceedings orderly and dignified and for protecting everyone in the courtroom.

Battery: An action creating unpermitted harmful or offensive contact to another and intent to cause such contact (tort). Similar to criminal assault.

Bill of Rights: The first ten amendments to the Constitution; guarantees United States citizens certain rights by limiting the power of government.

Booking: The entering of information, possibly including photographs and fingerprinting, of a defendant at the jail.

Briefing a case: Outlining a case.

Case law: Law based on decisions reached by courts in similar situations. Often referred to as "precedents."

Certiorari: See petition for certiorari.

Chain of custody: Documentation of custody of all physical evidence from the time it is found and collected to the time it is presented in court. Also called "continuity of evidence."

Challenge for cause: The objection to a potential juror by a lawyer for a specific reason.

Citation: A ticket.

Classical theory: Theory of delinquency tending to treat juveniles as adults, holding them more accountable for their actions by considering decisions to have been made via "free will."

Collective deep pocket: Possibility of an astronomical civil judgment by suing every possible party involved.

Common law: Judge-made case law that originated in England and reflects custom and tradition. It may or may not have been written at that time.

Complainant: A person who makes a charge against another person.

Complaint: A legal document drafted by prosecutors that specifies the alleged crime and the facts that provide the required probable cause.

Concurrent jurisdiction: Two separate courts having jurisdiction.

Contempt of court: Any act that embarrasses or obstructs the court, including insulting remarks or persistent arguments by the counsel, disorderly conduct by the defendant or spectators, and witnesses' refusals to be sworn in and testify.

Continuity of evidence: Documentation of custody of physical evidence from the time it is found and collected to the time it is presented in court. Also called "chain of custody."

Contraband: Anything that it illegal for people to own or to have in their possession, e.g., illegal drugs, illegal weapons.

Conviction: A verdict of guilt.

Coroner's jury: Investigates violent deaths where suspicion of foul play exists. Usually has six members.

Corpus delicti: The actual crime, the elements of that crime, and the fact that the crime occurred.

Corpus delicti evidence: Evidence establishing that a crime has been committed.

Crime: Statutorily defined wrong against the government with penalty.

Criminal justice process: That set of rules and procedures by which the government and the accused proceed in search of justice.

Criminal law: The principles and procedures which protect society and the community from the harmful acts of individuals.

Critical stages in justice system: Stages determined to be of such importance that specific legal rules must be satisfied. Includes the complaint or charge, the arrest, booking, preliminary hearing, the arraignment, the trial, and sentencing.

Cross examination: The most effective art of the skilled trial lawyer; interrogating witnesses by the opposing attorney by questions framed to test the accuracy and truthfulness of testimony on direct examination and to bring out the truth of the matter in issue; an absolute right in actions and proceedings.

Curtilege: That portion of property generally associated with the common use of land, e.g., buildings, sheds, fenced-in areas, and the like.

Custodial interrogation: Questioning initiated by law enforcement officers after a person has been taken into custody or otherwise deprived of his freedom of action in any significant way. Demands that the Miranda warning be given.

Defamation: Tortious conduct by which published statement injures the reputation of another (slander = speech; libel = writing).

Defendant: The person against whom an action or proceeding is brought.

Defense attorney: Same as defense counsel.

Defense counsel: A lawyer conducting or assisting in the defense in a civil action or criminal prosecution.

Demonstrative evidence: Serves as a visual aid to the jury in comprehending verbal testimony. Includes maps, charts, models, and actual demonstrations. Distinguished from ''real evidence.'' Has no probative value in itself.

Deposition: A written statement made by a witness under oath to be used in court.

Direct examination: The examination in chief of a witness by the party who called him to the stand, generally conducted by non-hostile, non-leading, open-ended questions.

Discovery process: A system that requires all pertinent facts be available to the prosecutor and the defense attorney before the trial, used to avoid surprises or ''ambush'' evidence.

Discretion: The ability to make choices or select alternatives.

Discretionary act: A duty calling for judgment.

Disposition: The final way that a legal matter is resolved.

District attorney: Governmental court officers representing the interests of the state, generally in criminal matters.

Due process of law: ''Due process of law'' implies the administration of laws equally applicable to all under established rules which do not violate fundamental principles of private rights, and in a competent tribunal possessing jurisdiction. A phrase is impossible to precisely define; one which asserts a fundamental principle of justice rather than a specific rule of law. The right to hear and to be heard.

Ecclesiastical law: Religious law.

Entrapment: The act of government officials or agents (usually police officers) inducing a person to commit a crime that the person would not have otherwise committed.

Equity: Fairness.

Evidence: Anything that helps to prove or disprove the truth of the point at issue.

Exclusionary rule: Demands that no evidence can be admitted in a trial unless it was obtained legally, that is, within the constitutional standards set forth in the Fourth Amendment.

Exclusive jurisdiction: Only that specific court can hear a specific case.

Exigent circumstances: Emergency situation. Includes danger of physical harm to an officer, danger of destruction of evidence, danger to a third person, driving while intoxicated, hot-pursuit situations, and individuals requiring "rescuing," for example, unconscious individuals.

False imprisonment: An action confirming or restraining someone to a bounded area and intent to do so (tort).

Felony: A more serious crime, generally punishable by a prison sentence of more than one year.

Field identification: A witness to or victim of a crime is shown one suspect for the purpose of identifying the perpetrator. Also called "showup identification."

Fleeing felon rule: A rule allowing police officers to shoot to kill any felon who fled to escape arrest. Made unconstitutional by *Tennessee v. Garner.*

Fresh pursuit: An uninterrupted, continuous chase.

Frisk: A reasonable search for weapons for the protection of the police officers and others, a "pat-down".

Fruit of the poisonous tree: Doctrine stating that evidence obtained as a result of an earlier illegality must be excluded from trial.

Good faith: Involves instances where police officers are not aware that they are violating Fourth Amendment principles.

Grand jury: A group of citizens, usually 23, convened to hear testimony in secret and to issue formal criminal accusations (indictments) based upon probable cause if justified.

Guardian ad litem: A legal counselor appointed for a juvenile by juvenile court.

Habeas corpus: A judicial order to bring a person being held in custody to court.

Harmless error: Instances where the preponderance of the evidence suggests the defendant's guilt and the "tainted" or illegal evidence is not critical to proving the case against the defendant.

Hearsay evidence: Secondhand evidence. A statement heard by someone else repeated by a witness during a trial.

Impeach: To discredit a witness by showing bias or lack of knowledge that would tend to negatively affect one's truthful testimony.

Indictment: A written accusation based on probable cause, returned by a grand jury charging an individual with a specific crime.

Inevitable discovery doctrine: Given time, an independent source would emerge with the same evidence. Also called "hypothetical independent source."

Inferior court: A court having lesser jurisdiction than that above it.

Informant: Any person who gives law enforcement officers information on criminal activity.

Informational probable cause: Information provided to police officers by others.

In loco parentis: Taking the place of parents.

Intentional infliction of emotional distress: An action that is extreme and outrageous conduct with intent to cause severe emotional distress.

Intentional wrong: Doing something against the law on purpose.

Interrogation: Questioning of a suspect.

Jurisdiction: In criminal cases, the power of courts to inquire into the fact, to apply the law, and to declare the punishment, in a regular course of judicial proceeding, embracing every kind of judicial action on the subject matter, from finding the indictment to pronouncing the sentence.

Jury: A group of citizens selected to determine, under the guidance of a judge, questions of fact arising in a civil or criminal trial.

Jury trial: A court proceeding to be determined by a jury, rather than only by a judge.

Kirby limitation: A suspect does not have the right to a lawyer in showup identification.

Law: A principle, standard, or rule made and enforced through consequences by a society.

Law of criminal procedure: Deals with the process of enforcing substantive criminal law.

Law of evidence: The body of rules that regulates the admission of proof in court.

Law of stop and frisk: Deals with that time frame during which officers follow up on their suspicions, but before the time that the requisite probable cause is established to justify an arrest.

Legal citation: Standardized way of referring to a specific element in the law. Has three basic parts: a volume number, an abbreviation for the title, and a page or section number. Sometimes followed by the date.

Libel: Written defamation.

Lifestyle, well-balanced: Equal emphasis on physical, mental/emotional, and spiritual health.

Lineup identification: A witness to or victim of a crime is shown several persons for the purpose of identifying the perpetrator of a crime.

Litigate: To maintain or defend an action as a party thereto; to sue or be sued.

Living law: Phrase describing the ability of our rules (laws) to change as the needs of the society it serves changes.

Lower courts: Used to refer to courts of lesser authority, or to all others than U.S. Supreme Court.

Magistrate: A judge.

Mala in se crimes: Offenses involving moral issues.

Mala prohibitum crimes: A crime not involving moral issues.

Malfeasance: Wrongful act.

Mandatory sentence: A minimal sentence required by statute.

Mens rea: An evil intent; a guilty mind.

Ministerial act: A duty whose performance is prescribed. It involves no discretion.

Misdemeanor: A lesser crime, generally punishable by a fine or a jail sentence not to exceed one year, or both.

Misfeasance: An act of misconduct.

Negligence: The existence of a duty to use due care, a breach of that duty that is both the actual and proximate cause of the injury and damages result to the plaintiff. The failure to use due care to prevent foreseeable injury that results in injury.

Nightcapped warrant: Search or arrest warrant that may be executed during the nighttime.

Nolle prosequi: A statement that a party will not proceed with a case.

Nolo contendere: "I do not wish to contend." An implied confession.

Nonfeasance: A failure to take action.

Observational probable cause: Data police officers become aware of through their senses.

Ordinance: Law passed by a local legislature or city council.

Original jurisdiction: Means the court has the authority to hear cases first, try them, and render decisions.

Overrule: To refuse to support an objection.

Parens patriae: Doctrine referring to the right of the government to take care of minors and others who cannot legally take care of themselves.

Peremptory challenge: The objection to a potential juror by a lawyer, for which no reason is necessary. Each side is entitled to a limited number.

Perjury: Willful and corrupt false swearing or affirming, often on oath lawfully administered in a judicial proceeding. Lying in court.

Petition for certiorari: A petition to a supreme court to review the decision of an appeals court.

Plain view evidence: Unconcealed evidence that officers inadvertently see while engaged in a lawful activity. Is admissible in court.

Plea: The response an accused gives to the court.

Plea bargaining: An agreement reached by both sides by which the accused pleads guilty, rather than take the case to trial.

Popular sources: Material written for the lay person, e.g., *Time* or *Newsweek*.

Positivist theory: Seeks to identify the reason a delinquent act was committed, proposing such factors as environmental, biological, or psychological influences as being at the root of the behavior, not simply "free will."

Precedent: A legal determination by a court that is to be followed by courts of the same or lesser status.

Preliminary hearing: A hearing permitted by statute, dealing with such preliminary matters as bail or the existence of probable cause.

Pre-sentence report: Information provided to the judge regarding the defendant or the offense which may influence the sentencing.

Preventive detention: Holding a juvenile in custody prior to a hearing when there is a suspicion that the youth may pose a threat to self or others or may not appear in court.

Primary sources: Raw data or the original information, e.g., the U.S. Constitution, state constitutions, statutes, and court decisions.

Privileged communication: Communication that need not be told to anyone else, including a judge during a trial. Includes communication between a defendant and his/her lawyer, doctor, etc.

Probable cause: The fact that it is more likely than not that a crime has been committed by the person whom a law enforcement officer seeks to arrest; or that items sought are where police officers believe them to be. Stronger than reasonable suspicion. The sum total of information and the synthesis of what the police have heard, what they know, and what they observe as trained officers.

Procedural due process: "A regular course of justice, which is not unreasonable or arbitrary, upon notice and hearing, in pursuance of an efficacious remedy secured by the law of the state." [16 An J.2d Const. L S 549] or, an orderly process which ensures the accused the right to hear and be heard. Fairness.

Procedural law: The legal requirements of how a case is to be pursued within the system.

Professional sources: Material written for the practitioner in a given field, e.g., *Police Chief* or *Law and Order.*

Proof beyond a reasonable doubt: The burden of proof required of the government for a successful prosecution.

Prosecutor: An elected or appointed official who serves as the public's lawyer.

Public safety exception: Allows police officers to question suspects without first giving the Miranda warning if the information sought sufficiently affects the officer's and the public's safety.

Reasonable: Sensible, rational, justifiable.

Rebuttal: The prosecution's last chance to prove its case. Follows the presentation of evidence by the defense.

Rehabilitation: Fortifying a witness who the opposing lawyer has attempted to discredit.

Rejoinder: The defense's last chance to prove its case. Follows the rebuttal of the prosecution.

Res gestae statements: Spontaneous declarations made as the direct result of some exciting or shocking event. Also called "spontaneous declarations." An exception to the hearsay rule.

Scholarly sources: Literature written for people interested in theory, research, statistical analysis, and the like, e.g., *Justice Quarterly.*

Secondary sources: Information based on raw data or original information, e.g., periodicals, treatises/texts, encyclopedias, and dictionaries.

Secular law: The law of governments.

Sequester: "to set apart"; to keep a witness out of court while others testify.

Showup identification: A witness to or victim of a crime is shown one suspect for the purpose of identifying the perpetrator of a crime. Also called "field identification."

Slander: spoken defamation.

Sovereign immunity doctrine: Protects certain governmental bodies from being sued.

Spontaneous declarations: Statements made immediately as the direct result of some exciting or shocking event. Also called "res gestae statements." An exception to the hearsay rule.

Standard of comparison: A measure, model, or object to which evidence is compared to see if both came from the same source.

Standing to raise exclusionary rule: Defendants cannot ask to have excluded evidence that was obtained through the violation of the constitutional rights of someone other than themselves.

Stare decisis: The legal doctrine or policy stating that courts will follow precedent by following decisions reached by prior courts of the same or greater authority.

Status offenses: Acts which are illegal if performed by minors, e.g., truancy, running away from home, curfew, incorrigibility, liquor violations and the like. The acts are illegal only because of the person's age.

Statute: Law passed by the United States Congress or by state legislatures.

Statutory law: Law based on legislation passed by governments.

Stop: A brief detention of a person based on "specific and articulable facts" for the purpose of investigating suspicious activity.

Strict liability: A wrongdoer is held liable to the injured party whether or not the wrongdoer actually did anything intentionally wrong.

Subpoena: A written legal document ordering a person to appear in court or to provide material to the court.

Substantive criminal law: Defines crimes and their penalties.

Substantive due process: "Freedom from arbitrary action coupled with the equal operation of the laws." [16 AMJ 2d Cont. L § 550].

Summons: In criminal law, an order to appear in court at a specific time.

Supreme Court: The highest court in the United States and the only court established by the Constitution.

Survival triangle: What it takes police officers to stay alive—mental/physical preparation, survival tactics, and shooting skills.

Sustain: To uphold an objection.

Syndrome evidence: Consists of facts presented by expert testimony that indicate existence of a specific conditions. e.g., child abuse.

Tort: Civil wrong against an individual.

Tortfeasor: A wrongdoer.

Totality of circumstances: Includes police conduct and all preceding factors.

Trespass: An action resulting in the physical invasion of the land of another and intent to do so.

Trial de novo: A new trial or new trial appeal.

Uniform Crime Reports: A key source of statistics in criminal justice. The FBI's compilation of reported crime nationwide.

Venue: The place a case comes to trial and the area from which the jury is selected.

Voir dire: Questioning of prospective jurors to determine their fitness as jurors.

Waiver: A purposeful, voluntary giving up of a known right.

Witness: A complainant, an accuser, a victim, an observer of an incident, a source of information, evidence technician, or other expert.

Writ of certiorari: A writ issued to a lower court for the record in order that corrections or reviews may be made. Also, certiorari must be granted by the U.S. Supreme Court before they will hear case.

Writ of habeas corpus: Basically, a writ to free those held with insufficient legal cause.

Writ of mandamus: An order by one court to an inferior court to carry out a legal duty.

Index